HIGH PRAISE FOR
MARK HERTSGAARD'S
A DAY IN THE LIFE

"AN EXCEPTIONAL STUDY, thoroughly researched and exhaustively documented." — *Publishers Weekly*

"IN BRISK, REFRESHING PROSE, he makes sense of the singers — and the success — by way of the song."
— *Entertainment Weekly*

"Hertsgaard painstakingly researches stories that you'd think had long ago sunk into legend." — *The New Yorker*

"Plenty of biographical background . . . incisive observations on Lennon and McCartney's songwriting process and the band's special chemistry." — *Booklist*

"Chronicles with vivid color and exacting detail the recording sessions that produced the group's albums, providing considerable insight into the thought processes of John, Paul, George, and Ringo as they created. . . . Lots of interesting facts, figures, and anecdotes."
— *Kirkus Reviews*

"A solid work, deftly using the tunes to tell the Beatles' story. The artistic discussion is reasoned and thoughtful."
— *Daily News* (New York)

A DAY IN THE LIFE

The Music and Artistry
of the Beatles

by Mark Hertsgaard

Delta
Trade
Paperbacks

A Delta Book
Published by
Dell Publishing
a division of
Bantam Doubleday Dell Publishing Group, Inc.
1540 Broadway
New York, New York 10036

Book design by Susan Maksuta

A portion of Chapter 1 first appeared in *The New Yorker*.

PHOTO CREDITS

1. © Apple Corps Ltd.
2. Steve Hale/Hulton Deutsch Collection
3. Peter Kaye/© Apple Corps Ltd.
4. Sotheby's, London
5. Brodie/Times Newspapers Ltd.
6. Henry Benson/Hulton Deutsch Collection
7. Philip Jones Griffiths/Magnum Photos
8. David Hurn/Magnum Photos
9. Rex Features
10. Tony Wale/Pictorial Press
11. Pictorial Press
12. Don McCullin/Magnum Photos
13. © Apple Corps Ltd.
14. Frank Herrmann
15. Hulton Deutsch Collection © Apple Corps Ltd.
16. Don McCullin/Magnum Photos
17. Hulton Deutsch Collection
18. David Magnus/Rex Features
19. Camera Press
20. Don McCullin/Magnum Photos
21. © Apple Corps Ltd.
22. © Apple Corps Ltd.
23. © Apple Corps Ltd.
24. Don McCullin/Magnum Photos

The trademark Delta® is registered in the U.S. Patent and Trademark Office and in other countries.

ISBN: 0-385-31517-1

Reprinted by arrangement with Delacorte Press

Manufactured in the United States of America
Published simultaneously in Canada

April 1996

10 9 8 7 6 5 4 3 2 1
FFG

A colei che amo

Contents

This book begins from the conviction that what matters most about the Beatles is their art. In the 1960s, John Lennon, Paul McCartney, George Harrison, and Ringo Starr affected everything from haircuts and fashion to the political and spiritual beliefs of a generation, even as their colorful private lives became a subject of endless media fascination. But in the long run it is the music, not the personal behavior of the four young men who produced it, that makes the Beatles important. This book offers a biography of that music, a brief account of how it was created, how it evolved over time, what the Beatles said and did inside the studio while recording it, which parts of which songs bear special listening, and what the Beatles themselves thought about what they had wrought. Although no artist creates in a vacuum, this book discusses the Beatles' personal backgrounds and such related topics as the role of their producer, George Martin, mainly insofar as they shed light on the music itself.

Besides the Beatles' commercially released song catalogue, my primary source materials for this book have been the rough drafts of the completed songs, as found in the Beatles archives at Abbey Road Studios in London and on bootleg recordings. I have also made cautious use of the public record on the Beatles. Cautious, because one simply cannot trust that the "facts" in most books about the Beatles are anything more than speculation, hearsay, or opinion. The daily media reporting about the Beatles over the years was often careless or simpleminded. Book authors then compounded the confusion by making vast deductive leaps that they presented as truth, or by using technically factual evidence in selective ways, or by surmising what a given person, usually one of the Beatles, *must* have thought in a situation and then putting those words in his mouth. Authors rarely bothered to document their conclusions; very few books on the Beatles contain a list of checkable citations in support of their claims.

In addition to sloppy journalism, there is the unreliability of human memory. During an interview at his AIR Studios building in London in 1993, George Martin told me about a disagreement that he and Paul McCartney had recently had about "a trivial fact—who thought of a line, or a word, from a song—and I said it was Ringo who said it, and Paul said no, it was George who said it. We looked at each other and Paul said, 'I *know* it was George.' I said, 'Paul, *I* know it was Ringo.' And we grinned at one another, and Paul said, 'You know now why history is bunk. If we can't get it right, who can?' "

No one can get everything right, but I have tried in these pages to be as scrupulous with evidence and its interpretation as possible. The sources and reasoning that support all factual statements can be found in the Notes section at the back of the book, along with extra detail and recommendations for further reading. Here I will simply note that the text is based mainly on first-person statements by named sources— whenever possible, by the Beatles themselves. It is not possible to write a book of texture and insight without the author's venturing a certain number of his own interpretations and occasionally even informed speculations, but these are usually apparent from the context and, if not, are identified as such in the Notes.

"Writing about music is like talking about fucking," John Lennon once complained. "Who wants to talk about it?" Lennon has a point, except that talking about it doesn't preclude doing it, and perhaps the greater one's knowledge, the greater one's enjoyment. This book is written in that spirit. It attempts to set the record straight (or as straight as possible) on central issues in the Beatles' work and lives. I have tried to achieve an organic connection between the chapters that explicate the music and those treating related topics so that over the course of the narrative the two spiral together like a vine around a sapling. American readers in particular should be aware that the music is discussed *in the order in which the Beatles originally recorded and issued it*; that is, according to the date of its release in Great Britain. In the United States, at least until the *Sgt Pepper's Lonely Hearts Club Band* album of 1967, record company caprice and greed resulted in "albums" that the Beatles did not oversee (and in fact detested) and that did not reflect their musical development. A full discography is provided at the back of the book. Finally, feel free to read with the music on. A principal aim of this book is to encourage readers to listen to the Beatles' music for themselves—separate from the myth—and to develop their own views accordingly.

And now, to paraphrase the bards themselves, I hope you will enjoy the show.

A DAY IN THE LIFE

C H A P T E R   1

Inside Abbey Road Studios ("A Day In The Life")

SOMEWHERE INSIDE LONDON'S ABBEY ROAD STUDIOS, HIDDEN BEHIND AN UNMARKED, TRIPLE-LOCKED, POLICE-alarmed door, are some of the most valuable artifacts of twentieth-century music: the raw tapes of every recording session in the nearly eight-year studio career of the Beatles. One of the most remarkable facts about the Beatles is that they released only ten and a half hours of music during their years together—the contents of the group's twenty-two singles and fourteen albums. Yet the tapes inside the Abbey Road archives, it turns out, contain more than four hundred hours' worth of Beatles recordings.

The collection extends from June 6, 1962, the date of the audition that narrowly persuaded George Martin, a producer at EMI Records, to sign the Beatles, to January 4, 1970, when Paul McCartney, George Harrison, and Ringo Starr (John Lennon was in Denmark on holiday) recorded the final overdubs for what amounted to the group's farewell album, *Let It Be*. In between are tapes of everything else, stored in red-and-white cardboard boxes the size of large telephone books. Pick a favorite Beatles song; the archives hold not only the master tape of that song as it is heard on the album but also the working tapes that trace the song's evolution from its first run-through to its polished final version. There are also lots of off-the-cuff jam sessions, argu-

1

ments, horseplay, and studio chat, as well as a few songs the general public has never heard.

In the course of the research for this book, I was fortunate enough to gain access to these archives on two occasions. While on assignment for *The New Yorker*, I spent the equivalent of six full days inside Abbey Road, listening to some fifty hours of tapes of the Beatles and of the solo work of John Lennon. I sometimes felt during those days as though I had been allowed to watch Picasso sketch, and never more so than on the afternoon I listened to all seven takes of "A Day In The Life," the closing song on the *Sgt Pepper's Lonely Hearts Club Band* album.

John Lennon recalled *Sgt Pepper* as "a peak" in the Beatles' career, a time when "Paul and I were definitely working together, especially on 'A Day In The Life.'" Indeed, "A Day In The Life" may be the ultimate Lennon–McCartney collaboration, a classic example of how the songwriting style of each man perfectly complemented that of the other. Although John would later confess that he and Paul wrote many songs "eyeball to eyeball," especially in the early days, their usual practice by this time, January 1967, was for one of them to provide the missing middle or accents to a song that the other had already almost completed. In the case of "A Day In The Life," it was Paul who made John's composition whole. Lennon had the melody and story line—the verses about a man who "blew his mind out in a car," the English Army that "had just won the war," the "four thousand holes in Blackburn, Lancashire"—but the song needed something more. Lennon didn't like laboring over songs, preferring instead the Zen purity of inspiration, so when he got stuck after completing the main verses he set the song aside. "I needed a middle-eight for it [the "middle eight" is the passage in the middle of a song where the tune changes before going back to the original verse], but that would have been forcing it," he later explained. "All the rest had come out smooth, flowing, no trouble, and to write a middle eight would have been to write a middle eight, but instead Paul already had one there."

Paul did indeed have the fragment "Woke up, fell out of bed . . ." lying around. The two partners agreed that its peppy portrait of the alienating hustle of modern urban life—based on Paul's memories of rushing to school in the morning—made the ideal counterpoint to John's gently ominous, dreamlike commentary on the hollow absurdity of status, order, and worldly attachments. The initial idea for the song had come, as it so often did with Lennon, from an item in the mass media. "I was reading the paper one day and noticed two stories," he recalled. "One was about the Guinness heir who killed himself in a car. That was the main headline story. He died in London in a car crash. On the next page was a story about four thousand potholes in the streets of Blackburn, Lancashire, that needed to be filled. Paul's contribution was the beautiful little lick in the song, 'I'd love to turn you on,' that he'd had floating around in his head and couldn't use. I thought it was a damn good piece of work."

The Guinness heir, whom the Beatles had happened to know, was born to a life of fantastic privilege. By conventional standards he was "a lucky man who made the grade." He had everything money could buy, but found himself no more immune to death's arbitrary, dispassionate arrival than the lowliest proletarian. A momentary, all too human lapse—"he didn't notice that the lights had changed"—and he was gone. In the moment of death, all delusion is shattered, everyone is equal. Lennon clinches the point with the wistful, mocking epitaph "Nobody was really sure if he was from the House of Lords." The gathered crowd knows they've "seen his face before" but they can't place it; in the broad scheme of things, he is barely a bit player. The wealth and position that seemed so important, to the heir *and* the larger society, is revealed as trivial and fleeting. Equally blinded by a different kind of triviality are the bureaucrats of the final verse, who insist on tabulating the precise number of holes in the roads of Blackburn, Lancashire, even "though the holes were rather small." No wonder the singer would "love to turn you on." To see his fellow human beings sleepwalking so numbly through the glorious richness that life offers is heartbreaking.

Musicologist Wilfrid Mellers has observed that "A Day In The Life" derives much of its power from the contrast between its relatively simple tune and the horrors described in its lyrics. But it is Lennon's *voice* as much as anything that puts the message across. In his 1992 behind-the-scenes documentary *The Making of Sgt Pepper*, George

Martin played an early version of "A Day In The Life." Referring to John, Martin said, "Even in this early take, he has a voice which sends shivers down the spine." Martin had just heard Lennon's entranced delivery of the opening lines—"I read the news today, oh boy / About a lucky man who made the grade"—and the deep gaze on his face and the slight glistening in his eyes suggested how moved he still was by the memory of his departed friend.

But when I listened to the working tapes of "A Day In The Life" at Abbey Road Studios, the first words audible as take one began were John murmuring, "Sugarplum fairy, sugarplum fairy." This was in lieu of a proper count-in to the song, something Lennon was incapable of, according to Mark Lewisohn, the EMI Beatles archivist who listened to all four hundred-plus hours of tapes in the Abbey Road vaults to write his official history, *The Beatles: The Complete Recording Sessions.* "While Paul or George's 1-2-3-4 count-ins were always appropriately sensible, John's—from the earliest surviving archive tape to the last—were anything but," wrote Lewisohn. "Only John Lennon could have devised so many demented ways of saying four simple numbers." But there was method to the madness in this case, and humor as well: "Sugarplum fairy" was sixties slang for the person who supplied one's recreational drugs.

I was listening to the tapes of "A Day In The Life" in room 22, the Sound to Picture Transfer Facility, which boasts Abbey Road's one remaining four-track tape machine—the only machine on the premises capable of playing recordings from the sixties. Room 22 is a small, cramped place, but its back window looks down on Studio One, by far the largest of Abbey Road's three main studios and thus the room where the orchestra overdub of "A Day In The Life" was recorded. But at this point, all I heard on the tape was Lennon's acoustic guitar, strumming lightly through the song's opening bars, backed by a piano, maracas, and, later, bongos. The tune was recognizable as "A Day In The Life," though it sounded much simpler, almost like a folk song. The goal of this first take was to get down a basic rhythm track upon which the Beatles could elaborate, but the others were still finding their way, and it was Lennon's vocal that stood out. Heavily echoed, it was as moving as Martin testified, and, in contrast to the occasionally tentative backing instruments, it was also perfectly controlled, its phrasing and delivery virtually indistinguishable from that found on the album.

At this point, McCartney's vocal was still lacking, and the Beatles apparently had yet to conceive of the hurricane of sound that would join his part of the song with Lennon's. Instead, after the "I'd love to turn you on" line, I heard the voice of Beatles assistant Mal Evans, loudly counting from one to twenty-four while Paul discordantly hammered the keyboard behind him. The purpose was to mark off the twenty-four bars that later would be filled by the still-unknown link to Paul's part of the song.

It took the Beatles four takes to achieve a rhythm track they were pleased with. The entire recording session, held on January 19, 1967, lasted from 7:30 P.M. to 2:30 A.M.; apparently most of the seven hours were devoted to untaped run-throughs aimed at finding the sound and tempo the Beatles were looking for. By take two, a much slower version, the piano was a far more confident element, no longer merely pounding out chords but fingering the climb-and-fall fills beneath Paul's still-absent vocal. Take three broke down after a false start, but take four was a winner: melancholy, purposeful, gathering from calm containment to resounding climax, it is the rhythm heard on the album.

The alarm clock that heralds the transition to McCartney's portion of the song was actually set as a joke, according to George Martin, who added, "We left it in because we couldn't get it off" the tape. But it is a sublime bit of serendipity; there couldn't be a more appropriate introduction to Paul's "Woke up, fell out of bed" lyric. Lennon was the more philosophical of the two, but McCartney showed more empathy for the daily life of the average person—think of "Lady Madonna," for example, or "Paperback Writer"—and here that perspective provides a reassuring anchor to Lennon's cosmic musings. McCartney's everyman seems oblivious to all but his own small concerns—a cup of tea, a quick cigarette on the way to work—yet he is not an unsympathetic character; he simply has enough trouble keeping his own life together without also trying to confront the moral issues raised in Lennon's part of the song. He represents each of us who retreats from full engagement of life; like us, he is the "you" in "I'd love to turn you on."

It was the "love to turn you on" line that caused "A Day In The Life" to meet a fate shared by numerous other Beatles songs: banning by the authorities. The British Broadcasting Corporation (BBC) contended that the song promoted drug-taking. It is true that by the time the Beatles made *Sgt Pepper's Lonely Hearts Club Band*, their use of mind-expanding drugs such as marijuana and LSD was copious and frequent, opening doors they had not even known existed, with obvious and beneficial effect on their creativity. McCartney later admitted that "A Day In The Life" was written "as a deliberate provocation to people. But what we really wanted was to turn you on to the truth rather than just bloody pot!" Critical of the Vietnam War and the narrow-minded conformity of modern consumer society, the Beatles sought to express countercultural values in their songs in an effort, George Harrison said, "to wake up as many people as we could."

The Beatles were rebels inside the recording studio as well. Armed with the clout of dozens of hit records, the Beatles constantly violated EMI's standard recording procedures, laughing all the way. "It wasn't a willful arrogance, it was just that we felt we knew better," recalled McCartney. "They'd say, 'Well, our rule book says . . .' And we'd say, 'They're out of date, come on, let's move!' " Lennon, for example, was particularly enamored of heavy echo on his vocals. Listening to take four of "A Day In The Life" with the rhythm section momentarily muted, I heard John's voice by itself, but somehow expanded. It turned out he had added three heavily echoed vocal overdubs onto the completed rhythm track, giving the song a choral, almost churchy feeling.

Meanwhile, in the back pew two naughty boys were giggling at a private joke. Paul and George, their voices pinched into pompous, indescribably accented weirdness, were slating the next take, a task that usually fell to an engineer. Take five, as one could barely make out before the ludicrous pair of voices dissolved into laughter, was not actually a new recording but a "four track to four track tape reduction," a technical procedure that clears space on a tape for additional overdubs. No one outside the studio was going to hear Paul and George's clowning, but that didn't stop their fun.

Takes six and seven were also reduction mixes, attempts to find the right blend of the already recorded rhythm and vocal tracks; take six was chosen as the best. The Beatles overdubbed Paul's bass, Ringo's drums, and Paul's vocal onto take six the following night, January 20, during the second session for "A Day In The Life." These additions were short of perfect, but they did bring the song very close to its final form. (Someone must have taken a copy of that night's work out of the studio, because it later became available on bootleg, including a funny moment when McCartney, having botched the last line of his vocal, muttered, "Oh, shit.")

The song was now complete, except for its two twenty-four-bar gaps. Obliterating boundaries between classical and rock and roll and avant-garde and the mainstream, the Beatles decided to punctuate "A Day In The Life" with a dark, tumultuous orchestra crescendo. Recollections differ on who came up with the idea of bringing in an orchestra and having it go musically crazy. It is the kind of innovation that people associate with John Lennon, supposedly the most "far out" of the Beatles, but Paul McCartney has more than once claimed credit for it, noting that it was he, not Lennon, who was most involved in the alternative art scene in London at this point, and adding that the crescendo "was based on some of the ideas I'd been getting from Stockhausen and people like that, which is more abstract." George Martin, on the other hand, has cited Lennon as the source, saying that John told him he wanted to hear "a tremendous build-up . . . from extreme quietness to extreme loudness, not only in volume, but also for the sound to expand as well."

Whoever fathered it, it is this stroke of audacity that catapults "A Day In The Life" beyond the level of splendid achievement to that of enduring masterpiece. Because Lennon and McCartney were musically illiterate—neither man ever learned to read or notate music—it was Martin who had to explain what the Beatles wanted to the forty outside musicians summoned to Abbey Road Studios on the evening of February 10, 1967. Martin, who had been trained at the Guildhall School of Music, wrote the musical score for virtually every Beatles song that employed classical instruments, and in his autobiography he described how he went about the task for "A Day In The Life": "What I did there was to write, at the beginning of the twenty-four bars, the lowest possible note for each of the instruments in the orchestra. At the end of the twenty-four bars, I wrote the highest note each instrument could reach that was near a chord of E major. Then I put a squiggly line right through the twenty-four bars, with reference points to tell them roughly what note they should have reached during each bar." To Lewisohn, Martin noted that in the studio he added some final instructions that struck the musicians as lunacy: "And whatever you do, don't listen to the fellow next to you because I don't want you to be doing the same thing. Of course they all looked at me as though I was mad." McCartney, who helped conduct the orchestra, recalled, "It was interesting because I saw the orchestra's characters. The strings were like sheep—they all looked at each other: 'Are you going up? I am!' and they'd all go up together, the leader would take them all up. The trumpeters were much wilder. The jazz guys, they liked the brief. . . . But it made for a great noise, which was all we wanted."

The orchestra's opening blast sounded portentously sinister when I listened to it isolated from the rest of the track, but in fact the recording session took place in a festive atmosphere. The Beatles had requested that George Martin and the orchestra wear full evening dress for the occasion, on top of which they were urged upon arrival to don silly party disguises; the leader of the violins, for example, wore a gorilla's paw on his bow hand. Mick Jagger and Keith Richards of the Rolling Stones and others from the London pop world were also invited to the session, and the entire wild scene was captured on camera as well. Ever the innovators, the Beatles had already made the world's first primitive music videos nine months earlier when they conceived and starred in two short films designed to promote the singles "Paperback Writer" and "Rain." Just days before the orchestra sessions for "A Day In The Life," they had gone a step further, shooting completely nonperformance-based films for "Penny Lane" and "Strawberry Fields Forever." ("In the future all records will have vision as well as sound," McCartney presciently predicted. "In twenty years time people will be amazed to think we just listened to records.") Now, the Beatles were planning a special television program depicting the making of *Sgt Pepper*.

The special was never broadcast, perhaps because of the BBC banning order, but the segment for "A Day In The Life" survived. Steeped in the double close-ups and liquidy fade-outs of the LSD era, the film shows the Beatles and company standing around in the semidarkness of Abbey Road's Studio One, chatting, drinking and goofily playing to the camera before the session begins. A dove flies back and forth across a darkened sky, strangely masked faces zoom in and out of the picture, Martin conducts the orchestra wearing a Pinocchio nose. In exquisite synchronization with the soundtrack, the film gradually builds to a fantastic climax, cutting faster and faster from image to trippy image as the orchestra madly charges up the hill to song's end—a riveting visual experience.

When the orchestra finished its crescendo, everyone in the studio burst into a spontaneous round of applause. "When we'd finished doing the orchestral bit, one part of me said, 'We're being a bit self-indulgent here,' " George Martin recalled. "The other part of me said, 'It's bloody *marvelous*!' " Afterward, the Beatles remained behind with some friends and taped four attempts at a long hum, intended as the song's ending. Inside room 22, I heard the group break down in laughter the first three times, with John teasing them, "Stop freaking out." At last they succeeded, but the hum lasted barely five seconds, a feeble anticlimax after the orchestra's huge, out-of-control buildup.

John had said he wanted the song to rise up to "a sound like the end of the world." Finally, the Beatles hit upon the idea of simultaneously striking an E-major chord on three grand pianos, the sound to be drawn out as long as possible with electronic enhancement. It took John, Paul, Ringo, and Mal Evans nine tries before they all hit the keys at precisely the same time. When that evening's overdub was attached to the end of the orchestra crescendo, John got his wish. The effect of the crashing E-major chord, followed by some fifty-three seconds of gradually dwindling reverberation, brings to mind nothing so much as the eerily spreading hush of the mushroom cloud.

To conclude a pop song with a sound evoking thermonuclear devastation, *the* late-twentieth-century human nightmare, would be pretentious in the hands of lesser artists. With the Beatles, it sounds as natural as a roaring waterfall, and as awe-inspiring. The rolling shock waves of the sustained E chord, at once terrible and magisterial, seem to go on forever, giving the listener ample time to absorb and ponder the many dimensions of meaning in the song.

A Day In The Life

"A Day In The Life" posits nothing so crude as a direct condemnation of militarism or the nuclear arms race, though its sensibility certainly encompasses a warning against such stupidities. The appeal of the song's poetry lies rather in its implicit articulation of the American Transcendentalists' credo "All is connectedness." Glorification of wealth, identification with hierarchy, fixation on the illusory trifles of existence—these values cannot be separated from the social structures that make nuclear war and other forms of organized violence possible. Yet for all its foreboding, the song offers redemption. The despair in "A Day In The Life," critic Tim Riley has pointed out, "is ultimately hopeful. 'I'd love to turn you on' is a motto of enlightenment, of Lennon's [sic] desire to wake the world up to its own potential for rejuvenation, not self-annihilation." "A Day In The Life" thus fulfills one of the holy missions of great art—awakening in its audience not only a reverence for the miracle of life but a renewed enthusiasm to go out and live it.

"A hundred years from now, people will listen to the music of the Beatles the same way we listen to Mozart," Paul McCartney was quoted saying in 1992. The claim is a grand one. Indeed, some people might regard it as no less blasphemously self-important than Lennon's notorious 1966 remark that the Beatles were more popular than Jesus. Yet a song like "A Day In The Life" gives a certain credence to McCartney's remark. Shortly after *Sgt Pepper's Lonely Hearts Club Band* was released, critic Jack Kroll likened "A Day In The Life" to T. S. Eliot's "The Waste Land," perhaps the greatest English language poem of this century. A separate comment by George Martin—that what the Beatles really did was paint pictures with sound—suggests an additional comparison: to the painting "Guernica," Picasso's 1937 masterpiece depicting the horrors of the Spanish Civil War. Like both "Guernica" and "The Waste Land," "A Day In The Life" is a work of sufficient beauty, power, and social relevance to rank among the outstanding statements of twentieth-century art. "A Day In The Life" remains as vibrant and affecting today, five years shy of century's end, as it was when first released in 1967. So why shouldn't it continue to thrill and inspire listeners in the decades and century to come?

CHAPTER 2

Four Lads from Liverpool

LONG BEFORE JOHN LENNON HAD HEARD OF MARIJUANA AND LSD, HE FOUND HIMSELF IN TUNE WITH ALTERNATE FORMS of consciousness. One day, when he was eight or nine years old, he walked into the kitchen and calmly announced that he had just seen God, quietly sitting by the fire. Years later, after taking acid and becoming acquainted with modern painting, he realized that he had always seen the world through what amounted to surrealistic, psychedelic glasses. But while he was growing up, he simply felt freakish, and was more often frightened by his special visions. He later explained that he came to identify with such artists as "Oscar Wilde or Dylan Thomas or Vincent Van Gogh—[with] the suffering they went through because of their vision. They were *seeing* and being tortured by society for trying to express ... that loneliness and seeing what *is*."

Lennon never seemed to escape the sense of loneliness that settled upon him in his early years. Although both he and Paul McCartney suffered the deaths of their mothers when the boys were teenagers, the emotional wounds appeared to be more painful and enduring for John, no doubt in part because John lost his mother twice: once at age five, when Julia Lennon gave John to her sister Mimi to raise, and again at seventeen, when Julia was struck by a car and killed. John's

13

life and work contain more than a few indications that he never got over the loss of his mother. In "Julia," the lovely ballad he wrote ten years after her death for the White Album, he admitted that "Half of what I say is meaningless / But I say it just to reach you / Julia." In "Mother," the opening song on John's first solo album, *Plastic Ono Band*, he bemoaned Julia's decision to give him away to Mimi, wailing, "I wanted you / You didn't want me." In the album's final song, he blankly lamented that "My Mummy's Dead." And in his private life, he habitually referred to Yoko Ono as "Mother" throughout their twelve years as a couple.

The adult that John Lennon would become was evident during his youth in other ways as well. Pete Shotton, John's lifelong best friend from the time they met at age seven, has noted that John could never "leave a word alone" even then. "As our relationship came to resemble that of Siamese twins, John renamed us 'Shennon and Lotton,' " Shotton recalled, adding, "Though I have yet to encounter a personality as strong and individual as John's, he always had to have a partner." And not just a partner, John himself later confessed, but "a little gang of guys ... who would play various roles in my life, supportive and, you know, subservient." Part of what drew followers to John was his quick-witted humor. While John "rarely told jokes as such, he was amusing virtually *all* the time," said Shotton. Once, when a twelve-year-old Lennon began a story by saying, "Pete and me," a boy named Turner dared to correct John's grammar. "You mean Pete and *I*," he pointed out. "Shut up, Turner," John riposted. "*You* weren't even there!"

Like the other Beatles, John Lennon was born during wartime, in a city under relentless aerial bombardment. The Beatles' hometown of Liverpool, located on the northwest coast of England, was one of Britain's chief ports and thus a prime target of Germany's air force. Indeed, when John Winston Lennon—the middle name was in honor of British prime minister Churchill—was born on October 9, 1940, Liverpool was in the middle of a punishing bombing raid. His aunt Mimi recalled being "literally terrified" as she ran to the hospital, dodging shrapnel and ducking into doorways, to see the infant that her sister had just delivered.

Ringo Starr, born Richard Starkey on July 7, 1940 (and thus the oldest of the four Beatles), also endured bombing raids in his infancy; his mother later told Hunter Davies, author of the Beatles' authorized biography, that during one such raid, young Ritchie cried and cried until she suddenly realized that, amidst all the fear and confusion, she was holding him upside down. The tide of the war had turned sufficiently that Liverpool was no longer enduring nightly attacks by the time Paul McCartney was born on June 18, 1942, and George Harrison on February 25, 1943, but life remained dangerous and pinched, with shortages of food, fuel, and even clothing. Years later, however, the Beatles reaped a vital windfall from their wartime birthdates; they were among the first generation of male Englishmen to benefit when mandatory military service was rescinded in 1960. Unlike Elvis Presley, the Beatles would not have to interrupt a burgeoning music career to learn to salute, march, and obey orders.

George was the only Beatle not deprived of one or both of his biological parents during childhood; John was the only one who tasted the fruits of middle-class affluence. Of the four, Ringo probably had the toughest lot. His parents had separated by the time he was born, and his mother had to work as a barmaid to make ends meet. She and her son lived in what was called the Dingle, an inner-city neighborhood considered one of the roughest in all Liverpool. Ringo suffered from poor health throughout his youth. At age six, his appendix burst, landing him in hospital for a year; at thirteen, just after his mother remarried, a cold turned into pleurisy and the boy spent two years recovering in a sanitorium. His absences from the classroom made learning difficult, and by the time he emerged from the hospital he could read and write only with difficulty. He never finished school. His stepfather, a housepainter, nevertheless managed to arrange an apprenticeship for him as a pipe fitter with an engineering firm. He also bought Ringo his first drum kit, on credit.

George Harrison's father supported a wife and four children on the modest pay of a municipal bus driver. When George, the youngest, was born, the family lived in a four-room row house in Wavertree, a working-class section of Liverpool. "The rooms downstairs were always extremely cold during the winter," George recalled, adding that there was only one heater in the entire house and the toilet was located outdoors. When George was six, the Harrisons, after eighteen years on a waiting list, moved to a larger, government-subsidized house in nearby Speke. "We got by well enough," his father, Harold, said. "But life was never easy." Material inadequacies were compensated for by emotional warmth and togetherness. The children "always knew the comfort and security of a very close-knit home life," said George's brother Harry. Young George was the only Harrison child to make it as far as grammar school, enrolling at the prestigious Liverpool Institute, but he found he had only disdain for his teachers—"Useless, the lot of them," he later huffed—and he rarely paid attention or applied himself. He duly failed all his classes except art and eventually accepted a job as an electrician's apprentice at a Liverpool department store.

Paul McCartney was also from a bona fide working-class background. Although his father's job as a cotton salesman was considered middle class, by the time Paul was born in 1942, Jim McCartney had been claimed for the war effort, working a lathe by day and fighting fires sparked by German bombs at night. After the war, he returned to the cotton business, but the market had deteriorated and his wages shrank accordingly. His wife, Mary, kept the family afloat (a second son, Michael, had arrived in 1944) by returning to nursing. Her job as a midwife for a public housing project not only paid wages equal to her husband's but secured a state-subsidized house for the McCartneys. Paul was a chubby youngster—"Fatty!" was his brother's favorite taunt—but the boys had a close relationship and family life was stable and loving. "We were very close, with aunties and uncles always coming in, sing-songs and parties," Paul recalled.

Like George Harrison, with whom he rode the bus in the mornings, McCartney attended the Liverpool Institute, but Paul excelled, becoming a favorite with classmates and teachers alike. He displayed wit, intelligence, and above all a charm that was "absolutely natural, quite extraordinary and quite irresistible," recalled one teacher. "He could deliver the sardonic, the *devastating*, comment even at that age. But because he's such a decent bloke, he wouldn't cultivate this . . . as John Lennon would. Lennon *loved* hurting people and stirring them up. Paul could do all that, too. . . . But he didn't." Even the sudden death of his mother from breast cancer when Paul was fourteen did not disturb his outward equanimity, though he did cry himself to sleep in the privacy of his bedroom. Mother Mary's death was an economic as well as an emotional blow. "What are we going to do without her money?" Paul blurted out, a nervous remark that later shamed him.

John Lennon was likewise fourteen when his surrogate father, Aunt Mimi's elderly husband, George Smith, died suddenly of a hemorrhage; it was neither the first nor last abrupt exit of a loved one from John's life. His biological father, a merchant seaman named Alfred "Freddy" Lennon, had been away at sea when John was born, and was rarely home thereafter. John spent his toddler years living with his mother in her father's house, closely attended by Julia's four older sisters. Julia had a fun-loving, exuberant personality and spent many evenings in the pubs, drinking and dancing with servicemen. In 1944, she had a daughter out of wedlock, but gave the child up for adoption. In 1945, she became involved with John Dykins, a hotel waiter with whom she eventually had two children, John's half sisters Julia and Jacqueline. The irregularity of Julia's domestic situation led her to hand young John over to his aunt Mimi to be raised.

When Freddy Lennon returned to Liverpool, Julia informed him that the marriage was over. Freddy was nevertheless allowed to take his five-year-old son on a holiday to the seaside resort of Blackpool, where the most traumatic event of John's young life soon took place. When Freddy did not return to Liverpool at the expected time, Julia traveled to Blackpool and demanded to have John back. An argument ensued. Finally Freddy presented John with a terrible dilemma: He had to choose whether to stay with his father or go with his mother. Tearfully, John twice replied in Freddy's favor. But when Julia, herself in tears, walked out the door, the little boy ran after and caught her on the street, pleading with her not to go. It was the last Freddy Lennon saw of his son until John became famous, and the breach between them was never healed.

But if young John expected to stay with his mother, he was mistaken. As soon as Julia and John got back to Liverpool, she deposited him at Mimi's house, where he remained until he was eighteen. Julia did visit her son—John later said he "saw her sporadically off and on all the time, I just didn't live with her"—but not until adolescence did he discover that his mother lived only a few miles away. John called Julia "Mummy" and Aunt Mimi "Mimi," though in fact their roles were exactly the reverse; Mimi, a stern authoritarian with bourgeois aspirations who despised anything "common," was the daily maternal presence, while Julia offered the carefree affections of a free-spirited aunt. Apparently puzzled by this arrangement, young John one day asked Mimi why he didn't call *her* "Mummy." But she was too quick for him, countering, "Well, you couldn't have two mummies, could you?"

As an adult, especially during his most militantly political period, John sometimes claimed to have grown up working class, but he knew otherwise. Aunt Mimi and Uncle George, he admitted in one of his last interviews, were homeowners who lived in the suburbs surrounded by doctors and other professional types. His uncle George owned rental properties and a dairy before he retired after the war, and a gardener came in twice a week. The Smiths were by no means rich, and when John was an adolescent, Mimi took in medical student boarders to boost the family income, but John's material circumstances were far cozier than those of his fellow future Beatles.

Like Mimi, with whom he was "constantly at loggerheads," according to Shotton, John was "headstrong, forthright and outspoken" and made little "effort to be superficially 'nice.'" His need to dominate others and be the center of any situation, as well as his keen intelligence, was obvious to classmates at both Dovedale Primary School and Quarry Bank Grammar School. Chronically disrespectful of authority, he was forever disrupting class, getting into fights, and generally making trouble; parents warned their children to stay away from him, and teachers regularly "caned" him. He was an avid reader, but his tastes—Lewis Carroll, Edgar Allan Poe, Robert Louis Stevenson—rarely coincided with school assignments; most teachers struck him as pompous bores, and his eyesight was as poor as his discipline, so his grades suffered. He had a fascination with deformities; physical afflictions or weakness of any kind invariably tempted his tongue to cruelty. For example, Julia's lover John Dykins had a recurrent nervous tic; John took to calling him Twitchy (though not to his face). "Anyone limping, or crippled or hunchbacked, or deformed in any way, John laughed and ran up to them to make horrible faces," said Thelma Pickles, one of his first girlfriends. "He would accost men in wheelchairs and jeer, 'How did you lose your legs? Chasing the wife?' "

Then came Elvis. Rock 'n' roll, John later said, "was the only thing to get through to me after all the things that were happening when I was fifteen." In September 1955, Bill Haley's "Rock Around The Clock" was released. The following spring, Elvis Presley burst onto the world stage with a string of hits: "Heartbreak Hotel," "Blue Suede Shoes," "Hound Dog," "Don't Be Cruel," "Love Me Tender." Elvis was "bigger than religion" in John's life, so he found himself torn when a friend played him Little Richard's "Long Tall Sally." John thought the song "so great I couldn't speak. . . . How could they be happening in my life, *both* of them?"

Unbeknownst to John, his future mates Paul McCartney, George Harrison, and Richard Starkey were themselves being swept up in the same rock 'n' roll craze. For countless thousands of British and American teenagers, it became imperative to talk like Elvis, dress like Elvis, sing and play music like Elvis. In England, the look was known as "teddy boy," with velvet jackets, drainpipe trousers, string ties, and brightly colored shirts. The music was called "skiffle," a hybrid of black folk and country and western. Made famous by British singer Lonnie Donegan, it could be played by nonprofessionals with do-it-yourself instruments: a guitar, tea chest bass, and washboard percussion. Julia, who played the banjo and had taken to rock 'n' roll as enthusiastically as her son had, taught John some chords and he was on his way. John drafted Pete Shotton and some other school chums to serve as backup players for a group he named the Quarry Men, after his high school, Quarry Bank.

It was during one of the Quarry Men's first engagements that John Lennon first met Paul McCartney. The date was July 6, 1957, a few days before John and Pete's high school graduation. The Quarry Men were performing at the St. Peter's Church garden fete, a neighborhood summer festival. Paul's friend and classmate at the Liverpool

Institute, Ivan Vaughan, who knew John from grade school and occasionally sat in with the Quarry Men, insisted that Paul, already a fervent rock 'n' roller, come hear the group. "I remember I was impressed," McCartney later said. "I thought, 'Wow, he's good.' " After the first set was over, introductions were made and it was John's turn to be impressed. Not only could Paul actually tune a guitar, he also knew more than three chords on it, as well as the full lyrics of songs. He regaled the group with Eddie Cochran's "Twenty Flight Rock" and copied down the words for John to keep before he left. Thus began the partnership that would change popular music forever.

McCartney had the advantage of coming from a musical family. His father had been the leader of a jazz band in his bachelor days and still enjoyed playing piano at family gatherings and parties. He gave Paul a trumpet on one of his birthdays, which Paul traded for a guitar after realizing that he couldn't sing if he played trumpet. He soon discovered that, while right-handed in everything else, he was left-handed on guitar, a condition he finessed by restringing the instrument upside down. "You lose a mother—and you find a guitar?" asked brother Michael about Paul's sudden musical immersion following his mother's death. "He didn't have time to eat or think about anything else. He played it on the lavatory, in the bath, everywhere." One regular location was the house of George Harrison, his schoolmate at the Liverpool Institute. Though Paul was a year older than George, a common obsession with the guitar cemented their friendship two years before McCartney met Lennon. "I can tell you we both learned guitar from the same book," Paul recalled.

Despite McCartney's obvious abilities, Lennon was not sure he wanted Paul to join the Quarry Men. "I'd been kingpin up to then," he explained. "Now I thought, 'If I take him on, what will happen?' " Eventually, Lennon's ambition triumphed over his insecurity: "Was it better to have a guy who was better than the people I had in, obviously, or not? To make the group stronger, or let me be stronger? The decision was to let Paul in and make the group stronger." A similar calculation led George Harrison to be admitted, though not until some months after McCartney. At fourteen, George was still a child in the eyes of the college-aged Lennon; to make matters worse, George seemed to idolize John, even tagging along when John stepped out with girlfriends. Unlike the chord-strumming Lennon and Mc-Cartney, however, Harrison could play solos; his renditions of "Raunchy" clinched him a spot as the group's lead guitarist. Sometime in mid-1958, the Quarry Men privately recorded a shellac disc containing Buddy Holly's "That'll Be The Day," copies of which surfaced many years later on bootleg tapes. The boys sound young and energetic on the scratchy disc, especially John's lead vocal. They play and harmonize in tune and tempo, but there is no real indication at this point of the glories that lay ahead.

By the end of 1958 at the latest, three quarters of the band that would soon shake the world were playing together on a regular basis. Paul's and George's parents warmly encouraged their sons' endeavors, but John's aunt Mimi was dismissive. She told John he was wasting his time and slammed the door in the other boys' faces when they called for him. Julia, on the other hand, gladly welcomed the boys into her home and even joined in the rehearsals that, for acoustical reasons, took place in her bathroom. "Our toilet was probably one of the tiniest in all of Great Britain, and to see John, Paul, George, Pete Shotton, Ivan Vaughan and Mummy all scrambling around inside trying to find a place to sit was truly a wondrous sight indeed!" recalled John's half sister Julia Baird.

John spent more and more time with his mother during his middle teen years, often sleeping over on evenings and weekends, and it was on one such evening that she was killed. On July 15, 1958, Julia was walking to the bus stop after visiting Mimi when she was struck by a speeding car driven by an off-duty policeman. An inexperienced driver, the man saw Julia crossing the road ahead of him but mistakenly hit the accelerator instead of the brake. She died on the way to the hospital. John was crushed. "It was the worst-ever thing that happened to me. We'd caught up so much, me and Julia, in just a few years. We could communicate. We got on. She was great. I thought, 'Fuck it! Fuck it! Fuck it! That's really fucked everything! I've no responsibility to anyone now.' "

John said little about his mother's death, Pete Shotton recalled, but he did begin "to drink heavily for the first time in his life." Foreshadowing a lifelong inclination, John showed himself to be a vicious and violent drunk. Subsisting on an art student's stipend, he would threateningly beg drinks off other customers in pubs. One night, said Shotton, John "took a dislike to a Semitic-featured piano player named Reuben, who seemed a pleasant enough gentleman to me. . . . John—stinking drunk, as usual—persisted in disrupting the performance with taunts of 'creepy Jewboy' and 'they should've stuck you in the ovens with the rest of 'em!' " until the man collapsed in tears.

Shotton feared that his friend "seemed destined for Skid Row," and many of Lennon's classmates at the Liverpool Art College agreed. Had John not become successful through his art, alumnus Michael Isaacson remarked to Lennon biographer Ray Coleman, "He might well have become a really nasty piece of work. . . . Where his energy was channelled into creative music, it would have gone into something destructive instead of creative. He was strictly an all-or-nothing kind of guy." Lennon himself later admitted that if it hadn't have been for the Beatles, he probably would have ended up a wandering ne'er-do-well, like his father.

Rock 'n' roll proved to be John Lennon's salvation. One effect of Julia's death had been to deepen John's connection with Paul McCartney, though the prevailing male code of behavior in mid-1950s Liverpool inhibited them from discussing their common sorrow. "That was one of the things that brought John and I very close together," McCartney recalled. "We'd both lost our mothers. It was never really spoken about much; no one spoke about anything real. There was a famous expression: 'Don't real on me, man.' " Instead, the two young men communicated through their music. Paul's Liverpool Institute was situated directly next door to John's Liverpool Art College, and the two of them, often joined by George Harrison, spent countless hours together pursuing their common love of rock 'n' roll.

Cynthia Powell, the demure art student who later became John's first wife, was "absolutely mesmerized" by the boys' lunchtime songfests, as were many of her schoolmates. John and Paul "seemed to have been friends for many years," she recalled. "George, being younger and not writing songs, didn't have the communication with them, but John and Paul couldn't stop playing together, practicing the chords of the latest

Elvis Presley song, the Everly Brothers, and getting the confidence to try writing their own words. . . . Their harmonies were so beautiful. John had this image of being the toughest boy in college but his music showed what all of us knew was underneath. He had a gentleness that needed to come out, and it did in those songs."

CHAPTER 3

Starting a Reputation (*Please Please Me*)

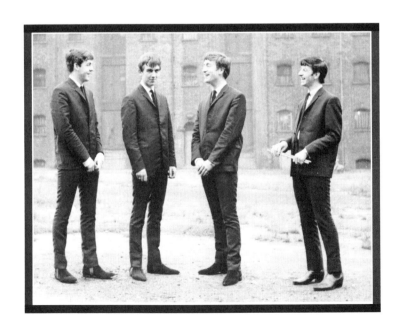

When John Lennon came out of semiretirement in 1974 to join Elton John on stage at New York's Madison Square Garden, he chose to conclude his three-song set with "I Saw Her Standing There," the very first song on the Beatles' very first album, *Please Please Me*. "I just wanted to have some fun and play some rock 'n' roll," Lennon explained. The other two songs he performed that night, his current number one hit, "Whatever Gets You Thru The Night," and his psychedelic era gem "Lucy In The Sky With Diamonds," also qualified as rockers, but for the encore Lennon wanted to "go all the way back." Apparently it was Elton John who suggested "I Saw Her Standing There," a selection Lennon readily seconded. With its instantly memorable opening couplet and its cheerful, rollicking beat, "I Saw Her Standing There" was not only a certain crowd pleaser but a rock 'n' roll classic.

"I Saw Her Standing There" was not the Beatles' first number one record—the single "Please Please Me" claimed that honor—but it was their first truly great song. By the time they recorded it for *Please Please Me* on February 11, 1963, it had long been a staple of their live stage act, and it remained so through their first visit to the United States in February 1964. With its signature "one, two, three, *fawr!*" count-in, its overt sexual yearning, and raw musical energy, "I Saw Her Standing

There" embodied the essence of rock 'n' roll. The rhythm made you want to dance, you felt the lyric in your pants, and the tune insisted that you sing along.

The song was one of the very earliest Lennon–McCartney compositions, written when John was still attending art college and Paul the Liverpool Institute. Although Paul wrote most of the song, it was John's small but crucial alteration of the song's second line that boosted "I Saw Her Standing There" to excellence. The two budding songwriters had skipped school one day and repaired to Paul's house to work on the song, recalled McCartney. "I remember I had the lyrics 'just 17, never been a beauty queen'—which John, it was one of the first times he ever went, 'What? Must change that . . .'—and it became, 'you know what I mean.' "

Lennon's insertion was as brilliant as it was basic. By adding five of the simplest words in the English language, he transformed the lyric from teenybopper cliché to sweaty groin-teaser. More than that, he made the listener complicit in the naughtiness. "You know what I mean" is the earliest example of a trait that would gain the Beatles both commercial success and heroic popular stature: their everyman identification with their audience. "You know what I mean" implicitly portrays the singer and the audience as equal parties, united against the adult world of propriety and responsibility. The listener *does* know what he means, and feels not only flattered by the vote of confidence but almost conspiratorially enlisted in the creative experience as well. Whether one is still a teenager or well past it, one's impressions of everything that the age seventeen represents lets the listener help write the rest of the song for him- or herself.

George Martin, the Beatles' producer, called "I Saw Her Standing There" a "potboiler"—straight-ahead, high-energy, irresistible rock 'n' roll. When Paul, singing lead, pauses a split second after asking, "So how could I dance with another," then leaps up to cry in unison with John, "Ohhhhh, when I saw her standing there," the anticipation is delicious, the exuberance overwhelming. Despite John's editing, the bulk of the lyrics is hardly sophisticated, yet the song's naiveté is so unaffected and its cumulative effect so ecstatic that it doesn't much matter. What counts is the overall sound, which is nothing less than joyous. A more fitting introduction to the music and persona of the Beatles is hard to imagine.

It is equally hard to imagine "I Saw Her Standing There" without McCartney's rampageous "one-two-three-*fawr*" count-in, but the un-released recordings of the song reveal that not until take nine does Paul actually cut it loose; before then, his count-ins are muffled, little more than whispers. Perhaps for that reason, the Beatles have some trouble hitting the right tempo on the song, a failing Paul uses to deflect blame when he flubs his vocal on take six. "She–I'll never dance with another," he sings, correcting himself in mid-word, but not quick enough to deceive George Martin up in the control booth, who signals for a new take. "Too fast," Paul interjects before Martin can say anything. When Martin points out the mistaken lyric, Paul again dodges, saying, "Yeah, but I mean it's too fast anyway." Later, in one of the very few overdubs on the album, the Beatles are adding handclaps to "I Saw Her Standing There." When one of them hits the wrong beat, it confuses the others and the pattern gradually dissolves into random clapping. Paul, already the de facto musical director of the group, murmurs that it should be "tidier." After a moment of quiet, a single pair of hands breaks into rapid, ironic applause, provoking boisterous snickers all around.

If "I Saw Her Standing There" marked a stunning debut, then "Twist And Shout," the closing song on *Please Please Me*, showed that it was no fluke. The Beatles didn't write "Twist And Shout," nor were they the first to record it, but they owned the song as surely as anything they ever played. From 1962, when they were still at Liverpool's Cavern Club, up through their American tour of 1965, "Twist And Shout" was a highlight of their live performances, and usually their showstopper. Raucous, rousing, raunchy, the song was a pulsating dance number that fairly screamed sex. The very phrase "rock 'n' roll" was, after all, black slang for making love. Beatles fans didn't know that, of course; they were virtually all white. But they were also mainly young and over-whelmingly female, and unconsciously they knew exactly what that music was about. The Beatles were never as overtly sexual as, say, the Rolling Stones, who projected more a sense of illicit danger. Yet despite the Beatles' clean image, sex was undoubtedly a large part of their appeal to the teenage girls who were their early core audience. One look at the films of their early concerts and the sweating, squirming, sobbing throngs of girls in various states of abandon confirms that.

The black rhythm-and-blues roots of rock 'n' roll were especially evident in "Twist And Shout," with its simple two-chord structure and call-and-response vocals. Lennon later said he preferred black songs "because they were more simple. . . . The blacks were singing directly and immediately about their pain and also about sex, which is why I like it." Separately, he also confessed that he hated to sing "Twist And Shout" when the Beatles were sharing the bill with black artists, because it was "their music" and "they can do these songs much better than us."

But even John, always the most self-critical Beatle, would have to admit that the Beatles do all right for a bunch of white boys, and John's lead vocal is the main reason. From the first syllable of "Twist And Shout," it's clear he's going for broke, and he pulls it off magnificently. It's not only the throaty roughness of his voice that rivets one's attention but the lustful urgency of his delivery when he tells the object of his desires to "C'mon and twist a little closer / And let me know that you're mine." The rest of the band is rightly caught up in John's frenzy, yet their playing is bright and steady. Although they do not match John's searing intensity, George and Paul's backing vocals reinforce his demands even as they egg him on. Leading into the last verse, all three stack their voices atop one another before finally exploding into manic shrieks as John sets off on a last dash around the track. When they repeat the exercise to conclude the song, the sense of climax is glorious, as if they have just enjoyed the orgasm of a lifetime.

In the years ahead, the Beatles would produce more mature works than "Twist And Shout" and "I Saw Her Standing There," but mature is not automatically better, especially as regards rock 'n' roll. When Lennon, speaking of the Beatles' early days, said, "What we generated was fantastic when we played straight rock, and there was nobody to touch us in Britain," he was talking about songs like "I Saw Her Standing There" and "Twist And Shout"—rock 'n' roll at its most basic and pure. It would be difficult to omit either of these songs from a list of the Beatles' all-time greatest musical achievements; each deserves a place in the permanent canon as much as any of the more sophisticated songs that appeared in years ahead.

To have produced such enduring, high-quality work is all the more extraordinary in light of the Beatles' extreme youth at this point. When they recorded *Please Please Me*, George Harrison was still nineteen. McCartney was twenty. Lennon and Ringo Starr, at twenty-two, were the group's elders. Yet they projected an aura of self-assured professionalism far beyond their years. They knew where they were going and had definite ideas about how to get there. Five months earlier, for example, when preparing to record their first single, the Beatles had rejected the song that George Martin wanted them to record. Although they had only narrowly passed their audition with Martin on June 6, 1962 (a story told in the next chapter of this book), the Beatles felt confident enough to tell him that, in McCartney's words, "It's a different thing we're going for, it's something new."

The song Martin had in mind was Mitch Murray's "How Do You Do It." He told the Beatles it was a guaranteed number one hit. Balking, they agreed that Murray's song might be commercial, but said it wasn't their style of music. "We figured, 'Now, wait a minute, we are now starting a reputation, a major reputation, hopefully, so we must be careful as to what we do,' " recalled McCartney. The Beatles said they wanted to record their own material. Martin replied that when the Beatles could write something as good as "How Do You Do It," they could record that; for now, he wanted them to follow his instructions.

Martin and the Beatles were both right. The Beatles did finally learn the song, and when they went inside Abbey Road's Studio Two on September 4, 1962, to record their first single record, "How Do You Do It" was the first thing they put on tape. A polished take of the song is still available, and it confirms the Beatles' wisdom in resisting Martin's wishes. Like most bubblegum songs, its melody is catchy enough, and the Beatles do a capable enough version of the song, with John singing lead, but the overall sound is pat, cloying, and safe—decidedly not what the Beatles were after. Nevertheless, it was the Beatles' arrangement of "How Do You Do It" that Gerry and the Pacemakers, a Liverpool pop group who had the same manager as the Beatles, copied when they recorded the song the following January. This version did indeed hit the top of the charts, just as George Martin had predicted.

The other song the Beatles recorded that evening was "Love Me Do." Like "I Saw Her Standing There," "Love Me Do" was one of the very earliest Lennon–McCartney compositions, written mainly by Paul. George Martin was never thrilled by the song, and it does not rank among the Beatles' finest efforts. Nevertheless, they themselves vastly preferred it to "How Do You Do It." The recording session itself was somewhat difficult, according to Lewisohn, who reports that it took fifteen takes to perfect the rhythm track alone, after which vocal overdubs also "took a long time." Foreshadowing a conflict that years later would spark nasty tensions within the Beatles, McCartney apparently felt that Starr's drumming on the song was not good enough. Others agreed with Paul, and a week later, on September 11, a second recording of "Love Me Do" was made, this time with session man Andy White handling the drums and Ringo relegated to the tambourine. White also played drums on "P.S. I Love You," another Lennon–McCartney original recorded that night.

"Love Me Do," backed by "P.S. I Love You," was duly issued as the Beatles' first single on October 5, 1962. It rose as high as seventeen on the British charts, a respectable but by no means earth-shattering showing, and even this was largely due to ten thousand copies that allegedly were quietly purchased by the Beatles' manager, Brian Epstein. The charting of "Love Me Do," McCartney later said, was what convinced him the Beatles were going to make it. But it was the next single that actually did the trick.

"Please Please Me" was a one hundred percent John Lennon composition, inspired by Roy Orbison's "Only the Lonely." John's original version of the song was very slow, almost dirgelike, and it went through dramatic changes before it was released. When George Martin first heard "Please Please Me," he felt it was too gloomy to succeed; he urged the Beatles to speed up the song and add some tight harmonies. It was the first of many times that Martin would show that "he could see beyond what we were offering him," said McCartney. The moment the Beatles finished recording the new, faster version of "Please Please Me," Martin recalled in his autobiography, "I pressed the intercom button in the control room and said, 'Gentlemen, you've just made your first number one record.' "

And so they had. "Please Please Me," recorded on November 26, 1962, and released on January 11, 1963, hit number one in the U.K. on February 22 and remained there for two weeks. Of course, the Beatles were thrilled. They had little time to enjoy their new success, however, for they were now fulfilling a punishing schedule of live performances across the length and breadth of Britain. Still, with "Please Please Me" on its way to number one by early February, it seemed wise to capitalize on the breakthrough by releasing a full album. The problem was when to record it. The Beatles were booked virtually every day for weeks. The solution was for the group to gather at Abbey Road on Monday, February 11, complete the album in a single day-long marathon session, and leave London in time to drive to gigs the next day in Yorkshire and Lancashire.

It was precisely because the Beatles made *Please Please Me* in one day that John Lennon later said it was one of his favorite Beatles albums. Actually, the Beatles had already recorded four of the songs that would go on the album: "Love Me Do" and "Please Please Me," plus their respective B-sides, "P.S. I Love You" and "Ask Me Why." Since albums usually contained fourteen songs, the Beatles had to record ten more numbers during the February 11 session. With their hectic performance schedule, there was no time to learn, much less write, any new songs, so Martin suggested they choose songs from their stage act, which was now regularly provoking hysteria among audiences, not only at their long-standing venue, the Cavern Club in Liverpool, but at dance halls throughout Britain.

The idea was to capture the energy and immediacy of the Beatles' live shows, to give listeners the feeling they were *inside* the Cavern. The studio technology of the era complemented this approach. With only two "tracks" available on a recording tape, there was room for only one "overdub" after the fact (and on February 11, the time deadline made such overdubs impractical). The upshot was that all four Beatles had to perform their parts perfectly on the same take of the song, or try it again. A further complication was the heavy cold that Lennon had picked up in the course of an especially bitter winter. "They had a big glass jar of Zubes throat sweets on top of the piano, rather like the ones you see in a sweet shop," said engineer Norman Smith. "Paradoxically, by the side of that, was a big carton of Peter Stuyvesant cigarettes, which they smoked incessantly."

Things got under way at ten o'clock that morning and, except for a supper break, the Beatles worked straight through until past ten that night. They even crammed in extra rehearsals during the lunch hour, astonishing George Martin and Norman Smith, who had adjourned to a local pub for "a pie and a pint." Smith recalled, "When we came back, they'd been playing right through. We couldn't believe it. We had never seen a group work right through their lunch break before." Printed estimates of exactly how long it took to record the album vary from nine and three-quarters hours up to sixteen hours, an instructive example of how factually unreliable most published accounts of the Beatles' lives and work can be. Lewisohn's analysis of EMI's internal studio recording sheets, however, pinpoints the total time beyond dispute. "There can scarcely have been 585 more productive minutes in the history of recorded music," he exults.

One can hear the hurried atmosphere of the recording session in a comment George Martin makes in the middle of take two of "Misery." Something doesn't sound right to the producer and he briskly whistles the band to a halt and asks whether George Harrison "has changed guitars now." Harrison says no, but "I've probably changed the tone." Martin asks him to change it back and play with "a little less volume, George." Then, all but immediately, Martin adds, "Okay, here we go," and the Beatles launch right back into the song. Progress is further delayed, however, by Paul, who repeatedly misstates the line "I won't see her no more." Paul keeps singing that he *wants* to see the girl. Finally, John finally spells it out for him: "I *won't* see her no more . . . I can see *other* girls."

Along with "There's A Place," "Misery" is one of the two sleeping beauties on *Please Please Me*. Both are Lennon–McCartney originals that were written primarily by John. What makes them exquisite is the sublime blending of Paul's and John's voices, especially on the stutter-step opening and sustained vocal phrases of "There's A Place." This song also offers the first hint of the free-thinking sensibility that John would later articulate more fully in such compositions as "I'm Only Sleeping" and "Tomorrow Never Knows." The place he sings about in "There's A Place" is one "Where I can go / When I feel low . . . And it's my mind." Not only is he never alone in his mind, but "there's no sorrow" and "no sad tomorrow," an idealized vision that starkly contrasts with the reality of his troubled childhood.

Lennon's childhood was also the source for the final Lennon–McCartney song on the album, "Do You Want To Know A Secret." When he was a baby, his mother, Julia, used to sing him the song "Wishing Well" from the Walt Disney movie *Snow White and the Seven Dwarfs*, which advised that if you want to know a secret, you had to promise not to tell. "Do You Want To Know A Secret" was given to George Harrison for his one lead vocal on the album (Ringo sang lead on the Shirelles tune "Boys"), and it was later released as a single in the United States as well, where it reached number two in the charts. In the U.K., however, it was a number one hit for Billy J. Kramer and the Dakotas, yet another Liverpool group managed by Brian Epstein.

As afternoon turned to evening and the Beatles supplemented their five original compositions with five additional "cover" versions of other artists' material, George Martin was amazed by their superhuman endurance. Without doubt, the high point of the entire session was Lennon's transcendent assault on "Twist And Shout." The song was left until the very end, for there would be no going back once it was begun. As Martin recalled, "There was one number which always caused a furor in the Cavern—'Twist And Shout.' John absolutely screamed it. God alone knows what he did to his larynx each time he performed it, because he made a sound rather like tearing flesh. That *had* to be right on the first take, because I knew perfectly well that if we had to do it a second time it would never be as good."

It was past Abbey Road Studios' usual ten o'clock closing hour by the time the Beatles took their places. Lennon seems to have psyched himself up for his performance the way that a boxer entering the ring would; one engineer recalled that he actually "stripped to the waist to do this most amazingly raucous vocal." Two minutes and thirty-three seconds later, it was over. With John leading the charge, the Beatles conquered "Twist And Shout" on the first take—an awesome display of guts, talent, and professionalism.

Please Please Me vastly accelerated the Beatles' impending rise to unparalleled fortune and fame. Even more remarkable than the speed with which the album was made were the musical quality, originality, and versatility it exhibited. In 1963, very few recording artists composed their own songs at all, much less songs of the caliber Lennon and McCartney wrote. Moreover, most album follow-ups to hit singles were marketing gimmicks that merely recycled the single, padded out with forgettable filler material. *Please Please Me*, by contrast, contained two all-time rock 'n' roll classics—"I Saw Her Standing There" and "Twist And Shout"—two number one hits—"Please Please Me" and "Do You Want To Know A Secret"—and a handful of such memorable originals as "There's A Place" and "Misery," all scattered amidst interesting cover versions of other songs.

Please Please Me was a runaway, record-breaking hit in Great Britain. Released on March 22, 1963, it took seven weeks to hit number one, but it remained there for an unprecedented twenty-nine weeks, riding the wave of mass Beatlemania that engulfed the country. In the United States, the album was released under a different title, *Introducing the Beatles*, and, oddly, it went nowhere. Capitol, the American division of EMI, deafly dismissed the Beatles as a British fad of no interest to American record buyers and refused to issue the album. Instead, the tiny Vee Jay label released it, and, deprived of publicity or air play, it sank without a trace. As spring turned to summer and then fall, *Please Please Me* continued its reign at the top of the British charts, and the Beatles followed it up with one number one single after another: "From Me To You," "She Loves You," "I Want To Hold Your Hand." By year's end, Great Britain was besotted with its four young heroes. In the United States, they remained all but unknown, but that would change, in a most spectacular way, soon enough.

C H A P T E R   4

Mach Schau!: The Hamburg–Liverpool Apprenticeship

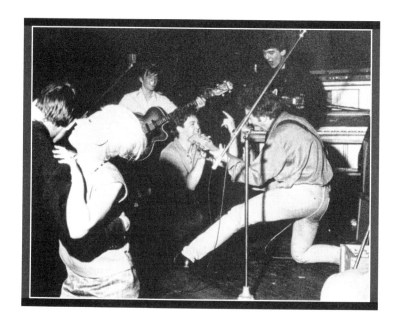

It was typical of John Lennon that his last remark on stage as a Beatle was a joke. The moment came at the end of *Let It Be*, the documentary film released in May 1970, a month after the Beatles officially disbanded. The film climaxes with the famous midday rooftop concert above downtown London, when the Beatles, if only briefly, seem to forget all that has come between them and get back to where they once belonged: playing rock 'n' roll like no one else. After the police arrive to stop the show, John steps to the microphone and says, with a smirk, "I'd like to say thank you on behalf of the group and ourselves, and I hope we passed the audition." Off-camera, hearty laughter erupts. After all, by the time *Let It Be* was shot, in January 1969, the Beatles were the biggest musical and show business phenomenon of their time; the idea of their having to pass an audition was absurd.

The irony is that the Beatles did fail their first big record company audition, with industry giant Decca, back in 1962. What's more, they nearly failed the subsequent audition with EMI that won them their first recording contract and made everything else possible. The Beatles had by then been turned down by virtually every major company in the British record business. Columbia and HMV, two prestigious, big-budget labels within the EMI corporate empire, had not even bothered

37

to give the group a studio test before saying no. Decca did send a man to hear the Beatles in Liverpool, and even followed up with a studio audition in London, but still reached the same conclusion. Dick Rowe, the head of the Artists and Repertoire department at Decca, explained to Beatles manager Brian Epstein that guitar-based groups were "on the way out." Later, at a press conference during the height of Beatlemania, McCartney remarked that Rowe "must be kicking himself now." Lennon added, "I hope he kicks himself to death."

George Martin, who eventually did sign the Beatles for EMI's tiny Parlophone label, nevertheless could see why his colleagues had passed on the group. The demonstration disc that Epstein had been playing for record companies was simply not that impressive. It contained an uninspired selection of old standards, along with a handful of unremarkable original compositions. Yet Martin was struck by "an unusual quality of sound, a certain roughness that I hadn't encountered before." He emphatically did not think the Beatles were "the greatest thing ever," but he reckoned it was "worth a shot" to hear how they sounded inside a studio.

The Parlophone audition took place on June 6, 1962, inside the square white two-story mansion on Abbey Road in north London that housed the EMI recording studios. Oddly, the Beatles themselves— who at this point still counted Pete Best, not Ringo Starr, as their drummer—were unaware that they were auditioning. On the contrary, they were under the impression that EMI had already signed them to a contract and that this was a proper recording session, intended to produce their debut single. According to archivist Mark Lewisohn's analysis of internal EMI documents, the confusion stemmed from the fact that George Martin had sent manager Epstein an EMI recording contract some weeks earlier, which Epstein had signed and returned to EMI on June 5. But this contract in fact committed EMI to nothing, for Martin himself had not signed it. Nor was he obliged to, unless he liked what he heard at the June 6 session.

As it happened, Martin's reaction to the Beatles' music at the audition was again lukewarm. Exactly how many songs the band played during the 6:00 P.M. to 8:00 P.M. session is unknown, but Martin later wrote that, "Frankly, the material didn't impress me, least of all their own songs. I felt that I was going to have to find suitable material for them, and was quite certain that their songwriting ability had no saleable future!"

The Beatles recorded a total of four songs that evening: "Love Me Do," "P.S. I Love You," and "Ask Me Why"—Lennon and McCartney originals that later were re-recorded for the *Please Please Me* album— and "Besame Mucho," an old Latin crooner that McCartney revived years later during the *Let It Be* sessions. Of the four, only "Besame Mucho" still survives on tape, and it offers an amusing aural snapshot of the group in early youth. The Beatles play "Besame Mucho" capably and with spirit, and McCartney does his best on lead vocal to put the song across, but there's no overcoming the mismatch between band and material. Try as they might, the Beatles sound earnestly silly, especially when Paul, apparently trying to kick some energy into the song's lolling Latin beat, punctuates its verses with the ludicrous exclamation, "Cha-cha-*boom*!" If this was typical of the day's output, it's no wonder Martin had mixed feelings about the group.

Or at least about their music. As people, Martin found the Beatles— specifically Harrison, Lennon, and McCartney—delightful. (Pete Best, according to Martin, didn't say a word the whole session.) Indeed, it seems that what ultimately won the audition for the Beatles was not so much their musical talent as their personal charisma. "It was love at first sight," Martin recalled. "That may seem exaggerated, but the fact is that we hit it off straight away. . . . The most impressive thing was their engaging personalities. They were just great people to be with." Liverpool was famous throughout England for its comedians, and it seems that the Beatles lived up to the image and then some. After the session, Martin lectured them on technical improvements they needed to make if they were to succeed as recording artists. Engineer Norman Smith recalled Martin concluding, " 'Look, I've laid into you for quite a time, you haven't responded. Is there anything you don't like?' I re-member they all looked at each for a long while, shuffling their feet, then George Harrison took a long look at George and said, 'Yeah, I don't like your tie!' That cracked the ice for us and for the next fifteen to twenty minutes they were pure entertainment. When they left to go home George and I just sat there saying, 'Phew! What do you think of that lot then?' I had tears running down my face." Separately, Smith added, "Let's be honest: they got that contract because of their enthusiasm, their presence, not because of their music. During that one conversation, we realized that they were something special."

Figuring he had nothing to lose, Martin decided to sign the Beatles to a (very stingy) recording contract. The first album they recorded together, *Please Please Me*, was, as already noted, a studio version of the wildly popular live shows the Beatles were then doing at Liverpool's Cavern Club. But the Cavern shows were, in turn, the fruit of the crucial apprenticeship the Beatles had already served in Hamburg. Beginning on August 17, 1960, the group made five visits to the German port city in the space of twenty-eight months, logging a grueling eight hundred hours on stage. If *Please Please Me* was the Cavern on tape, the Cavern was the Hamburg experience, writ large, polished and powerful.

"It was Hamburg that had done it," John Lennon said to Hunter Davies in the Beatles' authorized biography. "That's where we'd really developed. To get the Germans going and keep it up for twelve hours at a time, we'd really had to hammer. We would never have developed as much if we'd stayed at home." John exaggerated slightly about the Beatles playing twelve hours straight, but even the eight-hour shifts they did play were exhausting, for their audiences (and bosses) were tough, demanding types who insisted that the Beatles "Mach schau!"— Put on a show!—the louder and wilder, the better.

Hamburg was the vital crucible that transformed the Beatles from talented wanna-be's into entry-level craftsmen. Above all, it was in Hamburg that the Beatles began to find their own sound, a raucous yet melodious mixture of driving guitars, crashing drums, and screaming vocals, all cleverly counterpointed by the occasional romantic ballad. It was also in Hamburg that the Beatles became show business professionals who learned to work an audience, a skill that served them well in years to come. In Hamburg, the Beatles were like fairground barkers who sought to entice passersby into their show tent, McCartney once said. "People would appear at the door of the club and we were on stage and nobody [was] at the tables. . . . And we'd pretend we hadn't seen 'em and we'd rock out. And we'd find we got three of them in. . . . We eventually sold the club out and that, I would say, [is when] we started to know [we were] going to be big. . . . Then we went to another club; the same thing happened there. Then we went back to England and we started playing the Cavern, same thing happened there. . . . Each place we went, when we started there it was nothing, when we finished playing at that club, it was always like this incredible excitement had built up."

The initial Hamburg visit took place during what can be called Year One of the Beatles, 1960. In the Beatles' biography, Hunter Davies rightly singled out 1960 as "the vital year . . . . when they started using the name 'Beatles,' when they got their first professional tour, to Scotland, and when they made their first and all-important visit to Hamburg." These were key milestones, but the journey was far from easy.

John, Paul, and George had been playing together, accompanied by a changing cast of minor characters, since sometime in 1958, but the Quarry Men, as they were called, had so little luck attracting paid engagements that "for several months in 1959 [they] seem to have ceased existence altogether," according to Lewisohn. In January 1960, Stu Sutcliffe, a gifted, brooding painter who had become John's close friend and roommate at art college, joined the group. Though he had never played a musical instrument in his life, he tried, at John's urging, to learn bass guitar. Unfortunately, he never mastered it, and to hide this fact would habitually turn his back to the audience. The group was further handicapped by their perpetual lack of a drummer, which they would explain away by declaring, "The rhythm's in the guitars." When the chance came in May 1960 to tour Scotland as the backing group to a minor singer named Johnny Gentle, local drummer Tommy Moore was hurriedly drafted, but after nine days on the road, Moore had had enough. The tour was little short of disastrous, with funds so tight that meals often were missed, at least one hotel bill dodged, and tempers often frayed. Back in Liverpool, the band endured further indignity by playing instrumental backing music to a striptease act in July.

Though Stu Sutcliffe was no musician, he did make one major contribution to the development of the Beatles: helping to name them. The group began 1960 still called the Quarry Men, but in a letter

Sutcliffe wrote that January seeking employment for the band, he refers to them as the "Beatals." Over the next seven months, this name became first the Silver Beats, then the Silver Beetles, then the Silver Beatles and finally, simply, the Beatles. Actually, Sutcliffe shared paternity rights with John Lennon. Apparently Sutcliffe came up with the general theme of Beetles, inspired either by the name of rock 'n' roller Buddy Holly's backing group, the Crickets, or by the motorcycle gang called Beetles in *The Wild One*, the 1954 film starring Marlon Brando. Lennon, with his gift for wordplay, then made the suggestion of replacing the second "e" in Beetles with an "a," thus invoking not only the antiestablishment beatniks of the 1950s but also the beat, perhaps the primary characteristic that distinguished rock 'n' roll from mainstream pop music.

Although they appeared once as "The Beatles" in June 1960, the group did not adopt the name permanently until they went to Hamburg that August. By then, they had also acquired a drummer, Pete Best, who would remain with them for the next two years, up through the audition for George Martin at Abbey Road. Best was taken on literally days before the Beatles left for Germany; the Liverpool promoter of the deal, Allan Williams, refused to let the group go if they didn't find a drummer. At the time, Best was eighteen, owned his own drum kit, and hoped for a career as a professional. He was the son of Mona Best, who ran the Casbah Club in Liverpool, a basement hangout for teenagers where the Quarry Men had played in October 1959. Returning there by chance on August 6, 1960, the Beatles learned that Pete's group was about to disband. After a perfunctory audition, they invited him to join them and together they set off for Hamburg.

The Beatles played at four different clubs in Hamburg—the Indra, the Kaiserkeller, the Top Ten, and the All Star—each of which was located in the grungy, sex-soaked part of town known as the Reeperbahn. Not surprisingly, the clubs counted among their regular clientele large numbers of prostitutes, sailors, rock 'n' rollers, and street toughs; many of the latter came out to drink and fight as much as to hear music, thus obliging each club to employ its own protection in the form of switchblade-wielding waiters. The Beatles had seen plenty of violence at clubs back in Liverpool, usually courtesy of the notorious teddy boys;

in fact, they now dressed like teds themselves, with black leather jackets and boots. Still, this aspect of Hamburg sobered them. Experience taught them to stay well clear of the many British servicemen on shore leave. "We knew that by the end of the evening most of them would probably be lying there half dead," Harrison later said. "If the waiters or the patrons didn't gang up on them then the street toughs roaming around outside definitely would. . . . Most of the time they weren't just knocked about either, but bludgeoned or even knifed." Recalling the same scenes, Lennon remarked, "I've never seen such killers."

It was in this atmosphere that the Beatles learned to "Mach schau!"—to play as if their lives depended on it. Their initiation began at the Indra, a former strip club, where they played for forty-eight nights before complaints about the noise forced the owner to move them to the Kaiserkeller Club. Here, they shared the bill with Rory Storm and the Hurricanes, another Liverpool rock 'n' roll group, and got to know the Hurricanes' drummer, Ringo Starr. Eager to please, the Beatles literally threw themselves into their performances. Especially John but also Paul would leap about the stage like a madman, their frenzy fueled not only by the vast quantities of free beer sent up to the band, but also by pep pills the Beatles cadged from the old woman who minded the ladies' room. John often hurled insults at the audience as well, snarling that the customers were "fucking nazis" and asking where their tanks were. Undaunted, the crowd simply shouted for more.

Offstage, the Beatles' life was no less raucous. Their living quarters were so filthy and gloomy, they dubbed them "the Black Hole of Calcutta." Damp, chilly, and smelly, the rooms were located directly behind the movie screen of a run-down cinema, the Bambi. There was no bathroom; the Beatles had to wash in the men's room. They got little sleep; the blaring soundtrack of the Bambi's matinee show would invariably awaken them just hours after they had nodded off. The Beatles were onstage until at least two o'clock most mornings, did not get home for some hours after that, and often didn't go right to sleep. According to Pete Best, female fans often lay in wait inside the Bambi. It was common practice for the Beatles to share as many as six to eight girls a night, Best said, adding that they would often swap partners in the middle of the carnal activity they liked to refer to as "Gazunka!" Lennon later maintained, no doubt accurately, that the stories of the Beatles' exploits in Hamburg "built out of all proportion" over the years. Yet he himself was quoted in 1971 admitting that "Hamburg was fantastic. Between the whores and the groupies our dicks all just about dropped off."

Nevertheless, it was the Beatles' music, not their sex lives, that blossomed most impressively in Hamburg. They had arrived as raw and not very accomplished musicians; indeed, some Liverpool rockers already on the Hamburg circuit had tried to prevent their coming, protesting it would poison the well for everyone if a band as shoddy as the Beatles were brought in. But three and a half months of virtually nonstop performing changed all that. By the time the Beatles returned to Liverpool that December—minus Stu Sutcliffe, who remained behind with his German fiancée, Astrid Kirchherr, a photographer who later helped originate the "Beatle haircut"—they had improved so much that friends back home hardly recognized the band. They themselves didn't appreciate how much things had changed until the night of December 27, 1960, when their performance at Liverpool's Town Hall Ballroom provoked a near riot, as hundreds of fans suddenly rushed the stage, an outbreak of mass hysteria that foreshadowed the mania of years to come. "It was that evening," Lennon later said, ". . . when we began to think for the first time that we were good. Up to Hamburg we'd thought we were okay, but not good enough."

The significance of the Town Hall Ballroom show was immense. Hunter Davies calls it "the watershed" date in the group's history; Lewisohn writes that, "If any one live performance in the Beatles' career could be described as *the* turning point, it would be this." For the explosion at Town Hall led directly to a packed schedule of club dates in and around Liverpool; these not only kept the Beatles furiously busy during the first three months of 1961 but secured the fanatic base of local support that eventually propelled them onto the national and world stage.

One of the shows triggered by the Town Hall event was the Beatles' debut performance, on February 9, at the aptly named Cavern Club, a dank basement dance hall where, exactly nine months later, they met their future manager, Brian Epstein. From February 1961 to August 1963, observes Lewisohn, "the Cavern was like the Beatles' second home and, in Liverpool at least, the two names were synonymous." Often the Beatles played both the lunch and late-night shifts; queues of fans routinely stretched down the block, while inside the club it was common for audience members to faint from the combination of non-existent ventilation and hero-worship infatuation. The group played dozens of other venues in the following months, in Liverpool and beyond, but it was the Cavern Club that held first claim on their affections. "We probably loved the Cavern best of anything," George Harrison recalled. ". . . We were playing to our own fans, who were like us. They would come in their lunchtimes to hear us and bring their sandwiches to eat instead of having lunch. We would do the same, eating our lunch while we played."

The crowds and enthusiasm that greeted the Beatles grew by leaps and bounds throughout the rest of 1961 and into 1962, yet the group remained essentially a regional phenomenon. In June 1961, in Hamburg, they participated in their first professional recording sessions, providing rhythm and vocal backing for Tony Sheridan, an Elvis Presley sound-alike who also hailed from Liverpool. The record they made together, "My Bonnie," though by no means extraordinary, did later serve to bring the Beatles to the attention of Brian Epstein. Nevertheless, breaking out of the Liverpool ghetto and gaining the ears of the big London record companies proved an elusive goal until May 9, 1962. That day, the Beatles awoke in Hamburg (where they were making their third visit) to find a telegram from Epstein: "Congratulations boys. EMI request recording session. Please rehearse new material." The group returned to England May 31, and a week later presented themselves at Abbey Road Studios for what proved to be their historic meeting with George Martin.

Following the June 6 session, Martin told Epstein that before proceeding he wanted a different drummer for the group. The Beatles could do what they wished for live shows, but a session drummer would be used for studio recordings. Martin later wrote that his remarks inadvertently turned out to be "something in the nature of a last straw," because Paul, John, and George "already wanted Pete Best out and

Ringo Starr in." The three original Beatles had plausible reasons for their discontent with Best. Pete Shotton later wrote that John, Paul, and George had never considered Best a "real" Beatle; they had taken him on because they needed a drummer to go to Hamburg in August 1960, and the chronic shortage of drummers in Liverpool meant that beggars could not be choosers. There was no doubt that Best was popular with Liverpool audiences; commonly regarded as the best-looking Beatle, he enjoyed an especially large number of female admirers. Indeed, it was charged that he was gotten rid of precisely for this reason: Paul and John were jealous of his star power. McCartney later dismissed this as nonsense; as both a musician and a personality, Starr simply fit in with the original Beatles better than Best did. "I wasn't jealous of [Best] because he was handsome," McCartney told Hunter Davies. "That's all junk. He just couldn't play. Ringo was so much better. We wanted him out for that reason." Nor had Best really shared in the camaraderie of the group, McCartney said separately: "We were the wacky trio and Pete was perhaps a little more . . . sensible." Ringo, on the other hand, had hit it off with the Beatles ever since they had first met at the Kaiserkeller. For his part, Best was shocked and embittered by the decision to drop him from the group. The notion that he wasn't a good enough drummer naturally offended him, but years later he said that what hurt most of all "was that I knew they were going to be big. I could tell it. We all could. . . . I knew I was going to miss all the fun of that."

George Martin later speculated about how history might have been different had he rejected the Beatles like so many of his industry colleagues already had. "I was the last chance," Martin later wrote. "At that time I was very much the joker in the music-business pack, and if I, too, had turned them down, it's very hard to guess what would have happened. Possibly they would just have broken up, and never have been heard of again."

The available evidence suggests, however, that the Beatles were bound to break through before long. Martin was not, in fact, their last chance for a recording contract; the Philips company was going to be approached next. More to the point, the Beatles were experiencing enormous success as live performers. Their dream was to be "bigger than Elvis," and as their audiences grew steadily larger, louder, and more fanatically dedicated, this dream seemed less and less impossible. Why would they lose heart now? As John later explained, "We thought we were the best before anybody else had even heard of us, back in Hamburg and Liverpool . . . and believing that is what made us what we were."

C H A P T E R 5

Where Music Had to Go (With The Beatles)

JOHN LENNON WAS OF TWO MINDS ABOUT MANY THINGS IN LIFE, AND NOT LEAST HIMSELF. "PART OF ME SUSPECTS I'M A loser and part of me thinks I'm God Almighty," he said, laughing, in an interview with *Playboy* magazine just weeks before his murder in 1980. So it is not surprising that in that same interview Lennon expressed two contradictory views of the Beatles' early work. On the one hand, he asserted that the Beatles were the best band in the world during their Hamburg and Liverpool days. On the other, he disparaged some of the first songs that he and Paul McCartney wrote together, calling them "pieces of garbarge." Songs like "Little Child" and "Tell Me Why," which appeared on the Beatles' second and third albums respectively, were simply "knocked off" to satisfy the public's ceaseless demand for more Beatles records, said Lennon. John seemed most bothered by lyrical weaknesses in these and other early songs. Referring to his collaboration with McCartney, he said, "We were just writing songs à la Everly Brothers, à la Buddy Holly, pop songs with no more thought to them than that—to create a sound. The words were almost irrelevant."

But what a sound! To be sure, Lennon and McCartney wrote their share of what Paul—always the most carefully spoken Beatle—diplomatically called "work" songs. However, during the very months in 1963 when John and Paul were churning out "Hold Me Tight" and

49

other forgettable songs, they were also writing such gems as "All My Loving" and "This Boy," as well as the charming "From Me To You" and the musically intricate "It Won't Be Long." And of course their most striking creations during this period were "She Loves You" and "I Want To Hold Your Hand," two songs that not only were huge hits but which came to rank as enduring landmarks in the history of rock 'n' roll.

The Beatles had been avid students of rock 'n' roll since their schoolboy days. Because Liverpool was England's main Atlantic port, sailors were always bringing back records from America, giving the town a very rich musical life. As McCartney once recalled, "You'd hear about Big Bill Broonzy, Gene Vincent, Bill Haley, Ray Charles, Little Richard, Chuck Berry, Elvis, before a lot of people knew about it in America, really." The single most important influence was black music. "If the Beatles ever wanted a sound it was R&B," McCartney said separately. "That's what we used to listen to, what we used to like and what we wanted to be like. . . . Whenever we were asked who our favorite people were, we'd say, 'Black, R&B, Motown.' " The Beatles began by doing cover versions of songs by these and other forerunners. But especially when they moved on to write their own material, they brought their own intrinsic sensibilities to bear as well, producing a sound that was rooted in the past yet completely of the present, influenced by its predecessors yet utterly unique.

The Beatles' most important artistic contemporary, Bob Dylan, quickly recognized how special they were. By 1964, Dylan had acquired a reputation across America on the strength of such powerful folk songs as "Blowin' In The Wind," "Masters Of War" and "The Times They Are A-Changin'." He was driving through Colorado, he later recalled, when the lightning struck: "We had the radio on and eight of the Top Ten songs were Beatles songs. In Colorado! 'I Want To Hold Your Hand,' all those early ones. They were doing things nobody was doing. Their chords were outrageous, just outrageous, and their harmonies made it all valid." Dylan said he kept quiet about how much he admired the Beatles, but "in my head, the Beatles were it. In Colorado, I started thinking but it was so far out I couldn't deal with it—eight in the Top Ten. It seemed to me a definite line was being drawn."

If the Beatles influenced Dylan toward a more rock 'n' roll future, he in turn influenced them toward a more poetic approach to songwriting. But this development came later. In early 1963, when Lennon and McCartney were penning songs to follow up the Beatles' first number one single and album, their lyrics were still almost mindlessly simple, cliché-ridden expressions of puppy love or adolescent macho posturing. According to McCartney, this was a matter of simple commerce; the Beatles' lyrics were consciously designed to appeal to the group's main audience, teenage girls. He later explained, "A lot of our songs— 'From Me To You' is [one]—were directly addressed to our fans. . . . 'From *Me* To *You*,' 'Please Please *Me*,' '*She* Loves *You*.' Personal pronouns. We always used to do that."

"From Me To You," the first single after "Please Please Me," was released on April 11 and quickly became the Beatles' second number one hit. With its harmonica introduction and loping beat, "From Me To You" did not sound dramatically different from "Please Please Me," but McCartney saw it as a breakthrough for Lennon and himself. Instead of repeating the usual rock 'n' roll variations on the C chord— jumping three steps to F and four steps to G, or slipping into A minor, the minor chord equivalent of C—the middle eight passage of "From Me To You" shifted from C to G minor. The effect on the two fledgling songwriters was like that on a novice tennis player who has finally learned to hit a backhand. "That middle eight was a very big departure for us," McCartney said, adding, "Going to G minor and a C takes you to a whole new world. It was exciting."

The Beatles' next single, "She Loves You," broke even more ground. Written on twin beds in a Newcastle hotel room five days before it was recorded on July 1, "She Loves You" featured an infectiously unsophisticated chorus containing the famous "yeah, yeah, yeah" refrain that became the early Beatles' trademark. Although "She Loves You" became the biggest selling single in British history, Abbey Road recording engineer Norman Smith's first impression of it was far from favorable. "I was setting up the microphone when I saw the lyrics on the music stand," he recalled. " 'She Loves You Yeah Yeah Yeah, She Loves You Yeah Yeah Yeah, She Loves You Yeah Yeah Yeah Yeah.' I thought, Oh my God, what a lyric! This is going to be one that I *do not* like. But when they started to sing it—bang, wow, terrific, I was up at the mixer jogging around."

Not being a teenage girl, Smith may not have related to the lyrics of "She Loves You," but the song still enchanted him because it worked on so many other levels. As Lennon later emphasized, "It was the hook and the line and the sound we were going for." The hook of "She Loves You"—the "yeah, yeah, yeah" response to the title line—could not have been simpler, either lyrically or melodically, yet Lennon and McCartney sing it with such urgency that it can't be mistaken for pap. The overall sound, in turn, grows out of the hook, which is shrewdly positioned at the start of the song. Thus the opening explosion of vocal energy, riding atop a thumping drumbeat, thunders past like a herd of runaway horses. Things calm down as the first verse unfolds, telling the story of a young lovers spat that might yet be mended, but the horses come roaring back when the chorus returns after the second verse (and again after the third). But this time the listener is ready and feels the exhilaration of riding astride the herd instead of being overrun by it. The resulting mood is deliriously enthusiastic: She loves you, so don't be a fool—apologize and be happy again.

Even at this early date, it was not unheard of for Lennon and McCartney to write songs separately, but in later years both of them recalled "She Loves You" as a true collaborative effort. Indeed, when Lennon was asked in a 1971 interview, "Which songs really stick in your mind as being Lennon–McCartney songs?", he singled out "She Loves You," along with the two singles that immediately preceded and followed it—"From Me To You" and "I Want To Hold Your Hand." His memory of writing "I Want To Hold Your Hand" was particularly vivid: "I remember when we got the chord that made the song. We were in Jane Asher's house, downstairs in the cellar playing on the piano at the same time. And we had, 'Oh you-u-u . . . got that something . . .' And Paul hits this chord and I turn to him and say, 'That's it!' I said, 'Do that again!' In those days, we really used to absolutely write like that—both playing into each other's noses."

Like "She Loves You," "I Want To Hold Your Hand" showcased Lennon and McCartney's gift for instantly captivating melodies, as well as the Beatles' collective ability to translate these melodies into rousing pop music. Again, it was not the lyrics but the total sound that made "I Want To Hold Your Hand" a winner, a point well illustrated by the Beatles' recordings of the songs in German. Odeon, the West German division of EMI, had insisted that English-language records would not sell well in Germany, so the Beatles, after some resistance, agreed to re-record these two numbers in German. Aside from having lost some fidelity in the transferring process during "I Want To Hold Your Hand," the songs still succeed in the foreign tongue. Thirty years after the fact, it is a bit odd hearing German instead of English syllables coming out of Lennon and McCartney's mouths, but the overall effect of "Komm, Gib Mir Deine Hand" and "Sie Liebt Dich" is much the same as with the English-language originals.

The discovery of the third chord on Jane Asher's piano may be what made "I Want To Hold Your Hand" for John Lennon as co-composer, but what most grabs the listener is the brilliantly spirited, full-octave leap in melody on the words "I want to hold your *hand*." Suddenly, a song that begins as a pleasant stroll down the block is catapulted into hyperspace. The melody takes on added depth and breadth from its supporting elements: the rollicking drums, the handclaps accenting the beat, the discreet guitar riffs, the key change and hushed tone of the middle eight passage. Yet even these charms pale by comparison to the magnificent singing on the track. The full-octave leap was an inspired bit of songwriting, but the reason it packs so much punch are the raucous vocals of Lennon and especially McCartney. When Paul blasts onto that note, his voice nearly bursting with ecstatic, lustful energy, the song's title is immediately revealed as a polite misnomer. Anyone who sings with this kind of raw, unbridled exuberance will want to hold a lot more than a girl's hand.

Indeed, it was the Beatles' singing more than anything else that made their early sound so distinctive and appealing. George Harrison contributed more in this regard than is often realized, and, of course, Ringo Starr was allotted a solo on every album, but it was Lennon and McCartney who supplied the real firepower. Each was an extremely versatile singer, capable of delivering not only shouting rock 'n' roll but sensitive ballads; "I Want To Hold Your Hand," in fact, featured both talents in the same song. Each singer also had his own clearly recognizable sound, and if Paul had a sweeter voice, John's had more character. It was when they blended those voices together, however, that the greatest effects were achieved; each highlighted the qualities of the other without sacrificing any of its own appeal.

The vocal combination of Lennon and McCartney, augmented by Harrison, was potent when singing in unison, but was especially exquisite when singing harmonies. As Dylan observed, the Beatles' harmonies were what "made it all valid." The Everly Brothers and Motown were important influences in this regard, but the Beatles were blessed with enormous natural ability as well. Part of what made their harmonies work so well is that they were careful never to overdo them. As analyst Tim Riley has pointed out, "They know just where a harmony is needed and just where it would clutter an otherwise unfettered melody." Riley was referring to "From Me To You," but his comment also applies to "She Loves You," "I Want To Hold Your Hand," and other early songs in which the Beatles sing some lines in harmony, some in unison, depending on the musical effect they wish to achieve. (Riley's book, *Tell Me Why*, identifies these choices in detail.) Producer George Martin served as sounding board and adviser on these matters, but rarely did he find fault with the Beatles' choices. "They always experimented with close harmony singing, all I did was change the odd note," said Martin.

Certainly the outstanding example of close harmony singing in the Beatles' early career is "This Boy," the lovely ballad composed by John that became the B-side of "I Want To Hold Your Hand." Once again, it was a case of music taking precedence over words. Lennon was especially proud of the melody of "This Boy," explaining that the song was his "attempt at writing one of those three-part-harmony/Smokey Robinson songs. Nothing in the lyrics; just a sound and a harmony." McCartney later recalled that the Beatles "just loved singing that three-part," and it shows. John sings lead, but one almost wouldn't know it, the harmonies are so perfectly balanced. The mixture of John's voice with Paul's and George's is subtle yet strong; they sound less like a threesome than a single presence. John alone ascends to sing the middle eight, his voice full of impassioned pleading, but his partners return for the last verse, bringing the song to a sublimely understated conclusion. With its dreamy atmospherics, "This Boy" was the ideal counterpoint to the effervescence of "I Want To Hold Your Hand," but what record buyers did not know at the time was that both songs were recorded on the same night—further evidence of the Beatles' remarkable versatility.

"I Want To Hold Your Hand" was released in Great Britain on November 29, 1963, and went straight to number one; it literally entered the charts at the top position. One month later, it was released in the United States, where it sold a quarter of a million copies in the first three days, became the Beatles' first big record, and spent seven weeks at number one. The business plan worked out by George Martin and Brian Epstein called for the group to release four singles and two albums every year. With "I Want To Hold Your Hand," the Beatles fulfilled the singles quota and scored a fourth straight number one to boot. The album *With The Beatles*, released just a week earlier, on November 22, likewise satisfied the requirement for a second album (and also went to number one). Overall, it amounted to an impressive feat of industry, efficiency, and talent.

Perhaps the most astonishing thing about *With The Beatles* is that it was recorded at all. The Beatles were on the road virtually nonstop in 1963; recording sessions were squeezed in during one- or two-day stopoffs in London, songwriting sessions often took place in hotel rooms or in vans and buses while riding between gigs. After recording the *Please Please Me* album in a single marathon session on February 11, for example, the group set off on a three-week tour of one-night stands in western England. They returned to London for a day on March 5 to record "From Me To You," only to depart the next day for a BBC radio appearance in Manchester, the first date in a schedule that kept them traveling to a new town every day, with scarcely a day off, until the end of April. After a twelve-day holiday, they returned for another six weeks of one-nighters across England before slipping back to Abbey Road to record "She Loves You" on July 1. (One can hear the hurry they were in by listening to the middle eight of "I'll Get You," the often overlooked B-side of "She Loves You." It's a sweet, fetching melody—one suspects, but can't be sure, it's McCartney's—but one of the Beatles gets the words slightly wrong. However, the overall sound is right enough, and time short enough, that they don't go back and correct it.) Then it was another two and a half weeks on the road before the first recording session for *With The Beatles* took place on July 18, followed by a twelve-day interruption before the second session was held on July 30. And so it went for the rest of the year, excepting a second two-week holiday at the end of September.

It was an exhausting schedule, to say the least; 1963 was perhaps the most physically demanding year of the Beatles' entire career. "Paul always said—or was it George?—'The reason we were twice as good as anyone else is we worked twice as hard as anyone else,' " recalled Derek Taylor, the Beatles' former press officer. The Beatles were young and used to working long hours from their nights in Hamburg, but their stamina had less tangible roots as well. Ambition was part of it; they couldn't let up now, just when the success they hungered for was clearly within reach. But they were also having so much fun that the work often didn't *feel* like work. Recalling a spare afternoon he spent in a hotel room writing "She Loves You" with Lennon, McCartney exclaimed of the young Beatles, "God bless their little cotton socks, those boys *worked*! They worked their little asses off! Here I am talking about an afternoon off and we're sitting there writing! We just loved it so much. It wasn't work."

With The Beatles followed the same approach as *Please Please Me* had, mixing original compositions with American rock 'n' roll favorites drawn from the Beatles' live stage repertoire. But this time the originals outnumbered the covers, by eight to six, with the decisive eighth tune marking the songwriting debut of George Harrison. From the album's very first moment, the Beatles come out blazing, with John shouting the title line of "It Won't Be Long" and Paul yelling back "Yeah!" over and over and over again. The frenzy they whip up is finally reined in when John swings into the first verse, but the verses are mere interlude; the song is built around the hook, and after two quick verse lines, it's back to the frenzy. Most of Paul's replies are sung three notes above John's shouts, boosting the voltage that much higher.

Yet "It Won't Be Long" is no mere rock 'n' roll raver. When Dylan said the Beatles' chords were "outrageous, just outrageous," it's songs like "It Won't Be Long" he was talking about. Its chords go places they "shouldn't," according to conventional musical theory, but never having learned musical theory, the Beatles were free to disregard it in favor of what their ears told them worked. The middle eight of "It Won't Be Long" is a brilliant example. Until then, the song is basically in the key of E, which theoretically should resolve into the keys of A and B. It does, eventually, but not until the Beatles throw in various D-, C-, and F-sharps, as well as a peculiar but extremely simple hybrid of D and B minor, thereby giving the melody a whole new texture and direction.

The outstanding track on *With The Beatles*, however, is "All My Loving," a McCartney composition that ranks as one of the major works of the Beatles' early period. There is structural inventiveness here as well, but "All My Loving" is above all a melody song. McCartney said he remembered writing the words on a bus while the Beatles were on tour and working out the tune when they arrived at the gig; it was his first song where the lyrics came before the music. Perhaps the highest compliment paid to "All My Loving" came from Lennon, who confessed that he wished he had written it, "Because it's a damn fine piece of work." John made sure to add, though, that "I play a pretty mean guitar in back." Which he does. What he plays is not technically difficult, but his double-timing rhythm breathes rock 'n' roll energy into what would otherwise simply be a beautiful mid-tempo love song.

The other original compositions on *With The Beatles* are of lesser stature, as Lennon and McCartney themselves admitted. In fact, Harrison's "Don't Bother Me" may be the best of the bunch, a promising premiere from the guitarist who still had not turned twenty-one. The Beatles hit a decent groove on the song, and the hook is not bad, but George's voice lacks confidence, making the listener wonder how the song might sound in John's or Paul's hands. George does a far better job on the Chuck Berry tune "Roll Over Beethoven," and indeed the Beatles as a whole turn in first-rate performances on each of the songs covered on this album. With the exception of the McCartney-instigated "Till There Was You," from the Broadway musical *The Music Man*, each of the cover songs bespoke the Beatles' long-standing admiration for black American recording artists. Just as the Beatles had concluded their first album with one of their favorite black songs, "Twist And Shout," they ended *With The Beatles* with a blistering rendition of "Money (That's What I Want)." At a time when their records were selling furiously but relatively little money was trickling down to them, it was a sentiment embraced by all the Beatles, though before long they would have ample cause to question the song's assertion that money was the answer if you "wanna be free."

With The Beatles entered the British charts at number one, displacing the Beatles' first album, *Please Please Me*, which had spent the previous twenty-nine straight weeks at the top. *With The Beatles* then remained at number one an additional twenty-one weeks, setting a record for the longest continual stay at the top by any artist. Nor was it only the marketplace that was applauding the Beatles. On November 4, 1963, the Beatles put in an appearance before members of the English royal family at the annual Royal Variety Performance. On December 27, the London *Times*, long the voice of the English Establishment, became the first major newspaper to publish an article taking the Beatles seriously as artists. In the course of a glowing review, music critic William Mann called John Lennon and Paul McCartney "the outstanding English composers of 1963," and went on to praise their song "Not A Second Time" for its "Aeolian cadence," adding that the song featured the same "chord progression which ends Mahler's 'Song of the Earth.'" Lennon and McCartney were rather bemused by such inscrutably high-toned criticism; after all, said Lennon, "it was just chords like any other chords." (Years later, he told *Playboy*, "To this day I don't have *any* idea what [Aeolian cadences] are. They sound like exotic birds.") Two days after the *Times* article appeared, a review in the London *Sunday Times* went even further, saying that Lennon and McCartney were "the greatest composers since Beethoven."

Despite the imprimaturs of the *Times* and the royal family, and despite the unprecedented volume of record sales, the notion that these four young rockers from Liverpool were musically special was by no means unanimous. Perhaps because the Beatles burst onto the public stage as such an overtly *social* phenomenon, arriving amidst a ceaseless whirl of long haircuts and shrieking teenagers, many observers simply missed the point. Distracted by the hysteria in the streets, they failed to listen, really listen, to the music provoking it. The smug condescension voiced in a report by American television correspondent Alexander

Kendrick was typical. Deriding both the Beatles' "dish-mop hairstyles" and the mental capacities of their fans, Kendrick opined that the Beatles "symbolize the 20th century non-hero, as they make non-music, wear non-haircuts and give none-mersey."

Similar nay-saying would be directed at the Beatles for years to come, but for those who had ears to hear, it was clear that the fresh sound bursting forth heralded the beginning of a new era in popular song. As Dylan recalled, "Everybody else thought they were for the teenyboppers, that they were gonna pass right away. But it was obvious to me that they had staying power. I knew they were pointing the direction of where music had to go."

CHAPTER 6

Life with Brian: Manager Brian Epstein

OF ALL THE PHOTOGRAPHS SHOWING THE BEATLES TO-
GETHER WITH BRIAN EPSTEIN, PERHAPS THE MOST POIGNANT IS
the one in which a chamber pot is perched upon Epstein's head. It rests
there like a white bowler hat as Epstein, cigar and lighter in hand, looks
into the camera with a mischievous, giddy smile on his face. In the
background Ringo, George, Paul, and John laugh with evident affection. Sharing in the fun are George Martin and his future wife, Judy
Lockhart-Smith. The occasion was a private dinner at the George V
hotel in Paris in January 1964, convened to celebrate the news that the
Beatles' fourth single, "I Want To Hold Your Hand," had hit number
one in the United States.

For the man in the white bowler, it was perhaps the moment of his
greatest triumph and happiness during five and a half years as manager
of the Beatles. After years of toil, the Beatles had not only conquered
Britain but were on the brink of claiming America, the largest and most
important market in the world. Of course, the Beatles themselves had
worked very hard for this, and it was their music and charisma that was
exciting people, but Epstein's contribution had been vital as well. It was
he who packaged and promoted them, molding their public image,
selecting their live bookings with a strategic eye and persistently seeking and finally securing a national recording contract. The results

spoke for themselves, and the Beatles were well pleased. And there was nothing that made Brian Epstein happier than making the Beatles happy.

Yet for all the jollity in the photograph, the scene it captures is bittersweet. Epstein is playing the fool for the Beatles, a pose they found amusing at the time but one they later resented as an all too accurate description of his business persona. Epstein's promotional flair and tireless devotion to the Beatles notwithstanding, he later fumbled numerous financial opportunities, depriving the Beatles of untold millions of dollars that could have been theirs. Recording contracts, movie deals, live tours, merchandising rights, music publishing of the Lennon–McCartney song catalogue, tax shelters—virtually all the key business decisions that subsequently confronted the Beatles were to a greater or lesser degree mishandled.

As more and more of this truth became known to the Beatles, their displeasure with their manager grew and relations became more distant. Epstein's involvement with the group came to a tragic, ignoble end in August 1967, when he died of a drug overdose, but no fair evaluation can deny the key role he initially played in helping them achieve success. "Without Brian Epstein, the Beatles wouldn't have existed," George Martin once said. "Because he actually got them together and presented them in a way people really were to take notice of." John Lennon was, as usual, more blunt: "We'd have never made it without him, and vice versa."

It was by no means an obvious marriage, for Brian Epstein seemed to be everything the Beatles were not. He was wealthy, Jewish, fastidious, endlessly polite. He was a shopkeeper, a homosexual, a coat-and-tie man, initially a fan of classical rather than rock 'n' roll music. The Cavern Club where the Beatles regularly performed was located barely two hundred yards from Epstein's North End Music Stores (NEMS) record shop in Liverpool, yet Epstein had never ventured inside it, much less heard them play. And although the Beatles had been written up numerous times in the same local music paper for which Epstein regularly reviewed records, the *Mersey Beat*, he did not recognize their name on the fateful day in October 1961 when a young man entered his shop to request a record called "My Bonnie," which featured the Beatles as the backing group for Liverpool singer Tony Sheridan.

As soon as he discovered that they were a Liverpool group who literally performed down the street, he arranged to go and hear them, on November 9, 1961. He was repulsed by the loud, foul-smelling atmosphere inside the Cavern, but his reaction to the Beatles themselves was the same as George Martin's seven months later: love at first sight, fueled by their enormous personal charisma. "What was there was this presence," Epstein recalled. "Onstage they had this undefinable feeling. . . . They were not very tidy and not very clean. They smoked as they played and they ate and talked and pretended to hit each other. They turned their backs on the audience and shouted at people and laughed at their private jokes. But there was quite clearly enormous excitement. They seemed to give off some sort of personal magnetism. I was fascinated by them."

When Epstein approached the stage later to talk with them, it became apparent that while he had not known the Beatles, they did know him from having spent afternoons in his shop, listening to records. (In fact, Epstein, regarding them as "a scruffy crowd in leather" who never bought anything, had wanted to kick them out, but was dissuaded by his female clerks, who claimed that the boys did purchase the occasional disc.) Foreshadowing the initial encounter with George Martin once more, it was George Harrison's sarcastic wit that surfaced first in that initial, brief conversation with Epstein. "What brings Mr. Epstein here?" he challenged the well-dressed businessman, who, at twenty-seven, was six years older than the oldest Beatle, John Lennon.

Epstein explained that he sought information about their record "My Bonnie." But as Epstein's visits to the Cavern continued in the days and weeks ahead it was clear that something more was on his mind. He later said that the idea of managing the Beatles "was all part of getting bored with simply selling records. I was looking for a new hobby." Biographers later suggested that it was actually sexual interest, particularly toward John Lennon, that led him to befriend the group. Although Epstein never had the chance to respond to this speculation, there is evidence to support it, notwithstanding the rather hysterical manner in which the assertion was often phrased. (In his absurdly overdrawn *The Lives of John Lennon*, for example, Albert Goldman went so far as to claim that Lennon himself became a full-fledged homosexual under Epstein's tutelage.) After all, it was only natural that a group of rock 'n' rollers who were exciting near-orgasmic adulation from young women should prove attractive to a gay man as well. For his part, Lennon confirmed years later that Epstein "was in love with me," and it seems clear he and Epstein did have one sexual encounter; Lennon's best friend, Pete Shotton, later wrote that John told him that he allowed Brian to bring him to orgasm manually during a vacation together in Spain. However, to leap from this single episode to the notion that Lennon was himself a homosexual reflected as ignorant a view of homosexuality as did the assumption that Epstein, being gay, could not possibly have had any other motives for wishing to manage the Beatles. "I knew Brian Epstein well enough to know that he was in love with the Beatles as an entity," journalist Ray Coleman later wrote in his biography of Lennon. "He was fiercely protective of them all, ambitious for all four of them individually, and totally committed to make them the world's best-known pop act. It was something that went way beyond any sexual preferences."

Epstein's vision of how to make the Beatles famous reflected his salesman's background and entailed dramatic changes in the group's look, style, and mode of operating. Prior to signing with Epstein on January 24, 1962, the Beatles had been handling their own bookings after breaking from their first manager, Allan Williams, a year earlier in a financial dispute. Epstein brought efficiency and organization to what had been a haphazard process, instilling a greater sense of professionalism and direction along the way. Performance schedules were now typed out and faithfully delivered to each Beatle in advance. Higher fees were demanded and only certain venues chosen, depending on whether they figured to advance the long-term prospects of the group. "We were just in a daydream till he came along," Lennon said of Epstein. "We'd no idea what we were doing, or where we'd agreed to be. Seeing our marching orders on paper made it all official."

Epstein also sanitized their appearance, insisting that the Beatles exchange their leather jackets for coats and ties. They were still supposed to "Mach schau!", but the casual, anarchic stage demeanor of their Hamburg and Cavern days was out. No more eating and smoking onstage, no more horseplay and joking among themselves and the front rows, no more arguing about which songs to play or abruptly breaking off in the middle of them. From now on, the Beatles would play shorter, one-hour sets of material preselected to appeal to as wide an audience as possible. They would look and act like smooth show business professionals.

It was all in keeping with a dictum from Epstein's furniture salesman days: "If you show the public something lovely, they'll accept it." But what is lovely is, of course, a matter of taste, and while Epstein was eager to appeal to the tastes of the broad mainstream, Lennon, the group's leader, identified himself as a rebel outsider who had only contempt for orthodoxy. In Epstein's mind, image-making had nothing to do with deception or moral compromise—"I didn't *change* them," he said of the Beatles, "I just projected what was there"—but Lennon felt that Epstein's prescriptions went beyond mere cosmetic changes and altered the group's character and essence. Nevertheless, craving fame and fortune, he went along with Epstein's makeover, contenting himself with the "little rebellion" of keeping his tie askew and top button undone.

The same conflict arose when Epstein arranged the Beatles' first audition with a London record company. By exploiting his status and connections as a large-scale record retailer, Epstein persuaded the Decca company to send a talent scout to Liverpool to hear the Beatles perform at the Cavern in December 1961. The man liked their live show well enough to invite them to London for a proper studio audition. But the playlist Epstein prepared for that audition, though it did include three Lennon–McCartney originals, mainly highlighted middle-of-the-road numbers, thus playing away from the Beatles' natural strength as infectiously exuberant, powerhouse rock 'n' rollers— the very thing that had gained them the audition in the first place. After Decca turned them down, Lennon in particular blamed Epstein for having made the Beatles play it safe.

More rejections followed before Epstein finally got in touch with George Martin, the head of EMI's Parlophone label, who saw past the mediocre songs on the Beatles' demonstration tape and heard the "unusual quality of sound" that convinced him to offer them an audition. Getting the EMI recording contract was a crucial step toward fulfilling Epstein's oft-stated pledge that the Beatles were "going to be bigger than Elvis Presley," for it delivered them from the Liverpool backwater and gave them access to a national audience. But live performances remained vital to building the broad-based popular support that would make the group's records actually sell. Epstein kept the Beatles on a grueling schedule of live appearances throughout England in 1962 and 1963, thereby steadily extending their appeal and helping to propel all their early records (except the very first, "Love Me Do") to the top of the charts. Each successive number one in turn generated that much more interest in their live shows. This self-reinforcing process quickly attained critical mass and by October 1963 (at the latest) it had burst forth into the national hysteria known as "Beatlemania."

The Beatles' massive popularity in England gave Epstein the leverage necessary for the final step in his grand campaign, the invasion of America. In a master stroke, he arranged for the group to make three separate appearances on *The Ed Sullivan Show*, the most popular and influential variety show on American television. (Sullivan had apparently witnessed Beatlemania for himself in October 1963, when his flight from London to New York was delayed by an uproarious reception for the group at Heathrow Airport, welcoming them back from a tour of Sweden.) Epstein extracted a relatively low fee for these appearances, but the vast exposure provided by the Sullivan show was so decisive in making the Beatles' reputation in the United States that they could have performed for nothing and still come out well ahead. Seventy-three million people were estimated to have watched their first appearance on the show, on February 9, 1964, with similar numbers viewing the two subsequent broadcasts. Coverage by the print and electronic media was likewise extensive.

This was the height of Brian Epstein's glory. In the space of a year, he had gone from being an inexperienced pop group manager to being perhaps the most sought-after agent in show business, all at the tender age of twenty-nine. It seemed that everyone everywhere wanted the Beatles to appear on their stage, their radio show, their television broadcast, their front page. George Martin recalled it as a happy and heady time for Epstein: "He loved the helter-skelter of wheeling and dealing, the juggling of countries and dates, the hot kick of power."

Without question, Epstein deserved a good deal of credit for the Beatles' unparalleled rise to fame. "Brian contributed as much as us in the early days, although we were the talent and he was the hustler," Lennon later said. But Epstein, as Lennon also observed, "was a theatrical man, rather than a businessman." As business offers poured in from around the world, it was up to Epstein to choose among them and make the best deals possible. It was at this juncture, when his responsibilities as manager were shifting away from his natural talent of salesmanship toward the hard-nosed complexities of multimillion-dollar negotiations, that Brian Epstein began to find himself out of his depth.

One illustrative story comes from Pete Shotton, who wrote in his memoirs that Brian Epstein was a man of "extraordinary warmth, generosity and kindness" but "not a particularly astute businessman." Citing Lennon as his source, Shotton noted that sometime near the end of 1964, a tax adviser persuaded the Beatles to set up a tax shelter in the Bahamas, after which "Brian Epstein duly handed over 750,000 pounds sterling. According to John, neither the money nor the tax adviser was ever seen or heard from again." A second example concerns the contract for the Beatles' first feature film, *A Hard Day's Night*. The producers of the film were prepared to offer Epstein a twenty-five percent share of net profits, but first asked him what figure he had in mind. "I wouldn't consider anything under seven and a half percent," he replied. Only a review of the deal by Epstein's lawyer prevented the lower figure from being endorsed in the final contract.

Perhaps Epstein's most notorious misstep was the virtual giveaway of merchandising rights to the mountains of wigs, dolls, plastic guitars, coloring books, and countless other forms of Beatles paraphernalia that were produced to cash in on the public's seemingly bottomless appetite for all things Beatle. Epstein's NEMS company signed these rights away in return for a paltry ten percent of total sales. Since the Beatles owned ten percent of NEMS—a gift made to them by Brian, who said he did not ever want to appear to be taking advantage of the boys—this deal meant that they got one penny of every dollar's worth of these items that were sold under license. When Epstein realized what a poor deal had been struck, he demanded to renegotiate it. Beginning in August 1964, NEMS' take rose to forty-six percent, though of course by then untold sums had been lost; Epstein's business aide Peter Brown later estimated the total amount forgone to be $100 million. Mc-Cartney later remarked, "We got screwed for millions, but in the end it wasn't worth suing everybody. It was all Brian's fault. He was green. I always said that about Brian. Green."

McCartney was always the Beatle with whom Epstein had the most troublesome relationship, perhaps because McCartney had the most developed business sense and managerial ambitions. On the other hand, it was Lennon with whom Epstein was closest, despite John's often cruel treatment of him. When Brian asked what he should call his autobiography, for example, John shot back, "How about *Queer Jew*?" When Brian finally settled on the title *A Cellarful of Noise*, John satirized it as *A Cellarful of Boys*. Once Brian dropped into Abbey Road Studios while the Beatles were recording and dared, in front of a young male friend, to call down through the control room intercom in between takes, "I don't think that sounded quite right, John." Fixing him with a withering stare, Lennon riposted, "You stick with your percentages, Brian. We'll look after the music."

Epstein, who was prone to terrible temper tantrums, could be cruel as well, especially to anyone whom he felt threatened his relationship with the Beatles. Press officer Derek Taylor claimed that when he organized his first press conference for the group, Epstein "didn't want it to work," because then Taylor was certain to gain no control over the Beatles. Such possessiveness was apparently rooted in Epstein's massive personal insecurity and unhappiness, characteristics testified to by Taylor, George Martin, Beatles aide Peter Brown, and others who knew him well. According to Brown, Epstein had a depressive personality prior to meeting the Beatles, but the condition grew worse over time and reached a crisis point when the Beatles decided in 1966 to stop touring. The Beatles informed Epstein of their decision during a flight from New Delhi to London, after having narrowly escaped bodily harm in Manila. Brown recalled that the Beatles' decision "upset Brian so much that by the time the jet reached Heathrow Airport his body was covered with hives and welts," causing the pilot to radio ahead for an ambulance. After the Beatles' last concert, on August 29, 1966, in San Francisco, Epstein's friend and American business partner, Nat Weiss, said that Epstein, looking "pathetic" for the first time in their years of friendship, had rhetorically asked, "What do I do now? What happens to my life? That's it." According to Brown's eyewitness account, Epstein had no sooner returned to London than he made good on his implicit threat, attempting suicide with an overdose of sleeping pills.

Epstein's management contract with the Beatles was due to expire on October 9, 1967, and he had reason to fear it would not be renewed. Not only had the Beatles gotten wind of the various business missteps mentioned above, they were also grumbling more and more about the niggardly terms of their recording contract with EMI, their resentment fueled by the knowledge that their friends the Rolling Stones had recently pocketed a bonus of one and a quarter million pounds sterling after renegotiating *their* original contract with Decca. The terms of the Beatles' contract were, as George Martin himself admitted, appalling; for records sold in the North American market at three to four dollars apiece, the Beatles received a measly five cents; records sold in Britain earned them a single penny. Such terms were perhaps understandable when the Beatles first signed with EMI as raw unknowns in 1962, but utterly indefensible by 1964, when they were the biggest selling musicians in the world. Nevertheless, Epstein had not insisted on renegotiating the EMI contract and, more astonishingly, had even allowed it to remain in force for an additional seventeen months beyond its scheduled expiration date in June 1965. The contract he finally negotiated, signed by the Beatles in November 1966, did give them higher royalties, though again, as with the merchandising fiasco, it did not recoup the many millions of dollars already lost.

Brian Epstein prided himself on looking after the Beatles' interests, but in this November 1966 contract he protected his own interests as well. Although he knew that his management contract with the Beatles did not extend past October 1967, he inserted a clause in the EMI contract stipulating that all record royalties would continue to be paid to his company, NEMS, for the nine years duration of the EMI contract. In other words, he insured that he would continue to receive twenty-five percent of the Beatles' recording revenues for the next nine years, even if they abandoned him. According to Peter Brown, who secured each of the four Beatles' signatures on the EMI contracts, Epstein "never pointed this clause out to them."

By this time, Epstein's depressions were getting worse and more frequent. He was spending less and less time at the office, often not arriving until late afternoon, if at all, and was increasingly keeping himself going by relying on a witches' brew of pills—tranquilizers to put him to sleep, stimulants to wake him up. "Eppy seems to be in a terrible state," Lennon told Pete Shotton in August 1967. "The guy's head's a total mess, and we're all really worried about him. But we just don't know what the fuck we can do about it. It's time for us to go off in our own direction, and that's that." Lennon then played Shotton an audiotape that Epstein had made and sent him. "The recording was barely recognizable as that of a human voice," Shotton wrote, "alternately groaning, grunting, and shrieking—and occasionally mumbling words which, even when decipherable, made no apparent sense whatsoever."

Barely a week later, Brian Epstein was dead. Found lying in bed alone in his London home on August 27, he had succumbed to an overdose of tranquilizers. The coroner ruled that his death was accidental, a judgment accepted by his associates, who surmised that he had simply lost track of which and how many pills he had taken and ended up ingesting at least one too many. But if the death was not intentional suicide, it had every appearance of its subconscious equivalent. "Emotionally, it was suicide, even though I do not think he meant to do it at that time in that way," wrote Hunter Davies, who knew Epstein. "But I feel it would have happened, sooner rather than later." George Martin, who also doubted that Epstein meant to commit suicide, wrote in his autobiography, "The irony is that even if [Brian] had lived he would, I think, have had a very hard time coping with life. Because it was inevitable that he would shortly have lost the Beatles, and to him that would have been like losing his children, his whole reason for living. He could never have parted from them, as I did, with great friendship but no sense of loss."

The sense of loss felt by the Beatles after Epstein's death is difficult to gauge. Facing television cameras after receiving the news, John and George appeared subdued, even as they parroted the wisdom of their new guru, the Maharishi Mahesh Yogi, that death was an illusion and the best way to help Brian was to think happy thoughts. John privately repeated the same sentiments to Pete Shotton and to Ray Coleman in following days. Years later, however, he regretted these facile remarks and confessed that the death of the Beatles' manager had deeply shaken his faith in the future of the group. "I knew that we were in trouble then," he said. "I didn't really have any misconceptions about our ability to do anything other than play music and I was scared. I thought, we've fuckin' had it."

C H A P T E R 7

I Heard a
Funny Chord
(*A Hard Day's Night*)

WHEN JOHN LENNON WROTE "A HARD DAY'S NIGHT," THE TITLE TRACK OF THE FINEST ALBUM OF THE BEATLES' early period, he was twenty-three years old. Flushed with inspiration and fueled by ambition and adrenaline, he was living in a state of artistic grace where he was "creating without even being aware of how it's happening." Indeed, he composed "A Hard Day's Night" literally overnight, impelled by an off-the-cuff remark of Ringo Starr's. The Beatles were making their first film, and after weeks of twelve-hour days they were approaching completion, but they still lacked a title. After one such day, Ringo was in the midst of saying how hard they were working when he noticed that night had already fallen. "It's been a hard day's night," he quipped. It was all the help Lennon needed. He brought in the song the following morning.

Days later, on April 16, 1964, the Beatles slipped away from their film duties for a few hours and recorded the song at Abbey Road. This, too, was quick work; the Beatles needed only nine takes to get "A Hard Day's Night" down on tape. The atmosphere inside Studio Two that day seems to have been one of brisk yet casual professionalism. When an engineer calls out, "Take six!", for example, John is in the middle of saying something about the previous take, but he is drowned out by Paul, who is aimlessly singing, "Scoobie-doobie-doobie" and puttering about on his bass. John, always the least patient Beatle inside the studio, says, "Shh," waits a second for quiet, and in an intense, no-nonsense voice counts off, "One, two, three, four."

The band surges into motion, John's ardent vocal leading the way. The first two verses in take six sound quite similar to what is heard on the finished record; if the tempo is a bit sluggish, it is plainly only a matter of time before the Beatles get it right. The lead vocal passes to Paul during the song's middle eight—"When I'm home / Everything seems to be right"—then returns to John for the third verse. But just as John sings the line about "sleeping like a log," something in the rhythm section goes badly wrong. Inertia carries the band forward another few seconds before John is heard to declare, "I 'eard a funny chord." As the engineer breaks in to announce, "Take seven," John adds, "It was 'im." " 'Im" was very evidently McCartney, but Paul acts as if nothing has happened, even when John, more forcefully this time, tells George Martin up in the control room, "I heard a funny chord." Martin replies, "So did I." McCartney continues to play dumb, busying himself with rehearsing a harmony, but the last word is yet to come. An unidentified studio aide smirks a reply to Martin in a Cockney accent, "Not 'alf you didn't"—which is to say, "You certainly did." But Paul's error may have been just what the band needed, for after a few coughs to clear their throats, the Beatles launch into take seven, and this take, full of pep, is close enough to perfection that only two more tries are needed to complete the recording.

Record buyers, for their part, encountered quite a different kind of funny chord when they heard "A Hard Day's Night" for the first time. Struck but once on George Harrison's newly acquired twelve-string guitar, the strident opening chord of "A Hard Day's Night" immediately makes it clear that something powerfully new and exciting is in store. The chord is quirky, arresting, unmistakably original—the musical equivalent of the song's title. It is also complex (so complex that two leading Beatles musicologists disagree on whether it is a variant of F major or of G major 7th), as well as assertive, like a hijacked church bell announcing the party of the year. The chord reverberates alone for a full two seconds before John begins his vocal, then is brilliantly revived at the end of the song. "A Hard Day's Night" concludes with a guitar-picking of the opening chord's individual notes, a swirling fade-out that foreshadows the druggy electronic effects that will play such an important role in the group's music a few years hence, though at this point none of the Beatles had yet had a single puff of marijuana.

Martin later said that *A Hard Day's Night* represented the beginning of the second era in the Beatles' music; the title track is a good illustration of his point. Finding such an obscure yet powerful chord in the first place, then daring to use it to bookend an otherwise fairly straightforward pop song, was a sign of the Beatles' rapidly evolving creative mastery. This artistic evolution was in turn paralleled by a crucial technical advance, the record industry's move to four-track recording. Recording a fade-out as complicated as that on "A Hard Day's Night" would have been unthinkable on the two-track tape machines the Beatles had used for their first two albums. Having four tracks gave the Beatles and Martin twice as much space in which to elaborate on a song's basic structure, freedom they would use to increasing advantage in years to come.

The most significant improvement on *A Hard Day's Night*, however, was in the songwriting. The album marked a major advance beyond the Beatles' first two LPs not only because it was the first album to consist solely of original compositions but because so many of these compositions were of such high quality. Prior to *A Hard Day's Night*, the Beatles had issued perhaps half a dozen songs that seemed capable of standing the test of time: the singles "I Want To Hold Your Hand," "She Loves You," and perhaps "This Boy," and the album tracks "I Saw Her Standing There," "Twist And Shout," and "All My Loving." *A Hard Day's Night* nearly doubled this collection in a single stroke. It boasted five masterworks—the title track and the songs "Can't Buy Me Love," "And I Love Her," "If I Fell" and "Things We Said Today"—as well as the very accomplished "I Should Have Known Better" and a host of honorable mentions, led by "I'll Be Back."

What's more, the Beatles released an extended-play (EP) record three weeks before *A Hard Day's Night* that contained four additional songs, including one of the great vocal performances in rock 'n' roll history, Paul McCartney's brilliantly manic assault on "Long Tall Sally." The *Long Tall Sally* EP, combined with the *A Hard Day's Night* album and film and with the Beatles' wildly successful trip to America in February and their first extended foreign tour in June, made the first six months of 1964 a time of breathtaking creativity and achievement for the group, affirming their accomplishments to date as no mere public relations coup but the flowering of a huge and original talent.

As it happens, *A Hard Day's Night* was the only Beatles album to consist solely of Lennon–McCartney compositions. Lennon wrote the majority of the songs, serving as the principal composer on ten of the album's thirteen songs to McCartney's three, a discrepancy in keeping with what John later described as his "domination" of early Beatles records. "In the early days the majority of singles—in the movies and everything—were mine," he later boasted. John was especially proud of having written the title track of *A Hard Day's Night*, and with unseemly possessiveness went out of his way to declare that the only reason Paul sang on the track at all "was because I couldn't reach the notes" of the middle eight.

Judged purely by quantity, there is no question that Lennon won the *A Hard Day's Night* round of competition. At the same time, each of McCartney's compositions—"And I Love Her," "Can't Buy Me Love," and "Things We Said Today"—was a classic, every bit the equal of Lennon's three best songs, "A Hard Day's Night," "I Should Have Known Better," and "If I Fell." Moreover, both "A Hard Day's Night" and "If I Fell" would be greatly diminished without McCartney's vocal contributions, not to mention the tight, inventive backing provided by the band as a whole. Just who proposed the opening chord of "A Hard Day's Night" has never been documented (though had it been Lennon one presumes he would have asserted ownership); however, if creative credits are to be listed, that unknown person deserves considerable recognition for the song's overall sound, just as George Harrison merits special mention for the bouncy, full-bodied guitar lead that brightens the instrumental break. Moreover, if Lennon begrudged McCartney's singing the middle eight of "A Hard Day's Night," this was mere personal jealousy speaking, for there is simply no denying that Mc-Cartney's vocals enhance the song. Beginning with his discrete harmonies on the fifth and sixth lines of the verse, which boost the energy just enough, and culminating in his soulful homage to the pleasures of home in the middle eight, McCartney's vocals work precisely because of how they contrast with Lennon's. It's as if two gifted painters have each rendered half of the same landscape; the different colors, proportions and style favored by each artist only further highlight the virtues of the other.

"If I Fell," a tour de force of close harmony singing, is an even stronger example of the indivisibility of the Beatles' talents. Were it not Lennon who sings the sublime introduction to the song, the average listener would have no idea that he wrote "If I Fell," because throughout the rest of the song McCartney's harmony is at least as strong a presence as Lennon's melody; indeed, it is often hard to tell which is which. The mingling of their two voices is even more enchanting here than on the three-part harmony of the earlier "This Boy," for the melody and harmony in "If I Fell" blend in more intricate ways without sacrificing the illusion of simplicity. Like a pair of meadow hawks swooping to and fro across the sky, John and Paul mainly sing at a distance to one another, harmony to melody, but when they do soar in unison onto a joint melodic line, it is a lovely moment that makes their return to separate, overlapping orbits that much more moving. The underlying musical structure of "If I Fell," with its unexpected chord progressions and key changes, is interesting enough that the song would have succeeded without McCartney's vocals, but with them, the song ranks among the finest the Beatles ever recorded.

To stress McCartney's contributions is not to suggest that it was actually he who "won" the *A Hard Day's Night* creative contest but, rather, to put that contest in perspective. Knowing who wrote and created which parts of which songs is helpful to appreciating the Beatles' music, but to focus on it obsessively is to reduce great art to a sports event. At some point, keeping score misses the point, which is the music that the Beatles made as a unit. Having said that, it must be recognized that *A Hard Day's Night* represented an astonishing burst of creativity on Lennon's part. Without his compositions as starting points, there would have been far less for McCartney and the other Beatles to enrich.

John dominates both sides of *A Hard Day's Night*, writing five of the seven songs that constitute the film soundtrack of side one, and five of the six additional studio tracks found on side two. The strength of his songs at this stage remains their music—especially their melodies and impassioned energy—but the lyrics are beginning to improve as well. Lazy rhymes and sophomoric narratives remain the rule rather than the exception, but the exceptions hold promise. The opening verse of "A Hard Day's Night" is no teenage love lament; anybody who holds down a real j-o-b can relate to a song that complains about "working like a dog." In the song's bridge, the grown-up theme of Work gives way to the equally adult subject of Home. The treatment of Love also shows evidence of greater sophistication. Without question, "If I Fell" is primarily a musical triumph, but Lennon's lyrics have their moments. Shedding his two usual personae of cocksure grasping lover or angry loser, John reaches for greater emotional depth in "If I Fell"; he now seeks to *understand* before acting. Experience has shown him that love isn't as easy as the storybooks say. Almost as if intentionally referring back to "I Want To Hold Your Hand," he confesses to having learned that "love is more / Than just holding hands."

Having gotten the album off to a roaring start with "A Hard Day's Night," "I Should Have Known Better," and "If I Fell," John steps back for a moment to let George Harrison into the limelight. Lennon wrote "I'm Happy Just To Dance With You," but he gave it to George for his one lead vocal on the album. The tune is nothing special, but it gets elevated to respectability by John's and Paul's boisterous backing vocals before the band moves on to McCartney's radiant ballad "And I Love Her." Lennon claimed to have helped with the middle eight of "And I Love Her," but he clearly considered it McCartney's song and even went so far as to call it Paul's "first 'Yesterday,' " high praise indeed. It is a stunningly beautiful melody, tender, plaintive, awash in the mystery of romantic love. Lewisohn reports that the Beatles initially recorded a more energetic version of "And I Love Her," with a heavier drum sound and a guitar solo, but apparently this approach was abandoned after two takes. Instead, the Beatles give "And I Love Her" a completely acoustic treatment; Ringo switches to bongos, and they strip the song of all distracting ornamentation. The first four notes, plucked on guitar, establish the mood, and Paul sustains it with a serene yet stirring vocal; he sounds humbled by the wonder of falling in love. Years later, he still liked "And I Love Her," saying, "It was a nice tune, that one."

And it was followed—after a quick romp through "Tell Me Why," a Lennon composition rightly dismissed by its author as a mere knockoff—by "Can't Buy Me Love," the McCartney gem that concludes the soundtrack of "A Hard Day's Night." This song, too, underwent considerable alteration inside the studio. The studio in question, however, was not Abbey Road but rather EMI's Pathé Marconi Studios, in Paris. "Can't Buy Me Love" was the first of the *A Hard Day's Night* songs to be recorded, back in January 1964, when the Beatles were in Paris to overdub German vocals onto "She Loves You" and "I Want To Hold Your Hand."

The Beatles initially planned to begin "Can't Buy Me Love" with the verse line, "I'll buy you a diamond ring, my friend / If it makes you feel alright," but George Martin advised them to start with the chorus instead: "I said, 'We've got to have an introduction, something that catches the ear immediately, a hook.' " Tapes of the Pathé Marconi sessions reveal that the Beatles follow Martin's arrangement from the very start, yet the first two takes of "Can't Buy Me Love" still sound markedly different from the song as it was ultimately released on record. McCartney's vocal is bluesier, but the main difference is that John and George sing on the early takes as well, contributing very prominent backing vocals that give the song a sound somewhere between Buddy Holly and the Supremes. In a style reminiscent of Paul and George's supporting vocals on "Twist And Shout," John and George begin during the second verse of "Can't Buy Me Love" to echo the end of each of Paul's verse lines. Thus, when Paul sings, "I'll give you all I've got to give / If you say you love me too," John and George reply, "Oooooh, love me too." It's an interesting experiment, but the Beatles and Martin were right to discard it in favor of a more straightforward approach. This they did after two takes. Remarkably, they then required only two additional takes to perfect the version of "Can't Buy Me Love" that became the Beatles' fifth straight number one record. ("Can't Buy Me Love" was released as a single on March 20, prior to its inclusion on *A Hard Day's Night*.)

The second side of *A Hard Day's Night* inevitably pales next to its predecessor, but it contains some fine work nonetheless. "Any Time At All" is rough-and-ready and "I'll Be Back," with its splendid middle eight, provides just the right grace note as the album's finale. The main attraction, however, is "Things We Said Today." A crunching triple-strummed guitar kicks this McCartney ballad alive, imparting an urgency electrifyingly at odds with the wistful lyric and gentle melody. Critic Wilfrid Mellers has called "Things We Said Today" the Beatles' "most beautiful and deep song up to this point," adding that the import of the lyric "Deep in love / Not a lot to say" is "precisely that the love experience is too deep for words. [And the music] acts this out, creating an experience no longer just happy but full of awe." Even Lennon later gruffly conceded that his ex-partner's composition was a "good song." It was chosen as the B-side to the "A Hard Day's Night" single, but like "This Boy" with "I Want To Hold Your Hand" the previous November, "Things We Said Today" came close to outshining the top billing.

The album and single of "A Hard Day's Night" were released on July 10; both were immediate number ones. (American fans got *A Hard Day's Night* two weeks early, on June 26, but theirs was, as usual, a bastardized version; it included the film soundtrack but left out virtually the entire second side of the British edition. It would be another two years before releases in the States were finally synchronized to those in Britain, allowing Americans to hear Beatles albums the way they were intended to be heard.) *A Hard Day's Night* may have inaugurated the second era of Beatles music, but the work habits producing the music didn't change much. Once again, the album was recorded in a matter of days, scattered in bunches of twos and threes and squeezed in among the Beatles' other commitments. Chief among these, of course, was the filming of the accompanying movie, which began on March 2 and was completed April 24.

The foundation of the Beatles' appeal would always be their music, but the film *A Hard Day's Night* played a vital role in their rise to fame. The world had gotten its first glimpses of how funny and outrageous the Beatles were during the early press conferences of Beatlemania, when the four young Liverpudlians delighted in sending up one banal question after another. "The French seem not to have made up their minds about the Beatles. What do you think about them?" a BBC reporter asked in Paris in January 1964. "Oh, we like the Beatles," John Lennon quickly replied. "Why do you think you get more fan mail than anyone else in the group?" Ringo Starr was once asked. "I dunno," he replied. "I suppose it's because more people write me." But it was the *A Hard Day's Night* film, premiered in London on July 6, 1964, that clinched the Beatles' hold on the public imagination, turning what had been manic infatuation into an enduring love affair. In years to come there would be short-term rises and falls in the Beatles' popularity, depending on whether their most recent public act had been the release of a splendid new album or the utterance of a controversial remark about drugs or religion, but the sheer interest in what they were doing would never disappear.

A Hard Day's Night was crucial to this process, for the film provided the most concentrated, if contrived, exposure yet to the wacky humor and unpretentious likability that had previously captivated Brian Epstein, George Martin, and virtually everyone else who had come in contact with the Beatles. John, Paul, George, and Ringo came across on screen as four young men whom one could identify with, look up to, laugh at, envy, desire, and genuinely like, all at the same time. Charm, charisma, presence, magnetism—whatever one calls it, the Beatles had it. "Fame makes relationships difficult," George Harrison later observed while reminiscing about the popularity of the Beatles. "The difference is, we never lost our sense of humor. I think that's why people liked us, not just because of our music, but because we said funny and outrageous things and were real people."

The story line of *A Hard Day's Night* originated in a comment of Lennon's. When director Richard Lester asked him how he had liked the Beatles' recent tour of Sweden, John replied, "Oh, it was a room and a car and a car and a room and a room and a car," an offhand but revealing answer. Notwithstanding the glamour attached to international stardom, the Beatles were already prisoners of fame, unable to venture beyond guarded hotel rooms and police-escorted limousines for fear of being torn limb from limb by crazed fans. It was decided that the film would reflect this reality, albeit in a lighthearted way, so *A Hard Day's Night* featured many scenes of the Beatles being chased by screaming teenagers—up and down city streets, in and out of railway stations—all interspersed with the inevitable scenes of the group playing and singing together, usually in front of yet more screaming teenagers.

A Hard Day's Night was, in essence, a fantasy version of the Beatles' fantasy life that nevertheless conveyed a sense of how Beatlemania looked and felt from the inside. At one point in the film, the Beatles are playing music inside a dark cagelike enclosure, with a group of feverish teenage girls just the other side of the wire. One girl, plainly mesmerized, twice darts her hand through the wire to try to grab Ringo's hair. She looks at once frenzied and tentative, instantly withdrawing her hand the first time as if afraid her prey will bite, then plunging a second time as a startled Ringo jerks away. The effect on the viewer of this evidently unscripted moment is one of fascination, bemusement, and a degree of horror; one sympathizes immediately with the Beatles' plight: They are animals in a cage, constantly besieged by the animals outside the cage.

Lennon in particular came to resent the film's caricature of the Beatles as, to cite the usual cliché, "cheeky but lovable moptops." Yet, judging from their own comments and the comments of people who knew them well, the film's portrait of the Beatles as four happy-go-lucky, irreverent lads on the make was more one-dimensional than outright misleading. The Beatles did have "an independent, cussed streak about them, not giving a damn for anybody, which was one of the things I liked about them in the first place," George Martin later said, adding, "It was an expression of youth, a slight kicking-over of the traces, which found a ready response in young people. Curiously, it was a response that the parents, though they might not have liked the music themselves, did not seem to begrudge." The Beatles' devil-may-care attitude was key to their appeal. They were having a good laugh at life, and their sense of fun was infectious enough to make their audience feel it could do the same.

The music itself was the highest expression of this joie de vivre, and never was it more ecstatically expressed than in the title track of the *Long Tall Sally* EP. Even thirty years after the fact, listening to this track at high volume delivers a powerful jolt, like being injected with pure adrenaline. It's a completely physical experience, and not until it's over is there time to be amazed that the Beatles pulled it off on the first try, in a single blistering take.

First made famous in 1956 by the black American singer Little Richard, "Long Tall Sally" is one of the great songs of the rock 'n' roll genre. The heroine is a back-alley girl who's "built pretty sweet." She steps out with the singer's uncle John, who has falsely told Aunt Mary "he had the mis'ry / But he got a lot of fun / Oh baby." The song is about the pleasures of the flesh, and its virtually one-note melody requires a belting, physical vocal to succeed. Lennon covered similar ground with his searing "Twist And Shout" on the Beatles' first album, but "Long Tall Sally" was McCartney's song; in fact, it was one of the tunes he played to impress John the day they first met as schoolboys. After the Beatles broke up, Paul recalled that John always "liked it when I sang like Little Richard," adding that John would cheer him on whenever his screaming vocal threatened to "fall a little bit short" by urging, "Come on! Really throw it." There were no such problems this time around. McCartney sounds like a blast furnace of vocal energy, burning out of control but hitting every note dead on. The band is ferocious, especially the two Georges: Martin's nonstop piano is like a dangerously pounding heartbeat, and Harrison's lead guitar forces new breath into lungs already about to burst. The result is two minutes of unadulterated rock 'n' roll glory.

Put "Long Tall Sally" together with *A Hard Day's Night* and it's plain to see how the Beatles became the premier musical phenomenon of their time. Not only were Lennon and McCartney, in Ringo's words, "the greatest songwriters on earth at the time," they were also two of the most talented singers in rock 'n' roll. They had a fine supporting cast in Harrison, Starr, and Martin, but it was they who were irreplaceable. To ask who was the greater talent of the two is the wrong question. *A Hard Day's Night* coincided with an incredibly prolific period for Lennon, but at other times in the band's history it would be McCartney who carried a heavier load. Likewise, Lennon's "Twist And Shout" had made the first Beatles album a classic, but McCartney's "Long Tall Sally" was no less of a rock 'n' roll treasure. And so it would continue for the remainder of their career. One or both of them was always doing something extraordinary, which meant that the Beatles as a group rarely did anything less than special. Indeed, this may be what most set the Beatles apart from their musical contemporaries; they very rarely lapsed into mediocrity. They may have said funny and outrageous things and seemed like real people, as George Harrison said, but as artists they were in a class by themselves.

CHAPTER 8

The Burdens of Fame: Beatlemania

SAINT AUGUSTINE, WRITING IN THE MIDDLE AGES, OB-SERVED THAT THERE ARE MORE TEARS SHED OVER ANSWERED prayers than unanswered ones. The Talking Heads, singing in the 1980s, likewise warned, "Watch out! You might get what you're after." None of the Beatles were exactly get-down-on-your-knees types, so perhaps the updated, rock 'n' roll version of Augustine's lament is the more appropriate commentary for the crucial transformation the band underwent from 1963 to 1966. For this was the period when the mass phenomenon aptly christened Beatlemania went from being a thrilling, laugh-filled adventure to a suffocating, sometimes dangerous exercise in banality, decadence, and potential creative atrophy. That the four Beatles survived with their sanity intact is wonder enough. That they also managed, in the midst of so much craziness, to accelerate their growth as artists—producing by the end of the period an album, *Revolver*, that is arguably their greatest single work—is a tribute not only to their musical abilities but to their unshakable personal unity and the emotional toughness it engendered.

Virtually from the time they first picked up guitars, the Beatles had dreamed of being like Elvis Presley: rich, famous, lusted after, paid to do what they loved to do. Throughout their apprentice years in Liverpool and Hamburg, they had worked like demons to achieve this dream. Now the dream was their life, and everything seemed to have turned upside down. Instead of hustling to entice a few more customers into Hamburg dives, they were running for their lives before and after every show to escape surging, riotous mobs intent on seeing, touching, or just being near them. Instead of begging stories from indifferent local journalists, they were besieged by the media everywhere, and no matter how many interviews and press conferences they gave, it was never enough. Instead of daily face-to-face contact with fans who were more like them than not, they increasingly met only those people rich or influential enough to breach the walls they had defensively erected around themselves. In short, the unforeseen consequences of fame often made stardom feel more like prison than paradise. "Of course, at first we all thought we wanted the fame and that," George Harrison recalled in 1988. "But very shortly thereafter, we began to think twice. . . . After the initial excitement had worn off, I, for one, became depressed. Is this all we have to look forward to in life? Being chased around by a crowd of hooting lunatics from one crappy hotel room to the next?"

It was on tour that the madness was most oppressive, and by 1966 Beatlemania had driven the Beatles off the public stage for good; from then on, they would make music only in the calm of the studio. The year 1966 therefore marked the end of the first half of their career, the so-called touring years, and the start of the second half, the studio years. Their decision to forsake live performing was a risky one. In those early days of the consumer-electronics era, conventional show business wisdom still held that entertainers had to appear live if they wanted to build and keep an audience. Thus the news that the Beatles were giving up touring was widely interpreted as proof that they were breaking up. In fact, however, the decision was only further indication of their precocious self-assurance and free-thinking willingness to break rules that made no sense. Beginning with *Sgt Pepper's Lonely Hearts Club Band* in 1967, the Beatles would, in effect, let their albums, rather than themselves, go on tour.

It was not only the irritation factor that led the Beatles to abandon touring; it was also a conscious artistic choice, taken to safeguard their music and public standing. "It was wrecking our playing," Ringo Starr explained in the Beatles' authorized biography. "The noise of the people just drowned anything. Eventually I just used to play the off beat, instead of a constant beat. I couldn't hear myself half the time, even on the amps, with all the noise." Sometimes one or more of the Beatles would stop playing altogether, or simply mime the words, without anyone seeming to notice. "I reckon we could send out four waxwork dummies of ourselves and that would satisfy the crowds," John Lennon complained. Under the circumstances, the Beatles found it difficult to stay motivated. They were literally going through the motions, rushing through a half-hour set of the same ten or eleven songs night after night. That's when they knew it was time to quit. "You've got to give to receive," said Ringo. "Some nights we'd feel it had been terrible. We didn't give anything. That was when we decided we should give it up, before others started disliking it as well."

The precise date when Beatlemania began is a matter of interpretation, but the year was 1963. The term "Beatlemania" was coined by the mass-circulation Fleet Street newspapers of London after the Beatles' appearance at the prestigious London Palladium theater on October 13. That night's performance was broadcast live to some fifteen million viewers throughout Britain on what was then the nation's most popular television variety show, *Sunday Night at the London Palladium*, thus giving the general public its first glimpse of the hysterically screaming crowds that by now were a fixture at every Beatles live show. According to the reports and photographs that dominated the front pages of the next day's newspapers, bedlam reigned outside the theater as well, with hundreds of young fans blocking traffic, overrunning police lines, and chasing after the Beatles' getaway limousine.

It was later alleged that the crowds outside the Palladium were much smaller than reported, but whatever the actual numbers, Beatlemania was a social phenomenon that existed independent of and prior to Fleet Street's eager embrace of it. According to Mark Lewisohn's survey of local newspaper coverage, "Beatles-inspired hysteria had definitely begun by the late spring [of 1963], some six months before it was brought to national attention by Fleet Street newspapers." Nonetheless, the national media's sudden saturation coverage could not help but amplify the underlying frenzy, creating a self-reinforcing process whose immediate effect was an absolutely tumultuous welcome at Heathrow Airport when the Beatles returned from a quick tour of Sweden on October 31. The Beatles themselves cited this event as the beginning of Beatlemania. The spectacle of many thousands of screaming fans jamming the airport made news across the land, and for the next three years photos of the Beatles' well-attended departures and arrivals at Heathrow were a staple of British media coverage.

Four days after the Heathrow welcome, the Beatles clinched their hold on public affection with a performance before members of the English royal family at the Royal Variety Performance. To introduce the final number, "Twist And Shout," a surprisingly raucous selection for such a staid, upper-crust crowd, Lennon asked, "Will the people in the cheaper seats clap your hands? And the rest of you, if you'll just rattle your jewelry." When his jibe appeared on front pages throughout the country the next day, it solidified the Beatles' image as four cheeky but lovable lads from Liverpool.

Having captured Britain in 1963, the Beatles spent 1964 extending their dominion to the rest of the English-speaking world. They visited the United States (twice), Holland, Denmark, Sweden, Hong Kong, Australia, and New Zealand. In each country, the scenes of uncontainable mass excitement were similar enough to have been scripted by a single invisible master of ceremonies: boisterous airport welcomes, clamoring crowds outside the Beatles' hotels, shrieking audiences at their shows, all magnified by virtually nonstop media coverage. The single largest crowd gathered in Adelaide, Australia, where an estimated 300,000 people massed beneath the Beatles' hotel balcony in hopes of catching a glimpse of the conquering heroes. Young people were at the forefront of the international uproar, but their elders were also smitten, as evidenced by a sudden predeliction among middle-aged men to don Beatles wigs during the Beatles' first New York visit.

The 1964 touring schedule arranged by Brian Epstein—one tour of the United States, one of the United Kingdom, and one of Europe and/or Asia—was repeated in both 1965 and 1966 (except that the U.K. tour was dropped in 1966). But the tours became shorter each year as the Beatles got increasingly annoyed by the drudgery of it all. "We got in a rut, going round the world," Harrison said. "It was a different audience each day, but we were doing the same things." Touring was like the army, Lennon said: "One big sameness which you have to go through. One big mess."

Of course, it was not all hassles and hardship. The income generated by touring was fantastic, especially when the Beatles graduated from indoor arenas to outdoor football stadiums. The fees demanded by Epstein were the highest ever quoted in show business, yet local promoters were begging to do business with him. The infamous show at New York's Shea Stadium on August 15, 1965, for example, set a world record for both attendance (55,600 people) and gross revenue ($304,000 in 1965 dollars). In addition to the official receipts, Epstein regularly pocketed untold thousands of extra dollars in so-called brown paper bag money, which was skimmed off the top of proceeds by the local promoter and not reported to tax authorities. The Beatles soon became so blasé about the huge sums flowing in that when an eccentric American millionaire named Charlie Finley offered them $150,000 in clear profit for a single extra show in Kansas City on what would have been their day off, they barely looked up from their card game before telling Epstein to do whatever he wanted about the offer. Epstein accepted it.

Nor were the performances themselves invariably exercises in poor musicianship and mindless alienation. Accompanied by his future wife, Judy Lockhart-Smith, George Martin attended the Beatles' first concert in America, at the Washington Coliseum, on February 11, 1964. Having spent many hours with the group in the recording studio, Martin and Lockhart-Smith knew the Beatles as friends and co-workers, not as distant idols. Yet the spell cast by the Beatles was so powerful, Martin recalled, that when they played "I Want To Hold Your Hand," the entire "audience started singing with them [and] Judy and I just found ourselves standing up and screaming along with the rest . . . swept up in that tremendous current of buoyant happiness and exhilaration." On stage, Ringo felt the same spirit. "Some of them even threw jelly babies in bags and they hurt like hailstones but they could have ripped me apart and I couldn't have cared less," he later enthused. "What an audience! I could have played for them all night!" To be sure, this show took place early in Beatlemania, but undoctored tapes of other performances from 1964 through 1966 reveal a band whose singing and playing, though not necessarily inspired, were generally professional and respectably in tune and rhythm—no small feat, considering that the Beatles could barely hear themselves. (An acoustical expert who measured crowd noise during the band's Australian tour found that it was louder than a jet engine.)

"Look, when the Beatles did a tour, we hated it and loved it. There were great nights and lousy ones," Lennon later told journalist Ray Coleman. Separately, he admitted, "Oh sure. I dug the fame, the power, the money and playing to big crowds. Conquering America was the best thing." The Beatles had agreed among themselves to affect a pose of indifference about success, but the reception awaiting them in New York in February 1964 pierced this facade. There is a revealing piece of film, shot from inside the Beatles' limousine on the way into town from the airport, showing McCartney with a transistor radio to his ear, listening with the other Beatles as a local announcer rattles on excitedly about the Beatles programming his station is offering. (All day long, announcers had been giving the weather in "Beatle degrees," the time in "Beatle minutes.") Like the others, Paul is shaking his head in stunned, ecstatic disbelief, but he comes abruptly to attention upon hearing that "tomorrow night at seven the Beatles read their own poetry." Paul, for once not self-consciously "on," is genuinely surprised by this news and does a double-take at John before saying, with a startled grin, "Oh-oh? Oh, really?" Only then does he go into character, adopting a slow-thinking tone of voice to complain, "We ain't written no poetry."

And there were so many ways to have fun when the world lay at your feet! Big, wicked, high-octane fun—like the time the Beatles were in the Bahamas shooting their second film, *Help!* and they played bumper cars with four rented Cadillacs, leaving the cars total wrecks. "It was a terrific feeling, smashing up all those shiny new limos," John later told Pete Shotton. The party scene was no less wild. It was standard procedure for Beatles aides Mal Evans and Neil Aspinall to survey the crowd at concerts and ask four or more of the best-looking girls to meet the Beatles after the show. "Of course there were orgies!" Aspinall later admitted. "There was an orgy in every town. It's only a miracle the press didn't get a hold of it." Lennon told Shotton about one particular party, filled with starlets and models, where "I grabbed one and fucked her under the stairs—another one, fucked her in the bedroom—then another in the bathroom and one on the kitchen floor. . . . I've never seen anything like it—and it went on the whole night long. I had seven of them in all." Lennon separately likened Beatles tours to *Satyricon*, a film by Federico Fellini depicting the decadent hedonism of the late Roman Empire: "Wherever we went, there was always a whole scene going. . . . [Press officer] Derek [Taylor]'s and Neil's rooms were always full of junk and whores and who-the-fuck-knows-what, and policemen with it. Satyricon!" George Harrison, in one of the best songs of his solo career, aptly summed up the days "when we was fab" with the recollection, "And we did it aw-aw-aaw-all. . . . Fab!"

The Beatles' rock 'n' roll lifestyle—their rampant sexual promiscuity, the pills, booze and drugs they freely consumed—was no secret to the journalists covering them, yet never was it mentioned in news stories. "Everybody wants the image to carry on," Lennon later explained. "The press around with you want you to carry on because they want the free drinks and the free whores and the fun. . . . We were the Caesars. Who was going to knock us when there's a million pounds to be made?" The image of the four Beatles as clean, upstanding young Englishmen was reinforced most powerfully by the Queen herself when she named them Members of the British Empire in a ceremony at Buckingham Palace on October 26, 1965. Never before had pop stars received such an accolade from the Palace. Little did the Queen know that just prior to the ceremony, the Beatles had slipped into a Palace lavatory to smoke a quick joint.

It was all very seductive, flattering, and intoxicating, but it was also exhausting. "Those years did seem to be a thousand years long," Harrison later said. The problem, Lennon explained, was that "there was no switching off. The elevator man wanted a little piece of you on your way back to the hotel room, the maid wanted a little piece of you back at the hotel—I don't mean sexually, I mean a piece of your time and your energy." In self-defense, the Beatles developed a habit of speaking in code around strangers. People they wished to avoid they referred to as "cripples," a password derived from the fact that they were so frequently importuned to greet deformed, handicapped, or otherwise imperfect souls that George Martin has compared this aspect of their tours to a pilgrimage to Lourdes, adding, "There were people who actually wanted to touch the hems of the clothes they were wearing. . . . They can hardly be blamed for wanting to put up a barrier against the world."

To escape the masses at home, each of the Beatles (except Paul, who remained in town) moved to London's stockbroker suburbs, where distance and high walls afforded some protection from prying fans. On the road, however, they had little choice but to remain cloistered in tightly guarded hotel suites, where the claustrophobia and boredom were maddening. Even then they were not safe from the non-masses—the countless local personages who demanded access to the Fab Four. In his witty memoir, *As Time Goes By*, former press officer Taylor recalls an episode that took place in Milwaukee. It was the morning after the show, and the Beatles' entourage was still asleep. The hotel was in "the usual state of siege with the street scene spilling into the hotel lobby and armed guards everywhere . . . with shortsleeved white minds and thin grey thoughts." The mayor's wife, her nine-year-old daughter in tow, was allowed through, however, and escorted up to Taylor's room, where she insisted that he rouse the Beatles in order to meet her daughter. Over a wake-up screwdriver, Taylor listened to the woman disparage his bosses as "long-haired louts" who had no business sleeping at eleven in the morning but who nonetheless held a fascination for her daughter. With cunning foresight, the woman had brought with her a young local reporter, unschooled in the protective code of silence observed by the Beatles' traveling press corps; the woman threatened bad publicity if Taylor did not meet her demand. And so, Taylor concluded, "the daughter of the Mayor of M got to meet the Beatles later that day. Did you doubt she would?"

"The bigger we got, the more unreality we had to face," Lennon later recalled. Most humiliating, he said, were the events where upper-crust types "would be commenting on our work and commenting on our manners. . . . One has to completely humiliate oneself to be what the Beatles were, and that's what I resent; I didn't know, I didn't foresee. It happened bit by bit, gradually, until this complete craziness is surrounding you, and you're doing exactly what you don't want to do with people you can't stand—the people you hated when you were ten."

Sometimes the stress went beyond humiliation to outright physical danger. In 1966, when the Beatles failed to attend a party hosted by the wife of Philippine dictator Ferdinand Marcos, they learned just how severe the punishment for not playing the VIP game could be. Once again, the Beatles were asleep in their hotel rooms when policemen came knocking: What time would the group be appearing at the party? The Beatles knew nothing of any party, though an invitation had apparently been forwarded to one of their staff. Manager Epstein refused to have them wakened, despite a call from the British ambassador warning that this might invite retribution. After news reports trumpeted the story of the Beatles' insult to Mrs. Marcos and the national honor, Epstein tried to apologize, but it was too late; his televised statement was blocked from transmission. When the Beatles awoke the next morning, all the service employees and police protection had vanished from their hotel. At the Manila airport, they were confronted by armed troops and a mob that punched and kicked at them, and their entourage barely made it onto the plane. It was "incredibly frightening," Lennon said later, and it was during the flight out of Manila that he and the other Beatles decided that they had had enough of touring.

They had narrowly escaped bodily harm on a number of other occasions as well. Concert audiences sometimes became so rowdy that the police would halt performances in mid-show to calm things down. Crowds swarmed a Beatles limousine once, caving in its roof; the Beatles might have been killed, except they were actually inside an ambulance—the limousine was a decoy. At Houston's airport, thousands of fans went crazy when the Beatles' plane landed; when some ran onto the runway, the pilot made the mistake of coasting to a stop, and within minutes the aircraft was covered by kids eagerly banging on doors and peering through windows. Perhaps the scariest incident took place in Memphis, where the Beatles had received preconcert death threats after Lennon's infamous remark about the Beatles being "more popular than Jesus" (an incident described in Chapter Sixteen of this book). When a loud crack was heard during the show, each Beatle quickly checked himself, and then the others, to see which of them had been shot. The noise turned out to have been a firecracker.

More insidious than the prospect of assassination was the risk of creative and emotional death. Too much fame had been the ruin of their role model Elvis, reducing him from a magnificently wild, original talent to a pale Hollywood hack. That trajectory was by no means unique among show business success stories, yet the Beatles, the biggest success story of all time, managed to escape it. If the most striking thing about Beatlemania was the ability of four young musicians to spark such mass, spontaneous joy and excitement around the world, the second most striking thing was the survival of those musicians with their artistic powers enhanced. The Beatles' music continued its amazing progression in quality and sophistication throughout the years of Beatlemania, an achievement that reflected the extraordinary personal dynamic that existed among John, Paul, George, and Ringo. "There's four of us, so whenever one of us gets a little potty the other three bring him back to earth," Ringo said, explaining how the Beatles kept their balance.

"This isn't show business, it's something else," Lennon said in the midst of Beatlemania. "This is different from anything that anybody imagines. You don't go on from this. You do this and then you finish." By the time the Beatles gave their last live show, in San Francisco, on August 29, 1966, they had logged a career total of fourteen hundred performances. Their decision to stop touring was not yet public knowledge, but they documented their last appearance onstage with a group self-portrait, taken with a special wide-angle lens. "Ringo came off the drums and we stood with our backs to the audience and posed for a photograph, because we knew that was the last show," George recalled.

The crowd continued screaming, just like hundreds of other crowds had screamed the past five years, but the Beatles they were applauding no longer existed. John, Paul, George, and Ringo had been forced, by the pressures of Beatlemania itself, to grow up very fast, and in the process they had left some of their traditional audience far behind. "We live in a moving hothouse," John said shortly after the San Francisco concert. ". . . We had to be sort of more than four mopheads up on a stage. We had to grow up or we'd have been swamped." Indeed, by

August 1966 the Beatles were well on the way to becoming the foremost symbols of the emerging 1960s counterculture. By then, they had spoken out against the Vietnam War, and their use of marijuana and LSD had opened their minds to a deeper, richer reality, thereby making their Fab Four image seem all the more absurd. Above all, their music had become far more ambitious in every respect. They were consciously thinking of themselves and their art in lofty historical terms. "I'd hate the Beatles to be remembered as four jovial moptops," McCartney said in June 1966. "I'd like to be remembered, when we're dead, as four people who made music that stands up to be remembered."

CHAPTER 9

War Weary
(Beatles For Sale)

THE ONE CLEAR ARTISTIC CASUALTY OF BEATLEMANIA WAS *BEATLES FOR SALE*, THE ALBUM THE BEATLES RELEASED AT THE end of 1964; it had fatigue written all over it. Even its title, an empty and forgettable expression of unadorned commerce, sounded tired, as if no one had the energy to think of something better. The front and back covers featured matching photographs of the Beatles, and very somber photographs they were. Dressed in black, John, Paul, George, and Ringo stood huddled together, as if seeking protection from the outside world. Their pale, wan faces stared straight into the camera; not one wore anything approaching a smile. On the front cover, the Beatles looked glum and stricken, as if they had just been told a close friend has died; on the back, they peered dolefully upward, as if imploring mercy from above.

The Beatles were so famous by the time *Beatles For Sale* came out that the liner notes inside the album announced simply, "This is the fourth by the four." No one within earshot of the Western media could wonder which four; as the notes immodestly declared, the Beatles were now "the biggest attraction the world has ever known." Moreover, this fourth album was, according to a quote jointly attributed to John, Paul, George, and Ringo, "quite definitely" their best yet. All this was promotional hype, of course, but the man who wrote it, Beatles press officer Derek Taylor, was too talented not to rise above the conventions of the genre. Indeed, in the books Taylor published after the Beatles broke up, he showed himself to be the best pure stylist ever to write about the group. His prose rather resembled their music: witty, playful, and unpretentious, yet imbued with a keen, poetic intelligence—qualities that enabled him to place the Beatles in historical perspective without sounding pompous or puerile.

Thus Taylor went on in the *Beatles For Sale* liner notes to envision "a radio-active, cigar-smoking child, picnicking on Saturn" in the year 2000 who wonders what the Beatles craze was all about. The best way to explain, Taylor advised, will be to play the child a few tracks from this album. Generations to come, he predicted, "will draw from the music much the same sense of well-being and warmth as we do today. For the magic of the Beatles is, I suspect, timeless and ageless. It has broken all frontiers and barriers. It has cut through differences of race, age and class. It is adored by the world."

Those sentences offer as concise and insightful a summary of the Beatles' popular appeal and artistic stature as have yet been written. The irony is that Taylor summoned them on behalf of an album that was hardly the Beatles' finest work to date. (That honor plainly belonged to *A Hard Day's Night.*) Indeed, *Beatles For Sale* is probably the least impressive album the group ever released. George Martin has acknowledged that *Beatles For Sale* represented a lapse, explaining, "They were rather war weary during *Beatles For Sale*. One must remember that they'd been battered like mad throughout 1964, and much of 1963. Success is a wonderful thing, but it is very, very tiring. They were always on the go. *Beatles For Sale* doesn't appeal to me very much now, it's not one of their most memorable ones. They perked up again after that."

"War weary" is an apt phrase; the cover photos for *Beatles For Sale* made the Beatles look almost shell-shocked. Fame seems to have left them anxious, exhausted, and almost dreading whatever was coming next. On the album itself, the titles of the first three songs—"No Reply," "I'm A Loser," and "Baby's In Black"—all written mainly by John, struck a similarly despondent note. The Beatles still had their moptop haircuts, but their carefree image had cracked.

At the time, few outsiders seemed to notice. When *Beatles For Sale* was released on December 4, 1964, the Beatles fairy tale was still in first flower; how could its heroes possibly be having second thoughts? Not for the last time, the world was ignoring inconvenient truths about the Beatles. It was an easy mistake to make, and not only because the equivalent album in the United States, *Beatles '65*, featured completely different cover photos. After all, the single released a week prior to *Beatles For Sale*, "I Feel Fine," was a cheerful, upbeat rocker in the tradition of "She Loves You" and "I Want To Hold Your Hand." To no one's surprise, it became the group's seventh straight number one. *Beatles For Sale* also zoomed to the top of the charts, and not, one suspects, simply because of the momentum of Beatlemania. The flame of genius burned less brightly on *Beatles For Sale* than on other albums, but even its weariest flickerings validated Derek Taylor's observation that the music of the Beatles conveyed a "sense of well-being and warmth."

The best tracks on the album were the three that George Martin considered releasing as singles before Lennon came up with the clearly superior "I Feel Fine." These were "No Reply" and "I'm A Loser," the opening songs on side one, and "Eight Days A Week," which begins side two. Though none of these ranks among the best songs Lennon and McCartney ever wrote, each has charms, and the first two display evidence of Lennon's growing maturity as a lyricist. Needing extra ballast, the Beatles returned to their Cavern Club rock 'n' roll repertoire to fill out the rest of *Beatles For Sale*. Here, the standouts are Chuck Berry's "Rock And Roll Music" and the Little Richard–inspired medley of "Kansas City" and "Hey, Hey, Hey, Hey." However, Ringo is artlessly appealing on Carl Perkins's "Honey Don't," and George's delivery of "Everybody's Trying To Be My Baby," also by Perkins, allows the Beatles to close the album with a not-so-veiled comment on the oddities of living inside Beatlemania.

The abundance of cover versions on *Beatles For Sale* almost made it seem that the Beatles were paying homage to their American roots one last time, for (with four exceptions) they would record only original compositions during the remainder of their career. A mere eight of the fourteen songs on *Beatles For Sale* were Lennon–McCartney originals.

This constituted a retreat from *A Hard Day's Night*, back to the ratio found on their second album, *With The Beatles*. Yet how John and Paul found time to write even this many new songs amidst the white heat of 1964 is hard to fathom, and the recording of *Beatles For Sale* was no less rushed. Once again sessions at Abbey Road were crammed in among other commitments. The last four sessions took place in October, on what should have been days off for the Beatles, in order to finish the album in time for the Christmas season.

If this was not the most prolific or inspired period in the Beatles' songwriting career, it nevertheless witnessed continued artistic evolution. Most striking were the technical innovations that gave birth to new sounds, particularly the electronic flourishes that launched "I Feel Fine" and "Eight Days A Week." The Beatles had begun exploring the new vistas opened by four-track recording while making *A Hard Day's Night* earlier in 1964. The more they discovered about how studio tricks could alter a song's tone and texture, the more enamored they became of them.

The deep quivering feedback that introduces "I Feel Fine" was a source of particular pride to Lennon. "I defy anybody to find a record—unless it's some old blues record in 1922—that uses feedback that way," he later said. ". . . I claim it for the Beatles. Before Hendrix, before The Who, before anybody. The first feedback on any record." Such experimentation easily could have amounted to self-indulgent tinkering, but the feedback in "I Feel Fine" was no mere avant-garde statement. In service of the musical whole, it spun deftly into the funky guitar riff that turns the rest of the song into a toe-tapping cruise down back country roads in a sun-drenched convertible. Without the feedback, "I Feel Fine" might have been just one more hit single, catchy but fairly ordinary. As was so often the case with the Beatles, it was the mix of mainstream and avant-garde that yielded something memorable.

How the Beatles hit upon the feedback idea has never been adequately explained. Press reports from the time spoke of "an electronic accident," a notion curtly dismissed in Lewisohn's *Recording Sessions*, which declares, "It was no such thing. Right from take one the Beatles had perfected the curious sounding introduction . . . with Paul plucking a single bass string and John getting amplifier feedback on his guitar."

Yet surely the inspiration-giving "accident" could have occurred prior to the first take of the song, convincing the Beatles to incorporate a refinement of it later, when they began recording. After all, three separate entries in *Recording Sessions* note that the Beatles always took advantage of "accidents" in the studio, including one time when a certain organ note caused a wine bottle atop a speaker cabinet to vibrate in such an interesting way that the sequence was repeated specifically in order to get the odd sound down on tape.

In any case, "I Feel Fine" was a first-rate piece of work. It not only redeemed the general artistic shortcomings of this period in the Beatles' career, it foreshadowed the fascination with studio experimentation that would color so much of their future work. The B-side of "I Feel Fine," a throaty McCartney rocker called "She's A Woman," hinted at a different but no less important development: the Beatles' initiation (courtesy of Bob Dylan) into smoking marijuana. "She's A Woman" begins with one of the most awkward rhymes in the Beatles' catalogue: "My love don't give me presents / I know that she's no peasant." But four lines later, Paul sings that his lover "turn(s) me on when I feel lonely." It was the Beatles' first explicit reference to drugs. Listening to unreleased outtakes of the song, it sounds like the Beatles may even have had a few joints in the studio that day. Take seven of "She's A Woman" just keeps going, and going, and going, eventually becoming a spirited, if somewhat ragged, jam. In years to come, mind-expanding drugs would figure more and more prominently in the Beatles' work, not to mention their private lives and personal growth, but at this point John and Paul were simply voicing the wide-eyed joy of the newly awakened. "We were so excited to say 'turn me on'—you know, about marijuana and all that, using it as an expression," Lennon later recalled.

Had "I Feel Fine" not materialized, the song most likely to have been this period's single was "Eight Days A Week." In fact, "Eight Days A Week" was issued as a single in the United States, and spent two weeks at number one. Like "A Hard Day's Night" and the still-to-come "Tomorrow Never Knows," "Eight Days A Week" owed its title to an offhand remark of Ringo's. "He said it as though he were an over-worked chauffeur: 'Eight days a week,' " McCartney recalled. "When we heard it, we said, 'Really? Bing! Got it!' " A joint Lennon–McCartney composition, "Eight Days A Week" was later trashed by John as "lousy," an absurdly harsh judgment. In fact, its tune bounces along pleasantly and its lyrics, thanks to the injection of Ringo's unwitting wit, were a half step above those of many early Beatles songs.

But what most set "Eight Days A Week" apart was another studio gimmick. It had long been routine for record producers to conclude certain songs with gradual fade-outs rather than fully realized, discrete endings. On "Eight Days A Week," however, this practice was turned inside out; it became the first pop song ever to *begin* with a fade-in. This effect carried extra weight on *Beatles For Sale* because "Eight Days A Week" was the first song on the album's second side. Thus the listener, after turning the record over and waiting for the second side to begin, had the sensation of hearing the music before the song actually arrived; it was as if the sound arose out of the distance, like a flock of migrating birds that suddenly fills the sky. Such studio-wrought sleight-of-hand was, as George Martin remarked in a different context, "Very simple to do . . . but very effective."

Beatles For Sale also marked the beginning of what Lennon later referred to as "my Dylan period," a time when his lyrics became more realistic, introspective, and diverse. The song most commonly cited to illustrate this evolution, both by John and by critics, is "I'm A Loser," a song whose title speaks for itself. The verses offer the standard Lennon portrayal of romance as a war of possession and deceit that he has lost; indeed, to that extent, the song was no different from previous compositions. It was really only in the chorus that John's emerging sensibility revealed itself. "I'm a loser / And I'm not what I appear to be," he sang, a confession that paralleled the album's disquieting cover photos and would soon be echoed in such compositions as "Help!" and "Nowhere Man."

"No Reply" is actually a better example of Lennon's lyrical maturation, a fact remarked upon at the time by Dick James, the publisher of the Lennon–McCartney song catalogue. After James heard "No Reply," Lennon later recalled, he told John, " 'You're getting much better now—that was a complete story.' Apparently before that he thought my songs tended to sort of wander off." The story told in "No Reply" does resolve, but more impressive is the vivid scene that Lennon sketches along the way. A suitor is turned away from a young woman's house after being told she isn't home. But he learns otherwise when, looking up, he sees her peek through the window. Their eyes meet, and his sense of betrayal and humiliation is crushing. "I nearly died!" John wails, and Paul seconds the emotion with a powerful, desperate harmony. The pain is palpable, yet it is so fiercely and openly expressed that the ultimate effect is cathartic.

It was somewhat risky to open a Beatles album with two such despondent songs, and in fact Martin at one point toyed with the idea of putting "No Reply" on side two. But he was shuffling a deck with only a limited number of high cards, so he had to play them carefully. To be sure, there was no shame in such Lennon–McCartney originals as "Every Little Thing" and "I Don't Want To Spoil The Party," but what they illustrated above all was how the band, thanks largely to John and Paul's extraordinary singing, could make unremarkable material sound richer than it really was. Just how depleted the Beatles' songwriting reserves were at this point is indicated by a remark McCartney made years later about "I'll Follow The Sun," a pretty but slight ballad that is buried on side one. Paul wrote "I'll Follow The Sun" when he was only sixteen, but it did not appear on earlier Beatles records because, he confessed, "It wouldn't have been considered good enough. I wouldn't have put it up."

In the end Martin seems to have aimed to open and close each side of the album as strongly as possible while hoping that such undistinguished offerings as "Baby's In Black," "Mr. Moonlight," and "Words Of Love" would attract relatively little notice if snuck in amidst the rumbling herd. The mystery is why "Mr. Moonlight" made the cut at all. For on the same day that the Beatles recorded their cover of this 1962 non-hit by Dr. Feelgood and the Interns, they also taped a very animated rendition of "Leave My Kitten Alone," a R&B tune first recorded by Little Willie John in 1959. The unreleased recording of the Beatles' version of "Leave My Kitten Alone" reveals that it is in the same vein as their earlier covers of "Slow Down" and "Money (That's What I Want)"; that is, it boasts a shouting Lennon vocal over a rambunctious instrumental backing. It isn't as appealing as the two best covers on *Beatles For Sale*—"Rock And Roll Music" and the "Kansas City" medley—but it is vastly superior to "Mr. Moonlight" and could have injected some valuable pep into the album's second side. Whether it was the Beatles themselves or George Martin who vetoed "Leave My Kitten Alone" is unknown. The balance of power between group and producer was shifting at this point—Lewisohn reports that after listening to the discordant opening guitar twang on "Baby's In Black," Martin queries dubiously, "You want the beginning like that, do you?"—but the decision may have been mutual. In any event, it ranks as one of the Beatles' few instances of mistaken musical judgment.

It is largely because of the brilliance of the Beatles' career after *Beatles For Sale* that the album now stands revealed as the nadir of the group's recording efforts. It may have compared favorably with its contemporary competition, but measured against the total body of work accumulated by the Beatles, it is second-rate filler. As such, it can be regarded either as evidence that the Beatles were human after all or as a regrettable by-product of Beatlemania. No such charges were leveled at the time, of course, though had the Beatles followed this album with a second, equally weak release, the public might have started grumbling. Instead, however, the Beatles regained their feet and marched smartly forward. Indeed, from this point on, their career resembles nothing so much as a heaven-blessed, ever-rising shooting star.

CHAPTER 10

The Naturals: The Lennon–McCartney Collaboration

THE FOUNDATION OF THE BEATLES' EXTRAORDINARY POP-
ULAR APPEAL AND ARTISTIC STATURE WAS ALWAYS THE SONG-
writing of John Lennon and Paul McCartney. As a band, the Beatles
first attracted attention with their electrifying live performances of
American rock 'n' roll songs, and their talents as singers and musicians
remained huge assets throughout their recording career. But what set
the Beatles apart from such pop music greats as Elvis Presley and Frank
Sinatra was that the Beatles did not merely interpret other people's
songs, however skillfully; they also wrote their own, eventually compil-
ing a body of work that equals any in twentieth-century popular music.
Although George Harrison did contribute some fine songs to the
group's catalogue, it was above all the compositions of Lennon and
McCartney that made the Beatles the outstanding musical phenomenon of their time. "The song is what remains," Ringo Starr once
explained. "It's not how you've done it. I honestly believe in the song
more than the music. It's the song people whistle. You don't whistle my
drum part. And John and Paul wrote some amazing songs."

Oddly, Lennon and McCartney initially showed "absolutely no evidence that they were going to be great songwriters," said George Martin; indeed, the producer contended that it was the Beatles' all-absorbing rise to fame, and the competitiveness that this encouraged between Lennon and McCartney, that brought the duo's creative talents to fruition: "It was the pressure cooker process that made them into great songwriters. They learned very, very quickly and they spurred each other on—it was a competition, really, all the time."

The competitive nature of the Lennon–McCartney partnership was apparent from the very start, as illustrated by outtakes from the March 5, 1963, recording session for "From Me To You." On this day, the Beatles were returning to Abbey Road somewhat in the role of conquering heroes; it was their first time back in the studios since scoring their first number one hit with "Please Please Me," on February 22. Both songs were Lennon–McCartney originals; in fact, true to legend, "From Me To You" had been written in the back of the band's traveling van just five days before the March 5 session, while the Beatles were driving between gigs in York and Shrewsbury. Now, as Ringo settled in behind his drum kit in Studio Two and the other Beatles strapped on their guitars, the band was preparing to record what would soon become their second straight number one single.

It took seven full takes to get "From Me To You" right, but the Beatles had obviously been practicing it, for the song sounds very close to final form on the first take. John and Paul's dual lead vocals are expertly harmonized, George's guitar licks tag brightly along after the melody, Ringo's drums wheeze and shuffle as cheerfully as an aging merry-go-round. Indeed, additional takes might well have been unnecessary if a mysterious whistle had not sounded near the end of the third verse. A brief whistle was one of the signals routinely used to abort a take, and this one duly brought everything to a halt.

John and George stop playing first. Ringo's drums give another cough or two, and Paul trills a few more words before he, too, stops. In all apparent innocence, Paul then asks, "Wha' hap'nd?" There is silence, then a voice from the control room evenly replies, "What do you mean, what happened?" Quickly mounting his high horse, Paul answers in a lighthearted but accusatory tone, "I just thought I heard you talking, actually." Intense cross-talk between John and Paul follows, indecipherable except for John's query, "Did you play . . ." Seconds later, John declares in thick Liverpudlian, "I heard a whistle," but it is unclear whether he suspects Paul or someone else. In any case, no one admits to being the culprit, so John says, as if shrugging his shoulders, "Okay, come on," and the Beatles begin take two. This is another fine effort from start to finish—or so it sounds to a first-time listener. But the sharp-eared McCartney immediately detects what a rewind of the tape confirms: John's final vocal hits the wrong harmony. And so, with the last guitar notes still echoing through the amplifiers, Paul crows at John with obvious delight, "Ah-ah-ah-ah-ah-ah, you missed the ending."

Such affectionate competitiveness seems to have pervaded Lennon and McCartney's entire relationship. From their earliest days together, John and Paul were rivals as well as friends, competitors as well as partners, critics as well as soulmates. "Imagine two people pulling on a rope, smiling at each other and pulling all the time with all their might," George Martin told Lennon biographer Ray Coleman. "The tension between the two of them made for the bond." Their songwriting partnership was like a love affair, Lennon once said, but the affair always had an edge to it. "It wasn't resentment, but it *was* competitive," Lennon recalled. There was always "a little competition between Paul and I as to who got the 'A' side, who got the hit singles."

This rivalry not only drove Lennon and McCartney to write better and better songs over time, it also helped propel the astonishingly rapid musical progression that is so salient a feature of the Beatles' entire career. George Martin has suggested that had the two men never met, each would have become merely a good, but not "blisteringly great," songwriter. "Meeting John has made [Paul] try for deeper lyrics," Martin told Hunter Davies in the Beatles' authorized biography. "But for meeting John, I doubt if Paul could have written 'Eleanor Rigby.' " Paul himself later said of John, "He'd write 'Strawberry Fields,' I'd go away and write 'Penny Lane.' If I'd write 'I'm Down,' he'd go away and write something similar to that. To compete with each other. But it was very friendly competition, because we were both going to share in the rewards anyway. It was this—[he chops with his hands as if they are climbing an invisible ladder]—it really helped, step, so we were getting better and better all the time."

"Penny Lane" and "Strawberry Fields Forever" in fact offer one of the clearest juxtapositions of the differing sensibilities that made Lennon and McCartney such a potent songwriting team. With its jaunty, playful beat, warmhearted character sketches, and tongue-in-cheek humor, "Penny Lane" reflects McCartney's essentially sunny outlook on life. Paul's childhood "beneath the blue suburban skies" of Liverpool had dark moments, but overall it is a time he looks back on fondly. Lennon's "Strawberry Fields Forever," on the other hand, is a dreamy, almost haunted place, where "nothing is real" and John wonders whether it is he, or the world, that is crazy.

Lennon and McCartney were, in fact, just different enough in their temperaments and musical instincts to bring out more than the best in each other. It goes without saying that each was staggeringly gifted. But while McCartney was a songbird with a prodigious gift for melody, foot-tapping tempos, and uplifting sentiments, Lennon was a poet whose songs tended toward odd rhythms, melody lines of one or two notes, and a more angled, absurdist perspective on life. If McCartney tended to write about other people, Lennon was more inclined to write about himself. And if McCartney was responsible for most of the Beatles' mainstream standards—songs like "Yesterday," "Michelle," and "Yellow Submarine"—Lennon usually authored such philosophical statements as "All You Need Is Love," "Revolution," and "Nowhere Man." Left to themselves, these respective tendencies could be taken too far (a criticism sometimes leveled against each man's post-Beatles compositions). But within the Beatles, Paul's and John's individual proclivities were encouraged, usually without being overindulged. The dynamic was neatly summarized by Lennon's friend Pete Shotton, one of the very few outsiders with eyewitness knowledge of the Beatles' songwriting sessions. "Paul's presence did serve to keep John from drifting too far into obscurity and self-indulgence, just as John's influence held in check the more facile and sentimental aspects of Paul's songwriting," observed Shotton.

Ironically, the solo careers of Lennon and McCartney offered perhaps the clearest illustration of the strength of their partnership. As solo artists, both wrote numerous songs that were as good as those they wrote as Beatles; talent such as theirs does not simply vanish overnight. The problem was that John and Paul also wrote other, quite ordinary songs as well, songs that simply would not have been included on a Beatles album because they would have been outclassed by the competition. Here again, then, the competitive aspect was crucial. The mere fact that there was only so much space on each Beatles album meant that only the strongest offerings of each composer got recorded, whereas virtually every song they wrote as solo artists got released, either because there was no one around to tell them no or because they needed to pad out their albums. As McCartney remarked during his solo years, "You know, I could sit down [at a piano] and literally come back in three hours' time with about a hundred of those songs—and the terrifying thing is that ten of them might be big hits."

Yet it was not simply a matter of neutralizing each other's weak points; the melding of John's and Paul's contrasting styles also had the positive effect of greatly enlarging the emotional and musical canvas on which the Beatles expressed themselves. This was especially evident in songs that Lennon and McCartney composed together. In his 1980 *Playboy* interview, for example, John described how the process worked in reference to "Michelle." His explanation is illuminating in its own right, and it also punctures a common assumption among Beatles fans: that one can always tell who wrote a given song by listening to who sings its lead vocal. "Michelle" demonstrates how tricky such generally reliable rules of thumb can be. For while McCartney sings lead throughout "Michelle," he actually wrote only its verses; the middle eight passage was composed by John.

Recalling the scene, John said, "He and I were staying somewhere and he walked in and hummed the first few bars with the words . . . and he says, 'Where do I go from here?' " John had been listening to a blues record, and by reconfiguring a line from it he came up with the "I love you, I love you, I love you" phrase. "My contribution to Paul's songs was always to add a little bluesy edge to them," John explained. "Otherwise, y'know, 'Michelle' is a straight ballad, right? He provided a lightness, an optimism, while I would always go for the sadness, the discords, the bluesy notes." Thus in "We Can Work It Out," Paul's buoyant call for reconciliation takes on a persuasive measure of gravity from John's impatient warning that "life is very short, and there's no time for fussing and fighting, my friend." And in "She's Leaving Home," a song written primarily by Paul, John rounds out the lyric by forgiving the parents whose teenage daughter has fled their over-protective grasp: "What did we do that was wrong? / We didn't know it was wrong."

As much as fans and critics liked to speculate over who wrote what and who was the greater genius, it was the Lennon–McCartney partnership itself that was the point. As talented as each man was, it was their coming together, their influencing and challenging and complementing of one another, that elevated them to another dimension, producing music superior to what either man could consistently create on his own. To rank their respective contributions to the Beatles was impossible, said George Martin: "It's like asking what's the most important constituent in a sauce vinaigrette, the oil or the vinegar. Both were fundamentally important: one without the other would have been unthinkable in terms of the Beatles' success."

Nevertheless, over time, outside observers extrapolated the differences in Lennon's and McCartney's personalities and musical instincts into misleading stereotypes. Paul was cast as the mawkish lightweight who couldn't write a decent lyric, John as the rebellious artiste and abrasive bad boy. Both men were too complex and talented to be encompassed by such one-dimensional portraits, however. Paul was actually "quite a capable lyricist" when he put his mind to it, John argued, citing songs like "Yesterday," "The Fool On The Hill" and "Fixing A Hole." Yet the images stuck, in part because it wasn't only thickheaded critics who promulgated them; John in particular was less than generous in statements about Paul during the bitter post-breakup years of the early 1970s. Recalled McCartney, "I've become known as the soppy balladeer, and John of course did a lot to encourage that myth when we were having rows. He really tried to put that about but he knew otherwise." Indeed, it was McCartney who wrote and sang "Helter Skelter," a hyped-up, gut-churning song that kicked as hard as anything The Who ever did. And during the same session when Paul taped "Yesterday," he also recorded "I'm Down," a wildly raucous rock 'n' roller that featured his trademark power vocal. Likewise John, the screamer who demolished "Twist And Shout" in one take and later wailed "I Am The Walrus," was the same man who wrote the lush, sentimental ballad "Goodnight" and whose voice ached with loss on the tender, ethereal "Julia."

The ceaseless, often mistaken analysis of their work by fans and critics frequently annoyed Lennon and McCartney, and they in turn added to the confusion with statements that were often less than accurate or consistent. Dismissing the know-it-alls, Paul once said, "When we got in a little room it was me and John sitting there, it was me and him who wrote it, not all these other people who think they know all about it. It was me, I must know better than them. I was the one in the room with him."

Certainly McCartney has a point. Yet human memory is notoriously imperfect, as Paul himself once demonstrated when recalling the time that John supposedly told him that he liked Paul's songs better than his own. Paul remembered the conversation taking place in a hotel room when the Beatles were filming *Help!* He said John's comment came after the two of them had listened to a Beatles album that had three songs of John's and three of Paul's on the same side. The problem is, no such album was released prior to *Help!* Which doesn't necessarily prove that John never made the remark in question, only that at least part of Paul's recollection is faulty. John, for his part, intentionally used to foster the illusion that, despite the ever-present Lennon–McCartney credit line, he and Paul always composed separately. He later owned up to his deceit, confessing with a laugh, "I said that, but I was lying. By the time I said that, we were so sick of this idea of writing and singing together, especially me, that I started this thing about, 'We never wrote together, we were never in the same room.' Which wasn't true. We wrote a *lot* of stuff together, one-on-one, eyeball to eyeball."

The Lennon–McCartney collaboration in fact took various forms over the years, ranging from the fifty-fifty authorship of such early songs as "I Want To Hold Your Hand" and "She Loves You" to such completely individual efforts in later years as "Hey, Jude" and "Revolution." There were more joint compositions in the early years, explained Lennon, "partly because the demand on us was *tremendous*. They'd want a record, a single, every three months, and we'd do it in twelve hours in a hotel or a van." In those days Lennon and McCartney were, by their own admission, quite stylized and derivative composers, especially if they were writing for another singer or band. "We just knocked them out," said McCartney of such songs-for-hire. "In our minds there was a very vague formula and we could do it quite easily." Lyrics were unimportant back then, Lennon recalled: "When Paul and I wrote lyrics in the old days, we used to laugh about it like the Tin Pan Alley people would. And it was only later that we tried to match the lyrics to the tune."

Spurred by Bob Dylan's example, Lennon in particular came to realize that the words of a song mattered. John later said, "I remember the early meetings with Dylan, he was always saying, 'Listen to the words, man,' and I said, 'I can't be bothered. I listen to the sound of it, the overall sound.' " But Lennon was too smart to ignore the poet's advice for long. John had enjoyed wordplay since childhood; now he would consciously apply his verbal talents to devising lyrics that didn't just dress up a melody but actually *said something*. Entering what he later half-jokingly called his "Dylan period," Lennon began in late 1964 to craft such introspective, autobiographical songs as "I'm A Loser," "Help!", "In My Life," and "Norwegian Wood." It was the beginning of a new and lasting direction in his art, one that eventually manifested itself in such larger statements as "A Day In The Life," "All You Need Is Love," "Revolution," and, during his solo years, "Working Class Hero" and "Imagine."

In the Beatles' middle years the most common songwriting method, according to George Martin, was for John and Paul to help "each other out with little bits and pieces. One would have most of a song finished, play it to the other, and he'd say: 'Well, why don't you do this?' That was just the way their collaboration worked." However, even in the middle years quite a few of the Beatles' songs were written collectively, with George Harrison and Ringo Starr, and occasionally others as well, contributing bits and pieces to the finished product. "Eleanor Rigby," for example, which appeared on the *Revolver* album issued in 1966, was very much a group effort, according to Pete Shotton, who was at John's house the night Paul first played the song to the other Beatles. Paul seems to have had the tune well in hand before sharing the song with the others, but the lyrics had yet to gel, so the Beatles and Shotton "sat around, making suggestions, throwing out the odd line or phrase." The line about "darning his socks in the night," for instance, was apparently proposed by Ringo, while it was Shotton who suggested that the song end with Father McKenzie conducting Rigby's funeral service.

A similar brainstorming session took place when "Magical Mystery Tour" was first taking shape in April 1967, according to Hunter Davies, who wrote about it in the Beatles' authorized biography. More interesting than the "Magical Mystery Tour" session, however, is Davies's description of watching John and Paul work together on "With A Little Help From My Friends," the song they wrote for Ringo to sing on *Sgt Pepper's Lonely Hearts Club Band.* The basic tune and structure of the song had been worked out the day before Davies's visit; now John had come over to Paul's house "to polish up the melody and think of some words to go with it." For hours, as John played the guitar and Paul the piano, "each seemed to be in a trance until the other came up with something good, then he would pluck it out of a mass of noises and try it himself." The lyrics evolved through a similar process of trial and error. After singing "Are you afraid when you turn out the light?" John got the idea of starting each verse with a question. He next sang, "Do you believe in love at first sight?", but it had the wrong number of syllables—until Paul rephrased it as "Do you believe in a love at first sight." When John sang the line back to himself, the second half of the couplet came to mind instantly: "Yes I'm certain that it happens all the time." As they continued singing, John found himself changing the words to "Would you believe . . ." Next, they agreed to reverse the order of the couplets so that this line began the verse. These three lines alone took three hours to complete, though John and Paul spent some of this time doodling on their instruments and breaking into wild and funny versions of other songs, including "Can't Buy Me Love." Mostly, however, Davies wrote, "John and Paul were singing their three lines over and over again, searching for a fourth." At last John hit upon the idea of altering the third line to ask, "What do you see when you turn out the light?" This produced the final breakthrough, John's marvelous reply, "I can't tell you but I know it's mine."

Lennon and McCartney knew they were great songwriters, but where their songs came from was something of a mystery, even to them. And they liked to keep it that way, placing their faith in inspiration rather than perspiration. McCartney explained that he stayed away from any set formula for songwriting "so that each time, I'm pulling it out of the air." The best songs, he said, "are normally written in one go," and he added that "the good thing about working with John is he didn't like to hang about too much. Didn't like to be bored, which is always a good instinct." Having to sweat over a song, according to McCartney, is "nearly always a sign that it's not that good." For his part, Lennon said, "My joy is when you're like possessed, like a medium, you know. I'll be sitting round and it'll come in the middle of the night or at the time when you don't want to do it— that's the exciting part. So I'm lying around and then this thing comes as a whole piece, you know, words and music, and I think well, you know, can I say I wrote it? I don't know who the hell wrote it—I'm just sitting here and this whole damned song comes out." Among the songs that were given to Lennon in this way were "Nowhere Man," "In My Life," and "Across the Universe." The latter, John said, "*drove* me out of bed. . . . The thing *has* to go down. It won't let you sleep, so you *have* to get up, *make* it into something, and then you're allowed to sleep." McCartney had a similar experience with "Yesterday." He wrote the song one morning immediately after waking up. Or perhaps one should say that he transcribed it, for like Lennon, McCartney seems to have been given the song in completed form by an unseen source. Paul recalled, "I had a piano by my bedside and I . . . must have dreamed it, because I tumbled out of bed and put my hands on the piano keys and I had a tune in my head. It was just all there, a complete thing. I couldn't believe it."

Lennon once said that he and McCartney were both egomaniacs, yet he could speak quite humbly about this aspect of songwriting. It wasn't any particular genius that made Paul and him great composers, he maintained; they were merely vehicles that "the music of the spheres, the music that surpasses understanding" passed through on its way into the world. One had to be open to it—"You have to be in tune," John said—but in the end, he and Paul were just "channels" for music that was not really theirs. The trick was to get into the flow, the permanent Now, the zone where, "after you come out of [it], you *know*, 'I've been there,' and it was . . . just pure, and that's what we're looking for all the time, really."

Of course, songwriting was not always a cosmic experience; Lennon and McCartney were professionals who sometimes had to grind out songs on demand. "With A Little Help From My Friends" was one such composition, and it bears out McCartney's comment that such songs are "not necessarily worse than ones done out of imagination." But it also underlines the fact that, even on the songs they had to work at, Lennon and McCartney's instinctive approach was to trust their muse to show them the way. In "Eleanor Rigby," for example, the name "Father McKenzie" was selected by paging through a telephone book. "That's the beauty of working at random," said McCartney. "It does come up perfectly, much better than if you try to think it with your intellect." During one of the recording sessions for the *Let It Be* film, Lennon makes the same point to George Harrison. George was having trouble with the lyrics of "Something," his ballad that actually ended up on the *Abbey Road* album. He was stumped on the second line: "Something in the way she moves / Attracts me like . . ." First he asked McCartney, "What could it be, Paul?" and repeated the line for him. "Hmmm?" replied Paul. With a half-embarrassed chuckle, George explained, "I can't think what it was attracted me at all." John then broke in, advising George, "Just say whatever it is that comes into your head each time—'attracts me like a . . . *cauliflower*'—until you get the word."

"The nice thing about the way we worked was there were never any rules," recalled McCartney. "Any rules we found ourselves making we would generally try and break. It always seemed an unsafe idea to try and be safe, it never worked." Indeed, George Martin believed that not having learned the "rules" of music was central to the creative accomplishments of Lennon and McCartney. In his autobiography, Martin wrote, "I have often been asked if I could have written any of the Beatles' tunes, and the answer is definitely no: for one basic reason. I didn't have their simple approach to music. . . . I think that if Paul, for instance, had learned music 'properly'—not just the piano, but correct notation for writing and reading music—it might well have inhibited him. He thought so, too. . . . Once you start being taught things, your mind is channeled in a particular way. Paul didn't have that channeling, so he had freedom, and could think of things that I would have considered outrageous. I could admire them, but my musical training would have prevented me from thinking of them myself."

Indeed, the singular genius of Lennon and McCartney's songs was that they were simple without being simplistic and sophisticated without being obscure. John and Paul's free-spirited, almost anarchistic approach to songwriting gave their music a freshness and originality that made it both instantly recognizable and widely accessible. Somehow, the two of them tuned into the collective musical unconscious and brought back songs that resonated clearly and deeply among large numbers of their contemporaries. "They were the Cole Porters and George Gershwins of their generation, of that there is no doubt," wrote George Martin. "Somebody compared them to Schubert, which sounds a bit pretentious, but I would go along with that to the extent that their music was perfectly representative of the period in which they were living."

How the music of Lennon and McCartney will be regarded in decades to come remains to be seen, but the fact that the records of the Beatles continue to sell in large numbers, twenty-five years after the group disbanded, suggests that the appeal of Lennon and McCartney may not be limited to the generation whence they came. Dick James, the music publisher who initially owned the rights to the Lennon–McCartney catalogue, predicted in 1965 that the songs would "go on earning money well into the next century." Interviewed in the 1980s, long after he had sold the catalogue, he continued to stand by the prediction, declaring, "If the songs came around today, brand new, they'd still be world-wide smashes. The quality was amazing." McCartney offered a more personal perspective, musing in a 1984 interview that "the collaboration I had with John—it's difficult to imagine anyone else coming up to that standard. Because he was no slouch, that boy. . . . He was pretty hot stuff, you know. I mean, I can't imagine anybody being there when I go [sings]: 'It's getting better all the time.' I just can't imagine anybody who could chime in [sings]: 'It couldn't get much worse.' "

CHAPTER 11

Fresh Sounds (*Help!*)

THERE WAS ALWAYS A CERTAIN IRONY IN THE BEATLES BE-ING SEEN AS SYMBOLS OF THE 1960S COUNTERCULTURE. THEIR music did spread the sixties gospel of love, fun, and spiritual explora-tion, and they certainly consumed their share of mind-expanding drugs. But the Beatles also loved to make money—"Let's write a swimming pool!" John and Paul sometimes said when sitting down to write a song—and the idea of them "dropping out," of withdrawing from mainstream society and its competitive, hierarchical ethos to live a simpler life, was a dream not easily indulged when everyone from their record company to the public to the Beatles themselves expected them to keep turning out the music that had taken the world by storm. As Lennon once complained about the sixties, "when everybody else was just goofing off and smoking dope, *we* were working twenty-four hours a day." Years later, after retreating from public life for five years in the late 1970s, John celebrated the virtues of jumping off "the merry-go-round" of fame in one of the last songs he recorded, "Watching The Wheels." Deriding accusations that he was "crazy" or "lazy," he sang that he was "just sitting here / watching the wheels go round and round," adding with his usual dry humor, "I really love to watch 'em roll." But in 1965, when he was a twenty-four-year-old pop idol feeling trapped by the pressures and unreality of his apparently glamorous new life, he saw no such means of escape. All he could do was cry out for help.

Lennon wrote "Help!", the title track to the Beatles' fifth album and second feature film, in the spring of 1965. It was the first Beatles song in which the words were the point at least as much as the music. Few seem to have recognized the lyrics' full import at the time, however, not even the man who wrote them. The public heard only another beautiful pop song by the Beatles, and "Help!" quickly found itself on the usual fast track to the top of the charts. Lennon himself was unaware until much later that "Help!" was in fact a subconscious expression of the deep discontent he felt during his so-called fat Elvis period. In 1965, he was overweight, drinking too much, bored with his wife and their new house in the sterile suburb of Weybridge (a place he described as "like a bus stop, you wait until something comes along"), and fed up with the nonstop absurdities of Beatlemania. Nevertheless, the idea for "Help!" seems not to have originated with Lennon; rather, as with "A Hard Day's Night" a year earlier, he was probably told by director Richard Lester that *Help!* would be the title of the Beatles film then nearing completion, and he then rushed off to write a song with that title before McCartney could. But Lester's announcement acted on Lennon like a truth serum, triggering an outpouring of his underlying fears and unhappiness.

The result was a song whose lyrics were by far the best Lennon had written to date. Their strength is rooted in the unmistakable power of autobiographical confession, yet Lennon expresses his personal truths so simply and convincingly that he makes them universal. "Help!" may have sprung from Lennon's own alienation, but one did not have to be a rock 'n' roll star to share his yearning for a helping hand in times of trouble and a return to happier days. John contrasts a carefree past with a confusing present, when his "life has changed in oh so many ways." He responds by acknowledging the need for human connection. "Help me get my feet back on the ground," he pleads, his need so acute that he goes on to beg, in desperate falsetto, "Won't you please, please help me?"

Although the movie *Help!* was an artistic disappointment that the Beatles looked back on with disdain, the song "Help!" occupies a special place in the Lennon–McCartney catalogue, for it is one of a handful of songs that both men singled out for praise and affection after leaving the Beatles. Lennon said he liked "Help!" "because I meant it; it's real. The lyric is as good now as it was then." After Lennon's death, McCartney recalled "sitting there doing 'Help!' " as one of the "magic moments" in their songwriting collaboration, adding, "Those moments. That's what I cherish. No one can take it away from me." In keeping with their teenage routine of composing at each other's houses, Paul had driven out to John's place in Weybridge to work on "Help!" John seems to have had the song all but completed before Paul arrived, for John later said he wrote it "bam! bam!, like that, and got the single." Nevertheless, Paul's contribution was crucial, for it was he who conceived of adding the second vocal that makes the song both emotionally fuller and instantly ear-catching. This vocal, a cross between a countermelody and a call-and-response, is sung, unexpectedly, in *anticipation* of the verse, thus underlining the importance of the words even as it softens their sorrow with wistful nostalgia.

Had Lennon had his way, the words of "Help!" might have received even greater emphasis, for he originally wrote the song in a slower tempo, as befit its mood of doubting introspection. But "Help!" had to open the Beatles' new movie, so when it came time to record it, the tempo was speeded up to make the song more commercial, a decision Lennon later criticized. However, no such misgivings are evident on outtakes from the recording session for "Help!", which was held on the evening of April 13, 1965. Lennon was never the smoothest guitarist, and his playing here is more blustery than beautiful; it's no surprise that George Martin chose to mix it into virtual obscurity in the released version of the song. Yet in the early takes of "Help!", when the Beatles are concentrating on the rhythm track, it is above all John's rhythm guitar that drives the beat forward. Indeed, Lennon's is by far the most prominent instrument at this point, for Starr's drums and Harrison's lead guitar are audible only at pivotal moments and McCartney's bass, though forceful and constant, simply generates less noise than Lennon's thwacking strum.

The first take of "Help!" gets no farther than the opening refrain before John interrupts to yell, "Stop, stop, string broke." Take two, however, reveals that Harrison has already worked out his lead guitar part, the shimmering pattern of descending notes that rushes in like surf on a beach to fill the gap between the refrain and the verses. Starr's drum part, on the other hand, has yet to be fully developed; he gives a mere four loud crashes during the opening refrain and then contents himself with a barely noticeable backbeat during the verses. Indeed, at this stage, "Help!" recalls the claim from the Silver Beatles' drummer-less days that "the rhythm's in the guitars."

But not yet it's not, for during take five, the Lennon locomotive falters when, entering the second verse, he rushes the chord change. John then seems to lose his bearings and the beat nearly fizzles out entirely until, anchored by Paul's unswerving bass, John finds his way back. His recovery somehow brings the entire foursome powerfully to life; in the final half of take five, they surge together to hit the groove heard on the finished record. George Harrison's role is vital here. His guitar stabs, strong and precise, give the beat some needed punch during the refrain, yet what is even more noticeable about his playing during take five is what is *not* there. Harrison has temporarily abandoned his swirling guitar lead during this take, and the effect on the listener is like opening up a closet, knowing that something is missing but not realizing until later that it was a favorite pair of pants. When George overdubs a fresh version of his lead later, the missing item is returned and one is reminded of how important it was that the Beatles had a real guitarist in the band; Lennon simply could not have produced such a clean, rippling sound.

Having overcome the major hurdles, the Beatles now find it the proverbial work of a moment to finish "Help!" Between takes six and eight, a much fuller drum sound is added, thus bringing the rhythm track to completion. Take nine augments this with the addition of a tambourine in the refrain, but the main attraction is the introduction of the vocals, which John, Paul, and George sing almost flawlessly. By take twelve, these, too, have been perfected, and when George re-records his guitar lead, one of the Beatles' early masterpieces is ready to be mixed and released.

Lennon said that "Help!" reflected his "fat Elvis" period, but in fact it was also a product of his "Dylan" period, for the two overlapped. Although Lennon himself never remarked on this simultaneity, his own recollections make it clear: Physically and emotionally, he was floundering in late 1964 and 1965, just as the bloated king of rock 'n' roll would a decade later, yet artistically he was increasingly stimulated by the young American troubadour's practice of inserting real poetry into the framework of popular song. McCartney and especially Harrison also became admirers of Dylan at this time, but it was Lennon whose work was most obviously affected, as the *Help!* album illustrates. Nascent signs of Dylan's influence had been evident on the previous *Beatles For Sale*, but on *Help!* those first tentative efforts have developed into fully realized musical achievements. In addition to the unprecedented lyrical richness of the title track, there is McCartney's warm, cheerful folk-rock treasure "I've Just Seen A Face," as well as two more Lennon compositions, the mainly acoustic "It's Only Love" and the completely acoustic "You've Got To Hide Your Love Away."

Lennon said he always hated "It's Only Love" because of its "abysmal" lyrics, a harsh judgment that does an injustice to the song's lovely lilting melody. Nevertheless, "You've Got To Hide Your Love Away" is plainly the superior song, even if it finds Lennon once again in a downcast mood. Its straightforward major chord patterns and sawing strum could hardly be more Dylanesque, and if the lyrics fall short of Dylan's poetic depth and linguistic richness, they are still vivid and affecting, and project a sensibility far more human and approachable than Dylan's snarling put-downs. One felt respect bordering on awe for Dylan, for he seemed to speak for all humanity; one felt respect warmed by affection for Lennon, because he seemed to speak for you personally.

In "You've Got To Hide Your Love Away," a Lennon racked by self-doubt reflects on a troubled romance, but the lyrics hint that the love affair is merely a cover story for a deeper, more pervasive anomie. How else to explain his unsparing paranoia—"Everywhere / People stare / Each and every day / I can hear them laugh at me"—in regard to what, after all, is a private matter? His self-esteem is so low that he is left "feeling two foot small," a line originally written as "two foot tall" until the serendipity of accident, or perhaps the intervention of Lennon's unconscious mind, improved it. (When he first sang the song to McCartney, the line came out "two foot small," a phrasing John immediately preferred.)

"You've Got To Hide Your Love Away" was later called the first gay love song, and it did express the sort of fear, shame, and hopelessness that many homosexuals have felt in the face of the larger world's disapproval. However, this interpretation is worth noting not because it sheds light on Lennon's sexual orientation—it doesn't—but because of what it says about his ability to reach inside himself and articulate larger human truths, truths that reach across barriers of age, race, class, and other categories and speak to people who otherwise feel isolated from one another. Like those of "Help!", the lyrics of "You've Got To Hide Your Love Away" are compelling because of the honesty and directness of their self-revelation; at the same time, they are inclusive and open-ended enough to accommodate alternative interpretations that others may assign them. As McCartney said in another context, "You put your own meaning at your own level to our songs, and that's what's great about them."

The flutes whose mellow tones bring "You've Got To Hide Your Love Away" to such a sublime conclusion make the song significant in one last respect, for they mark the first time that an outside musician was brought in to play on a Beatles recording (with the exception, of course, of George Martin's occasional piano playing and his insistence, back in 1962, on drafting a session drummer for the group's first single). In fact, the entire *Help!* album represents a major acceleration in the Beatles' ongoing search for fresh sounds. Previous landmarks on this path include "A Hard Day's Night," "Eight Days A Week," and "I Feel Fine," songs that owed their distinctive sounds mainly to innovative recording techniques. Now, on *Help!*, the Beatles begin exploring what could be achieved by experimenting with new instruments.

The string quartet employed on "Yesterday" is the best-known example, but in fact fully half of the fourteen songs on this album feature one or more instruments not previously employed by the Beatles. For example, Lennon plays electric piano on both McCartney's "The Night Before" and Harrison's "You Like Me Too Much"; McCartney and Martin, sitting astride the same acoustic piano, join John on the latter, giving the song its strongest single feature. Harrison plays a tone pedal guitar for the first time on "I Need You," his other composition on *Help!*, a catchy pop tune that demonstrated that he had now matured into the kind of pleasantly stylized, if innocuous, songwriter that Lennon and McCartney had been in their early days. Last but not least, it was on the movie set of *Help!* that Harrison first picked up a sitar, the Indian stringed instrument that would figure so prominently in the music on the *Rubber Soul, Revolver,* and *Sgt Pepper* albums.

Not everything the Beatles touched at this time turned to gold. Indeed, two of the songs recorded during the *Help!* sessions were judged too poor to release at all; today they remain locked away in the Abbey Road archives. Both are Lennon–McCartney compositions. The first, "If You've Got Trouble," was written as Ringo's vocal turn on the album and recorded on February 18, 1965. The Beatles did only one take of the song, perhaps realizing that no amount of extra work could salvage the poor thing. Outtakes from the session reveal "If You've Got Trouble" as a fast-paced rocker, in the tradition of "I'll Cry Instead" from *A Hard Day's Night* or "What You're Doing" from *Beatles For Sale*, but lacking even the modicum of melody found on those songs. The tune, such as it is, is monotonous, clunky, and repetitive, and gains nothing from lines like "If you've got trouble, then you've got less trouble than me." Ringo seems to sense he is piloting a sinking ship, for as the band heads into the instrumental break, he shouts in resigned, almost disgusted desperation, "Ah, rock on, anybody." McCartney, admitting that he and Lennon did not take Starr's songs as seriously as their own, later confessed that "If You've Got Trouble" was a song "we just couldn't get behind." Eventually, Ringo chose to record the country-and-western song "Act Naturally" for his contribution to *Help!*

The other song rejected by the Beatles is by no means such a clear-cut case. "That Means A Lot" is no jewel—indeed, there are no undiscovered Beatles masterpieces still secreted away in the Abbey Road archives—but it is quite an agreeable song, fully the equal of others the band had previously released. With a lead vocal from McCartney that recalls his cover of "Till There Was You" on *With The Beatles*, "That Means A Lot" is a mid-tempo love song in which Paul gives encouraging advice to a lovesick friend, à la "She Loves You." The song's high point is a raucous vocal fade-out, but the Beatles themselves were not pleased with their efforts, and after twenty-four takes they abandoned the song on March 30. It was soon recorded by another singer, P. J. Proby, but did not become a hit.

The Beatles scored a big success, however, with "Ticket To Ride," the thumping rocker that concludes the film soundtrack and side one of the *Help!* album. "Ticket To Ride" was first released as a single, backed by the three-part harmony ballad "Yes It Is," and it duly became the group's eighth straight number one. "Ticket To Ride" is the most radical piece of rock 'n' roll on *Help!*, but not because of the introduction of new instruments; the song's unconventional sound comes instead from the Beatles playing their usual instruments in unusual ways. When Lennon called this song "one of the earliest heavy-metal records made," he was exaggerating, but only slightly; "Ticket To Ride" does kick up a storm of rude, thrusting energy.

Two things instantly stamp the song as original: the glistening opening guitar riff that establishes the beat, and the jagged, whack-and-jump drum pattern that rams that beat forward. "Ticket To Ride" is a Lennon composition, but what it illustrates above all is the fertility of the Lennon–McCartney collaboration. For it is McCartney who contributed both of these rhythmic ideas. Without them, John's song would be a shadow of itself, just as "Help!" would be a lesser work without McCartney's invention of the second vocal. In a break from routine, Paul plays the lead guitar part on "Ticket To Ride" himself. It is not that the riff in question was beyond Harrison's ability, for it is actually an extremely simple phrase, like much of McCartney's best work. The trick, rather, was to hear that phrase in the first place, a point that applies to the drum pattern as well. Obviously, Ringo could have created his own pattern, but it almost certainly would have been less powerful and memorable than the one suggested by McCartney, the natural musical arranger in the group.

John Lennon's lyrical maturation is rightly stressed in most accounts of this period in the Beatles' history, but McCartney was making important strides artistically as well, as "Ticket To Ride" illustrates. He still had a penchant for writing standard-issue throwaways like "The Night Before" and "Another Girl," but within a few months the impulses that gave rise to these sorts of facile pleasures would instead yield such *Rubber Soul* standouts as "Drive My Car" and "I'm Looking Through You." Meanwhile, there was the magnificent achievement of "Yesterday," the all-time classic that more than any other song extended the Beatles' appeal beyond their initial core audience of young people and forced remaining mainstream skeptics to acknowledge that this band was no mere fad but a musical force to be reckoned with.

The high regard in which other musicians hold "Yesterday" is indicated by the large number and variety of them who have chosen to perform and record it; the song is one of the most frequently covered in history. The Beatles themselves, however, seem to have been unsure about it at first, perhaps because it departed so sharply from their traditional sound. Remarkably, "Yesterday" was not released as a single in the United Kingdom, nor even selected for the film soundtrack of *Help!* Instead, it was relegated to the second side of the *Help!* album, where it was placed, incongruously, just ahead of the final track, the Beatles' whoop-it-up cover of "Dizzy Miss Lizzy." Indeed, the big mystery about "Yesterday" is why the Beatles waited so long to record the song in the first place.

"Yesterday" was the song that came to McCartney in a dream, in January 1964 when the Beatles were staying at the posh George V hotel in Paris. Soon thereafter he played the tune for George Martin, confiding that he was thinking of giving it a one-word title—perhaps "Yesterday," if that wasn't too corny. Martin told him it wasn't. The other Beatles, too, heard the song around this time, and they liked it, according to McCartney. Nevertheless, another eighteen months passed before the song was recorded, on June 14, 1965. True, it did take Paul some time to write proper lyrics. His working title was "Scrambled Eggs," in keeping with his opening line of "Scrambled eggs / I love your legs." But this can only explain why the song was not included on the *A Hard Day's Night* album recorded in the spring of 1964, for surely McCartney did not need a year and a half to complete the lyrics. Moreover, the Beatles dearly could have used a gem like "Yesterday" when assembling the less than impressive *Beatles For Sale* album that autumn. So why was the song held back? The closest any of the principals has come to answering the question is McCartney's two-pronged remark to Lewisohn in 1987 that "Yesterday," like the subsequent "Michelle," was never released as a single "because we didn't think it fitted our image. . . . They might have been perceived as Paul McCartney singles and maybe John wasn't too keen on that."

" 'Yesterday,' " McCartney observed separately, "is the most complete thing I've ever written." Paralleling Lennon's "Help!", it contains the finest lyrics Paul had yet written; it was almost as if he realized the song was too beautiful to send into the world tarnished by the clichés that dominated most of his lyrics at this point. There are other similarities to "Help!" as well (though not because of any conscious or unconscious duplication, since "Yesterday" was written many months earlier). McCartney, too, refers back to an innocent, happier past, when all his "troubles seemed so far away." And while not autobiographical like "Help!", "Yesterday" does touch the common person in much the same way through its unaffected recounting of a love affair that for some reason did not work out, leaving the singer thinking sadly back to yesterday, when "love was such an easy game to play."

The melody of "Yesterday" is gorgeous enough to be sung a cappella and still enchant—indeed, after leaving the Beatles, McCartney performed it live accompanied only by his acoustic guitar—but the addition of a string quartet during the second verse gives the song an almost heavenly quality. Had this step been mishandled, "Yesterday" could have been badly marred. But the playing of the quartet is a model of tasteful discretion; it highlights the natural beauties of the song without succumbing to ostentation or mawkishness. It was George Martin who originated the idea of a string quartet and who did most of the scoring for it, but it was another sign of McCartney's rapidly evolving musical mastery that he worked closely with Martin throughout this process. The result was, quite simply, one of the quiet masterpieces of twentieth-century popular music.

June 14, 1965, was a red-letter day for McCartney, not only because he finally recorded "Yesterday" but because of two other songs he taped that day. The first was "I've Just Seen A Face," the delightful folk-rock ballad that precedes "Yesterday" on *Help!* With its thigh-slapping beat, sing-along melody, and cheerful, isn't-love-great lyrics, "I've Just Seen A Face" is fetching, vintage McCartney. The spiraling acoustic guitar introduction and energetic middle eight give the song a sophistication uncommon to the genre, yet "I've Just Seen A Face" remains the musical equivalent of an armful of freshly picked daisies. As such, it could not be more different from Paul's third song of the day, "I'm Down." Issued as the B-side to the single of "Help!", "I'm Down" is a rock 'n' roll raver, pure and simple. Paul's screaming vocal recalls "Long Tall Sally" and foreshadows "Helter Skelter," and the three other Beatles turn in a splendid, blistering performance as well, with John's organ all but literally catching fire.

That McCartney could not only write but in the space of less than eight hours brilliantly perform three such varied songs demonstrates an extraordinary musical versatility, and the point goes double for the Beatles as a whole. The range of musical styles displayed on *Help!* and its accompanying singles extended from upbeat pop through confessional folk-rock to country and western to archetypal ballad to down-and-dirty rock 'n' roll. The three finest songs on the album—"Yesterday," "Ticket To Ride," and "Help!"—are themselves as different as east, west, and south. To attempt such a diverse selection of songs in the first place is an indication of impressive ambition, but what set the Beatles apart was their ability to execute each of these styles with power, grace, and style. Their songs were the equal of any produced in these various fields, yet they always retained the Beatles' own particular sound. *Help!* thus represented a key stage in the Beatles' development, a sort of staging ground where they consolidated the growth and influences of their early years in anticipation of a future uniquely their own. Beginning with their next album, *Rubber Soul*, they would leap from one artistic summit to the next, accumulating in their four remaining years together a body of work whose quality, diversity, and originality were nothing short of breathtaking.

CHAPTER 12

Four-way Synergy: That Inexplicable Charisma

THE MAGIC OF THE BEATLES, AS THEY THEMSELVES WELL KNEW, WAS SOMETHING BIGGER THAN THE FOUR OF THEM. Talented as they each were, there was an alchemy in the way they came together that made two plus two equal not four but forty. "It is absolutely true that the sum of the four of them was much, much greater than the sum of the individual parts," George Martin said. Indeed, the Beatles themselves sometimes said they felt like four aspects of the same person. "We're individuals, but we make up together The Mates, which is one person," McCartney explained. "We all add something different to the whole." To an amazing degree, their collaboration canceled out the weaknesses while magnifying the strengths of each member; collectively, they projected an irresistible personal charisma. "If you put together all the personalities of the Beatles, it worked perfectly," said George Harrison. "It was magic." And the charisma carried over to the art; the Beatles' personal chemistry was indivisible from their musical creativity. "Beatlemusic is when we all get together," said John. "The Beatles just go into a studio. And IT happens!"

Unfortunately, most of what the Beatles did and said inside recording studios has been lost to history. There are, it is true, more than four hundred hours of Beatles recordings in the archives at Abbey Road

Studios in London. Yet even the four hundred hours of working tapes exclude most of what took place when the Beatles were in the studio and IT was happening. The reason is that only actual takes of songs— conscious attempts to record them—were committed to tape. The talking and joking around between takes, the exchange of ideas and critiques, the rehearsals to try out these ideas or simply to let the Beatles practice a song until all four performed their parts properly— all this generally occurred without being permanently recorded. Thus a six-hour recording session might eventually yield a mere ten or fifteen minutes of taped music. "I was saving money," explained George Martin. "If you're a trained producer, you've got your eye on the budget all the time, and why have a tape running? No one told me in those days it would be of great historical value."

There was one occasion, however, when Martin did keep the tape running between takes, and the result is both illuminating and amusing. The Beatles were working on George Harrison's song "Think For Yourself" for the *Rubber Soul* album. The night in question was November 8, 1965, a late autumn date that helps explain why Martin departed from normal procedure that night. The Beatles had not yet recorded their 1965 Christmas gift for fan club members, an annual flexi-disc that contained spoken messages and, in later years, skits and music; apparently Martin thought he might graft some of the Beatles' studio banter onto this giveaway disc. It didn't work out that way—the Beatles recorded a separate Christmas message later that night—but the moments captured by Martin still make for fascinating listening.

Like the 1970 film *Let It Be*, the studio chat from "Think For Yourself" offers an inside look at the Beatles at work, but with a crucial difference: In 1965, the Beatles clearly took joy in one another's company. The lyrics of "Think For Yourself" are intelligently serious, proclaiming the quintessential Beatles message that one should wake up and live life with eyes open, but the Beatles are anything but solemn while recording the song. Half the time, they can barely stop laughing long enough to try another take, and it's often hard to tell whether they are trying to work or just having a good time. The "Think For Yourself" tapes are not merely entertaining, however. Especially when heard in conjunction with the Beatles' annual Christmas records, they shed revealing light on the personal dynamics of the band: John as the gang leader everyone looks up to; Paul as the perfectionist workaholic always urging the others back to the job; George as the younger brother, eager to be included but too proud to say so; and Ringo as the best friend whose easygoing nature is a vital steadying influence within a swirl of mammoth egos.

The Beatles have apparently just taken a tea break when the "Think For Yourself" tape starts, for one hears McCartney say in a thick-tongued, quasi-American accent, "I *will* have a cup." The band has been working on the song's vocals, and John simply cannot get them right. "I already did it once wrong on the first take, you know," he explains with a grin in his voice. "Now I've got it in me bleedin' mind for remembering it." Strumming his acoustic guitar, John then launches vigorously back into the line from the last verse, "About the good things that we can have if we close our eyes." Toward the end, he is interrupted by George Harrison, who instructs him, "No, play *major*." He and John try the line again, but this time when they get to "close our eyes," John goes mute and George sings the notes alone. John then tries to follow George's example but fails, so George repeats the notes and they start over. Once again, John goes slightly off on the word "eyes," so George sings it yet again, this time adding the exhortation, "That chord. Play that . . ." But his correction is cut short when either John or Paul (it's impossible to tell which) lets loose a cry of strangled but good-humored frustration—"Ee-yaah-aagh"—and everyone laughs.

"You'll just have to bear with me or have me shot," chortles John after a few more mistakes. Calling up to the control room, he tells George Martin, "All right, we'll just have to have a go of it, you see." Martin, wonderfully deadpan, replies, "Yes, I know *exactly* what you mean." John explains, "It could be there, or it couldn't." "Could be where?" asks Martin. "There," John answers in a brisk, disembodied tone. Then, switching to a slow and kindly grandfather's voice, he adds, "All right, Paul, come along now." Two takes later, after John, Paul, and George almost get it right, John jokes, "If that works, I'm in for it!" The next take is a bust, however, and John and George go practice some more. Finally John announces, "All right, I think I *might* have it now." Martin teases him, "Oh, you're a right piggler, aren't you, John?" One can almost see the smile on John's face as he agrees, "I know. I get something in me head, you know, and all the walls of Rome couldn't stop me," a line that provokes yet more giggles from the other Beatles.

The Beatles did a lot of giggling that night, and marijuana was probably at least part of the reason. The Beatles were very frequent smokers at this point, both inside the studio and out. This was no secret to Martin, but out of respect for his known disapproval—and perhaps a certain boyish preference for feeling sneaky—the Beatles took pains not to light up in his immediate presence, stealing away instead to the canteen or toilet. In fact, besides all the giggling, the clearest hints that the Beatles were getting high this night come in remarks delivered by John and Paul after they had briefly excused themselves from the session. Returning with a conspicuous case of the sniffles, Paul quips to the other Beatles, "I just got in from Olympia. I lit the torch." At another point, as John, George, and Paul gather around the micro-phone, there is a muffled whisper from one of them that seems to say, as if in reference to a shared joint, "There's still some left." And John, after disappearing for some minutes, returns confident that he will at last get the harmony right, winking, "I've just been singing it in the toilet, so I think I *might* get it now."

The atmosphere of the session is pure adolescent boys' club, com-plete with farting noises and jokes about bodily functions. When John says he stinks and primly confesses, "I've been waiting for someone to say something about it," Paul invents a ditty on the spot about the "B.O.-derant, that great big B.O.-derant" John is using. As if on cue, John sniffs that Cynthia, his wife, "licked it clean before we left." Later in the session, heading to the toilet, John is heard singing, to the tune of "Do You Want To Know A Secret," the words "Do you want to hold a penis?" But for now, John contents himself with a different musical joke. The phrase "close our eyes" in "Think For Yourself" has three syllables that are sung on two notes, the first syllable on one note and the second and third syllables on the next note down the scale. John is singing this phrase to himself without words—DAH-

dah-dah—when he realizes that much the same pattern occurs at the start of "Yesterday." So without missing a beat, he goes straight from the DAH-dah-dah of "Think For Yourself" into a boisterous, intentionally off-key version of "Yesterday": DAH-dah-dah (pause), dah-dah-dah-dah-dah-dah-DAH-dah-dah. He only breaks off when Paul, imitating a nervous nightwatchman, urgently whispers, "Shhhh, keep quiet."

Next Paul and John get in a mock argument about whether it's Paul's fault that John keeps going wrong on "Think For Yourself." Paul finally shouts John down with the challenge, again in an American accent, "Do you wanna fight?" Suddenly meek, John murmurs, "No," and Paul says, "Okay. Let's settle it, other ways." John first suggests snooker, then tennis, but Paul changes course and asks with a snicker whether John saw Rocky Marciano, the former American boxing champion, on television the night before. Apparently the retired champ was less than razor-sharp mentally, for John starts laughing and says, "The whole conversation's about everything else, and he goes, 'I remember the great Joe Louis' " (Marciano's most celebrated foe).

John assumes a plodding cadence while reciting Marciano's punch-drunk recollection, but a moment later he is shouting like a revivalist preacher, "Somebody up there likes me!" George Harrison asks, "Hoo-izit?" and John bellows, "It's Jesus, our Lord and Savior, who gave his only begotten bread, for us to live and die on. And that's why we're all here, and I'll tell you, brethren: There's more o' them than there are of us. And that's a-why there's so few of us left." Another voice asks, "Why such fury?" but John loudly barrels on, "Condemn thou the thoughts of man." George tries to spark off with the question, "What is this wrath?" but falters when his follow-up line, "The B.O.-derant," fizzles into a weak giggle. Paul, laughing, tries to restore order, urging in a normal voice, "Okay, let's go," but John isn't ready to stop. Yelling full-out now, he declares, "And *he* called, and *they* bloody well *come!*" George tries again with, "Yes, but if you look in your Bible," but he has no punch line, so Paul is able to jump back into the fray, and get everybody back to work as well, by despairing in an impatient, upper-class accent, "I can't go on, I really can't. Come on, let's *do* this bleeding record."

Although "Think For Yourself" was written by George, it is obviously John who is the center of attention, humor, and energy throughout the session. Conversely, Ringo is not heard at all on the "Think For Yourself" tapes, for the simple reason that he did not contribute to the song's vocals. His role within the Beatles is more evident on the Christmas records, where he tends to play the kind, unassuming fourth fiddle who often serves as the butt of the others' jokes but manages to contribute his share of fun all the same. On the 1963 disc, for example, Ringo is in the middle of mentioning that he played in other bands before joining the Beatles when Paul interrupts and, like a parent urging a child to hurry up on a long-distance phone call, tells Ringo, "Just wish the people a happy Christmas." Taking no offense, Ringo offers heartfelt holiday wishes. Paul then tells him to sing "Good King Wenceslas." Again Ringo obeys. The mike then passes to George, who adds a dig of his own, intoning like an audition master, "Thank you, Ringo. We'll phone *you*." On the 1964 disc, when Ringo observes, "It's been a funny year," one of the other Beatles suppresses a snort of laughter at this seemingly banal remark. But Ringo cheerfully carries on and soon gets a laugh by intentionally losing track of which countries the Beatles visited in 1964 and listing some of them, like Australia, twice.

Ringo Starr had to be one of the luckiest people in the history of show business. He himself marveled at how fate had given him a first-class seat in the Beatle fame train just as it was leaving the station. Nevertheless, Lennon maintained that Ringo "would have surfaced as an individual" even without the Beatles; he had a certain intangible flair. Moreover, said John, "Ringo [was] every bit as warm, unassuming, funny and kind as he seems. . . . He was quite simply the heart of the Beatles." If the other Beatles, especially John and Paul, seemed too talented to be true, Ringo was the average guy with a good nature whom everyone in the audience could identify with. During the seven years (1963 to 1969) that the Beatles issued Christmas discs, Ringo was the only one whose holiday greetings were consistently warm, rather than merely funny or clever. He was a born straight man: if the Beatles were, as some said, the English rock 'n' roll equivalent of the Marx Brothers, Ringo was a more lovable version of Zeppo. Yet he was by no means a doormat for the other Beatles. "John, that's crap," he might suddenly tell Lennon in the studio, according to George Martin, who added that John would then "look up over his glasses and murmur, 'Oh really?' and change it. Either that or he'd make a rude remark back, and then change whatever it was that Ringo had picked up on."

Nowadays, when the Beatles exist as a public presence only through their musical recordings, it is easy to forget how funny they were in their heyday. John and Paul in particular were gifted mimics, and all four of them boasted quick, original wits; indeed, this was a large part of their charisma. Yet while Paul could keep up with John's acerbic lunacy at times—"if I was in a bad enough mood!" Paul later joked—day in and day out, it was John who most excelled at wordplay, verbal put-ons, and sly, offbeat humor. Sometimes his comedy was unintentional, such as the night he was dining with George Martin in a fancy restaurant and Martin tried to get him to try mange-tout peas for the first time. "All right, then," John replied without enthusiasm, "but put them over there, not near the food." More often, however, John took active delight in his gift for droll wickedness. Journalist Ray Coleman recalled boarding a Lufthansa flight once with Lennon and hearing him wise-crack, twenty years after World War II, "It's good to fly Lufthansa to London, all the pilots know the way."

John was always "idolized" by the other Beatles, according to Paul, who recalled, "He was like our own little Elvis in the group. Not because of his looks or his singing—although he was a great singer— just his personality. He was just a great guy. Very forceful guy. Very funny guy. Very bright and always someone for us to look up to." Even when John's repeated errors during the "Think For Yourself" re-hearsals oblige the rest of the band to do their parts over and over again, they react with good humor, albeit tinged with exasperation. At one point, for example, Paul pokes fun at John by singing, "Why do you fuck up everything that you do?" John laughs and in a commanding, computer-like voice declares, "I will be *pleased* to see the earth men disintegrated."

When yet another take breaks down, George asks in a singsong tone, "What is wro-ong?" This time John slips into the rapid, fluttering speech of a well-bred but embarrassed English matron: "Oh, I'm so sorry, I feel so stupid, I don't know what to do." Paul lashes into him like a schoolmaster whose patience has finally run out: "Look, Terence! If you want to resign from the amateur dramatics, *do!*" Stifling a laugh, John whimpers, "It's not that, I put a lot of money and thought into the whole thing." "Yeah," Paul blusters, "but let's face it, you're *crap*! Aren't you?" Fighting off another giggle, John shouts back, "Whose father was it got the hall in the first place, eh?" Paul gets the last word, charging, "Yes, you were only doing walk-ons with your farting nose up," but within seconds it's clear that John is still top dog. As soon as Paul, still in character, says, "Let's take it from the top and run it," John impatiently shoots down the idea, countering in his normal voice, "*Don't* take it from the top." Paul quickly corrects himself, and the Beatles return to the same verse they were struggling with before.

All these studio fights were shams, of course. Yet even when genuine quarrels broke out among the Beatles, they seemed only to underscore the deep connection among them. Ringo once said of the others, "They are my brothers, you see. I'm an only child, and they're my brothers." It was a telling remark. When the Beatles did clash, it was with the familiarity and bluntness of brothers whose unshakable underlying bond let them voice complaints freely, secure in the knowledge that they would remain brothers no matter what. "[John and I] were once having a right slagging session," Paul once said, "and I remember how he took off his granny glasses. I can still see him. He put them down and said, 'It's only me, Paul.' Then he put them back on again, and we continued slagging." External threats immediately provoked a united front. As Astrid Kirchherr, their close friend from Hamburg days, recalled, "Even when things were pretty rough they all stuck together. They often argued amongst themselves, but just let an outsider have a go at one of them and the sparks would fly. At first they were close out of necessity; later it was out of love."

Their love and loyalty intensified during the madness of Beatlemania, for only the four Beatles themselves knew what life was like in the eye of the hurricane. As Paul later recalled, "When we actually got in that limo, big blacked-out windows, there were really only ever four of us in the back of that car. And what went on then, that was the real thing. That was where we drew our strength from. We were able to withdraw into this private world of our own." After the Beatles quit touring, the bonds forged amidst the hysteria endured. As Pete Shotton later maintained, "There never was, and probably never will be, a group more self-contained or tightly knit than the Beatles were" in the mid-1960s.

The special aura the Beatles projected was visible even during the period of growing discord in 1968 and 1969. On April 26, 1969, for example, a young engineer at Abbey Road Studios named Jeff Jarratt was getting ready to work his first session with the Beatles, who were then recording tracks for *Abbey Road*. George Martin was unable to attend, but Martin tried to prepare the nervous Jarratt for what he was about to experience. Jarratt recalled Martin saying, "There will be one Beatle there, fine. Two Beatles, great. Three Beatles, fantastic. But the minute the four of them are there, that is when the inexplicable charismatic thing happens, the special magic no one has been able to explain. It will be very friendly between you and them, but you'll be aware of this inexplicable *presence*."

"It was a brotherhood," Martin later explained. "It was like a fort, really, with four corners, that was impregnable. Nobody got inside that fort once they were together, not even Brian Epstein, nor I. We were not part of that. They'd been together through thick and thin, the craze of their meteoric rise—that only happened to them. . . . I traveled with them sometimes on their tours, and they were complete prisoners of their fame. They only had each other to turn to for support and comfort in those times, and consequently they had an empathy and a kind of mind-reading business, an almost kinetic energy, such that when they were together they seemed to become another dimension."

Whatever dimension that was, the Beatles were clearly aware of the special energy they tapped into together. In fact, they so took for granted the powers at their disposal that they could laugh at failure, confident it was a temporary condition. At one point during the "Think For Yourself" session, for example, John, Paul, and George are making yet another effort to coordinate their harmonies. John requests that this time they sing only the "And you've got time to rectify" line, for despite the dozens of previous rehearsals, he has "forgotten what it was." Following his count-in, the three singers try the line a cappella, but they're not in sync at all and Paul finally demands of John, "What *key* are you in, Jack?" George then sings the line again properly to guide them and the three try it again. This take flops so badly that Paul spoofs it, and them, by crooning, "Maaaa-gic." This sends John into another fit of giggles, but George immediately begins another take and, amazingly, this time all three hit it perfectly. "That was *it*," Paul says in awed surprise. John, a swagger in his voice, says, "You should'a got me then, boy, I was movin'."

"When the four of us got together, we were definitely better than the four of us individually," McCartney later said. "One of the things we had going for us was that we'd been together a long time. It made us very tight, like family almost, so we were able to read one another. That made us *good*. It was only really toward the very end, when business started to interfere . . ." Indeed, the *Let It Be* film, which showed the Beatles recording together in January 1969, demonstrates just how central emotional harmony was to the group's music. The Beatles were not getting along well at this point, and it was reflected in the sloppy, lethargic way they played—at least inside the studio. Yet when they assembled on the roof of the Apple building to "do it to a live audience" one last time, as Paul put it, their spirited performance confirmed that the old magic was still there, lying dormant, waiting only to be unleashed again.

And the connection apparently remained intact even after the group disbanded. Ringo, who recorded with each of his former bandmates after the breakup, said, "We could play real well together, even in 1981." Once, in the mid-1970s, Ringo, John, and George happened to jam together. Afterward, Paul said, "I think it was John who said to me, 'Man, it was great, we're a great band.' Because that was the great thing about the Beatles, we really were a great band. I mean, *really*. I know now from playing with other people that it's not always you can sit down and actually get in a groove. With the Beatles, it nearly always was. We could sit down and do any old piece of crap, and we'd generally hit a groove. And that is something you cannot buy."

Or manufacture. The Beatles were living proof that it is not necessarily the greatest musicians who make the greatest music. "The worst band I ever played with in my life had Eric Clapton, Elton John, Keith Richards, Ronnie Wood, and I all playing in my studio in Tittenhurst in 1985," Ringo once said. In terms of sheer musical ability, the team of Clapton, Richards, and Elton John was superior to that of Paul, George, and John Lennon. But the superstar band sounded awful, explained Ringo, because it had "too many leaders. It just didn't work." Of course, the Beatles eventually had their own problems with egos, but for the bulk of their career, their talents and personalities combined in fruitful equilibrium. Though there was a clear pecking order in the band, with Harrison and Starr ranking below Lennon and McCartney, the major business and artistic decisions were made collectively, in the spirit of all for one and one for all. The result was a combination of one-man, one-vote democracy and musical meritocracy, leavened by the mutual respect and affection of being best friends.

"None of us were technical musicians," John said of the Beatles in one of his last interviews. ". . . But as pure musicians, as inspired humans to make noise, they're as good as anybody!" Of the four, George and Paul were by far the strongest instrumentalists, capable of holding their own with the best players in rock 'n' roll. Paul in particular was "an excellent musical all-rounder," said George Martin—"probably the best bass-guitar player there is, a first-class drummer, brilliant guitarist and competent piano player." John and Ringo, on the other hand, played like brilliantly inspired primitives, to use John's word. Asked once to rate himself as a guitarist, John's candid, accurate assessment was "I'm not very good technically, but I can make it fuckin' howl and move." Likewise, Ringo was not, in George Martin's words, "a 'technical' drummer. Men like Buddy Rich and Gene Krupa would run rings round him. But he's a good solid rock drummer with a super steady beat, and he knows how to get the right sound out of his drums. Above all, he does have an individual sound. You can tell Ringo's drums from anyone else's." Again, it was the mixture of elements that produced the magic. There was just the right proportion of technique and rawness, of virtuosity and soul, to make music that sparkled.

The two dominant figures were plainly Lennon and McCartney, with their prodigious singing and songwriting gifts. Indeed, one reason the group remained stable so long may have been that John and Paul's superiority was so obvious that there was no disputing it. Yet George and Ringo were by no means interchangeable spare parts or obedient yes-men. "We know that John and Paul wrote the bulk of the songs," Martin later said, but George and Ringo were "very much part of the magic. If any one of them, George or Ringo, would express a critical view of a song John or Paul might be writing, they would be heard. And that would be changed, or it would be dropped." For his part, Lennon said, "I think it's possible for John and Paul to have created the same thing with two other guys. It may *not* have been possible for George and Ringo to have created it without John and Paul." Yet John went on to muse that, "On the other hand, who knows? It mightn't have worked without them."

In the years since Lennon's murder, in 1980, a myth has grown up that John was the all but sole creative force behind the Beatles. As McCartney observed of his soulmate nine years after John's death, "There are certain people who are starting to think he was the Beatles. There was nobody else. George just stood there with a plectrum [guitar pick] waiting for a solo. Now that is not true. George did a hell of a lot more than sit waiting for a solo. John would be the first to tell you that." It is true that the Beatles were always John's group. It was he who invited first Paul, and later George and finally Ringo, to join, and it was he who announced at the end that he was disbanding the group. But it was the group, the special dynamic among those four individuals, that made the Beatles what they were. Their astonishing synergy was partly a matter of conscious design, as Lennon himself once explained: "We reckoned we could make it because there were four of us. None of us would've made it alone, because Paul wasn't quite strong enough, I didn't have enough girl appeal, George was too quiet, and Ringo was the drummer. But we thought that everyone would be able to dig at least one of us, and that's how it turned out."

Coming of Age
(*Rubber Soul*)

"HOW DIFFICULT IT IS TO BE SIMPLE!" EXCLAIMED VINCENT VAN GOGH IN ONE OF THE LAST LETTERS OF HIS LIFE. The Dutch painter was writing to his friend and fellow nineteenth-century giant Paul Gauguin, but he was identifying a challenge common to artists down through the ages. To create a work of art that is simple yet still beautiful and compelling is indeed difficult, for it means expressing the core essence of reality, uncluttered by what is superficial and secondary. The reward for success, however, is a creation all the more powerful, not to mention accessible, because of its very purity.

A gift for this type of sophisticated simplicity lay at the heart of the Beatles' genius, and perhaps never was it more brilliantly and consistently displayed than in the songs produced for their landmark sixth album, *Rubber Soul*. Recorded in October and November 1965 and released early that December along with the single "Day Tripper"/"We Can Work It Out," *Rubber Soul* was "the first album to present a new, growing Beatles to the world," observed George Martin. With the Beatles becoming increasingly disenchanted with inaudible live performances before hysterically screaming crowds, they had begun concentrating their energies on studio work. Prior to *Rubber Soul*, Martin added separately, "we had been making albums rather like a collection of singles. Now we were really beginning to think about albums as a bit of art on their own."

Rubber Soul was plainly the Beatles' finest album to date and, some say, their finest album ever. With *Rubber Soul*, the Beatles offered for the first time an album with virtually no weak spots. It was made up all but entirely of songs that were immediately captivating and enduring. The chord patterns of "Day Tripper" and "We Can Work It Out," and of such album highlights as "Norwegian Wood," "I'm Looking Through You," "Nowhere Man," and "In My Life," could hardly be more elementary, but the Beatles fashioned from them songs whose beauty, depth, and freshness remain fully intact thirty years after the fact. Partly this was a reflection of the Beatles having reached musical maturity. But their lyrical abilities and poetic sensibilities had also taken a giant step forward in the four months since their last album, *Help!* Now, in addition to the traditional romantic themes of popular song, the Beatles began to make significant statements about the society around them. From *Rubber Soul* onward, their music would no longer merely entertain their audience. It would also speak to and for that audience—leading, encouraging, amusing, teaching, inspiring. In short, without losing their youthful exuberance, the Beatles had come of age.

Perhaps the outstanding expression of this new artistic mastery is "We Can Work It Out," a song that ranks second only to "A Day In The Life" as an example of Lennon and McCartney's collaborative brilliance. It is Paul who wrote the verses to "We Can Work It Out" and John the middle eight, but in both cases the music is simplicity itself— so simple, in fact, that any intermediate-level guitarist can easily see how the two writers most probably discovered the chords of the song. Paul begins the verse—"Try to see it my way"—in D major. He then accents this briefly by placing his pinkie finger on the guitar's highest string, adding a G, before reaching over with his index and middle finger to briefly play a variation of C major. Both of these are among the most basic gimmicks on the guitar, and the rest of the verse is no more complicated: G major, back to D major, once more to G major before concluding with A major.

Writing the middle eight, John, too, seems to have let his fingers do the walking. He starts his passage—"Life is very short"—in B minor, the natural complement of Paul's D major. After that, his hand barely moves; he simply slides his fingers over one string, or up or down one fret, to form slightly but resoundingly different variations of the initial chord. So little structural variety could lead to musical cliché in the wrong hands, but the melodies that emerge from Lennon and Mc-Cartney are anything but banal. Light yet insistent, fluid yet weighty, they are the ideal complement to the lyric's mixture of urgency and hope.

It took the Beatles just two takes to record "We Can Work It Out," but this is misleading, for the takes were preceded by a considerable amount of rehearsing and then augmented by overdubs. The entire recording session lasted from two-thirty in the afternoon until eleven forty-five at night on October 20, 1965, with a mere half-hour supper break. Judging from an exchange between John and Paul prior to the first take, the Beatles seem to have spent quite a bit of time that afternoon practicing the shift to a near-waltz tempo that temporarily slows the song at the end of the middle eight, a marvelous effect that adds texture but seems to have taxed John's ever erratic memory. In the final seconds before the take, as Ringo gives his drums a few last warm-up smacks and Paul's bass rumbles around aimlessly, Paul asks, "So you remember the ending?" John, witty even when giving a straight answer, replies, "I know how it goes. It's when it comes."

Take one is only instruments—John plays rhythm guitar and George the tambourine—and sure enough, it's during the waltz passage that the take breaks down. The mistake, however, is not John's but Ringo's; he adds an extra drum stroke during the second pass. Off-mike, one of the Beatles, probably Ringo, says, "Sorry," but another—John?—says, "That was the right tempo, though," and Paul agrees. A voice from the control room remarks with quiet admiration, "It was *great* up to that last bit." And so it was, though at this stage the song sounds rather subdued compared to its final incarnation.

The missing spark becomes apparent with take two, when John adds a harmonium, an instrument that resembles an organ crossed with an accordion. This fills out the rhythm track nicely and prepares the song for vocal overdubs, which John and Paul add during the evening session. Typically, these are nothing short of superb. Indeed, the bare rhythm track of take one reveals just how much "We Can Work It Out" owes to Lennon's and McCartney's vocals. Impassioned yet controlled, John and Paul sing as if their message is too important to express with anything less than total clarity, and their testimonies give the song an energy and emotional power far beyond what the unadorned instrumental track would indicate.

The lyrics are, in fact, what matter most about "We Can Work It Out," and they triumph because they work on so many different levels. Listening to them in retrospect, one cannot help but be struck by their eerie foreshadowing of events in the Beatles' own lives. Four years later, as Paul struggled to keep the band from breaking up, he would in effect tell his mates, especially John, "While you see it your way / There's a chance that we might fall apart / Before too long." And eleven years after that, John's sudden death at the hands of a pistol-wielding madman would provide tragic confirmation of his warning that "Life is very short, and there's no time / For fussing and fighting, my friend."

Yet these lyrics touched listeners back in the 1960s for the same reason that they continue to resonate today: In a concise, moving way, they address a problem common to all human beings—how to get along with one another. At one level, "We Can Work It Out" is a love song, in which one partner urges the other not to give up on their relationship. But Paul's plea for compromise and reconciliation, reinforced by John's rejection of needless feuding, applies equally well to human relationships in general, from the individual scale of children who've grown estranged from parents or two old friends who've had a falling-out, to the social scale of strife between classes and races, to the global scale of defusing wars and preventing nuclear and environmental self-destruction. ("We can work it out / And get it straight or say good night.") What's more, the message of "We Can Work It Out," like so much of the Beatles' work, is ultimately affirming: We, you, all of us, can indeed work it out if we really try.

This same duality between individual romantic and larger social concerns is evident in *Rubber Soul* as a whole, where "love" songs like "Girl" and "Michelle" coexist with "message" songs like "The Word" and "Nowhere Man." In a less obvious way, it is also embodied in "Day Tripper," the companion song issued with "We Can Work It Out" as a double A-sided single, a rarely employed category that indicated both songs were deemed strong enough to become hits.

Lennon and McCartney later said that "Day Tripper" was a forced composition, created under deadline pressure, but one would never know it from listening to it. In fact, "Day Tripper" is one of the very best pure rock 'n' roll songs the Beatles ever created. Its opening guitar riff is one of the most distinctive in rock, a sleek powerhouse of compressed energy that gets better with each listening. A groove this natural doesn't need much ornamentation, but the Beatles nevertheless chose to build in a climax after the second verse that propels the song to breathtaking heights. George's lead guitar initiates the ascent, punctuating it with tension-building bursts of energy. John and Paul enter next, working their usual vocal magic, goading each other step by step further up the scale. Finally Ringo, whose splendidly muscular drumming has been anchoring the song, boosts the excitement one last notch with a shattering assault on his drum kit before the band slides back to the original riff and rides the song into the sunset.

It was Lennon who discovered the "Day Tripper" riff and had the wit to write an entire song around it—another case of exploiting the power of simplicity—and though he later shrugged it off as "just a rock 'n' roll song," he also said that there was more to the lyrics of "Day Tripper" than first met the eye. "Day trippers are people who go on a day trip, right?" he explained. "Usually on a ferryboat or something. But it was kind of—you know, 'you're just a weekend hippie.' "

Weekend hippies is something Lennon and the other Beatles definitely were not by late 1965. Smoking marijuana had become an all but daily practice by then—Lennon later said they were smoking pot for breakfast while filming *Help!* in early 1965—and all of them but Paul had taken LSD at least once. The *Rubber Soul* album cover hinted at the transformation all this had set in motion. Beneath the album title, which was rendered in weirdly elongated, puffed-out letters, a photo of the four Beatles showed each of them with substantially longer hair and John and Paul with knowing looks of private amusement. The photo was taken with a fish-eye lens and tilted diagonally on the page, as if to emphasize that the Beatles were no longer what hippies referred to as "straights." Even more obvious was a reference inside the album, an in-joke inserted in the chorus of the song "Girl." Lennon's long, sharp intake of breath after singing "Ah, Gir-ir-ir-irl" was, of course, the unmistakable sound of pot smoke being sucked into the lungs. ("Girl" also featured background vocals repeating the word "tit" over and over. However, because these two pranks succeeded first and foremost on musical grounds, many listeners never realized quite what they were hearing.)

Smoking marijuana was part and parcel of a larger evolution for the Beatles, one encompassing the first stirrings of their social and political consciousness. For example, *Rubber Soul* included "Nowhere Man," a composition that Lennon said was all but involuntarily bestowed upon him; after struggling for hours to write a suitably meaningful song, he had lain down in frustration to rest, whereupon the completed words and music suddenly materialized in his head, a gift from the great beyond. As in "Help!", Lennon is singing about himself in "Nowhere Man," but in the process he expresses feelings common to many. Along the way, he makes an argument against the kind of apathy and self-absorption that leaves the status quo unchallenged: to not have a point of view about the world, the opening verse suggests, is to be nowhere.

The Nowhere Man, concerned only with himself, is "as blind as he can be" and thus "knows not where he's going to." Lennon follows the latter observation with the question, "Isn't he a bit like you . . ." but is careful to soften the accusation by adding "and me," thus implicating himself as well as the listener and demonstrating the egalitarian inclusiveness that was so central to his mass appeal. In contrast to, say, George Harrison, whose tendency to lapse into self-righteousness could leave one feeling judged and inadequate, Lennon's songs made your shortcomings clear but left you feeling empowered to do something about them. You may have been nowhere in the past, but now is now and "the world is at your command."

In "The Word," Lennon employs much the same psychological modus operandi. The Beatles sing here for the first time about love in the universal sense, declaring it to be "so fine / It's sunshine," and promising listeners that if they, too, spread the word, it will set them free. The song's proselytizing lyrics could have been irritating, except that John first admits his own faults—"In the beginning I misunderstood"—before going on to describe his enlightenment—"But now I got it, the word is good." With this as prologue, the final, vintage Lennonism—"Now that I know what I feel must be right / I'm here to show everybody the light"—conveys not so much arrogance as the enthusiasm of the newly liberated.

The exuberant three-part harmonies and instrumental work that reinforce the joyful mood of "The Word" are typical of *Rubber Soul* as a whole. One hesitates to overuse the phrase, but each of the first six songs on the album is a tour de force of harmony singing; Lennon, McCartney and Harrison display a vocal inventiveness and technique equal to any period in their career. Likewise McCartney's bass playing on "The Word"—especially at the end, where he seems almost to snap and juggle the notes in a dazzling cascade of virtuosity—is magnificent, and all the more so when the feverish counterpoint of George Martin's harmonium is added. The harmonium was a favorite new toy at this point, an instrument the Beatles used not only on "The Word" and "We Can Work It Out" but also apparently on Harrison's "If I Needed Someone." The opening riff of "If I Needed Someone" is an ear-catching delight that the Beatles then modified with electronic effects, giving it what McCartney called "that jangly thing." This sound was borrowed from The Byrds, the California band then making a name for itself with electrified, harmony-laden covers of "Mr. Tambourine Man" and other Dylan songs. Further bolstered by yet another display of fine harmony singing, "If I Needed Someone" was clearly Harrison's best song to date.

A different kind of musical effect brought novelty to "In My Life," the beautiful autobiographical ballad on side two of *Rubber Soul* that Lennon called "my first real major piece of work" as a songwriter. The song was actually more collaborative than John's comment suggests; he himself admitted that Paul wrote the music for the middle eight passage, and McCartney said that he actually wrote *all* the music for "In My Life." In any case, it was indeed a major piece of work, a poignant meditation on the passage of time and the comforts, and sadness, of memory. In the face of life's impermanence and inevitable losses, it is love that remains and sustains, enriching the present by honoring the past: "I know I'll never lose affection / For people and things that went before / I know I'll often stop and think about them . . ." Again, it is an expanded definition of love that is invoked, one including but not limited to romantic attachments. With lines referring to "lovers and friends I still can recall / Some are dead and some are living," it's a song that could just as easily be sung by soldiers around a campfire as by a sweet-voiced coffeehouse singer.

What neither of these renditions could reproduce, however, was the graceful piano solo that unexpectedly appears during the middle eight of "In My Life." This solo is played by George Martin, who in turn was interpreting the typically vague yet inspired instructions of John Lennon. Quite what led Lennon to envision "something baroque-sounding" to spice up the middle eight of "In My Life" is unclear. It was Martin who composed the Bachlike solo, which he initially tried to play on an organ before switching to piano. In order to attain the desired tempo, the solo was recorded at half speed and played back at double speed. The sound thus produced resembles that of a harpsichord, an eighteenth-century allusion that subtly underlined the song's preoccupation with the bittersweet relationship between the present and the past.

Such musical enterprise was one more of the unifying themes that validated George Martin's remark about *Rubber Soul*'s being the first true Beatles *album*. What gave the album a noticeable internal consistency was not simply the imaginative use of such instruments as the harmonium, or the sitar that George Harrison plays for the first time on "Norwegian Wood" and "Girl," or the fuzz bass with which Paul applies extra heft to George's "Think For Yourself." More broadly, it was that the music, despite its simplicity of form, was growing more sophisticated in content, more a matter of shades and crosscurrents, a development that in turn paralleled the greater depth and scope of the lyrics. It wasn't the kind of music you danced to, but then neither was jazz; it was music you listened to. "Day Tripper" proved that the Beatles could still rock with the best of them, but the music on *Rubber Soul*, by contrast, spoke above all to your heart and your head. In the words of critic Tim Riley, the material on *Rubber Soul* "is still powerful, but the tug of the record is intelligent and cunning, not brazen or manic."

And yet with the arguable exception of "Michelle," the Beatles by no means became precious. They maintained their sense of humor and cocksure cheekiness; in a word, they still had attitude. The album's opening song, "Drive My Car," for example, is a hip, wisecracking put-down of grasping ambition, of the selfishness and falsity that often accompany dreams of "making it." It is McCartney's song, but Lennon did an editing job on the lyrics that recalls his alteration of "I Saw Her Standing There," way back on the Beatles' first album. It seems that Paul had the tune of "Drive My Car" under control from the start, but his original lyrics went something like, "I can give you golden rings / I can give you anything / Baby I love you." Lennon rightly dismissed these as "crap" and together they devised the quirkier story line of a girl in a hurry on her way to the top who consents to take the singer along with her for the ride—as her chauffeur. In the end, it turns out she doesn't actually have a car yet, a plot twist that sets her up for the droll, self-inflicted ridicule of her exit line, "But I've found a driver and that's a start." As the song winds down, the Beatles cannot resist getting in one last dig, gaily chirping "Beep-beep, beep-beep, *yeah*!" as if it is they who are driving off and leaving the girl in the dust.

The humor is tongue-in-cheek, but not innocently so, and it illustrates one of the peculiarities of *Rubber Soul*: In an album that marks the onset of the Beatles' peace-and-love phase, the sentiments expressed about women are remarkably harsh. With the exception of the empty sweetness of "Michelle" and forgettable formulaics of "Wait," the emotions directed toward women in the "love" songs of *Rubber Soul* are angry, cutting, and occasionally even violent. Beginning with the least caustic, the girl in "You Won't See Me" refuses "to even listen," while the one in "I'm Looking Through You" is jeered and dismissed as "down there" and "nowhere." The heroine of "Girl" is the kind "who puts you down / When friends are there" while that of "What Goes On" (Ringo's one vocal on *Rubber Soul*) finds it easy to lie. More menacingly, the object of desire in "Norwegian Wood" has her flat set on fire after failing to sleep with the singer, while the "little girl" in the self-explanatorily titled "Run For Your Life" is told that she will be killed if she chooses another man over the singer.

"I'm Looking Through You" does, it is true, sound milder in an earlier, unreleased version. The song was remade three times during the *Rubber Soul* sessions, and the first take in particular is markedly different from what is heard on the finished record. The words and tune are the same, but the tempo is slower, the mood more subdued, the overall tone less of an attack and more of a disappointed revelation. After Paul's 1-2-3-4 count-in, the first sound is handclaps, a rhythmic device that remains in the finished song but nowhere near so prominently. These are backed by a discreet maraca and joined after the first two bars by an equally demure acoustic guitar, setting the stage for Paul's lead vocal. Here, too, the phrasing is similar to the final product, except there is less anger. Indeed, the only place where this take really catches fire is at the end of the verse—"You're *not* the same!"—and even there the pounce of the organ is positively restrained compared to the shrilly whistling electric guitar that replaces it on the finished version. None of this is to suggest that the first take of "I'm Looking Through You" is unappealing, far from it. Lewisohn, for example, nominated it as one of the best alternate takes in the entire Abbey Road collection. But the statement it makes is undeniably different from that of the released version of the song. On this first take, the singer sounds like he still loves his sweetheart, despite having come to see her in a less idealized way. Amidst the accusations, there is acceptance more than resentment, a posture that has vanished by the time the rowdier version of the song goes on the album.

An even more nuanced assortment of emotions are expressed in "Norwegian Wood (This Bird Has Flown)," the pop masterpiece that more than any other song sums up the achievements of *Rubber Soul*. What makes "Norwegian Wood" so representative is, first of all, its remarkable musical simplicity. A classic sing-along song, its melody derives from yet another case of Lennon's taking the easy way out—in this instance, by planting his hand on the D chord and then moving his pinkie and index fingers around to pick out the tune. (The Beatles recorded "Norwegian Wood" in E major, but Lennon played his guitar in the D-major form and raised it to E major with a capo.) Likewise, his transition to the bridge of the song—"She told me she worked in the morning"—is as easy as it is unorthodox; John simply shifts from D major to D minor, a sin of musical theory that he turns into virtue by concluding the bridge in G and A major, the "natural" companions of the original D major.

In keeping with the rest of the first side of *Rubber Soul*, the bridge of "Norwegian Wood" is also enhanced by some of the most beautiful harmonies Lennon and McCartney ever sang together, and in another characteristic touch, the song is further lifted out of the ordinary by an exotic new instrument, Harrison's sonorous, oddly cheerful sitar. Perhaps the most impressive thing about their use of the sitar is how cleverly it is deployed; the Beatles are careful not to overdo it. Indeed, the most striking difference between the first take of "Norwegian Wood" and the released version concerns the sitar. On take one (which is also slightly slower), the sitar crops up everywhere, overwhelming the guitar during the introduction, filling all the gaps not occupied by vocals (for example, after the line "and she told me to sit anywhere") and generally being overplayed. This remains the case during take two, though in fairness to Harrison, he had just started learning the instrument at this point. By take three, someone has realized the problem and the sitar is set aside for a moment (along with all percussion instruments) in favor of an arrangement that features only two acoustic guitars and McCartney's bass. This take provides the perspective necessary to reintroduce the sitar on the fourth and final take, where Harrison's playing admirably illustrates the truth that less is more.

Poetically, "Norwegian Wood" is heartfelt, witty, and, in the best sense of the word, enigmatic. With lyrics that are by turns perceptive, wicked, and funny, it offers observations on both the singer and the ways of the world. Loosely based on a real-life extramarital liaison of Lennon's, it tells of a mutual seduction that comes to naught, and in the process it deftly illuminates some of the changes in male–female relations that accompanied the sexual liberation of the 1960s. As if to mock his own machismo, Lennon makes it clear from the opening lines that the joke is on him. After beginning with the near cliché "I once had a girl," he turns the tables on himself with the brilliant correction "or should I say she once had me?"

He goes on to sketch a scene of coolly self-conscious urban sophistication: two young singles adjourn to her place, which apparently is furnished with floor pillows ("I noticed there wasn't a chair") and Norwegian wood, a fashion rage of mid-sixties London. Yet beneath the enlightened veneer, both he and she remain hesitant about how this new game gets played. He assumes they'll have sex—she asked him to

159

stay, after all—if only he is hip enough to be patient, so instead of making an immediate pass at her, he sits there, "biding my time, drinking her wine." The moment of truth comes at two o'clock, when she announces, "It's time for bed." It's now or never, and the Beatles exquisitely play up the uncertainty by bringing the sitar front and center for a solo while she makes up her mind.

John's and Paul's vocals return on the bridge to reveal that the woman has either misread her guest's passivity or lost her nerve, for she backs off, explaining with a nervous laugh that she has to work in the morning. After spending the night in the bath, the singer awakens to find her as good as her word; "This bird"—English slang for girl—"had flown." He takes revenge by setting fire to her apartment, but this is hinted at so obliquely that one would never guess it had McCartney not later disclosed it in an interview. On the contrary, the lasting impression of "Norwegian Wood" is not animosity but wistful regret at the lost opportunities and miscommunications that impede human connection.

That is a theme as timeless as wheatfields in the spring, and the Beatles evoke it with an ease that recalls Van Gogh's dying lament to Gauguin. It *is* difficult to be simple, but the satisfaction it brings is unsurpassed. At the start of the fourth and final take of "Norwegian Wood," Lennon twice falters on the fingering of the opening guitar strum. "Wrong," he softly admonishes himself after the second mistake, before immediately plunging in to try it again. This time is perfection all the way through, and John knows it. No sooner has he struck the last chord than he declares, as if to the universe itself, "I showed ya!"

"Think Symphonically": Producer George Martin

LIKE THE CREATIONS OF THE GREATEST ARTISTS, THE WORK OF THE BEATLES IS INSTANTLY RECOGNIZABLE. JUST AS A few sentences of *Light in August* are enough to identify the rich, brooding prose of Faulkner, so the sound of what John Lennon called "Beatlemusic" is unmistakable within seconds. Artistic greatness depends not only on aesthetic excellence but on personal style; there must be something in the art that makes it unique to the artist who created it. The songs and voices of Lennon and McCartney are part of what gave the Beatles their distinctive sound, but only part. The Beatles were also masters of what might be called musical architecture. Their tunes are catchy enough to sing in the shower, yet there is far more going on within the typical Beatles song—more embellishments, more layers, textures, and dimensions of (unusual) sounds—than in most popular music. Listen, for example, to the staccato scraping of violins that marches the beat of "Eleanor Rigby" forward so insistently. Listen to the wheedling sitar that mimics Lennon's melody line on "Norwegian Wood," the handclaps in the breaks of "Here Comes The Sun," the melting mélange of strings and synthesizer that gives "I Am The Walrus" its strange, lugubrious start. These and countless other embroiderings are like musical fingerprints, each proclaiming, "The Beatles were here."

There is of course no one explanation for the unique sound of the Beatles. By the time they began recording together in 1962, they had absorbed a wide array of musical sources, ranging from country and western to rhythm and blues, from rock 'n' roll to show tunes, from English folk songs to dance hall sing-alongs; as McCartney once said, his musical influences extended from Big Bill Broonzy to Fred Astaire. A second factor was the magical synergy among the Beatles themselves. And of course there was the huge songwriting talent of Lennon and McCartney, which ensured that the group consistently began the creative process with raw material that was second to none.

But it was also what they did with that raw material that set the Beatles apart. As superb as the songs were to begin with, their ultimate expression depended on what happened to them inside the recording studio—how they were arranged, elaborated upon, and presented; which instruments were used where, how, and when; how vocal melodies and harmonies were structured; what special effects were added; how it was all captured on tape; and finally how this amalgam of sound was mixed together onto the master reels that yielded the records (and later the cassette tapes and CDs) that people actually bought in shops.

The Beatles' essential partner in this respect was producer George Martin, who in turn was aided by the many engineers and technical assistants who worked at EMI's Abbey Road Studios in London. Besides passing initial judgment on the Beatles' compositions and serving as a sounding board for their ideas, it was Martin who introduced them to the classical instruments that became such a vital component of their overall sound; it was also he who arranged those instruments into scores of grace and power. Above all, it was Martin who urged the Beatles to "think symphonically," to create and structure pop songs that borrowed the grand forms and techniques found in symphonies but without sacrificing the urgency and clarity of rock 'n' roll. Martin was at once a mentor whose guidance helped the Beatles channel their prodigious natural gifts into commercially successful records, and a colleague whose enthusiasm and technical expertise helped them realize their grandest artistic visions. "If the Beatles hadn't found George Martin, they would have had to invent him—find some poor bastard who wasn't as good and whip him into shape," Derek Taylor commented years later.

The defining characteristic of Martin's relationship with the Beatles was his vastly different musical background; their partnership was almost a case of opposites attracting. While the Beatles were musical illiterates who could neither read nor notate music, Martin had graduated from London's prestigious Guildhall School of Music, where he had studied musical theory, composition, orchestration, piano, and oboe. And although Martin came from a modest background—his father was a carpenter who was reduced to selling newspapers on the street during the Depression of the 1930s—he looked and sounded distinctly upper class, thanks to a self-possessed bearing and polished accent. What Martin had in common with the Beatles, however, besides musical talent, was an open-minded eagerness to explore new ideas and unconventional means of expression. This freethinking attitude, combined with his unimpeachable classical background, made George Martin an ideal collaborator for the Beatles.

In the Beatles' eyes, Martin was "very twelve-inch," said Ringo, referring to the premium record format used in England during the 1950s (when most records were ten-inch). John said of the Beatles' partnership with their producer, "We did a lot of learning *together*. We'd say, 'We wanna go [shaking his fists in front of him] "Oo, oo" and [shaking his arms to the right] "Ee, ee," and he'd say [in calm, upper-class delivery], 'Well, look chaps, I thought of *this* this afternoon. Last night I was talking to' . . . whoever he was talking to . . . 'and I came up with this. And we'd say, [big, enthusiastic smile], 'Oh, great, great, oh, we'll put it on here.' But he'd also come up with things like, 'Well, have you heard an oboe?' 'No, which one's that?' 'It's this one.' *'That'd* be nice.' So, really, we grew together."

Just how vital Martin's contribution to the Beatles' sound was can be gleaned from listening to unreleased early takes of "I Am The Walrus," the Lennon composition that appeared on the *Magical Mystery Tour* EP of 1967. Hearing a song like "I Am The Walrus"—or "All You Need Is Love," or any number of other Beatles productions—without the orchestration and classical instruments that Martin supervised is like watching a talented actor perform in street clothes rather than stage costume. The essence of the performance is still there, but part of the magic that makes it soar is missing.

The Beatles spent six hours on the evening of September 5, 1967, recording the basic rhythm track of "I Am The Walrus"; the track featured drums, bass guitar, electric guitar, electric piano, and an over-dubbed mellotron synthesizer. Sixteen takes were required before everyone was satisfied, but most of these were incomplete; indeed, most of the session seems to have been spent on incremental improvements rather than major revisions to the song. By take nine, the Beatles clearly had matters well in hand. The electric piano carried most of the load, but Ringo's drums already stuttered and burst in most of the right places and the tempo was close enough to the released version that one can easily sing along. One night later, on September 6, Ringo perfected his drum part, Paul added a stronger bass line and John recorded his magnificent lead vocal. With a little polishing, the song could easily have been released at this point.

But Lennon and Martin had other ideas. On September 27, two additional overdub sessions were held at Abbey Road. The first, an afternoon session, focused on additional instruments: outside musicians were summoned to play eight violins, a contrabass clarinet, four cellos, and three horns, all conducted by Martin. Martin also wrote the score these instruments play (though with how much direction from Lennon is unknown), and a brilliant score it was. For a man who had never done, and indeed seemed to frown upon, hallucinogenic drugs, Martin did an amazing job of reproducing the elongated, liquidy sense of time and space one experiences on LSD. At the same time, in keeping with his classical training, Martin's score was tight and purposeful, never lapsing into dead-ended esoterica. The vision articulated in Lennon's lyric was cosmic, almost infinite in its dimensions, and Martin's deep, rumbling score reinforced this perspective, asserting a grand sense of scale so confidently that the unadorned rhythm track sounds puny by comparison.

It was also Martin who masterminded the choir of voices that swoop in and out of the song, sounding like cathedral gargoyles suddenly come alive to torment parishioners with keening wails and mocking laughter: "Ho-ho-ho, hee-hee-hee, ha-ha-ha." These vocals were supplied by sixteen outside singers brought in for the evening session on September 27; Martin fit their voices into the song just as if they were instruments. "We got in the Mike Sammes Singers, very commercial people and so alien to John that it wasn't true," Martin told Lewisohn. "But in the score I simply orchestrated the laughs and noises, the whooooooah kind of thing. John was delighted with it." Lennon later added the final touch—snippets from a BBC radio performance of *The Tragedy of King Lear*—and the song was complete.

Martin later called "I Am The Walrus" a piece of "organized chaos" of which he was proud. Certainly the song fulfilled what Abbey Road engineer Ken Scott recalled as the Beatles' guiding principle during the *Magical Mystery Tour* sessions. "They half knew what they wanted and half didn't know, not until they'd tried everything," Scott said. "The only specific thought they seemed to have in their mind was to be different." In fact, since their earliest days as a band, one of the cardinal rules of the Beatles had been to sound not just good but different from everybody else. Thus, in Liverpool and Hamburg the songs they covered were often obscure B-sides no one else had ever heard of. After scoring their first number one hit in 1963 with "Please Please Me," McCartney later said, "We decided we must do something different for the next song. We'd put on one funny hat, so we took it off and looked for another one to put on."

This obsession with constant change and growth helped fuel the artistic progression that characterizes the Beatles' entire career, but it became especially pronounced around the time of *Rubber Soul*. It was then, Lennon said, that the Beatles finally "took over the studio. In the early days we had to take what we were given. We didn't know how you can get more bass. We were learning the technique on *Rubber Soul*." Said McCartney of the Beatles' attitude inside the studio, "We were always pushing ahead: '*louder, further, longer, more, different.*' "

Martin has offered a similar account of the Beatles' studio development, writing in his autobiography that over the course of his seven and a half years of collaborating with them, their mutual relationship "moved in two different directions at once. On the one hand, the increasing sophistication of the records meant that I was having a greater and greater influence on the music. But the personal relationship moved in the other direction. At the start, I was like a master with his pupils, and they did what I said. They knew nothing about recording, but heaven knows they learned quickly: and by the end, of course, I was to be the servant while they were the masters. . . . Although at the end I still clung to putting in my two cents' worth, all I could do was influence. I couldn't direct."

When the Beatles stood Martin up for a recording session in Paris in January 1964, for example, the infuriated producer ran out of the studio, jumped into a taxi, and, minutes later, barged into the Beatles' opulent hotel suite. There he found a scene "straight out of Lewis Carroll. . . . Around a long table sat John, Paul, George, Ringo, Neil Aspinall and Mal Evans, his assistant. In the centre, pouring tea was [Paul's girlfriend] Jane Asher, a beautiful Alice with long golden hair. At my appearance, the whole tableau exploded. Beatles ran in all directions, hiding behind sofas, cushions, the piano—anything that gave them cover." After making sheepish apologies and turning on their irresistible charm, the Beatles dutifully went ahead with the recording.

By 1968, on the other hand, the Beatles had long since stopped acting like schoolboys toward Martin. "With the 'White Album,' they'd come back from India with thirty-two songs and they wanted to record every one of them," Martin recalled, adding, "I really didn't think that a lot of the songs were worthy of release, and I told them so. I said, 'I don't want a double album. I think you ought to cut out some of these, concentrate on the really good ones and have yourself a really super album. Let's whittle them down to fourteen or sixteen titles and concentrate on those.' " Needless to say, this advice went unheeded.

According to both Martin and the Beatles, the turning point in the Beatles' relationship to the studio came in 1965. Lennon saw *Rubber Soul*, released that December, as the album where the Beatles began dominating the recording process; Martin cited *Help!*, released that August, as the album where, he later wrote, "I started to leave my hallmark on the music, when a style started to emerge which was partly of my making." Martin was referring particularly to "Yesterday," the song on which the Beatles employed classical instruments for the first time, in the form of a string quartet. (Contrary to Martin's memory, however, outside musicians were used first not on "Yesterday" but on "You've Got To Hide Your Love Away," also from *Help!*). It was also in 1965 that new recording techniques were adopted by the Beatles team. The advent of four-track recording in late 1963 had opened vast new vistas that only now were being fully explored. "With four-track one could do a basic rhythm track and then add on vocals and whatever else later. It made the studios into much more of a workshop," explained Ken Townsend, an EMI balance engineer who performed many feats of technical wizardry for the Beatles.

Prior to "Yesterday," Martin recalled, the Beatles' songs were too simple to accommodate orchestration. When Lennon and McCartney brought in new compositions, Martin would seat himself on a high stool and listen while they played the songs on their acoustic guitars. He might suggest improvements, after which John and Paul would run through the song again before bringing in George and Ringo to begin the actual recording process. The only real arranging Martin did at this point was to make sure the song was the right length to get on the radio, that it was in the right key for the Beatles' voices, and that the beginnings, middles, and endings were tidy and well placed. On "Can't Buy Me Love," for example, Martin suggested that the song begin with the chorus, since it was more ear-catching than the verse.

The Beatles seem to have realized they had a good thing going with Martin, for when he resigned from EMI in 1965 to become an independent producer, they insisted that he continue to produce their records, despite the extra costs thus imposed on EMI. It was a respectful and affectionate collaboration. For example, there was the time the Beatles wanted to conclude "She Loves You" with a chord they were sure no one had heard before. Martin, who knew this wasn't quite true, later said the chord was "an odd sort of major sixth." According to McCartney, Martin laughed when the Beatles played it for him, and told them they couldn't use it because, " 'It's too like the Andrews Sisters!' And we said, 'Alright, we'll try it without,' and we tried it without and it just wasn't as good. And this is what I mean about George—then he conceded. 'You're right, it's great.' But we were both very flexible. . . . There was good to and fro."

There was also plenty of joking and horseplay, judging from the studio chat recorded on November 8, 1965, while the Beatles were making *Rubber Soul*. As described in Chapter 12, the Beatles were taping George Harrison's "Think For Yourself" that night, but they, and especially John, were having trouble getting the harmonies right. At one point, they have lost track of which part of the lyric they are supposed to be singing. Martin offers via the control room intercom to let them hear the tape again before the next take, but Harrison quickly demurs, saying, "It's okay, we know, I think we know," and John speaks up to predict, "I think this [take] might be it." But of course it isn't, because John still isn't sure what he's supposed to be singing. Like a schoolboy who has been caught not paying attention, he turns to Harrison and murmurs, "Which bit are we doing?" Before Harrison can answer, a laughing Martin calls down from the control room, "Honestly, John. You *know*, don't you."

Moments later, however, it is Martin's turn to make a mistake, when he inadvertently records over the passage that John finally gets right. When Martin confesses this to Harrison, the latter replies, "Aah, naughty." After yet more confusion among the Beatles about what they are supposed to be singing, Martin again asks if they want to hear their words played back to them. "God, no!" Lennon erupts in mock anger. "We've never heard them once, ya fool, no wonder we've been getting 'em wrong." Playing along, Martin says sweetly, "I'm hearing them here." Lennon snorts, "Wonderful for you," and Martin adds with a smirk, "Very lovely."

To be sure, the collaboration had its bumpy moments as well, though at this stage they were mainly rooted in the fact that the Beatles and Martin spoke different musical languages. Having had no technical training, the Beatles could only stare blankly if Martin started talking about suspended ninth chords. To make things easier, Martin endeavored to learn guitar, but soon gave up when it became clear that John and Paul were learning his instrument, the piano, much more quickly. Nevertheless, moments of incomprehension continued to pop up. During the overdubbing session for Lennon's song, "Good Morning Good Morning" on *Sgt Pepper*, for example, John insisted on correcting Martin in front of outside musicians. John was playing notes on his guitar that Martin was translating into notes for saxophone players. John kept contradicting Martin's instructions because John didn't realize that some saxophones were pitched in E-flat, some in B-flat, and so forth. When Martin explained this, John replied, his voice heavy with disgust, "That's bloody silly, isn't it?"

Such brazen technical ignorance caused some professionals to disparage the Beatles as musical impostors, a criticism that confused mere expertise with creativity. The Beatles needed George Martin to translate their ideas into proper musical terms, but the ideas were theirs to begin with. To his great credit, Martin was both intelligent and emotionally healthy enough to accept that "theirs was the greater talent" and to recognize that in most cases "an idea coming from them was better than an idea coming from me." Recalling his collaboration with McCartney on the high, piccolo trumpet overdub that brightens the middle of "Penny Lane," Martin wrote, "It is true that I arranged it, but . . . if I had been left to myself, I honestly do not think I would have written such good notes [as Paul did]."

Moreover, precisely because the Beatles didn't know what they didn't know, they could suggest innovations that never would have occurred to better-trained but more conventionally minded colleagues. "We were always forcing them to do things they didn't want to do," McCartney later said of the technical engineers at Abbey Road. "We would say, '*Try it*. Just try it for us. If it sounds crappy, okay, we'll lose it. But it just might sound good.' " It was this insistence on experimentation that produced the pathbreaking, often peculiar sounds that did so much to distinguish the Beatles' music from everyone else's. The Beatles, for example, would overrecord an acoustic guitar so that it sizzled like an electric one. They would reverse the tape of a cymbal so that its shimmering expansiveness was transformed into a sharp, sucking intake of electronic breath. They would deliberately record songs overly fast or slow so that they would assume a different texture when played back at normal speed. They would move drum sets into the corridor to achieve an odd echo effect— anything to sound different. Lewisohn's *Recording Sessions* is filled with stories of the Beatles working with one or another Abbey Road staffer, most often engineer Geoff Emerick or technical engineer Ken Townsend, to distort the sound of their voices and instruments in fresh and interesting ways. Recalled Emerick, "The Beatles would say, 'We don't want the piano to sound like a piano, we want it to sound like a guitar. But we then want the guitar to sound like a piano.' We used to sit here thinking, 'Well why play the wretched thing in the first place?"

Lennon in particular was obsessed with altering the sound of his voice. On one occasion, Emerick suspended a plastic bag–encased microphone inside a milk bottle filled with water to give him an unusual vocal sound; on another, Lennon lay flat on his back to record his vocal for "Revolution." When Ken Townsend invented a way to artificially double-track vocals, thus attaining the fuller, more echoed sound that Lennon craved without the need for laborious overdubs, Lennon was thrilled. Yet he continued to pester the engineers for other ways to make him sound different—"like somebody from the moon," he once said. Perhaps the culminating moment came when John ventured into the control room to ask whether his voice could be injected directly into the recording console, the way guitars sometimes were. "Yes, if you go and have an operation," replied George Martin. "It means sticking a jackplug into your neck!"

Although all the Beatles loved experimenting, George Martin later singled out George Harrison in particular in this respect, remarking that besides his guitar playing and songwriting, "his main influence [within the Beatles] was in coming up with ideas for sounds." As Harrison himself recalled, "A lot of time in 1967 in the studios was spent actually just trying to get sounds. We'd spend hours and hours trying to invent sounds. Nowadays it's pretty easy because there's so many sounds available just by hitting a button—in fact it's too easy." Martin agreed, arguing that overreliance on machinery and technology has taken the soul out of much of today's popular music. Quoted in 1993, he said, "All the sounds we were making in 1967–68 you can now get by pressing a button. So people *select* rather than *create*. Nobody's *playing*, just assembling digital information, and we get a lot of sterility, which is why music is going down the pan and Nintendo and Sega are taking over."

Martin referred to the work he and the Beatles did together as "trying to paint pictures in sound." Like Picasso with a canvas, they would begin with a central motif—a drum and bass guitar rhythm track, say—and then stack additional layers of sound on top of it to give extra dimensions and vitality to the original idea. The highest expression of this collaboration was *Sgt Pepper's Lonely Hearts Club Band*. But precisely because Martin's contributions to *Sgt Pepper* received so much praise from outside critics, seeds of resentment were planted. The Beatles felt offended, McCartney said, adding, "I mean, we don't mind him helping us, it's . . . a great help, but it's not his album, folks, you know. And there got to be a little bitterness over that." Speaking to *Rolling Stone* in 1970, Lennon accused Martin of thinking he had "made" the Beatles when in fact he had not even produced all of their albums. "I'd like to hear George Martin's music, please, just play me some," said John. It was the angriest interview Lennon ever gave, and though Martin was hardly the only one he attacked, Martin later said that "I hardly ever forgave him. It was completely unwarranted. I met him in Hollywood in 1974 and spent an evening with him. I said, 'I don't know if you want to see me, John,' and he replied, 'Oh, come on, George! I was out of my head when I said a lot of those things. Take no notice of what I said.' It was a kind of apology which I was grateful for. But John was a strange person and he did change enormously from the early days."

As the Beatles' career continued, "the workers took over the tools more," as McCartney put it, and Martin's role diminished. By the time of *Magical Mystery Tour*, in autumn of 1967, "the Beatles had taken over things [in the studio] so much that I was more their right-hand-man than George Martin's," recalled balance engineer Ken Scott. On the following album, *The Beatles*, Martin did not even attend some of the recording sessions; in effect, the Beatles often produced themselves. With tempers fraying among the four, relations with Martin also grew more strained; on at least one occasion, McCartney directed harsh words at the producer. Things got even nastier during the sessions for what became *Let It Be*, and afterward Martin decided not to work with the Beatles anymore. He was, however, enticed back to work on *Abbey Road* by McCartney, who promised that the Beatles would behave and that Martin would be allowed to "produce an album like you used to." The result, a tour de force of studio sophistication, confirmed the Beatles' renewed faith in Martin; he himself was especially proud of the segues that turned the second side of the album into one continuous piece of music.

Neither Svengali nor lackey, George Martin was nothing less than an integral part of the Beatles' artistry. "In all those years I worked with the Beatles there were no clear lines of demarcation," he wrote in his autobiography. "It was more a question of being a good team than of isolating individuals as being a producer, arranger or songwriter. . . . Without my arrangements and scoring, very many of the records would not have sounded as they do. . . . But equally, there is no doubt in my mind that the main talent of that whole era came from Paul and John. George, Ringo and myself were subsidiary talents. We were not five equal people artistically: two were very strong, and the other three were also-rans. In varying degrees those three could have been other people. The fact is, we were not."

CHAPTER 15

Listen to the Color of Your Dream (*Revolver*)

SOMETIME AFTER THE BEATLES' *SGT PEPPER'S LONELY HEARTS CLUB BAND* ALBUM CAME OUT, IN JUNE 1967, PAUL MC-Cartney paid a self-described "homage visit" to Bob Dylan at the Mayfair Hotel in London. Dylan was holding court in a back room at the Mayfair, and McCartney waited for an hour, chatting with Keith Richards and Brian Jones of the Rolling Stones, before being ushered into the inner sanctum. Once there, the Beatle took the opportunity to play Dylan some of *Sgt Pepper*. Dylan and the Beatles had known each other for almost three years by then, during which time they had influenced each other's work considerably. Dylan's reaction to *Sgt Pepper*, according to McCartney, was, "Oh, I get it. You don't want to be cute anymore." McCartney saw it as an astute comment, explaining later, "Whereas we'd been artists with a cute edge, because that was what . . . was required, we'd really always preferred to not have to do the cute thing. It started to be art, that was what happened."

Yes, but when? McCartney recalled that he played *Sgt Pepper* for Dylan "a bit late," and indeed the same can be said of their mutual citation of *Sgt Pepper* as the beginning of the Beatles' artistic period. It takes nothing away from the accomplishments of *Sgt Pepper* to suggest that the Beatles' music *started* to be art at least one album earlier, with their masterpiece *Revolver*, released in August 1966. *Revolver* was the first album of the Beatles' psychedelic period, but the reason it qualifies as art is the indisputable quality and sophistication of song after song like "Eleanor Rigby," "Tomorrow Never Knows," "Here, There And Everywhere," "Got To Get You Into My Life," "She Said She Said," and "Taxman." And there was also "Paperback Writer" and "Rain," another in the Beatles' continuing string of double blockbuster singles. None of this was cute music.

With *Rubber Soul*, the Beatles had made their first real album, a coherent, full-length musical presentation in which virtually every song was a gem. *Revolver*, however, took the achievements of *Rubber Soul* to another level. Not only were the songs on *Revolver* uniformly superb, they were performed in ways that had never before been realized in pop music. McCartney may have been boasting when he told a reporter in 1966 that *Revolver* contained "sounds that nobody else has done yet . . . *ever*," but he wasn't exaggerating. The Beatles' tireless experimentation with backward tapes and other technical tricks, the results of which delighted the world on *Sgt Pepper*, actually began in earnest during the *Revolver* sessions.

And the lyrical sophistication of their songs also reached new heights on *Revolver*; clever, thought-provoking lyrics were now the rule rather than the exception. More and more, the Beatles were expanding beyond straightforward love songs to venture the kind of philosophical declarations that caused them to be seen as spokesmen for their generation. All this was managed, moreover, without losing the sing-along quality that had made their music so popular to begin with. The tunes were as catchy as ever, but now they floated within richly wrought pieces of music that made statements in and of themselves. Indeed, there was so much going on within most of the songs on *Revolver* that they could not be fully absorbed immediately. *Revolver* thus did not merely invite repeated listenings, it demanded them, and like the best art, it yielded fresh joys and insights with each additional encounter.

Just how far the Beatles had progressed from their days as beloved moptops was evident in the album's first song, "Taxman." The Beatles would make one final concert tour after completing *Revolver*, visiting Asia and the United States in the summer of 1966, but they had long since grown disgusted by the musical travesty of their live performances and now made real music only in the privacy of Abbey Road. "Taxman" hints at the Beatles' transition from stage band to serious recording artists by opening with the sounds of the studio: George Harrison's gruff 1-2-3-4 count-in, McCartney's throat-clearing cough, and some high-pitched electronic doodling. Listeners didn't know it at the time, but the sleight-of-hand began even here; George's count-in was actually patched on separately after the song was completed, as were the nose-tweaking catcalls at the then prime minister and leader of the Opposition, "Mr. Wilson" and "Mr. Heath."

Harrison's biting complaint about the ninety-six percent tax bracket that the newly wealthy Beatles found themselves in—"There's one for you, nineteen for me"—was also miles away from previous Beatles concerns. But "Taxman" demonstrated Harrison's maturation into a songwriter of genuine stature, for his anger gave rise to some of the best lines he ever wrote: "Now my advice for those who die / Declare the pennies on your eyes." Like numerous other Beatles songs of this period, incuding "Tomorrow Never Knows" and "Paperback Writer," "Taxman" was a virtually one-chord song. While earlier Beatles compositions had derived much of their sound and vitality from the chord combinations they embodied, now the music was coming from somewhere else. On "Taxman," it came from the guitar. The rhythmic bursts at the end of each verse line were like the sharp splat of eggs hurled against the windows of high government officials, and the solo in the middle eight (reprised briefly in the fade-out) was an eruption of bristling fury. Rousing, provocative, original, "Taxman" was an inspired album-opener.

But the most musically daring song on *Revolver* is "Tomorrow Never Knows," the bizarre, hypnotic, LSD-inspired John Lennon composition that concludes the album. With its avant-garde sentiments and otherworldly sounds, "Tomorrow Never Knows" is the summit to which the entire album ascends. It was actually the first song recorded for *Revolver*, and both its cosmic lyrics and wide-ranging studio effects set a tone that permeated the whole *Revolver* project as it unfolded over ten weeks in the spring of 1966. "*Revolver* very rapidly became the album where the Beatles would say, 'OK, that sounds great, now let's play it backwards or speeded up or slowed down,' " recalled engineer

Geoff Emerick. "They tried everything backward, just to see what things sounded like."

The recording of "Tomorrow Never Knows" began on April 6, 1966, following the first three months of public inactivity the Beatles had enjoyed since their days as Quarry Men, back in early 1960. Lennon had apparently spent quite a bit of his time off exploring the wonders of psychedelia, and the results were immediately evident in the songs he wrote; five of the six songs he composed during this period were either about or inspired by drug experiences. The lyrics to "Tomorrow Never Knows," for example, were drawn almost verbatim from LSD-guru Timothy Leary's guidebook, *The Psychedelic Experience*. On *Rubber Soul*, Lennon had urged his audience to "spread the word" about love; now he was doing the same with LSD, advising listeners to "turn off your mind, relax and float downstream" if they wanted to learn "the meaning of within." Yet this new message enhanced rather than supplanted the old one, for among the things one realized during an LSD trip was that "love is all, that love is everyone."

Lennon's messianic impulse was expressed quite specifically in a request he made to George Martin before recording "Tomorrow Never Knows." Lennon told the producer that he wanted his vocal to sound as though he were "the Dalai Lama, singing from the highest mountain top." Further underlining the spiritual import of the song, Lennon also envisioned thousands of monks chanting in the background. The latter was deemed impractical, but Martin did find a way to satisfy Lennon's first request. He had John sing his vocal into the microphone as usual, but before the vocal reached the tape machine it was routed through an organ, inside of which was a revolving loudspeaker. It was this speaker that gave the organ's notes a swirling sound, and it had a similar effect on Lennon's vocal. As Martin later recalled, "It actually did come out as that strangled sort of cry from the hillside."

The most arresting sounds on "Tomorrow Never Knows," however, were neither the ethereal vocals nor the muscular rhythm track, but the cacophony of strange noises that rushed in and out of the song, seemingly materializing out of nowhere before plunging back into the void whence they had come. The first such noise, sounding like manic seagulls, or perhaps angry wasps, appears just eight seconds into the song, before Lennon's vocal begins. Another eleven seconds later, after he sings, "It is not dying," a noise like a shimmering magic carpet arises out of the distance, but within seconds the carpet metamorphoses into a clutch of wildly disharmonious trumpets. Soon the wasps and seagulls return, and so it goes throughout the rest of the song, as these and other sounds—including a squirming lead guitar played backward by Harrison—soar through and around one another like the disjointed thoughts and images of the unconscious mind.

All these noises were produced with tape loops, pieces of recording tape that had been recorded over many, many times until the tape had been saturated with sound. The seagulls noise, for example, was a tape loop of a distorted guitar; other "looped" sounds were produced from a wineglass and from the laughter of Paul McCartney. The tape loops were added to the rhythm track of "Tomorrow Never Knows" during an overdub session on April 7. The Beatles had done only three takes of the rhythm track the day before (the second of which was a break-down), and of the two completed versions take three was chosen as the best. It is hard to imagine, given the epic grandeur of the finished song, but the first take of "Tomorrow Never Knows" apparently was even heavier. Lewisohn writes in *Recording Sessions* that "take one was a sensational, apocalyptic version . . . a heavy metal recording of enor-mous proportion, with thundering echo and booming, quivering, ocean-bed vibrations."

Part of what gave "Tomorrow Never Knows" such overpowering force was yet another technical trick, this one related to Ringo Starr's drumming. First the microphone was moved much closer to the bass drum than ever before, and a woolen sweater stuffed inside the drum to muffle it slightly. The recorded sound was then fed through a series of limiters and compressors to further distort it. "It became the sound of *Revolver* and *Pepper* really. Drums had never been heard like that before," said engineer Geoff Emerick, who came up with the idea.

Emerick, in fact, was the technical brain behind many of the studio innovations initiated during the *Revolver* sessions. A mere twenty years old at the time, he had recently been promoted out of the disc-cutting department at EMI; under the tutelage of George Martin, he quickly became an eager partner in the Beatles' constant quest to expand the frontiers of recordable sound. One of his earliest and greatest achievements was the liberation of McCartney's bass sound, for which he shared credit with technical engineer Ken Townsend.

It was on "Paperback Writer," the thumping McCartney rocker recorded a week after "Tomorrow Never Knows," that the bass was first "heard in all its excitement," Emerick told Lewisohn. Part of the secret was McCartney switching to a new bass, the smaller and lighter Rickenbacker that became his trademark. But Emerick and Townsend also figured out how to boost the Rickenbacker's sound even further by recording it through a loudspeaker rather than a mere microphone. McCartney compounded these effects by adopting a much more active and melodic style of bass playing, thus making the instrument more interesting to listen to on purely musical grounds as well. Suddenly, the bass that had lumbered along all but unnoticed on previous Beatles songs became a vivid, unmistakable part of their sound.

Lennon, though not in the habit of complimenting his former partner, contended in 1980 that McCartney "was one of the most innovative bass players that ever played bass," and "Paperback Writer" is a good illustration of his point. The Beatles begin the song a cappella, swirling the voices of John, Paul, and George around one another in a lovely cascade of harmonies that suddenly explodes into rock 'n' roll with the arrival of Starr's drum smacks and Harrison's stinging lead guitar. These opening moments validate Lennon's separate reference to "Paperback Writer" as the "son of 'Day Tripper' . . . meaning a rock 'n' roll song with a guitar lick on a fuzzy, loud guitar." But then McCartney's bass enters, and Lennon's comparison is revealed as almost faint praise. For just as the verse is about to begin, Paul sneaks in a pulsing flurry of notes, kicking off a bass line that gives "Paperback Writer" a fluid yet pounding undertow and an identity all its own. Indeed, the bass instantly becomes the song's most ear-catching instrument, despite some fine playing by George and Ringo. Beatles records would never sound the same again.

McCartney's bass is even more prominent in "Rain," though it shares instrumental pride of place with Starr's self-described "amazing . . . drumming." Looking back on his Beatles work, Ringo singled out "Rain" as the best drumming he ever did, marveling, "I know me and I know my playing, and then there's 'Rain.' " From the moment he spanks the song to life with five lightning raps on his snare, Ringo's drumming is a whirlwind of energy and unexpectedness. The supple groove he hits with McCartney's bass and Harrison's squalling lead guitar is filled to bursting with intensity—the musical equivalent of a gathering thunderhead racing across the sky, preparing to drench all in its path.

For all its power, though, the sound of "Rain" is by no means crisp. Like an impressionist painting, the tone of both the instruments and the lead vocal is agreeably blurry, as if to reinforce the song's lyrical message that the dimensions of reality are less clear-cut than commonly thought. (Lennon's backward vocals in the closing reprise, the first backward vocals on any Beatles record, make the same point.) This impressionist effect was created by yet another instance of electronic manipulation. As Geoff Emerick explained to Lewisohn, the Beatles had discovered while making "Tomorrow Never Knows" that certain instruments took on a different depth and texture when their sound was slowed down. So it was decided to record both the rhythm track and Lennon's lead vocal for "Rain" at a very fast speed, and then slow them down when it came time to mix the various tracks into the finished record. Indeed, the Beatles now began for the first time to routinely attend mixing sessions, precisely in order to oversee these kinds of last-minute touches.

Besides being a powerhouse of musical ingenuity and studio experimentation, the "Paperback Writer" and "Rain" single was, on lyrical grounds, the nonexception that proved the rule about Lennon and McCartney as songwriters. Stereotypes are not always wrong, after all, nor always pejorative. In "Paperback Writer," McCartney may have been writing "about boring people doing boring things," as Lennon later remarked, but he was also describing the everyday life of postwar English society, a preoccupation that would animate some of his finest work, including "Eleanor Rigby," "Penny Lane," and "She's Leaving Home." Lennon, meanwhile, ran no less true to form in "Rain," with his cosmic musings about the nature of reality. Just months earlier, he was a self-confessed Nowhere Man. Now he was smirking at the unenlightened, singing that "they might as well be dead" and proffering the conviction that reality is "just a state of mind." What's more, he was going beyond description to prescription. With the promise "I can show you," he was personally reaching out to his audience as he had on "Tomorrow Never Knows" and, before that, "The Word," but with his follow-up question—"Can you hear me?"—he seemed almost impatient that listeners follow in his footsteps. Years later, John would play down the Beatles' significance as leaders during the sixties, but with lines like these, it's no wonder people looked to them for answers.

Like so many songs of the *Revolver* era, "Rain" was, in short, a multilayered masterpiece. Paul's bass playing, Ringo's drumming, George's guitar work, John's lyrics and lead vocal, the joint backing vocals of ecstatic, almost falsetto timbre—each was compelling enough on its own terms to command the listener's full attention, yet all blended together in perfect, synergistic harmony, rather like the Beatles themselves did.

The same kind of magic was evident in "Eleanor Rigby," the second song on *Revolver* (after "Taxman"), even though not a single Beatle played on it. The double string quartet brought in to back McCartney's lead vocal was deployed with such skill that the finished recording seems to contain two complete songs in the space of one. And although Paul did virtually all the singing on "Rigby," the behind-the-scenes creation of the song was very much a collaborative effort.

"Eleanor Rigby" began when Paul stumbled upon its opening melody one day while dabbling at the piano. To maintain the creative flow, he plugged in the words "Miss Daisy Hawkins" where "Eleanor Rigby" would later appear, just as he had initially sung "Scrambled eggs" at the beginning of "Yesterday." And the tactic worked, for the next line that popped into his head—"picks up the rice in a church where a wedding has been"—starkly revealed his heroine's character and thus suggested the rest of the story. She was a lonely spinster, so utterly cut off from the lifeblood of human contact that she "lives in a dream," a phrase that evoked her isolation with astonishing brevity and power.

Though McCartney soon changed her name to the "more natural" sounding Eleanor Rigby (after seeing the name Rigby in a shop window in Bristol), it is unclear how much of the overall lyric he wrote himself. Lennon later claimed to have written many of the words, but this assertion is doubtful, for it was denied not only by McCartney but by Lennon's friend Shotton, who was there when Paul first played the song on guitar to the other Beatles one night at John's house. McCartney seems at that point to have gotten no farther than the basic tune, plus at least some of the first verse and a plan to feature a clergyman in the second verse. It is a measure of how thoroughly wrapped up in their own creative world the Beatles were at this point that they found nothing odd about Paul's initial idea of calling the clergyman "Father McCartney." It took Shotton to point out that listeners would naturally assume that Paul was singing about his real-life father. The clergyman's name was then changed to "Father McKenzie" and his loneliness deftly sketched with Ringo's line about "darning his socks in the night when there's nobody there."

The crowning lyrical glory of the song—the uniting of the two lonely characters in a closing death scene—was apparently also proposed during the brainstorming session at Lennon's house, but by Shotton, not one of the Beatles. But Lennon, perhaps seized by a fit of jealousy, shot down Shotton's suggestion with a snide remark. Only later was it resurrected for a final verse that was unsentimental yet laced with compassion. Eleanor Rigby gets "buried along with her name," as if she had never existed. Father McKenzie is seen "wiping the dirt from his hands as he walks from the grave," the futility of it all captured in the singer's detached observation, "No one was saved." Apparently the lyrics were given one last polish at Abbey Road, for Lennon had a specific memory of being there when McCartney and Harrison came up with the song's opening lament, "Ah, look at all the lonely people."

Meanwhile, George Martin's instrumental backing for "Eleanor Rigby" could not have been more appropriate to the somber, searching tenor of its lyrics. The violins, cellos, and violas he orchestrated proved that the Beatles' use of classical instruments the year before on "Yesterday" had been no passing phase; in "Eleanor Rigby," the Beatles fully incorporated classical instrumentation into their musical palette, heralding a trend that would take on increasing relevance in months to come. Martin received some general direction from McCartney on the score to "Eleanor Rigby," and he took additional inspiration from the strident strings heard on the sound track of François Truffaut's film

Fahrenheit 451. The result was a tour de force of emotional expressiveness. The loneliness and waste of lives like those of Eleanor Rigby and Father McKenzie, and the larger world's brisk indifference to such mundane tragedies, fairly scream out behind McCartney's wonderfully restrained, almost matter-of-fact vocal. Between the gravity of its symphonic effects and the superb simplicity of its melody, the completed "Eleanor Rigby" ranks as one of the very finest songs the Beatles ever recorded, an enduring piece of art that deeply touched contemporary hearts and minds.

The full magnitude of *Revolver* was, alas, lost on American listeners. Continuing its practice of releasing cannibalized versions of the Beatles records, Capitol Records issued a *Revolver* that lacked what should have been the album's next song, John's "I'm Only Sleeping," as well as two additional Lennon compositions, "Doctor Robert" and "And Your Bird Can Sing." (The songs instead appeared on the *"Yesterday" . . . And Today* album.) Thus, Americans missed what appeared to be the Beatles' first use of backward guitars, as well as the splendidly ironic lyrics of "I'm Only Sleeping." With lines about "staring at the ceiling / Waiting for that sleepy feeling," Lennon was hardly singing about napping, but in 1966 LSD remained sufficiently unpublicized for the true meaning of the song to escape most people. Drugs informed the album's next song as well, Harrison's "Love You To," though what caught most people's interest was the exotic rhythm track. The opening descent of shimmering harplike notes beckoned even those who resisted Indian music, while the lyrics melded the mysticism of the East—"Whole world in a plan"—with the pragmatism of the West, and the hedonism of the youth culture. The response to the precious fleetingness of time was to affirm and celebrate life: "make love all day long / make love singing songs."

Romantic love hadn't disappeared entirely from the Beatles' repertoire, however, as the album's next song, McCartney's "Here, There And Everywhere" exquisitely demonstrated. An instant classic, "Here, There And Everywhere" enjoyed the distinction of being both Paul's and probably John's favorite McCartney composition. The song was, not surprisingly, the epitome of simplicity. Paul wrote it by John's pool in Weybridge one day, and with its step-by-step, gently ascending basic chord structure, it's easy to see how it could have been started and finished in the time it took John to wake up and get dressed. The melody was another McCartney jewel, set off by gorgeous block harmonies from John, Paul, and George.

Besides love, McCartney seems also to have had childhood much in his thoughts at this time. On "Paperback Writer," he had asked John and George to sing a high-pitched, greatly attenuated version of the nursery rhyme "Frère Jacques" as backing vocals. Now came an entire song written specifically with children in mind, "Yellow Submarine." Sung by Ringo, "Yellow Submarine" became one of the Beatles' best-known songs ever, inspiring an animated feature film that, like the song itself, appealed to young and old alike. Although Paul and Ringo both stressed that there were no hidden meanings in "Yellow Submarine," the song's childlike lunacy and charming escapism were not inconsistent with the antiwar sentiments sometimes ascribed to it. The most striking part of the song, besides its catchy chorus, were the bombastic sound effects. The Beatles, assisted by various aides and friends, spent a full twelve hours inside Abbey Road's Studio Two on June 1 making these effects by dragging chains through tubs of water, shouting through echo chambers, blowing bubbles, directing a traditional brass band, and taping increasingly raucous versions of the song's chorus. Upon sober consideration, most of these noises were pruned from the finished song, but it was a wacky and enjoyable day's work. At the end of the session, Beatles assistant Mal Evans strapped a bass drum to his chest, the entire entourage formed a conga line behind him, and they marched around the studio singing, "We all live in a yellow submarine."

The final song on side one, John's "She Said She Said," was a vintage Lennon mind game enlivened by some great guitar work by Harrison. The song grew out of John's recollection of his second LSD trip, taken at a party "with the Byrds and lots of girls" the previous August while the Beatles were on tour in California. The acid had been supplied by Peter Fonda, the actor who would soon make the classic sixties movie, *Easy Rider*. At one point in the party, Fonda, recalling a time he had nearly died on a hospital operating table, said, "I know what it's like to be dead." Lennon was unnerved by the remark, but it stayed with him and he turned it into the opening line of "She Said She Said."

Indeed, for some time it was the *only* line of "She Said She Said," judging from John's raw composing tape. Accompanying himself on acoustic guitar, John begins the song by repeating the line, "He said, 'I know what it's like to be dead,' I said" over and over, apparently waiting for inspiration to suggest the next line. He is playing the song in G major (on the record it is in B-flat) and the melody has not yet taken shape; instead of an upward leap from a brief "He" to an extended "said," as on the record, the rather nondescript tune hops quickly from "He" down to an equally clipped "said."

Eventually John decides to slow the tempo and echo his vocal; this brings him closer to the final melody and also leads to the line "I know what it is to be sad." Switching next to B major and a faster tempo, he changes "He" to "She" and adds the piercing third line, "And it's making me feel like I've never been born." Now the lyric becomes a battle of wits, with John asking, "Who put all that crap in your head?" and trumping the woman's opening claim about death by riposting, "I know what it is to be mad"—no mere boast on Lennon's part, one imagines. He concludes the verse with the throwaway line, "And it's making me feel like my trousers are torn," but the important thing is that the melody has now fallen into place—except for the still-missing opening hook, but including the beginning of the middle eight, where he will later sing, "She said, 'You don't understand what I said.' " The tape ends at this point, but John later explained that he completed the middle eight some days later by writing the first thing that came into his head. The result was the eneverating, midbreath flight of nostalgia that suddenly lands the story back in John's childhood, which he inexplicably idealizes as a time when "everything was right."

One of the best things about the Beatles' music is that it makes you feel happy, and side two of *Revolver* begins with a classic case in point, "Good Day Sunshine." McCartney once said that he wrote his best songs "in one go . . . inspiration just comes quickly, it falls in place," and it's easy to imagine this being true for "Good Day Sunshine," despite the song's underlying structural complexity. "Good Day Sunshine" was another song that Paul wrote by the side of Lennon's pool, and it is not hard to picture him there with his guitar on a beautiful late spring morning, opening himself to serve as a "channel" for "the music of the spheres," as Lennon would put it. A reverence for the life-giving warmth of the sun has been a human constant since time immemorial (especially in such northern climes as England), and Paul seems to have tuned in to this sentiment to produce a song whose joy is irresistible. His first line speaks for everyone—"I need to laugh"—and then he reminds us how easy it can be: The simple blessing of a shining sun is "something I can laugh about." The middle of the song is standard boy–girl love story, but the end returns to sun worship; the rising half-step key change in the fade-out generates, in the words of Wilfrid Mellers, "a timeless, upward-lifting ecstasy."

Next comes Lennon's "And Your Bird Can Sing," a song that is remarkable above all for its creator's dislike of it. John later dismissed "And Your Bird Can Sing" as "a horror," a ridiculous self-flagellation, for the lyrics certainly make their statement (despite the weird bird metaphor) and the song has plenty of musical bite, especially in Harrison's guitar work. John, however, got more of a kick out of "Doctor Robert," his tongue-in-cheek tribute to a New York doctor who gave special injections to the rich and arty of Manhattan for less than medical reasons. Celebrating a drug-dispensing Dr. Feelgood in a mainstream pop song appealed to Lennon's bad boy self-image; Shotton later reported that John "seemed beside himself with glee over the prospect of millions of record buyers innocently singing along."

Yet John also appreciated the restrained beauty of "For No One," the melancholy ballad he later referred to as another of his favorite McCartney compositions. The opening lines of "For No One" announce the theme of lost love with vivid economy: "Your day breaks / Your mind aches / You find that all her words of kindness linger on. . . ." McCartney then demonstrates his skill as a musical arranger in sustaining this effect, first with a clavichord that he overdubbed onto his piano rhythm track and then with the sublimely understated French horn solo contributed by famed symphony player Alan Civil. McCartney's musical director role is even more evident on Harrison's "I Want To Tell You." All but single-handedly, Paul transforms what would otherwise be a somewhat dreary song into a memorable piece of music, first with the descending instrumental fade-in, next with his prominent harmonies that almost amount to a countermelody, then with his discordant two-note piano hammers, and finally with the bouncy bass line he overdubbed after the song was complete.

"Got To Get You Into My Life" was another McCartney song that Lennon especially admired. John even went so far as to speculate that the lyrics were about Paul's first experiences with LSD. Allowing for the fact that John may have been engaging in psychological transference here, the opening lines do support his interpretation: "I took a ride / I didn't know what I would find there / Another road where maybe I / Could see another kind of mind there." At that point, however, the lyric reverts to a straight love call, and since Paul had, in fact, not yet tried LSD at this point, John's speculation has to be discounted.

It was Paul's idea to add the brass that reinforces the lyric intensity of "Got To Get You Into My Life," and the lads he recruited from the London club scene did not disappoint; their horns bubble over with good-time energy. Geoff Emerick used the same trick in recording the horns that he had used with the strings on "Eleanor Rigby," placing his microphones extremely close to the instruments. The classical musicians who performed on "Rigby" were horrified, but the jazz players on "Got To Get You Into My Life" seem not have minded at all. Their sounds leap out of the speakers with a vitality that suggests that the album, as magnificent as it has been so far, is actually picking up pace as it nears the finish line. Indeed, the horns are the perfect fanfare for the awe-inspiring finale of *Revolver*, John's "Tomorrow Never Knows."

"That *was* an LSD song," McCartney had to admit afterward about "Tomorrow Never Knows." But to dismiss "Tomorrow Never Knows" as just "a drug song" would be a foolish mistake indeed. Like jazz players before them, the Beatles were engaging in the musical equivalent of abstract painting with "Tomorrow Never Knows" (even if they did not think of it in those terms). And along with the overpowering mélange of sounds they created came a very interesting set of lyrics. Like those of many Lennon songs, "you don't realize what they mean till after," as John once said, and even then "Tomorrow Never Knows" is open to a wide range of interpretations. The eerie closing line about "play[ing] the game existence to the end / Of the beginning," for example, can be read as a direct endorsement of reincarnation, a theory Lennon actively explored in later years; its larger value, however, lies in its serene invocation and welcoming acceptance of the most basic of human truths, the endless cycle of life and death. The most self-revealing lyric in "Tomorrow Never Knows," on the other hand, is John's suggestion to "listen to the color of your dream." One could scarcely find a more poetic shorthand for the magical workings of the Beatles' creative process, especially as it was manifested in *Revolver*, an album that on purely musical grounds may well be the greatest triumph of their career.

C H A P T E R   1 6

We All Want to Change the World: Drugs, Politics, and Spirituality

Although their music was always the basis of the Beatles' mass appeal, what made them larger-than-life figures—what made them matter so much to so many people—went well beyond beautiful lyric and melody. Calling them "an abstraction, like Christmas," Derek Taylor once observed that the Beatles "represented hope, optimism, wit, lack of pretension, [the idea] that anyone can do it, provided they have the will to do it. They just seemed unstoppable." By virtue of their own example, the Beatles gave people faith in their ability to change themselves and the world around them: *you* could do it, because *they* had done it. After starting out as four seemingly average lads from a backwater town in northern England, they had become a worldwide sensation, but along the way they had also made themselves into more creative, empathic, and interesting individuals. Their dizzying rise to fame and fortune may have been difficult for the average person to identify with, but their search for truth and personal growth was not. As Lennon sang in 1967, "There's nothing you can do that can't be done."

When the Beatles first burst onto the global stage in 1964, they did not appear much interested in the larger world or deeper questions of life, but they soon became very interested. Asked during a press conference at the height of Beatlemania to define success, for example, all four replied in unison, "Money." The threat of nuclear war, on the other hand, provoked only such self-absorbed banalities as Lennon's remark that "now that we've made it, it would be a pity to get bombed." Within a few years, however, the Beatles had evolved into leading figures of the 1960s counterculture, extolling a philosophy of love, peace, spiritual exploration, and social change. "For a while we thought we were having some influence," recalled George Harrison, "and the idea was to show that we, by being rich and famous and having all these experiences, had realized that there was a greater thing to be got out of life—and what's the point of having that on your own? You want all your friends and everybody else to do it, too."

The crucial catalyst for the Beatles' transformation from lovable moptops to high-minded rebels was their involvement with consciousness-raising drugs, specifically marijuana and LSD. No one liked fun more than the Beatles, but for them drugs were not simply about having a good time. Marijuana and LSD were also and more profoundly tools of knowledge, a means of gaining access to higher truths about themselves and the world. Indeed, it was above all the "desire to *find out*," as Harrison later put it, that lay beneath their involvement not only with mind-expanding drugs but with Eastern philosophy as well. In their own ways, each of the Beatles had resisted received wisdom ever since their days as defiant young rock 'n' rollers back in Liverpool; the wonder is that their rise to superstardom did not extinguish their natural curiosity and independence of thought. They remained seekers, and their quest for enlightenment, despite moments of stumbling and naiveté, spurred countless others to stretch the limits of their own horizons.

It was marijuana that came first and triggered "the U-turn," as McCartney put it, in the Beatles' attitude toward life. Of course, as far as "drugs" in general were concerned, the Beatles had been heavy consumers for years, beginning with their swilling of beer and popping of pills in Hamburg. But after Bob Dylan introduced them to the green goddess of marijuana in August 1964, "we dropped drink, simple as that," said Lennon.

The magic moment took place in the privacy of a New York hotel room during the Beatles' first tour of the United States. It was the first time the Beatles and Dylan had met one another, and it turned out to be a very amusing and enjoyable evening. Like many novice pot smokers, the Beatles simply couldn't stop giggling. For his part, Dylan was surprised to learn that the Fab Four had never smoked pot before. After all, he'd heard them sing about it, hadn't he? What about those lines in "I Want To Hold Your Hand" about "I get high, I get high, I get high"? Dylan's error was understandable; the Beatles' voicing of "I can't hide" did sound a lot like "I get high." In any case, once Dylan turned them on, the Beatles started getting high every chance they got. "We've got a lot to thank him for," Lennon later acknowledged.

By the spring of 1965, when they were shooting the movie *Help!*, the Beatles were smoking marijuana on a daily basis. It offered them welcome relief from the all-engulfing pressures of Beatlemania—they were "in our own world" when smoking grass, John recalled—and it made them laugh even more than usual with one another; indeed, "Let's have a laugh" reportedly became their code phrase for stealing away for a quick smoke. But the larger significance of their embrace of marijuana was that it further stimulated their already prodigious creativity, and it made them think, really think, for the first time in their lives. With their physical senses heightened and their mental faculties unlocked, they experienced reality in a fuller, more vivid way, which in turn yielded fresh realizations about what kinds of art were possible and what kind of life was desirable. "It was a move away from accepted values and you thought it out for yourself rather than just accept it," said McCartney.

If marijuana left the Beatles feeling, in Derek Taylor's phrase, "taller and broader of mind," psychedelic drugs took that taller, broader mind to places it would never forget. "It was like opening the door, really, and before you didn't even know there was a door there. It just opened up this whole other consciousness," George Harrison explained, adding, "I had such an overwhelming feeling of well-being, that there was a God, and I could see him in every blade of grass. It was like gaining hundreds of years of experience within twelve hours. It changed me, and there was no way back to what I was before."

Harrison cited 1966 as the year LSD came into the Beatles' lives, but in fact all four Beatles except Paul had taken acid at least once by the time they started recording *Rubber Soul* in October 1965. John and George had the first experience, though not of their own volition. They and their wives were having dinner one night with their dentist when the dentist secretly drugged the coffee. Not knowing what to expect from LSD, the four guests naturally felt frightened when its effects began to kick in. They fled to a London discotheque, screaming, laughing, and hallucinating, and eventually drove back to George's house, which looked to Lennon like a giant submarine. "It was just terrifying, but it was fantastic," John said afterward.

Sometime later (the date of the dentist encounter has never been fixed), John and George took LSD again, but under far more hospitable circumstances, and this time joined by Ringo. It was August 1965 and the Beatles were renting a house in the posh Los Angeles neighborhood of Benedict Canyon during a few days off from their second American tour. The acid was supplied by actor Peter Fonda, and although Fonda's comments about death (recounted in "She Said She Said") unsettled Lennon, John later recalled the scene in idyllic terms: "The sun was shining and the girls were dancing and the whole thing was beautiful and Sixties." Paul, however, stayed straight that day, despite heavy pressure from his bandmates to join in.

Indeed, another twenty months would pass before the cautious McCartney investigated LSD firsthand, on March 21, 1967. By this time the Beatles had completed their first acid-soaked album, *Revolver*, and had nearly finished *Sgt Pepper*. Although they frequently smoked marijuana in the studio, the Beatles never dropped acid while working, except on this one occasion, when John took some by mistake. After announcing that he felt ill, John was taken up to the open, railingless roof of Abbey Road Studios by George Martin to get some air. When Paul and George Harrison, who knew why John felt odd, learned where he was, they dashed up to retrieve him and Paul drove him home. In the car, Paul asked if John had any more LSD, and soon the two partners were tripping together.

Years later, Paul said he took acid that night mainly to keep John company, but in the immediate aftermath of the event he spoke far more exuberantly about what he had experienced. He and John had taken "this fantastic thing," he told Derek Taylor, after which they sat staring "into each other's eyes . . . and then saying, 'I *know*, man,' and then laughing." Publicly, Paul declared that LSD had "opened my eyes. It made me a better, more honest, more tolerant member of society." Pete Shotton, who, like McCartney, had long resisted Lennon's urgings of LSD, nevertheless offered a similar view of the drug's effect on John. LSD "brought enthusiasm back into his life," wrote Shotton. ". . . It also served to smooth away some of the rough edges of his personality, virtually curing him of his arrogance and paranoia." It was because of reactions like these that Derek Taylor later said, "We felt liberated by the experience of taking LSD, and that's why it's hard to see it lumped with addictive drugs and other things. I think if you were doing it all the time it would be a madhouse. You couldn't raise children or hold a job. . . . [But for exposing one to] other verities, other structures than the usual, I think it was very helpful."

For four individuals as creatively inclined as the Beatles, it was only natural that the personal growth sparked by marijuana and LSD would affect their art. "It started to find its way into everything we did, really," Paul said of the Beatles' experiences with drugs. "It colored our perceptions. I think we started to realize there weren't as many frontiers as we'd thought there were. And we realized we could break barriers." The Beatles' first musical reference to marijuana came a mere six weeks after their hotel room encounter with Dylan, when John and Paul inserted the line "turns me on" into the song "She's A Woman," recorded on October 8, 1964. It was another year before the next hints—John's imitation of a pot smoker on the background vocal of "Girl" on *Rubber Soul* and his song about a "Day Tripper." But to tally only the direct mentions of drugs in the Beatles' music misses the point, and not simply because outsiders often surmised drug allusions where the Beatles didn't intend them. The Beatles had too light an artistic touch to reduce their songs to any one gimmick, be it a drug, a new musical instrument, or a clever studio trick; the influence of LSD and marijuana on their art was more subtle than that.

The drugs "didn't write the music," Lennon once said. "I write the music in the circumstances in which I'm in, whether it's on acid or in the water." What marijuana and LSD did was to change the sensibility that the Beatles brought to their music. "We found out very early on that if you play it stoned or derelict in any way it was really shitty music, so we would have the experiences and then bring that into the music later," explained Ringo. The first stirrings of an alternate awareness were evident on the *Help!* album, where songs like the title track and John's "You've Got to Hide Your Love Away" foreshadowed the greater depth and meaning that would characterize the Beatles' work in years to come. On *Rubber Soul*, probably the single most marijuana-flavored album, the songs became more consistently sophisticated and the Beatles began to articulate the cheerful, humanistic sensibility that became a central element of the 1960s zeitgeist. "The Word" in particular on *Rubber Soul* was later identified as a product of "the marijuana period" by John, who said it was "about— gettin' smart . . . the love-and-peace thing." *Revolver*, of course, was the first psychedelically inclined album, as much in its sounds as its subject matter. And then came *Sgt Pepper*, the biggest barrier-breaker of them all.

Despite the ever more obvious indications that the Beatles, like generations of artists before them, were lubricating their natural creativity with mind-altering substances, the world at large remained blissfully ignorant of their transformation until *Sgt Pepper*. Indeed, George Martin himself, though he knew the Beatles smoked pot, "had no idea they were also into LSD." The first whiff of controversy came on May 19, 1967, thirteen days before *Pepper* was released, when the BBC banned its closing song, "A Day In The Life," from the public airwaves on the grounds that it might promote drug-taking. But the fact that the Beatles themselves took drugs remained unknown for another month, until Paul disclosed, in reply to a reporter's question, that yes, he had taken LSD and was not ashamed of it. The uproar was immediate, and it only intensified when John, George, and Brian Epstein, in reply to further press inquiries, said that they, too, had taken acid to positive effect. (Indeed, John and at least one other Beatle were tripping—or "flying," as John put it—during the photo session for the *Sgt Pepper* album cover.)

It was difficult to make a convincing argument that drugs had ruined the Beatles' lives, for they had just issued an album of breathtaking genius, widely recognized as the most impressive achievement in popular music for many years. Indeed, the period of the Beatles' heaviest drug use coincided with the three albums that may well be their finest: *Rubber Soul*, *Revolver*, and *Sgt Pepper*. Nevertheless, the sense of shock and betrayal felt by the Establishment that had previously celebrated the Beatles was palpable, and the ensuing counterattack extended from news media vilification to police harassment. In separate incidents, both John and George were arrested months later for possessing illegal drugs. Each protested that the drugs supposedly found in his house did not belong to him, and there is reason to believe their claims; the arresting officer, London police sergeant Norman Pilcher, was later sentenced to six years in prison for planting evidence on suspects in other cases. Amidst all the criticism, the Beatles nevertheless stood by their beliefs. When leading figures from the British arts and entertainment world placed a full-page advertisement in the *Times* of London on July 24, 1967, calling the laws against marijuana "immoral in principle and unworkable in practice," the Beatles both signed the petition and guaranteed its costs.

Yet, exactly one month later, the Beatles shocked the world anew by announcing that they were now giving up drugs. Their image remained under a cloud, however, for their announcement came in the context of a newfound enthusiasm for the spiritual teachings of an Indian guru, the Maharishi Mahesh Yogi; in the eyes of many, the Beatles had merely replaced one set of weird beliefs with another. The following February, the Beatles made a much publicized journey to the Maharishi's meditation center in India and came away doubting that he was as holy as they first thought. But while they distanced themselves from the messenger, they did not discard the message. In their view, mind-expanding drugs and spiritual practice were simply different paths to the same goal of higher consciousness; neither was an answer in itself. Drugs and meditation could "open a few doors," said McCartney, but it was up to you to walk through them: "You get the answers yourself." Distinguishing themselves from the passive, socially unengaged stance of some sixties hippies, Lennon and Harrison, previously the two heaviest drug-users in the Beatles, argued that "worshiping" a drug was wrong, just as withdrawing from society was selfish and irresponsible. "It's not drop out, it's drop in and change it," said John. George added, "It's drop out of the old established way of thought . . . [and] drop in with this changed concept of life and try to influence . . . people."

"In a way we'd turned out to be a Trojan Horse," John later said of the Beatles. "The Fab Four moved right to the top and then sang about drugs and sex and then I got more and more into the heavy stuff and that's when they started dropping us." The first "heavy stuff" to cause trouble had been John's remark that the Beatles were "more popular than Jesus." First mentioned in a long profile article in the London *Evening Standard* on March 4, 1966, the remark occasioned no particular comment until it was quoted out of context in an American teen magazine some five months later. On factual grounds, Lennon's observation was quite possibly true, but the outrage it provoked among Christian fundamentalists led to boycotts and public burnings of Beatles records in some parts of the American southern Bible Belt, as well as death threats against the Beatles themselves. At a press conference in Chicago on August 11, on the eve of the Beatles' third American tour, as hostile reporters insisted that he apologize, John tried to explain that he had been misinterpreted. He pointed out that he had not said the Beatles were "greater or better" than Jesus, only more popular. "I believe that what people call God is something in all of us," he said. "I believe that what Jesus and Mohammed and Buddha and all the rest said was right. It's just that the translations have gone wrong." The reporters deafly continued to demand an apology. Finally Lennon said, "If that will make you happy, then okay, I'm sorry."

Yet minutes later, Lennon delved into more "heavy stuff" by coming out against the Vietnam War, *the* hot-button issue of the 1960s. Close friends Derek Taylor and Pete Shotton later cited 1966 as the year that the Beatles, and John most of all, took a sudden new interest in political issues—another consequence, it seems, of the growth in awareness stimulated by their use of marijuana and LSD—and this new awareness was followed by a desire to change their behavior accordingly. According to John, the Beatles had opposed the Vietnam War privately for some time, but manager Epstein had dissuaded them from speaking out on such a controversial issue. However, John and George in particular had grown impatient with silence—"The continual awareness of what was going on made me feel ashamed I wasn't saying anything," said John—and they duly warned Epstein prior to the 1966 tour that, in John's words, "When they ask next time, we're going to say that we don't like that war and we think they should get right out." This the group did, and not just once. Moreover, they went beyond condemnation of the war to a critique of the larger social and economic structures that lay behind it. In April 1968, when Lennon blasted the Vietnam War as "another piece of the insane scene," his interviewer asked what he thought should be done about "the Establishment." "Change it," John replied, "and not replace it with another set of Harris tweed suits. Change it completely." He was honest enough to add, "But how you do that, we don't know."

Of course, the most powerful weapon at the Beatles' disposal was their music. George later explained, "We felt obviously that Vietnam was wrong—I think any war is wrong, for that matter—and in some of our lyrics we expressed those feelings and tried to *be* the counter-culture, to try and wake up as many people as we could to the fact that you don't have to fight. You can call a halt to war and you can have a laugh and dress up silly, and that's what that period was all about. . . . It was all part of our retaliation against the evil that was taking place and still is taking place."

With the exception of Lennon's 1968 song "Revolution," the Beatles were never as outspokenly topical as, say, Dylan in his early years. Nevertheless, their music was by no means without political implications and effect. Precisely because the messages of their songs were stated less explicitly, the Beatles were able to reach people who would not have responded to more overt forms of address. They did not sing about racism, war, and injustice directly, but there was no doubt how they felt about such issues; the sensibility that permeated their music rejected such barbarisms. The outstanding example was *Sgt Pepper*, an album praised by the American radical activist Abbie Hoffman as "Bee-thoven coming to the supermarket! . . . It summed up so much of what we were saying politically, culturally, artistically, expressing our inner feelings and our view of the world in a way that was so revolutionary."

"They had, and conveyed, a realization that the world and human consciousness had to change," poet Allen Ginsberg said of the Beatles. But that was only part of their significance. The essence of the Beatles' message was not simply that the world *had* to change, but, more importantly, that it *could* change. There is nothing particularly original about thinking that things *should* be different; as John pointed out in "Revolution," "We all want to change the world." The truly radical first step is believing it can actually happen. In their public statements and their music, usually subtly and implicitly, the Beatles proclaimed that it was indeed possible to break the old patterns and forge a kinder, more peaceful reality, that it was important to care not just about the war in Vietnam but about other manifestations of evil, and that it was important to try to do something. It was up to you—which is to say, all of us—to make changes, and you could do it. That message resonated deeply and powerfully in the mass psyche, for it put people in closer touch with their higher selves and made them feel part of a larger project of human renewal. The Beatles, in short, brought out the best in people, which is a large part of why so many people cared, and still care, so passionately about them.

The Beatles' evolution into cultural radicals—their use of drugs, their adoption of long hair and colorful clothing, their dissent from the official policies of the day, their promotion of an alternative worldview—made them heroes to some and outlaws to others, but above all it made them socially relevant in a way few artists ever manage to be. The individual Beatles would later deny having been the architects of the vast sea change in social attitudes that occurred during the 1960s, claiming they were simply being swept along by a larger momentum. "Maybe the Beatles were in the crow's nest shouting 'Land Ho!' or something like that, but we were all in the same damn boat," exclaimed Lennon. But part of their genius as artists was to be in touch with the spirit of their age, to give voice to the underlying, inchoate human yearnings of their time and place. The Beatles, Yoko Ono once said, "were like mediums. They weren't conscious of all they were saying but it was coming through them." Or, as George Martin put it, "The great thing about the Beatles is that they were of their time. Their timing was right. They didn't choose it, someone else chose it for them, but their timing was right and they left their mark in history because of that. I think they expressed the mood of the people and their own generation."

CHAPTER 17

Rock 'n' Roll as Art (*Sgt Pepper's Lonely Hearts Club Band*)

JOHN LENNON OFTEN FOUND IT DIFFICULT BEING JOHN LENNON. HE WAS NOT BOASTING WHEN HE SAID, "GENIUS IS A form of madness." He had realized as a child that he was different, that he saw things others did not, that he had been given the ability, as he once put it, to "see through walls." But his special gifts sometimes seemed more curse than blessing, for they imposed the twin burdens of knowledge and responsibility. Lennon could not escape the deeper questions of existence, could not help asking what purpose his life on earth was to serve. "Why in the world are we here?" he cried in his 1970 solo single "Instant Karma." Years earlier, at the height of the Beatles' success, he had posed the question in more anguished, personal terms. One night, he literally got down on his knees and yelled, "God, Jesus, or whoever the fuck you are—*wherever you are*—will you please, just once, just *tell* me what the hell I'm supposed to be doing?"

It was this very question that gave rise to one of Lennon's greatest compositions ever, "Strawberry Fields Forever," the first song recorded for the album that instantly became known as the Beatles' masterwork, *Sgt Pepper's Lonely Hearts Club Band*. Of course, "Strawberry Fields Forever" did not appear on *Sgt Pepper*; along with McCartney's "Penny Lane," it was released some three months earlier, on February 17, 1967, as a double A-sided single. (The Beatles' record company had insisted on having some kind of product on sale while waiting for the album to be completed.) But both songs underscored that *Sgt Pepper's Lonely Hearts Club Band* was originally intended to be an album about the Beatles' childhood. Penny Lane was a bus round-about in suburban Liverpool, Strawberry Field was a former orphanage whose leafy grounds hosted summer festivals. "[Strawberry Field] was the place right opposite [John's house]," Paul later recalled, "where he used to go and play in the garden kind of thing, so it was a kind of magical childhood place for him. We transformed it into the sort of psychedelic dream, so it was everybody's magic childhood place, instead of just ours."

The Beatles began recording "Strawberry Fields Forever" on November 24, 1966, and "it set the agenda for the whole [*Sgt Pepper*] album," said George Martin. However, the version of "Strawberry Fields Forever" that the Beatles completed four weeks later was miles away from Lennon's original conception of the song. Indeed, perhaps no other Beatles song changed more dramatically during the recording process. Depending on how one counts, the Beatles recorded two or three decidedly different versions of "Strawberry Fields Forever." By the time the song was released, it had become an absolutely monumental production that utilized all the tricks and talents the Beatles recording team had developed in the past two years.

Lennon nevertheless maintained until the end of his life that "Strawberry Fields Forever" had been "badly recorded," a shortcoming he seemed to blame on McCartney's supposed interference in the studio. According to George Martin, Lennon had initially envisioned "Strawberry Fields Forever" as "a gentle dreaming song," a view confirmed by John's privately recorded rough drafts. The raw composing tapes feature Lennon alone with an electric guitar and, briefly, an organ. Whether this minimalist version is superior to that found on the album is a matter of taste, and even Lennon conceded that the released version of "Strawberry Fields Forever," a song he considered one of the most honest and important of his career, still worked. But one thing must be said for the demo versions of "Strawberry Fields Forever." Lacking the barrage of fantastic embellishments later added in the studio, they focus the ear on what Lennon is actually saying in

"Strawberry Fields" and the lovely tune he uses to say it. Indeed, they offer a window on Lennon's soul and the existential questions he was wrestling with that the final version of the song simply does not provide.

Perhaps the most striking aspect of the demo versions of "Strawberry Fields Forever" is how precise and articulate Lennon is about his uncertainty and confusion. The song had, in fact, been born during a time when he was wondering what to do with his life now that the Beatles had decided not to tour anymore. To fill his days and feed his ego in that autumn of 1966, John had accepted a small role in the film *How I Won the War*, which was being shot in southern Spain. During the long hours of waiting around the set, he had strummed his guitar endlessly, waiting for the right chords and words to fall into place.

And so they had, though at that point the song did not open with the disquieting invitation to "Let me take you down." Instead, it began with the lines that later became the second verse but which state the central dilemma of the song: "No one I think is in my tree / I mean it must be high or low." His point, John later revealed, was that nobody else seemed to be on the same wavelength he was, "therefore I must be crazy or a genius." But Lennon does not sound half so flip as that when he sings these lines on the demo tape. Particularly in the weary stress he gives the word "must," he seems almost to be appealing to a kind of heavenly tribunal, pleading that surely some mistake has been made—for how else to explain his strangeness in the world, his failure to fit in? He tries to assure himself that "it's all right" anyway, but he's too smart not to recognize that this is faith not facts speaking, so he quickly retreats to the timid suggestion that he thinks (but isn't sure) "it's not too bad."

He then proceeds immediately into the next verse, choosing his words even more carefully, trying to decide how much of his restless anomie is his own fault. No sooner has he begun this verse, however, than he stops to correct himself, though the resulting wordplay makes his intent somewhat hard to grasp: it's not that he *always* knows, but rather, "Always, no, sometimes think it's me." Two lines later, after claiming to know the difference between reality and "a dream," he again revises himself in midthought—"I *think* I know, I mean"—before throwing up his hands in despair: "But it's all wrong." Yet he can't sustain even this much conviction, so the verse concludes with another tentative dissent: "That is, I think I disagree." Only then does he launch into the refrain, though in contrast to the final version of the song he now wants to take us "back," not "down," to his childhood—Strawberry Fields.

"Absolutely lovely" was George Martin's reaction the first time he heard John play "Strawberry Fields Forever" on acoustic guitar at Abbey Road. In fact, Martin later wished he had taped and released that simple version of the song. Searching, aching, ethereal, John's melody floats above a chord structure that is a typical Lennon mixture of simplicity and unorthodoxy. Although the Beatles would play the song a tone and a half lower, in his demo version John begins the verses in G major. He then makes a series of technically "wrong" chord choices that nevertheless produce a musical foundation light yet strong, unobtrusive yet distinctive. With just a lightly strummed electric guitar behind his dreamy voice, Lennon achieves a sound not unlike that of such subsequent songs as "Julia" and "Dear Prudence."

By the time Martin hears "Strawberry Fields Forever," John has added a final verse as well, though he places it at the start of the song. In typical Lennon fashion, this verse connects his own predicament with that of the larger society. Life would be simpler if he were like everyone else—"Living is easy with eyes closed"—but the price is too high: "Misunderstanding all you see." Having been not only vilified but threatened with death some months earlier for saying that the Beatles were more popular than Jesus, he has learned that it is indeed "hard to be someone" of substance and integrity. He tries to pretend that none of this matters—since "nothing is real," there's "nothing to get hung about"—but the rest of the song calls his bluff; the fact is, he can't stop chewing away at these questions. Yet at the end of "Strawberry Fields Forever," he remains in flux. There is no solution, not even the kind of affirmation of faith that concludes "Tomorrow Never Knows." He doesn't know where he stands, except that he'd like to escape, perhaps to an idealized childhood of summer parties, perhaps to a psychedelic dream life represented by the stunning visual image of green fields and red strawberries, stretching out to infinity.

Lennon's lyrical message is not indecipherable in the released version of "Strawberry Fields Forever," but it is inevitably more difficult to absorb amidst so much musical decoration. The ornamentation, it turns out, commenced with the very first take. The Beatles had a new toy at their disposal, a mellotron synthesizer, an electronic marvel that could mimic wind, string, and a variety of other instruments. Although played by Paul, it was John who first proposed using the mellotron, according to George Martin—which, if true, puts a question mark over John's blaming Paul for the song's arrangement. In any case, the mellotron is the dominant instrumental presence during take one, though not until take two does Paul hit upon the *whoo-whoo, whoo-whoo, whoo-whoo, hoo-oo* introduction that announces, in the words of Martin, "It's 'Strawberry Fields,' immediately." Take two is also the first time that the song begins with the "Let me take you down" refrain rather than the verse; the drum fills and guitar backing that Ringo and George Harrison had begun exploring on take one also move much closer to final form. Indeed, although there will be important refinements during the next five takes, take two is quite similar to what is heard on the finished record—or at least during the first sixty seconds of the finished record.

Lennon, however, is dissatisfied. He approaches Martin some days later to ask if they can record the song again. Perhaps recalling what a string arrangement had done for "Eleanor Rigby," John asks if some orchestration can be devised for "Strawberry Fields Forever." Martin obliges, scoring the song for trumpets and cellos and engaging the necessary musicians. Meanwhile, the Beatles record a completely new rhythm track, this one even heavier than the first. Its most ear-catching sound is the sharp slurp of cymbals recorded backward, the Beatles' latest studio trick. Fifteen takes are required to perfect the new rhythm track, and even then the best version is actually a splice of two separate takes. Onto this are superimposed the frenzied trumpets and lugubrious cellos heard on the record, as well as the shimmering glissando of notes that precede "No one I think is in my tree" and "Always, no sometimes, think it's me." This latter effect was produced by Harrison playing a swordsmandel, a harplike Indian instrument. A fine new vocal from Lennon is also added.

The mind-bending musical inventiveness and power surging through this new rhythm track make it difficult to swallow John's subsequent complaints about "Strawberry Fields Forever." Once again, Martin's score does such an uncanny job of expressing the drug experience that one is almost tempted to doubt his assurances that he never tried LSD. Other high points are the backward cymbals, cleverly accelerated to double time on the second half of the verses, and the piano that suddenly floats in from nowhere at the very end of the vocal, recalling the magic carpet of sound from "Tomorrow Never Knows." Although his exertions drive the song even farther away from the tranquil mood he initially wanted, John throws himself into these proceedings wholeheartedly. Toward the end of the new vocal, he ad-libs a stream of nearly incomprehensible babbling, including two phrasings of "cranberry sauce" that sound enough like "I buried Paul" that a surprising number of people later see them as proof of a silly rumor that McCartney had secretly died.

The Beatles now had recorded two markedly different versions of "Strawberry Fields Forever." But rather than choose between them, John told George Martin that he liked parts of each. Could not Martin meld the start of the first together with the end of the second? Well, not really, the producer said, explaining that the two were in different keys and tempos. Unfazed, John replied, "Well, you can fix it."

Lennon's reply reflected not only his notorious ignorance of musical and recording theory, but also the boundless creative optimism he shared with his fellow Beatles. "There's one thing they always used to say," Abbey Road engineer Phil McDonald told Lewisohn. "There's no such word as *can't*. What do you mean *can't*? The word just wasn't in their vocabulary. . . . If they had an idea—any idea—they thought it must be possible to do it." Certainly it proved possible in this case. While preparing to mix and balance the various recorded tracks of "Strawberry Fields Forever" into a final version, Martin and engineer Geoff Emerick discovered that if the first, lighter version (take seven) was sped up slightly and the second, orchestrated version (take twenty-six) slowed down substantially, they would match. The stitch job explains why no orchestration or backward cymbals are heard during the first minute of the song, and also why John sounds a bit more druggy during the second part of the song. It was also during the mixing process that "Strawberry Fields" was given its falsely premature fade-out. Although this edit was done for technical reasons, it effectively underscored the song's claim that "nothing is real."

The pairing of "Strawberry Fields Forever" and "Penny Lane" may have been dictated by commercial greed, but it resulted in an artistic triumph. With their radically different treatments of the common theme of childhood, the two songs complemented one another perfectly. Together, they communicated a full range of human emotions, from joy and ironic nostalgia to mystery, fear, and melancholy, all conveyed through rhythms and melodies that were by turns merry, bombastic, self-confident, cautionary, ominous, and serene. For his part, Martin considered the single of "Strawberry Fields Forever" and "Penny Lane" to be the best record the Beatles ever made; others have called it the greatest pop single ever released by *anyone*. It is high but plausible praise. Not only were the Beatles as a unit now functioning at the peak of their talent and creativity, John and Paul were writing some of the greatest songs of their career. Indeed, it would be hard to argue that Paul ever wrote a song better than "Penny Lane"; it may be his single finest composition.

Although McCartney had had the idea of writing a song called "Penny Lane" since November 1965, he seemed to require the competitive impetus of Lennon's "Strawberry Fields Forever" to turn his thought into action. John later recalled Paul's feeling full of confidence during this period of their collaboration, and it shows in "Penny Lane." The music is full of McCartney's usual optimism and exuberance, but there's more to it than that; his sure lyrical touch proves that the sophistication of "Eleanor Rigby" earlier that year had been no fluke. Like a painter in full command of his canvas, Paul captures entire personalities with single strokes. His character sketches are specific enough that the individuals spring to life instantly in our mind's eye, yet archetypal enough to summon up an entire social reality.

Although John apparently helped with some of the words to "Penny Lane," the song is basically Paul's and there are simply too many good lines for John to have written all of them: "The little children laugh at him behind his back," referring to the banker too concerned with social appearances to wear a raincoat, even in a downpour; "In his pocket is a portrait of the Queen," nine words that say everything you need to know about the sturdy fireman, while also alluding to a key aspect of the English identity during the years of imperial decline; and, most wittily, "And though she feels as if she's in a play / She is anyway," about the "pretty nurse . . . selling poppies from a tray." McCartney celebrates the people of Penny Lane even as he laughs at some of their behavior: "Very strange!" But because his satire never descends to meanness, we feel comfortable laughing along with him, recognizing in his characters people we know, perhaps even ourselves. And despite the huge distance the Beatles have traveled since their youth, Paul also hints that they are still Liverpool boys at heart by including a risqué joke in local dialect, "Four of fish and finger pies."

McCartney has never been quoted explaining how the music of "Penny Lane" came to him. Was he composing on the piano or the guitar? did the melody come first or the chords? did he write it in B major, the way the Beatles play it, or some other key? What is known is that eight sessions were required to record the song, and that along the way Paul made extensive use of pianos and flutes, as well as a variety of classical instruments. It takes more than one listen to fully appreciate the beauty of each, but one mark of the greatness of "Penny Lane" is that it withstands repeated playing; the song never tires.

Begin with the vocals, where Paul's good-humored worldliness makes an ideal match for his wryly nostalgic lyrics, while John's backings show that the two partners remain as harmonically in sync as ever. Next, the instruments, a trickier proposition. In the opening seconds of "Penny Lane" it is Paul's joyous bass that commands attention most, but notice also the flutes crisply piping away at the end of each beat. Then, before you know it, a metallic piano joins in, but its entrance, half a beat before the word "known," is so smoothly disguised that it's not immediately distinguishable from the flutes. And at that same moment, either those flutes or others (there are a total of four on the song) also blow, further delighting the ear and covering the piano's tracks. At the end of the verse about the people who "stop and say hullo," the flute(s) do a pretty figure eight, like a hummingbird pausing to ponder a lilac bush, and at that very moment, the baton passes to Ringo, who swats his drums high and hard while Paul sings about the "banker with a motorcar." All these elements are then consolidated for a few bars, creating an equilibrium that is freshly burst when the trumpets come blasting in on the refrain, just after Paul sings "Penny Lane is in my ears and in my *eyes*."

The pièce de résistance comes after the line about the fireman and his "clean machine," when suddenly a very high trumpet rises out of the din like a bird taking wing at dawn. The sense of freedom, energy, and sheer happiness is glorious. This solo, played on a piccolo trumpet, is so unmistakably a part of "Penny Lane" that it is incredible to realize that it was added almost as an afterthought, at a point when anyone else but Paul McCartney would have considered the song finished. But the night before the seventh (and supposedly final) recording session for "Penny Lane," Paul was at home watching television, a BBC broadcast of Bach's Brandenburg Concerto, when he heard what he later described to Martin as "this fantastic high trumpet." The trumpeter in question, David Mason of the New Philharmonia Symphony, was summoned to Abbey Road some days later, where McCartney described, via Martin, the sounds he wanted on "Penny Lane." "Paul sang the parts he wanted, George Martin wrote them out, I tried them," Mason recalled. After three hours of experimenting, they found what Paul was looking for and finished the recording in two quick takes.

They were "jolly high notes, quite taxing," said Mason, whose fond memories of the session include the interesting fact that John, George, and Ringo were present throughout, even though musically they had no need to be there. The Beatles, it seems, remained as tight-knit as ever. Ironically, the media at this time was proving itself as mindless as ever by running stories citing the Beatles' abandonment of live shows as evidence that the band was breaking up. In fact, they were simply hiding out. The studio was the Beatles' clubhouse now. It was the one place where they could go and be themselves, unhassled by the ever-pressing outside world. It was also the place where they could do the one thing that at this point still turned them on more than any drug, woman, or other possible claim on their attentions: create great music together.

The baying of the press hounds was heard again in February 1967, when "Strawberry Fields Forever" and "Penny Lane" became the first Beatles single not to hit number one since "Love Me Do." But the Beatles remained serene, partly no doubt because of their cosmically expanded consciousnesses, but also because of their growing conviction that they were creating a masterpiece. John, for one, had never been so happy in the studio as during the making of *Sgt Pepper*. Notwithstanding his subsequent criticisms of the album, at the time he "plainly felt [that it] was far and away the greatest thing the Beatles had ever done," according to Pete Shotton. For his part, Paul later recalled taking "great glee" in reading press claims during these weeks saying that "the Beatles have dried up . . . they're stuck in the studio, they can't think what they're doing. And I was sitting rubbing my hands, saying, 'You just wait.'"

The Beatles did not panic even when "Strawberry Fields Forever" and "Penny Lane" were summarily removed from the album in mid-project; they simply began recording what was probably their most accomplished and important song of all time, "A Day In The Life." Like both "Strawberry Fields" and "Penny Lane," "A Day In The Life" was nothing less than a modern symphony within the pop format; in the space of three minutes, it conveyed the kind of musical experience and emotions that a hundred years before had been communicated in the span of an hour. Yet impressive as that was, it did not encompass the entirety of the Beatles' achievement. For at the same moment when they were creating music for the ages, they were also vigorously avant-garde, not only in the sounds they made but in the forms of expression they pioneered. Today's music videos, for example, can be traced back to the Beatles and the inventive promotional films they made to accompany the three songs just mentioned.

Yet nothing could have prepared the world for the Beatles' most audacious and inspired leap into the avant-garde: their decision to present themselves as fictional characters called Sgt Pepper's Lonely Hearts Club Band. This reinvention of self was an artistic statement in its own right, just as creative in its way as some of the Beatles' songs. Here they took a central, and oppressive, reality of their lives as artists, turned it inside out, and used it in their art in quite a witty, humorous way. By pretending to be someone else (and a somewhat hapless bunch at that), they both escaped and deflated their media image while laughing at both themselves and the public. They punctured the absurdity of stardom by stepping outside it.

Recollections differ on who dreamed up this masterstroke, but it was McCartney who ran with it the hardest; in particular, it was he who pressed most insistently for the extraordinary cover photo and design that encapsulated the concept and became the *Sgt Pepper* album's trademark. (Despite his straight image, McCartney was the Beatle most inclined toward the avant-garde at this point, though he was always careful not to let his experimental enthusiasms overwhelm his keen sense of the commercial. Unlike John in later years, Paul preferred to incorporate avant-garde elements into music that was still aimed at a mainstream audience.)

Sgt Pepper's Lonely Hearts Club Band assured the Beatles of their place in history. Although they had certainly made their mark on pop music and society by 1967, they would not have been remembered in quite the same larger-than-life way in later years had *Sgt Pepper* not been the radical groundbreaker it was. "If you want to know about the Sixties," the composer Aaron Copland once remarked, "play the music of the Beatles." Of no album was this more true than *Sgt Pepper. Revolver*, for example, though musically superior, had nowhere near the same social impact. The release of *Sgt Pepper's Lonely Hearts Club Band*, on June 1, 1967, was a huge cultural event; the album was seen to herald a new era of alternative values, fresh energy, and renewed promise. The critic Kenneth Tynan went so far as to call it "a decisive moment in the history of western civilization."

Everything about *Sgt Pepper*, from the flamboyantly colored outfits worn by the Beatles on the front cover to the song lyrics printed (for the first time on a rock album) on the back, said that here was something unprecedented. *Sgt Pepper* was that rare work of art that captures its historical moment so well that it transcends it. With its seemingly effortless articulation of the Flower Power ethos of freedom, fun, and creative possibility, it was very sixties. Yet its operatic format, innovative production techniques, and high musical quality made it far more than a mere period piece. In the words of George Martin, *Sgt Pepper's Lonely Hearts Club Band* was the album that "turned the Beatles from being just an ordinary rock 'n' roll group into being significant contributors to the history of artistic performance. . . . [It] changed the recording art from something that merely made amusing sounds into something which will stand the test of time as a valid art form: sculpture in music, if you like."

Song for song, *Sgt Pepper* may not have boasted the greatest music the Beatles ever recorded, but the way those songs came together! More than on any other Beatles album, the songs of *Sgt Pepper* reverberated off one another, gaining strength and meaning from their relationship to the larger creation. Thus the album mirrored the Beatles themselves, in that its whole was greater than the sum of its parts. Perhaps because of the great acclaim the album received, Lennon later debunked this notion, calling *Sgt Pepper* the concept album that wasn't. John pointed out that his own songs on the album had "absolutely nothing to do with this idea of Sgt. Pepper and his band, but it works 'cause we *said* it worked." Well, exactly; it's called suspension of disbelief, and it's a sign of the album's strength, not its fraudulence. Likewise, when Ringo remarked that the "musical montage" idea of *Sgt Pepper* "went out the window two tracks in, after 'Sgt Pepper' and 'Little Help From My Friends,' " he was overlooking the fact that by then the Beatles had so powerfully set the mood that subsequent songs could sustain and expand it without having to reiterate it.

The audience murmurs and instrument tunings that open *Sgt Pepper* immediately proclaim the album's originality by creating the transparent illusion of a live performance; already we feel as if we're in a play, and we are anyway. This conceit is then elaborated by a title track whose crunching guitars and throaty McCartney vocal take us back to the Beatles' hard-rocking roots in Liverpool. (The song also unconsciously foreshadows the Beatles' reputation after their breakup with the line "They've been going in and out of style / But they're guaranteed to raise a smile.") One of the successes of *Sgt Pepper* is how it conjures up a spellbinding succession of visual images, beginning here with four brightly costumed lads arrayed on stage, singing their hearts out. Paul then introduces the singer, the beat changes, and suddenly alone in the spotlight is "the one and only Billy Shears."

The ultimate Everyman, Shears begins apologetically, pledging to "try not to sing out of key." But the moment he swings into the uplifting, sing-along refrain about getting by "with a little help from my friends" it's clear that he'll do just fine. This song, one of the Beatles' most irresistible, was written intentionally for Ringo to sing, and only he could do its heartwarming message full justice. As critic Wilfrid Mellers has written, "He's the least talented, the least articulate, 'inferior' member of the group; nonetheless he has his own unassailable identity: which will be enough, given a modicum of love." It's a message that cements the tie not only between band and audience, but among all of us; taking care of each other is in everybody's interest.

Having established a foundation of trust and togetherness, the Beatles can now take off in strange new directions. First stop is the psychedelic world of "Lucy In The Sky With Diamonds," where "cellophane flowers of yellow and green" grow "so in-*cre*-di-bly high." Lennon always insisted that this song had nothing to do with LSD, explaining that it had actually been inspired by a drawing his young son Julian had made at school. Yet even John conceded that his acid experiences came through unconsciously in the song. The title formed an acronym of LSD (the reason cited by the BBC when it banned "Lucy") and the imagery was straight out of an acid trip, with music to match. The otherworldly tone is set instantly, with an introduction that ranks among the most distinctive in the Beatles' repertoire. Played by McCartney on an organ altered to sound like a celeste, the opening notes of "Lucy In The Sky With Diamonds" were later described by Martin as "a most wonderful phrase. If Beethoven were around, he wouldn't have minded one of those." Paul's bass notes enter next, dripping and sliding like slow-motion raindrops, joined by the low buzzing of Harrison's tamboura and fuzzed lead guitar. Both Paul and John later maintained that the song's lyrics had been modeled on *Alice in Wonderland*, but wherever they came from, they added a third vivid picture to the tableau of *Sgt Pepper*; this one a scene of fantastic adventure in a never-never land that somehow didn't seem all that far away.

From a purely technical standpoint, *Pepper* was the greatest achievement of the Beatles' career, according to engineer Geoff Emerick. Despite having only four-track technology at their disposal, the Beatles recording team crammed the album full of layer upon layer of intriguing noises. Quoted in the late 1980s, tape operator Jerry Boys said that some of these noises "are still impossible to make, even with today's computerized forty-eight track equipment." Perhaps the outstanding example is the marvelously shrill rhythm that opens the album's next song, "Getting Better." Bright and piercing as an icepick, this sound was produced by a piano, the trick being that instead of playing its keys, George Martin reached inside and struck the actual strings with a mallet. It gets the song off to a ripping start, and Paul keeps things moving with a melodically bobbing bass line before the vocals claim center stage.

"Getting Better" is both a classic meeting of the minds of Lennon and McCartney as composers and a showcase of their rare chemistry as singers. Paul's lead vocal is strong, cheerful, brimming with optimism; John's falsetto backing is thin, wickedly droll, imparting just the right amount of cynicism to ground Paul without sinking him. Lennon's "It can't get no worse" line was, as Paul fondly recalled, "Typical John." Indeed, the line was so typical that Lennon wrote it virtually without thinking, the moment he first heard the song, according to Martin. The producer recalled Paul sitting at a piano inside Abbey Road's Studio Two, playing "Getting Better" so that Martin, Harrison, and Starr could learn it, when John suddenly walked in, began singing, and contributed his legendary line on the spot. It must be said that Martin's recollection of this scene is contradicted by the Beatles' authorized biography, but it's the kind of story that should be true, even if it's not.

"Getting Better" was originally intended to lead into yet another product of Lennon and McCartney's extraordinary yin and yang partnership, the magnificent "She's Leaving Home." Indeed, the sequence of the entire first side of *Sgt Pepper's Lonely Hearts Club Band* was configured differently until virtually the last minute, when the running order was changed and "Fixing A Hole" was placed next. This was Paul's song alone, and was praised by Martin for its fine bass and lead guitar lines and by John for its lyrics. As with so many Beatles songs of this era, the emphasis is on taking matters into your own hands and making the world a better place. Free-thinking exploration—"I'm taking the time for a number of things / That weren't important yesterday"—alternates with self-acceptance: "It really doesn't matter if I'm wrong, I'm right / Where I belong I'm right. . . ."

From a happy daydreamer in his colorful room, the scene now shifts dramatically to the heartbreaking predawn runaway of a lonely teenage girl. "She's Leaving Home" was inspired by an item in a London newspaper, but as with "Penny Lane," McCartney portrays the feelings and behavior of the imaginary parents and daughter in such vivid yet universal terms that they could live anywhere. The beautiful melody and lush string arrangement tug at one's heart without cloying, and the emotional balance struck by the lyrics is just right, full of compassion yet absolutely clear-eyed. The story contains enough drama to amount to a play within the play of *Sgt Pepper*. In act one, the girl knows she has to go off and live her own life, yet she is nearly as sad about leaving as the mother will be upon finding the farewell note that the girl "hoped would say more." In act two, while "father snores," the nightgowned mother reads the letter and "breaks down," her lament—"Daddy, our baby's gone!"—expressing the very overprotectiveness that drove the daughter away. In act three, the girl has made good her escape and is preparing to enter the adult world by meeting a prospective employer "from the motor trade."

"She's Leaving Home," one of only three orchestrated Beatles songs not scored by George Martin, features only outside musicians and only John and Paul on vocals. If Paul's verses side with the girl, John's responses make sure the song is true to the complexity of human relationships. Speaking for the parents, John leaves no doubt about their devotion to the girl even as he takes them to task for defining love in monetary terms. His final line warns the rest of us against casting the first stone, though, for the parents are not malevolent so much as blind: "What did we do that was wrong? / We didn't know it was wrong." Forgive them, in other words, for they know not what they do. Wise lyrics, superb singing, a timeless melody—"She's Leaving Home" is one of Lennon and McCartney's finest creations.

Listening to John's last "Bye-bye," one assumes the curtain is about to fall on side one, but there is one last song, John's "Being For The Benefit Of Mr. Kite!" This song was a favorite of Martin's, which explains its placement; the producer believed in starting and ending album sides "with a bang." John himself was less enamored of the song, complaining that its lyrics were "a straight lift" from a nineteenth-century publicity poster he had found in an antique shop. "Mr. Kite" was, in fact, above all a triumph of production; it was the cheerful blend of sounds more than the lyrics that transported the listener to this new make-believe world.

John had told Martin that he wanted a circus atmosphere for the song, adding, "I want to smell the sawdust." The initial rhythm track relied on a harmonium, organs, and harmonicas, but Martin felt some-thing was missing; a fairground just wasn't a fairground without a calliope. The problem was that importing a huge calliope into Abbey Road for a single recording session was extravagant even by Beatles standards, and all the archive tapes that Martin found with calliopes featured military marches. The producer cleverly circumvented this problem by transferring the archive marches onto a single new tape, which he then had engineer Geoff Emerick snip into small bits. Then, in what Martin recalled as "a wonderful moment," he told Emerick to throw these bits into the air so that "it snowed pieces of tape all over the control room." The fragments were then reassembled in random order until they formed the "chaotic mass of sound" that forms the calliope background of "Mr. Kite."

Given Martin's belief in strong openings, it might seem odd that he chose Harrison's "Within You Without You" to lead off side two. After all, he himself referred to the song as "rather dreary" and "a dirge." Yet in fact, just as *Moby-Dick* would not be the same novel without its sometimes tedious chapters on whaling, so *Sgt Pepper* would not be the same album without "Within You Without You." Martin and the other Beatles genuinely admired the song. Musically, it added an unusual flavor, with its Indian tabla, dilruba, and tamboura, and its lyrics contained the album's most overt expression of the Beatles' shared belief in spiritual awareness and social change. Warning against those who "gain the world and lose their soul," Harrison reminded his listeners that "No one else can make you change," and urged contemplation of the implacable truth that we humans are "really only very small / And life flows on within you and without you."

If "Strawberry Fields Forever" and "Penny Lane" *had* been included on *Sgt Pepper*—and Martin later called their exclusion "the biggest mistake of my life"—it is the next two songs that would have been jettisoned to make room. Both were McCartney compositions. "When I'm Sixty-Four" was one of the first songs Paul ever wrote, on the family piano when he was a mere fifteen or sixteen. He sounds about that age on the *Sgt Pepper* version; his vocals were speeded up during the mixing process to give them a more youthful air. The song had a quaint old English music hall charm that was saved from preciousness, according to Martin, by the clarinets. As idiosyncratic in its way as "Within You Without You," "When I'm Sixty-Four" became one of the Beatles' best-known songs.

"Lovely Rita," on the other hand, had to be one of the most fun to record. Many of the incidental noises on the song were produced by blowing on combs covered with toilet paper. (Ludicrously enough, each sheet of the stuff at Abbey Road was stamped, "Property of EMI.") The combs surfaced during the final overdub session, when harmonies were being added to "Lovely Rita." By this time, the Beatles had long since taped the exuberant rhythm track, with McCartney's pounding bass and Harrison's upward-sliding guitar, and overdubbed Martin's jolly piano solo. Before the night was over, the Beatles—following the lead, not surprisingly, of Lennon—got more than slightly carried away with the sound of their own voices, striving to outdo each other in wackiness. Hence, the various groans, panting, and other vocal oddities that pepper the song, especially during the fade-out.

Plenty of sound effects were added to "Good Morning Good Morning," too, ranging from the crowing cock that opens the song to the avalanche of animals that close it, but this Lennon song was no mere collection of gimmicks. Foreshadowing the themes of the album's approaching finale, "A Day In The Life," "Good Morning Good Morning" cast a jaundiced eye on the banalities and everyday tragedies of modern urban life. Its first line writes off an anonymous man at death's door with stunning casualness; the next recites the tired small talk that two acquaintances—or worse, friends—have exchanged for years. This is how we look, trudging numbly through the daily grind, implies Lennon, and one can almost hear him smirking during the refrain that he adapted from an insipid breakfast cereal commercial. (In fact, he does giggle once during the demo version of "Good Morning," which reveals him writing the song on piano, not guitar.) And yet . . . the raucous opening shouts of "Good morning," the pumping brass, and especially the scorching guitar solo from McCartney simultaneously animate the song with the constant, throbbing vitality of life. It's possible to smile after all, particularly when work is done, and even romance is not inconceivable with a little luck. Anyway, it was ever thus, so there's no point in complaining: "I've got nothing to say, but it's okay."

And then it is suddenly getting very near the end. In an extremely lucky edit—"Sgt Pepper himself was breathing life into the project by this time," claimed Martin—the final hen cluck of "Good Morning Good Morning" turns into the opening guitar note of the reprise of "Sgt Pepper's Lonely Hearts Club Band." As the last song recorded for *Sgt Pepper*, the reprise has the adrenaline rush of a sprinter crossing the finish line in record time. It is briefer and faster and rocks harder than the earlier version, and it is immediately followed by "A Day In The Life," the encore to end all encores. What more proof was needed that the Beatles were, as the Pepper band sang, the one and only?

If, as George Martin said some years later, *Sgt Pepper* was not the Beatles' strongest album musically, it was certainly their most important album artistically and historically. It displayed every quality that made them the premier musical artists of their time: creativity, intelligence, humor, daring, inventiveness, relevance, versatility, accessibility, and, of course, brilliant songwriting and inspired performing.

Nothing in popular music was the same after *Sgt Pepper*; it ranks as one of the cultural landmarks of the twentieth century. In its closing line, John Lennon summed up the album by singing, with world-weary gentleness, "I'd love to turn you on." But the truth is, he and his mates already had.

CHAPTER 18

Organized Chaos (*Magical Mystery Tour*)

IN THE WEEKS FOLLOWING THE STUNNING TRIUMPH OF *SGT PEPPER*, THE BEATLES LITERALLY HAD THE WORLD AT THEIR command. On June 25, 1967, they starred in planet Earth's first global television show, a two-hour program that was transmitted live to all five inhabited continents and broadcast in twenty-four countries. Two years before, the Beatles had set a live performance record by playing to an audience of 55,000 people in New York's Shea Stadium. Now, thanks to the wonders of satellite technology, they would be seen by an estimated 350 *million* people. How they responded to this unprecedented opportunity to reach people says a great deal about their self-image as artists. Having just issued the most earthshaking album in the history of rock 'n' roll, they now took another leap forward by performing their most political song yet, "All You Need Is Love." Indeed, much of what later caused John Lennon in particular to be remembered as a humanitarian hero began with this song.

The "All You Need Is Love" broadcast marked the onset of a curious period in the Beatles' career. During the ten months between completing *Sgt Pepper* in April 1967 and departing to study meditation in India in February 1968, the Beatles recorded a collection of songs whose quality varied widely. Most of these songs were intended for the two films the band was involved in making at this time: the children's cartoon *Yellow Submarine* and the surreal travelogue *Magical Mystery Tour*. The latter was an apt title for this phase in the Beatles' career; artistically, they seemed to be on their own magical mystery tour during these ten months. How a group capable of creating "Eleanor Rigby," "Strawberry Fields Forever," and the many other gems of the *Revolver–Sgt Pepper* period could record some of the dreck found on the *Yellow Submarine* and *Magical Mystery Tour* soundtrack albums was indeed a mystery. Yet their magic touch did not completely desert the Beatles during this period: "All You Need Is Love" ranks among their all-time greatest songs, as does "I Am The Walrus," while "Lady Madonna," "Hey Bulldog," and "Hello, Goodbye" are also first-rate.

"All You Need Is Love" was written specifically for the so-called *Our World* global television broadcast, but not until the very last minute. "Oh, God, is it that close?" asked Lennon when someone at Abbey Road mentioned that the show was only days away. "I suppose we'd better write something." The idea was to show the Beatles in the studio, recording their next single, and as it happens, both John and Paul composed songs for the occasion. But there was no doubt who won this round of their perpetual competition. The song Paul came up with was apparently "Your Mother Should Know," a tuneful but slight piece of nostalgia, devoid of larger social significance. The two partners agreed that "All You Need Is Love" was plainly the superior choice.

Unfortunately, nothing more is known about how Lennon composed the song, although he obviously wrote it quickly. Nor is it known who contributed the idea of beginning "All You Need Is Love" with the opening bars of the French national anthem. But it was probably either John or Paul, because the song started that way from the very first studio take, giving "All You Need Is Love" yet another of the Beatles' very distinctive introductions. (Indeed, from then on, many non-French listeners who heard "La Marseillaise" during, say, the Olympic Games would half expect it to give way to "All You Need Is Love.")

Structurally, "All You Need Is Love" seemed an extremely simple song, with its "Three Blind Mice"–like opening refrain and its virtually single note melody in the sing-along chorus. But beneath the surface, it was trickier than that, thanks to a vintage Lennonism: the dropping of a beat at the end of each verse line. This twist subtly imparted extra speed and momentum to the song, though this seems to have been unintentional on John's part. Citing the skipped beats in "All You Need Is Love" as an example of his bandmate's "amazing" sense of timing, George Harrison once said, "But when you question [John] as to what it is he's actually doing, he really doesn't know. He just does it naturally." Lennon's music wasn't called "bumpy" for nothing.

Despite its simplicity, "All You Need Is Love" went through fifty-seven takes and numerous overdubs before the Beatles played it live for the world. One reason for the unusually large number of takes may have been that the Beatles took to heart John's line "There's nothing you can do that can't be done." During the first recording session for "All You Need Is Love," held on June 14, John, Paul, and George all insisted on playing instruments that were, to put it mildly, strange to them. John played a harpsichord, Paul a double bass, and George scraped away at a violin (which he had never played before that night). Thirty-three takes were recorded. Take ten was chosen to receive vocal and instrumental overdubs on June 19, as well as orchestral backing some days later.

The goal of these prebroadcast sessions was to record a basic rhythm track that could be played behind the Beatles' live performance on June 25, thus reducing the chance of an egregious error in front of millions. Even so, much of what the world heard that day was performed completely live, including John's lead vocal, some of the backing vocals, Paul's bass, George's lead guitar solo, and parts of the orchestra and Ringo's drums. That left plenty of room for mistakes, and unlike the howling stadium crowds of the Beatlemania era, viewers of the *Our World* program would be able to hear those mistakes. The Beatles had agreed years before always to feign indifference in public, no matter how high the honor or great the pressure, but Abbey Road staffers saw through the pose in this case. "Lennon was very nervous that day, too," recalled tape operator Richard Lush. "He might not have looked it, but I was used to working with him and you get to know when someone is nervous."

On camera, however, Lennon was the picture of nonchalance, perched on a stool, chewing gum, warbling off-key snatches of the Beatles' old hit "She Loves You" while waiting for the final take to begin. The other Beatles seemed no less calm and collected. Why not?

It was a party. The BBC's film of the event calls to mind the festive atmosphere of four months earlier, when the orchestra crescendo of "A Day In The Life" was recorded. Multicolored balloons and streamers abounded inside Abbey Road's huge Studio One, along with placards spelling out "Love Is All You Need" in English, French, German, and Spanish. The orchestra members wore evening dress, while a contingent of pop luminaries including Eric Clapton and Mick Jagger sat on the floor, clapping and singing along.

The song went off without a hitch, with John delivering an especially splendid, moving vocal. Paul blinked a look of good-humored surprise at one point when the backing track caught him about to go wrong, but otherwise the performance was virtually flawless. Obviously, the Beatles could still play live when they wanted to. In the fade-out, while John repeated "Love is all you need" over and over like a mantra, Paul called out, "All together now" and "Everybody," encouraging the Beatles' studio guests, and doubtless millions of viewers around the world as well, to join in. "Pop music never really had a finer moment," Derek Taylor later said.

The song "cannot be misinterpreted," declared Brian Epstein some days later when "All You Need Is Love" was issued as a single. At the time he seemed to be right. "All You Need Is Love" was embraced as *the* anthem of the sixties counterculture, a perfect articulation of its cheerful faith in love's power to transform the world. Yet the song also appealed to mainstream audiences, causing "people who'd never really liked the Beatles to say they were among the great treasures," recalled Taylor. The combination made "All You Need Is Love" a number one hit worldwide.

But despite the popular acclaim for the song, Brian Epstein's confident assertion about its transparent meaning was later proven wrong by many biographers and music critics. Rather than a song of hope and possibility, "All You Need Is Love" has been portrayed in most written accounts of the Beatles' work as little more than an embarrassing, if pleasant-sounding, banality. It is faulted on musical grounds for being simplistic and unimaginative, and on poetic/political grounds for being naive, self-satisfied, and irrelevant. At most, the naysayers concede that "All You Need Is Love" expresses a sentiment characteristic of its era. But that era, they are quick to add, was long ago. Everyone has grown up a lot since then and, having put away childish things, recognizes that the world doesn't really work like that.

In fact, the condescending dismissals of "All You Need Is Love" as a silly sixties relic are themselves rather simplistic, for they fail to recognize a distinction between shallow and utopian. It is certainly utopian to proclaim, as Lennon does, that the world does not have to be this way, that change is possible, that love can triumph over wickedness. After all, human history can be read as proving quite the opposite; at the very time when the Beatles were spreading their message of love, the United States was raining bombs on Vietnam, a short but brutal war had just ended in the Middle East, and the nuclear arms race had quietly brought the world to within thirty minutes of Doomsday. But history is a record of progress as well as ruin, and in times when justice does prevail, it is often in pursuit of goals that were previously considered utopian, be it abolition of slavery, voting rights for women, democracy in South Africa, or the collapse of Soviet communism. Love is not all you need to change the world, that was Lennon's natural hyperbole coming through. But one may as well complain that Martin Luther King was a poor singer as criticize Lennon on fine points of political strategy; his role was the Poet, not the Political Organizer. And as the poet, he knew instinctively that love—in the universal sense of loving one's neighbor as oneself—was the surest foundation for honest and lasting participation in the eternal struggle against evil and suffering, for sustaining one's efforts in the face of failure, and for resisting the insidious temptations of apathy and self-interest.

"You may say I'm a dreamer / But I'm not the only one," Lennon sang in "Imagine," and he stood by his convictions until his dying day. Invoking a popular song of the day, John said in an interview just days before he was shot that "I still believe in love, peace and understanding, as Elvis Costello said, and what's so funny about love, peace and understanding?" In a second interview, completed six hours before his death, John emphasized that wishing for a kinder world was not enough; one also had to act. "Maybe in the Sixties we were naive and like children," he said, "and later everyone went back to their rooms and said, 'We didn't get a wonderful world of flowers and peace. . . . The world is a nasty horrible place because it didn't give us everything we cried for.' Right? Crying for it wasn't enough. The thing the Sixties did was show us the possibility and the responsibility we all had. It wasn't the answer. It just gave us a glimpse of the possibility."

Who knows how different Lennon's views might have been had he lived through the sobering events of the 1980s, with their celebration of greed and materialism, like everyone else? Who knows how different the eighties might have been had he been around for them? In any case, his murder in December 1980 was widely seen as symbolic of the death of the sixties "dream," thus further reinforcing the cynicism he had fought against while alive. But not everyone surrendered to despair. Shortly after Lennon's death, Václav Havel, the Czech playwright whose lonely dissent against totalitarian orthodoxy in the 1980s would seem hopelessly futile until the so-called Velvet Revolution of 1989 suddenly made him the country's president, wrote, "I do not believe that certain values and ideals of the Sixties have been discredited as empty illusions and mistakes; certain things can never be called into question, either by time or by history. . . . I only think that everything today is somehow harder and rougher, that one has to pay more dearly for things and that the dream of a freer, more meaningful life is no longer just a matter of running away from Mommy, as it were, but a tough-minded, everyday confrontation with the dark powers of the new age."

Tough-minded it wasn't, but the *Yellow Submarine* film that was being created in the summer of 1967 certainly applauded the idea of good guys—the Beatles—doing battle with the forces of evil, as represented by the Blue Meanies. Nevertheless, the real-life Beatles were decidedly unenthusiastic about the film during its production (though they warmed up to it after its release, in July 1968). Brian Epstein had sanctioned the *Yellow Submarine* project in order to conclude the group's three-film contract with United Artists. The cartoon format let the Beatles avoid acting in the film, but they were still bound to supply a soundtrack. Apparently resentful of the obligation, the Beatles scarcely involved themselves in the production and, according to George Martin, contributed only "bottom of the barrel" songs to the project. Harrison's "Only A Northern Song," for example, had understandably been rejected as not good enough for *Sgt Pepper*; while his "It's All Too Much" was little more than formless shrieking. McCartney's "All Together Now" was harmless fun but nothing more. "Baby, You're A Rich Man," a joint composition of Lennon and McCartney, had its moments but was unexceptional, and in any case was quickly reassigned to the B-side of the "All You Need Is Love" single. The one diamond in the rough of "Yellow Submarine" was "Hey Bulldog," a great, growling rocker recorded just days before the Beatles left for India in February 1968. All four Beatles play this Lennon composition with tight, ferocious intensity, whiplashing its simple groove to a fever pitch. The barking and maniacal laughing between John and Paul during the fade-out not only confirm engineer Geoff Emerick's recollection of the session as "really fun," they also indicate how fond of each other the Beatles still were at this point.

By this time, the *Magical Mystery Tour* film had come and gone, after being savaged by critics who pronounced it the Beatles' first real failure. Here it is important to distinguish between the film, which was indeed a plotless flop—"We goofed really," admitted McCartney—and the album, which featured such Beatles classics as "I Am The Walrus" and "The Fool On The Hill." These classics, however, were offset by the four other songs on the *Magical Mystery Tour* EP (which was actually a double EP disc, containing only the six songs featured in the film). Although the title track and McCartney's "Your Mother Should Know" were likable, they could not compare to the superb quality of the *Pepper*, *Revolver*, and *Rubber Soul* era. Meanwhile, the instrumental "Flying" and Harrison's "Blue Jay Way" were downright tiresome—examples of the "disorganized chaos" that George Martin said infected this cycle of Beatles recordings. "If the Beatles' professional career were to be plotted on a graph," Martin later wrote, ". . . *Magical Mystery Tour* was a definite dip."

For all its later problems, the *Magical Mystery Tour* project had actually started promisingly enough. After *Sgt Pepper* was completed, McCartney had traveled to the United States, where he apparently took notice of the Merry Pranksters, a group of LSD-inclined, anarchist hippies who roamed the country by bus and staged occasional "happenings." On the airplane ride home, Paul sketched the idea of making a film about a different kind of traveling troupe. Recording of the *Magical Mystery Tour* title track duly began on April 25, just days after Paul's return to London, during the Beatles' first Abbey Road session after *Sgt Pepper*. It took four sessions to bring the song to virtual completion on May 3. Then the Beatles were distracted by "Yellow Submarine" and the "All You Need Is Love" broadcast, after which they took two months of holiday, the result being that work on *Magical Mystery Tour* did not resume until August 22, with the taping of "Your Mother Should Know." Days later, the sudden death of Brian Epstein threw a question mark over the future, but on September 1 a meeting was held at McCartney's house during which the four Beatles decided to press on with the *Mystery Tour* project. Initial signs were encouraging: In the first two days of work, much of "I Am The Walrus" was recorded, as was a demo version of "The Fool On The Hill."

Paul had started "The Fool On The Hill" back in the spring; in fact, he played an early version of it to John while they were composing "With A Little Help From My Friends." At that point, "The Fool On The Hill" was a guitar song, and judging from Hunter Davies's eyewitness account, Paul had written only a handful of lyrics for it. In the demo version taped at Abbey Road on September 6, however, Paul plays piano and sings a virtually complete set of lyrics. The performance is completely solo and very similar to the final version in tone and tempo while lacking the flutes and other backing instruments. "The Fool On The Hill" went on to become a well-loved song, despite lyrics that recall Lennon's criticism of "Yesterday": The individual lines are good, but they don't add up. McCartney's Fool has rejected society's constraints in favor of solitary communion with the natural world, a choice that is portrayed as knowing and noble. But beyond watching sunsets, how is he so different from the people who snub him? Paul either can't or doesn't bother to explain. The lovely slow melody, however, conveys such an enchanting mood of childlike wonder that it redeems his lyrical laziness.

There are childlike aspects to "I Am The Walrus" as well, though they are hard to detect without knowing the story behind the song. The opening affirmation of human unity—"I am he as you are he / As you are me and we are all together"—came to Lennon during an acid trip. But many of the subsequent verses were triggered by a fan letter he received from a student at his old high school. Pete Shotton recalled how he and John were taking one of their "lucky dips" into the fan mail bag one day when out came a letter from a lad describing how a Quarry

Bank literature teacher was pontificating on the real meaning behind the Beatles' lyrics. John, already exasperated by the often mistaken analysis of Beatles songs by journalists, critics, and fans, was seized by a brainwave. Asking Shotton to recite their shared boyhood rhyme "Dead Dog's Eye," a listing of the kind of grotesqueries that adolescent boys seem to find irresistibly hilarious, Lennon reconfigured the words into, "Yellow matter custard / Dripping from a dead dog's eye." Likewise the words "Semolina pilchard" referred to types of pudding and sardines, respectively, that he and Shotton remembered from childhood. After scribbling down these lines, John looked up with a smile and said, "Let the fuckers work *that* one out, Pete."

There were other influences as well. In fact, "I Am The Walrus" is an excellent illustration of Lennon's conception of songwriting as "doing little bits which you then join up." Thus the main melody was his approximation of the two-note rhythm of a police siren—"*Mis*-ter *cit*-y *p'lice*-man *sit*-ting"—which he had heard one day outside his house near London. The character of the walrus was borrowed from Lewis Carroll's anticapitalist poem, "The Walrus and the Carpenter." The line about "Element'ry penguin" was a veiled slap at American poet Allen Ginsberg's overly zealous (in Lennon's eyes) conversion to the Hare Krishna religion. Deliberate obscurities aside, there were also such penetrating one-liners as "Don't you think the joker laughs at you?" and "Man, you should have seen them kicking Edgar Allan Poe." (Was the latter a blast at the trendiness of so much artistic criticism?)

Finally, there was the overdubbing of parts of Shakespeare's *King Lear*, most notably the infinitely sorrowful lament "Oh, untimely death!" This masterstroke was apparently a product of pure intuition; the idea of putting Shakespeare on "Walrus" seems not to have occurred to Lennon until he arrived at Abbey Road for the song's final mixing session on September 29. But once inside the control room of Studio Two with George Martin (whose orchestration of "Walrus" is described in Chapter Fourteen), John began dialing across the radio band. Happening upon a performance of *Lear* on the BBC, he threaded it directly into the mix, another case (like "Eleanor Rigby") where random chance surpassed anything that could have been scripted. John's patch job may have been an impromptu whim, but artistically it was an innovation.

A Day In The Life

Some fifty years earlier, Picasso and his fellow Cubist Georges Braque had devised new means of commenting on the nature of art by pasting bits of cloth, newspaper, and cigarette packs onto their painted canvases. Lennon, in a less structured way, was exploring the possibilities of matching two different but related forms of electronically generated sound: the deliberate form of a studio-recorded popular song and the spontaneous form of a live spoken-word performance.

Lennon resented that "I Am The Walrus" took a backseat as the B-side to McCartney's "Hello, Goodbye" on the Beatles' next single, issued in November 1967. Yet if there was no question which song was more impressive on artistic grounds, it was also clear which boasted a more commercial sound. "Hello, Goodbye" was another in the long line of crowd-pleasing potboilers that McCartney seemed to turn out effortlessly. In fact, he later said that the song "almost wrote itself" with its yes–no, black–white lyrical exchanges. The song was given a very polished production and an impassioned McCartney vocal, especially in the fade-out, and it went straight to number one. (It was also the subject of another Beatles promotional film, a slapdash affair featuring dancing girls in Hawaiian skirts that was salvaged only by some ludicrously spastic dancing by Lennon.)

The final song in this cycle is "Lady Madonna," recorded in February 1968, just days before the Beatles left for India. The idea was to put out a single in absentia that would keep fans and the record company happy while the Beatles occupied themselves with spiritual explorations. On the B-side, Harrison's "The Inner Light," anticipated the Indian journey both lyrically and musically, but McCartney's "Lady Madonna" was not without its own humanistic concerns. Behind a boogie-woogie beat driven by a fine piano lick, Paul once again champions the Everyman, though this time it is an Everywoman. His lyrics express a sympathy and empathy for the harried, economically trying life of single mothers decades before they were discovered by journalists and sociologists. There are no weekend getaways, romantic or otherwise, for Lady Madonna—"Friday night arrives without a suitcase"—and the question of how she makes ends meet is no mere rhetorical query. Perhaps she has to rely on public assistance, which would explain why "Tuesday afternoon is never ending" and why the failure of her check—the "Wednesday morning papers"—to come leaves her worried about a mere run in her stockings; she can't afford to just run out and buy a new pair. Yet she is not defined solely by her troubles. When she lies down to rest for a minute, there is music playing in her head.

Although "Lady Madonna" became yet another number one hit, the larger *Magical Mystery Tour* period was later seen by many as the beginning of the end for the Beatles. Brian Epstein's death the previous August, it was said, had left the group to its own devices managerially, the dangers of which were soon made plain by the disaster of the *Magical Mystery Tour* film. Epstein's death, moreover, was portrayed as opening the door to domination of the group by McCartney, whose sometimes overbearing manner in turn caused resentment on the part of John, George, and Ringo.

This interpretation of events was not without foundation, but it overlooked key facts. First, by 1967, Epstein no longer controlled the Beatles; he had not wanted them to stop touring or to issue the luxurious *Sgt Pepper* cover, for example, but had been overruled in both cases. Certainly his organizational skills were missed, but the Beatles had long since begun charting their own course. Moreover, while it is true that Paul was the driving force behind the *Mystery Tour* project, his bossiness was nothing new; the other Beatles were quite used to it, and quite used to standing up to it. Of course the four of them had disagreements, as they always had, but whatever strains existed among the Beatles when they left for India in February 1968, unity and affection remained the dominant characteristics of their group dynamic. They continued to have a good time with one another in the studio; one listen to their off-mike laughing and joking while recording "Lady Madonna," or their hilarious 1967 Christmas fan club disc—where they send themselves up as "The Ravellers," singing nostalgically about "Plenty of jam jars, baby"—confirms that. Their togetherness, in fact, was so extreme that they seriously considered buying a Greek island where they would all live together with their wives and children. And, of course, the Indian trip was a communal adventure as well. In short, most of the evidence suggests that, as of the start of 1968, the Beatles were not, in fact, destined to break up. Not yet.

CHAPTER 19

The Ballad of John and Yoko

JOHN LENNON ONCE REMARKED THAT IN THE COURSE OF HIS CAREER HE HAD CHOSEN TO WORK WITH ONLY TWO PART-ners, Paul McCartney and Yoko Ono, adding proudly, "That ain't bad picking." To Lennon's great annoyance, however, he was virtually alone in this opinion, at least when it came to Yoko Ono. The world adored the artistic partnership of Lennon–McCartney, but it barely tolerated that of johnandyoko, as John christened them, and not simply because of resentment of Ono's supposed role in breaking up the Beatles. While John was "overawed by her talent" and what he called her "sixteen track voice," the public was more often bewildered and appalled by Ono's baffling kookiness and onstage shrieking. What in the world did he see in her?

One important exception was John's friend Pete Shotton. Although Shotton had ample experience with Ono's difficult personality, having felt the lash of her wrathful, manipulative arrogance more than once, he nevertheless maintained that "she was the best thing that ever happened to [John]." Not only was Yoko the love of John's life, maintained Shotton, she liberated him to be what "he'd always most wanted to be: an Artist, with a capital A." A second important excep-tion, though only a partial one, was Paul McCartney. Affirming the latter half of Shotton's opinion, Paul said that Yoko had freed John to explore the avant-garde in ways that had not been possible during John's married years in suburbia. "In fact she wanted more," said Paul. "Do it more, do it double, be more daring, take all your clothes off! She always pushed him, which he liked, nobody had ever pushed him like that."

It was ironic that McCartney made this comment, for of course he himself had pushed John very hard during their years of collaboration, albeit in a very different way. Yet Paul was John's friend as well as his partner, and as a friend, he could not help but see how deeply in love with Yoko John was. Indeed, John always felt that Paul tried to say as much in "Hey, Jude," the magnificent ballad-cum-anthem that Paul wrote shortly after John and Yoko became a couple.

"I know I'm sounding like one of those fans who reads things into it, but you *can* hear it as a song to me," John later said. When John mentioned his suspicion to Paul, Paul denied it, explaining that "Hey, Jude" was actually about himself (and in fact, Paul's future wife, Linda Eastman, did enter his life at about this time). Yet John persisted in his interpretation, and not without reason. Although Paul had started writing "Hey, Jude" one day while driving out to comfort John's son, Julian, during the divorce of his parents, many of the lyrics do seem directed more at a grown man on the verge of a powerful new love, especially the lines "you have found her now go and get her" and "you're waiting for someone to perform with." As John saw it, "The words 'go out and get her'—subconsciously [Paul] was saying, Go ahead, leave me. On a conscious level, he didn't want me to go ahead. The angel in him was saying, 'Bless you.' The devil in him didn't like it at all, because he didn't want to lose his partner."

Paul's losing his partner was the last thing anyone would have expected when Yoko Ono first appeared on the scene. According to McCartney, it was actually he who met Ono first, when she asked him for old songwriting manuscripts for a project she was doing with avant-garde composer John Cage. Paul declined but suggested she check with his mate, John. Ono and Lennon met for the first time on November 9, 1966, in London, at the avant-garde Indica Gallery that McCartney had helped found, the night before an exhibit of Ono's work. Ono then pursued Lennon relentlessly, seeking patronage. Lennon's wife

Cynthia recalled that Yoko not only barraged their house in Kenwood with dozens of phone calls and letters but would also wait in the driveway, no matter the weather, hoping to snatch a few words with John. Eventually she must have succeeded, for one day John instructed Shotton, who had been appointed a director of the Beatles' new company, Apple, to meet with Ono. When she nervously requested two thousand pounds to finance her next exhibit, Lennon told Shotton to grant it.

Shotton's recollections are invaluable to understanding the romance of John and Yoko, for he was at Lennon's house the night John and Yoko say they first became lovers, and he was the first person John confided in the morning after. Shotton had assumed that Yoko was merely a casual sexual conquest, a night of fun for John while Cynthia was away on holiday, but John's reverential demeanor the next morning quickly disabused Pete of such notions. "This is *it*, Pete," said John, gulping down a cup of tea and a boiled egg, in a hurry to return to Yoko upstairs. "This is what I've been waiting for all me life." He then asked Shotton to go find a new house where he and Yoko could live together.

Shotton was flabbergasted. He didn't doubt his friend's resolve, but how long would it last? John had always been a man of intense but often fleeting enthusiasms. Moreover, he had been acting quite peculiarly recently, even by the eccentric standards of John Lennon. Barely twenty-four hours earlier, for example, he had decided in all seriousness that he was Jesus Christ, come back again. This revelation had come to John during an LSD trip, but he was no less convinced of it when he woke up the following day, and he was determined to tell the world. He insisted on immediately convening a meeting of the Apple inner circle—the three other Beatles, plus Shotton, Neil Aspinall, and Derek Taylor. When John announced his news, the others were stunned into silence; they could see that he meant it. Thus no one laughed or challenged his declaration. Rather, they agreed that this development was too important to deal with hastily; what was needed was time to absorb its significance and reflect upon its implications. And meanwhile, couldn't everybody use a quick drink or three?

John soon forgot his Christ fixation, as the others no doubt hoped he would. Yet the story is important beyond illustrating Lennon's colorful unpredictability, for it also sheds light on the other Beatles' states of mind at the time they learned of John's liaison with Yoko: To them, the Japanese artist must have seemed yet another example of John's fascination with the bizarre, a fad that would run its course, probably sooner rather than later, and be forgotten. They soon found out otherwise. The exact date of John and Yoko's first night together is unknown, but it was sometime in the latter half of May 1968, just days before the Beatles began recording the so-called White Album, officially titled *The Beatles*. Whether John introduced Yoko to any of the Beatles separately is unknown, but certainly everyone met her when they assembled at Abbey Road on May 30 for the first day of work, for John now insisted on having Yoko by his side at all times.

And not just by his side. Beginning with that very first session, Yoko also took part in the recording process. The song of the day was John's "Revolution," his most explicitly political composition yet. The Beatles eventually released three separate versions of "Revolution"—two appeared on the White Album and one as the B-side to the "Hey, Jude" single—but the two White Album versions actually began life as a single track. It was that track the Beatles were taping this day; its first four minutes were the slow guitar-shuffle later titled "Revolution 1," its last six minutes the chaotic instrumental and vocal jamming that became the montage titled "Revolution 9." Not until take eighteen was the freak-out part added, however; until then, each take had averaged only five minutes in length and concentrated solely on the song proper. But for some reason, take eighteen just kept going, the other Beatles bashing away on their various instruments as John and Yoko screamed and moaned and Yoko offered such enigmatic utterances as "You become naked."

Lennon later attributed the montage idea to Ono's influence, and his original demo tape of "Revolution" confirms his remark. Shortly before the May 30 Abbey Road session, the four Beatles had met at George Harrison's house to tape demo versions of some twenty-three new compositions, most of which ended up on the White Album. John's "Revolution" demo contains no hint of the weirdness later appended to the song, and it is revealing in other respects as well. At a time when student revolutions were raging throughout Europe and the United States, John wanted "Revolution" to be the Beatles' next single, a statement of the band's views on the Vietnam War and the ways and means of social change. Paul and George, however, contended that the slow version of the song was not upbeat enough to succeed as a single. John disputed this, but his demo tape seems to side with Paul and George, for its version of "Revolution" is considerably faster than the version taped on May 30. In fact, it is nearly as fast as the blistering version taped in July and released as a single, though it sounds much less raucous, since the only instrument it features is John's chugging acoustic guitar, charmingly augmented by handclaps and falsetto backing vocals from the other Beatles.

George, Paul, and Ringo added various overdubs to the ten-minute version of "Revolution" during the June 4 session as well, but two days later John and Yoko took the last six minutes of the take and began adding the many sound effects and tape loops that would transform it into the baffling "Revolution 9." Although George Harrison helped briefly, this recording was essentially John and Yoko's baby; Paul and Ringo did not participate, and Paul apparently disapproved of its being included on the White Album at all. This divergence of opinion was a good illustration of McCartney's remark about his and Lennon's differing attitudes about avant-garde work. Certainly Paul had no animus toward experimental recordings; as Lewisohn points out, Paul had led the Beatles' creation of a similar sound montage some seventeen months earlier, in January 1967. But that montage had been given to a London theater group, not released on record as part of the Beatles' formal body of work, as John proposed for "Revolution 9." But John, fortified now by Yoko's example and encouragement, would have it no other way.

As the Beatles moved on to subsequent White Album songs, beginning with Ringo's first solo composition, "Don't Pass Me By," it became increasingly clear that Yoko was there to stay. John's message to the rest of the Beatles recording team, George Martin recalled, was "Yoko is now part of me. In other words, as I have a right and left hand, so I have Yoko, and wherever I am, she is. That was a bit difficult to deal with. . . . To begin with, everyone was irritated by it." And not least because Ono did not merely keep John company in the studio, she also weighed in freely with comments and criticisms of the Beatles' work. By her own admission, she knew nothing about rock 'n' roll music, but that didn't stop her. When the Beatles were recording John's "Sexy Sadie," for example, Yoko interjected after one take that she thought they could do better. John, caught between his new love and his longtime mates, quickly stepped into the breach, saying, "Well, maybe *I* can."

John regarded Yoko as his artistic equal, if not superior, but it was plain that he was a minority of one in this respect, even if the other Beatles were careful not to say so directly. (The closest any of the Beatles inner circle came to speaking on the record about Yoko's musical abilities was George Martin, who commented after the Beatles broke up that Yoko Ono was not a substitute for Paul Mc-Cartney any more than Linda Eastman was a substitute for John Lennon.) John took the Beatles' coolness toward Yoko as a personal affront, conveniently overlooking that it was he who was changing the rules on *them*. Prior to Yoko, outsiders had generally been prohibited from eavesdropping on the Beatles in the studio; even close associates like Brian Epstein and publisher Dick James were encouraged to transact their business and leave. Now John was not only unilaterally ignoring these strictures, he was all but installing Ono as a de facto member of the group. Her constant presence and frequent intrusions annoyed the other Beatles, undermining the lighthearted togetherness and extraordinary synergy that had always been so vital to their studio magic. Lewisohn, not a writer given to speculative or pejorative judgments, has observed that the union of John and Yoko "had an undeniably negative bearing on the functioning of the Beatles as a unit," for it "inhibit[ed] the others and ma[de] them feel uncomfortable and ill at ease in what had always been their ideal environment and refuge away from the madness outside."

John being John, he apparently thought he had the right to do whatever he wanted; the Beatles, after all, were his group. And John being in love with Yoko, he could not fathom how anyone could fail to share his worshipful attitude toward her, both as a woman and as an artist. Rejecting John's assertions that the staff at Apple hated Yoko,

Derek Taylor said, "No one in this building *hates* her. *Hate!* That's a very strong accusation and an extreme assumption. I can't say as I blame him for thinking that sometimes, but the reason he feels that way is because we don't *love* her." John's feelings for Yoko were so obsessive that he felt compelled to warn Paul—quite unnecessarily, Paul later emphasized—not to make a play for her. And Yoko herself later explained that the reason she accompanied John everywhere at Abbey Road, even into the toilet, was not because she wanted to, but because John was afraid to leave her alone in a roomful of men, since surely they would desire her as much as he did.

To John, Yoko was "this goddess of love and the fulfillment of my whole life." After years of feeling that no one was in his tree, he was ecstatic to discover someone who was "as barmy as me!" In John's eyes, he and Yoko were so much alike that she was "me in drag." Each had an eccentric, alienated, irrepressible perspective on reality that left them feeling alone in the world, "with a real need to do something to act out your madness," as Yoko put it. Thus they recognized each other as soulmates, sharing a connection so deep and transcendent that even John's wife had to acknowledge it. When she walked in on John and Yoko after their first night together, Cynthia recalled, "I knew immediately I saw them together that they were right for each other. I knew I'd lost him. . . . It was a meeting of two minds and nobody could fight that."

John claimed in one story that he and Yoko had been on the same wavelength from the very first time they met, some eighteen months before they apparently became lovers. When he offered her an imaginary five shillings to hammer an imaginary nail into one of her art pieces at the Indica Gallery, said John, "She got it and I got it and the rest, as they say in all the interviews we do, is history." But John told a lot of stories, and like most people he believed what he liked to believe, especially when it came to him and Yoko. Perhaps it did happen the way John said it did, for him anyway; but then he was the one that fell for her, not vice versa. In the very interviews that John referred to, for example, one does not find Yoko talking about falling in *love* with John, certainly not in the passionate, all-consuming sense that he did with her. For her, the attraction seemed to be more a matter of companionship and intellect; she had finally met someone who understood who she was, and loved her for it. He, on the other hand, had met "Don Juan," his spiritual guru.

Yoko was a mother figure to John, as she herself admitted, filling the gaping hole left in John's life after the double loss of his biological mother. "I was probably the successor to Aunt Mimi," Ono told Lennon biographer Ray Coleman. John had been the boss in previous relationships, often imposing his will through physical violence. The lines "I used to be cruel to my woman / I beat her and kept her apart / From the things that she loved" in *Sgt Pepper*'s "Getting Better" were autobiographical, John later confessed, adding, "I will have to be a lot older before I can face in public how I treated women as a youngster." Although John abused Cynthia more than once, Yoko denied that he ever hit her, and it is unlikely she would have stood for such behavior; she was the dominant one in this relationship.

It was a role she had been accustomed to since childhood. Born into a wealthy Tokyo family, she had grown up in a house with dozens of servants; at school, she forced her classmates to vote again when she wasn't given the role she wanted in the school play. As soon as she realized how smitten John was with her, recalled Pete Shotton, the nervousness Yoko had initially displayed evaporated and she revealed herself as "a strong-willed, domineering tigress." One night, as Shotton was driving both John and Yoko home, Shotton took a wrong turn and briefly lost his bearings. From the backseat, Ono erupted in rage, shrieking, "What's wrong with you, I want to go home," as if Shotton were her chauffeur. Later, when Pete was good enough to offer to help John and Yoko clean up their apartment in the minutes before a police drug squad was due to arrive, Yoko hissed at John to get rid of him. In 1976, when Shotton happened to be passing through New York and hadn't seen John in five years, John had to get permission before inviting Pete over for the evening. When John wanted to repeat the occasion one more time before Pete returned to England, Yoko actively opposed it, in keeping with her pattern of discouraging contact between John and his oldest friends, including the other Beatles, who she claimed merely upset him.

Although John denied the oft-made accusation that Yoko controlled him, the evidence is difficult to interpret any other way. Referring to the famous photo of John and Yoko that was taken the day before his death, showing a naked John curled in the fetal position around a distant Yoko, critic Robert Christgau commented, "As both of them were happy to make clear to Annie Leibovitz's camera, Yoko encouraged in her husband an infantile or even fetal dependence." Moreover, John was the first to admit that it was *Yoko* who kicked *him* out prior to their separation in 1973 (though he was silent about her dispatching their twenty-three-year-old Chinese secretary, May Pang, to serve as her eyes, ears, and sexual substitute during John's notorious "lost weekend" of drunken rowdiness). Furthermore, it was John who begged Yoko repeatedly to let him return. But she was the teacher who "taught me everything I fucking know," he said, and he was the pupil. She didn't let him come back, John said, until he had learned what he was supposed to learn.

In one of his last songs, "Woman," John professed that he would be forever in Yoko's debt. She had literally saved his life. Specifically, she had woken him up and liberated him from the suffocating self-indulgence and lethargy he associated with being a Beatle. "That's how the Beatles ended," John later maintained. "Not because Yoko split the Beatles, but because she showed me what it was to be Elvis Beatle and to be surrounded by sycophants and slaves who are only interested in keeping the situation as it was. And that's a kind of death." As usual, John was overstating the point, and in any case it was not the other Beatles' fault that the world surrounded them with madness. But listen to the love songs on John's *Imagine* album, where he sings that "for the first time in my life . . . I see the wind / Oh, I see the trees," and his rejuvenation is unmistakable. He is experiencing life anew, as if reborn.

Yoko also helped John return to the outrageous, impassioned, devil-may-care abandon of his youth. Although he and Yoko were sincere about their peace campaign, John confessed to Shotton that many of their public events—their nude album cover, their bed-ins, the news conferences they held from inside bags—were simply adult versions of the practical jokes John and Pete used to play as kids, except that John and Yoko now passed them off as avant-garde art. If the outside world blamed Yoko for leading John astray, those who knew him well recognized that in fact it was "just John being John," as Ringo put it.

If Yoko Ono did not directly cause the disbanding of the Beatles, she plainly was the catalyst that initiated John's inexorable withdrawal from the group. Reflecting on the Beatles' breakup, Paul later said, "Looking back, it was largely that John needed a new direction that he went into headlong, helter skelter. . . . He wanted to live life, do stuff and there was no holding back with John. And it was what we all admired him for. So we couldn't really say: 'Oh, we don't want you to do that, John. Stay with us.' You'd feel so wimpy. It *had* to happen." John agreed: "The old gang of mine was over the moment I met her. I didn't consciously know it at the time, but that's what was going on."

Nevertheless, despite the tensions that arose during the recording of the White Album, there remained a lot of affection between John and the other Beatles. While rehearsing "Hey, Jude" in front of television cameras that July, for example, John teased Paul after one take by intoning in a mock-sentimental voice, "Well, I felt closer to it that time, Paul, I felt closer to it." When Ringo complained that he kept getting his trousers caught in his drum kit, John shot back, "Take 'em off!" And during a live televized performance of the song, an unmistakable look of loving friendship passed between John and Paul after John tried to make Paul break into laughter in the middle of his vocal. These are the kinds of moments that give credence to what John later hinted at separately: that he would not necessarily have chosen to break completely from his three longtime friends and partners. But on the other hand, if he did have to choose, there was no doubt which partnership was most important to him. "You see, I presumed that I would just be able to carry on and just bring Yoko into our life [as Beatles]," John explained in 1970. "But it seemed that I had to either be married to them or Yoko, and I chose Yoko, and I was right."

CHAPTER 20

Inner Turmoil, Creative Abundance (*The Beatles*)

IF IGNORANCE IS BLISS, ADMIRERS OF THE BEATLES WERE IN A STATE OF NIRVANA DURING THE SUMMER OF 1968. THE outside world knew, of course, that the Beatles had gone to India together over the winter and that John Lennon was now running around with some Japanese woman named Yoko Ono. The more sharp-eared had also heard about Apple, the company the Beatles had founded in the fall of 1967 to manage their future creative endeavors. But no one outside the Beatles' inner circle knew about the turmoil that Ono and Apple had engendered within the band during the recording sessions for what later became known as the White Album. Both Lennon and McCartney later cited the White Album sessions as the time when the Beatles' breakup really began. Starr and Harrison shared in the disenchantment; Ringo went so far as to quit the band in frustration for a couple of weeks in August 1968. All these unhappy tidings were kept secret at the time, however. Indeed, the release of the *Yellow Submarine* cartoon movie on July 17 only reinforced the prevailing image of the Beatles as a united, fun-loving foursome.

Then, on August 30, came the release of "Hey, Jude" and "Revolution." It had been nearly six months since the Beatles had been heard from musically, but the "Hey, Jude"/"Revolution" single made the wait seem worth it. One advantage of ignorance was that because the public was not distracted by the ego battle between Lennon and McCartney over who got the A-side of the single—Paul prevailed with "Hey, Jude"—it was free to respond purely to the music. And on musical grounds, there was only cause to rejoice, for John and Paul were both right: "Hey, Jude" and "Revolution" were each good enough to warrant A-side recognition, just as "Strawberry Fields" and "Penny Lane" had been.

The Beatles filmed live—actually, semilive—performances of both songs for television audiences in Great Britain and the United States, and the excitement they generated is palpable even at a distance of more than twenty-five years. Although only the vocals were truly live, no one who saw these clips could doubt that the Beatles could rock with the best of them. The clip of "Revolution" showed John, George, and Paul in front of microphones playing their guitars, with Ringo and his drum kit occupying a raised podium behind them. John in particular was a serious longhair by then, his center-parted locks falling down to his shoulders, and both his vocals and his subject matter further under-lined how far he had traveled since the moptop days. His opening howl, coming on the heels of a fiercely insistent, very fuzzy lead guitar, was more a call to arms than a joyful shriek, and his lyrics proclaimed his readiness for a radical change in the existing social order. The only question was how to make it happen.

Astonishingly, some on the militant left attacked "Revolution" as not revolutionary enough, but Lennon's lyrics stand up to history's scrutiny far better than such criticisms do. Though less trusting and idealistic than the previous summer's "All You Need Is Love," "Revolution" continued Lennon's insistence that political actions be judged on moral rather than ideological grounds. Thus he refused to support "people with minds that hate." At the same time, practicality mattered, too; whatever one thought of Mao's China, it was self-defeating to preach his brand of revolution to Western masses who feared him. But if you had a better idea, Lennon was all ears; in fact, he'd *love* to see the plan. In the opening lines of the song he didn't shy away when his unnamed counterpart advocated revolution as a means of curing society's ills; on the contrary, John was eager to hear him out. After all, as he sang twice in reply, he wanted to change the world as much as anyone.

And if that meant violence? The question of whether the ends justify the means is one of the oldest in political ethics, and Lennon was understandably uncertain about how it should be answered. On his demo tape back in May, he had sung "you can count me out" of any revolution that entailed destruction. He soon changed his mind, however, and not just once. Overdubbing his vocal to the slow version of "Revolution" on June 4, he had sung "you can count me out [and] in." On July 10, when taping the faster version of "Revolution" that was released as a single, he reverted back to "out." But when the Beatles did the fast version on television that September, he switched back again to both "out" and "in"—perhaps the best answer possible, for it recognized both the desirability of nonviolence and the reality of what actually happens during most revolutions, as well as during "just wars" waged against the likes of Hitler, which is that the bad guys usually don't give up without a fight.

With Lennon becoming more political with each passing day, not to mention more determined to reassert his leadership within the Beatles, it could not have been easy for him to concede the A-side of the single to McCartney's "Hey, Jude." But John could see that the song was a "masterpiece," as he later put it, and in the face of apparently unanimous agreement from the rest of the Beatles recording team he eventually gave way. "Hey, Jude" went on to become one of the biggest-selling singles in pop music history. And competitiveness aside, Lennon's fondness for the song was such that he passionately defended one of its key lines when McCartney wanted to cut it. When playing "Hey, Jude" for John (and Yoko) the first time, Paul had bashfully explained that the phrase "the movement you need is on your shoulder" was mere filler; he'd replace it later. But John vetoed Paul's idea. In a mirror image of his reaction years before to "I Saw Her Standing There," when he insisted on replacing Paul's clichéd second line with the phrase "you know what I mean," John exclaimed that the shoulder line in "Hey, Jude" made perfect sense. Like so many Beatles lyrics, it told you to believe in yourself; everything you needed to turn sadness into joy was right there, as close as your shoulder.

As befit one of the great anthems in rock 'n' roll, "Hey, Jude" was also a model of the Beatles' gift for simplicity. The verse unfolded over three basic chords, F major, C major, and B-flat. This 1, 5, 4 chord progression was then flipped on its head, as it were, during the song's refrain; the initial top chord of C was replaced by E-flat, with B-flat becoming the base of the new triangle. Meanwhile, the lyrics of the refrain were literally simple beyond words—just line after line of "nah, nah nah nah-nah-nah nah, nah-nah-nah nah, Hey, Jude." But by then the song had acquired enough levels of emotion that the listener could put his or her own meanings to these sounds while singing along with everybody else.

At over seven minutes in length, "Hey, Jude" was the longest song the Beatles ever released. It began quite gently, with Paul singing alone to his own piano accompaniment, but it gradually grew into a massive musical force. As more and more instruments and backing vocals were layered around the basic melody, the song swelled like a mighty river being fed by one tributary after another. In addition to the Beatles themselves, a thirty-six-piece orchestra was employed to give extra depth and breadth to the long fade-out. Besides playing their various violins, flutes, and trombones, the outside musicians were also encouraged to clap and sing along during the refrain. Finally, on top of this huge rolling wave of sound came McCartney's fade-out vocal, a series of manic yelps, screams, stutters, and oral explosions that ranks among the most inspired performances of his career.

Also singing along during the televised performance of "Hey, Jude" were some three hundred lucky fans, recruited at the last minute to serve as the Beatles' live audience inside Twickenham Film Studios. Young, old, male, female, black, brown, and white, the extras began the session grouped in a large circle around the Beatles. But as the song proceeded further and further into the fade-out, the circle gradually tightened until Ringo and Paul in particular were so tightly hemmed in by clapping, swaying fans that they could hardly move, much less play their instruments. Neither seemed to mind. It was a quintessential sixties moment, a touching tableau of contentment and togetherness.

What the audience didn't know was that the Twickenham performance was virtually Ringo's first day back at work after having quit the Beatles on August 22. He had apparently felt taken for granted by the other Beatles, superfluous to the group effort, and weary of the increasing bickering within the band. Many were the evenings when Ringo would arrive at Abbey Road on time only to be kept waiting and waiting while the others showed up whenever they felt like it. Probably most disconcerting was Ringo's feeling that he wasn't drumming very well, a feeling that Paul in particular had done much to encourage. Not only was Paul in the habit of lecturing Ringo on how to drum, he sometimes even shunted him aside and did the drumming himself. Indeed, it was after Paul had been hectoring Ringo about his drumming on "Back In The U.S.S.R." that Ringo walked out of Abbey Road in midsession. After a few days passed and the other Beatles realized that this was no overnight tantrum, they invited Ringo to a meeting at George's house to implore him to return to the group. He was as much a Beatle as anyone, they assured him, and the greatest drummer the band could ever have. It took a while to soothe Ringo's feelings, but on September 3 he returned to Abbey Road, where he found his drum kit surrounded by flowers.

Ringo's defection was symptomatic of deeper troubles within the group, however. Besides Paul's bossiness, there was John's obsession with Yoko. The other Beatles felt slighted by John and irritated by Yoko's interference; John, in turn, resented their resentment. "There was a definite strained relationship right from the White Album, there was a lot of alienation between us and him," George recalled, adding, "There was alienation amongst all of us." The recording sessions that used to be orgies of fun and creativity were now often dour, humorless affairs, punctuated by Apple business meetings and darkened by lost tempers, swearing, and shouting matches. By no means was every session unpleasant, but for a group whose extraordinary personal chemistry had always been such a strength, it was a bad sign. The deterioration in civility cost the Beatles a key member of their recording team. Engineer Geoff Emerick, whose ingenuity had been vital to the accomplishments of both *Revolver* and *Sgt Pepper*, resigned on the spot after one nasty outburst too many.

The Beatles were also confronting the paradox of having too much talent for their own good. The internal competitiveness that had previously propelled the group to ever greater heights of achievement now began turning brother against brother. Paul remained as prolific a songwriter as ever. And now that the trip to India and the arrival of Yoko had reawakened John's artistic energies, he was composing songs at a rate not seen since the *Hard Day's Night* period. John was also growing increasingly critical of what he ridiculed as Paul's weakness for "granny music"—songs like "Martha My Dear" and "Honey Pie." Meanwhile, George was feeling taken for granted almost as much as Ringo was. He, too, was writing more and better songs, but the others seemed too wrapped up in their own egos to pay much attention. Indeed, according to Harrison, the other Beatles even turned a deaf ear to "While My Guitar Gently Weeps," the first great composition of George's career and perhaps the single most impressive song on the White Album.

"While My Guitar Gently Weeps" was one of twenty-three songs the Beatles taped during demo sessions held at George's house prior to the White Album, along with such other standouts as "Revolution," "Julia," "Back In The U.S.S.R.," "Dear Prudence," and "Blackbird." But while most of these songs emerged on the album in relatively similar form, "While My Guitar Gently Weeps" underwent a spectacular transformation, as radical as what had happened to "Strawberry Fields Forever" eighteen months before.

The Beatles didn't get around to recording "While My Guitar Gently Weeps" until July 25, nearly two months after the White Album sessions had begun, and their attitude toward the song left George distinctly unimpressed. "I worked on that song with John, Paul and Ringo one day and they were not interested in it at all," Harrison later recalled. "And I knew inside of me that it was a nice song." George responded by taping a solo version of the song during the July 25 session, and "nice" doesn't begin to describe its beauty and power. Plaintive and spare, it was the first formal take of "While My Guitar Gently Weeps."

Virtually the only sounds on this take are Harrison's flawlessly picked and strummed acoustic guitar and his aching, meditative vocal. The sadness is overpowering when he sings of "the love there that's sleeping" within all of us; the chasm between the world as we know it and the world we could create is heartbreaking. He comforts himself with the thought that "with every mistake we must surely be learning," but this is a plea for progress, not an affirmation, and his guitar cannot keep from crying. And there is a last verse, later dropped, in which the singer, resigned to the idea that the world will go its own way no matter what, moves beyond mourning to acceptance. This last verse contains two of the most poetic lines Harrison ever wrote; it's a shame they were cut from the final version of the song. In any case, take one of "While My Guitar Gently Weeps" was a spine-tingling performance, made all the more poignant by its contrast with the electric version of the song found on the White Album, featuring Eric Clapton's shimmering lead guitar.

Apparently Harrison invited Clapton to contribute to the song partly as a retaliation against the other Beatles' apathy and quarreling. The two guitarists were driving into London together from their respective homes in Surrey on September 6 when George proposed the idea. Clapton was taken aback: "I can't do that. Nobody ever plays on Beatles records." But if John could bring Yoko into the Beatles more or less permanently, surely George could draft the finest lead guitarist in Great Britain to sit in for a single session. And as it happens, Clapton's presence in the studio that evening did put the other Beatles on their best behavior.

By this time, the band had recorded forty-four takes of two different arrangements of "While My Guitar Gently Weeps." Take twenty-five had already been selected as the basic rhythm track, and notwithstanding Harrison's complaints, it did not sound like the work of apathetic musicians. Listen to the opening seconds of the released version of the song: McCartney's strident, almost single-note piano riff and Starr's vehement, imploding cymbal come from take twenty-five. Now, over-dubs were being added to this take. In the course of seven hours of work inside Abbey Road's Studio Two, George taped his lead vocal, backed by Paul's harmonies, Paul played a fuzz bass, and Ringo spiced his drum track with extra percussion. Nevertheless, it was Clapton's magnificent lead guitar that dominated the session. Meaty, fluid, restrained, urgent, it was the work of a master.

Whether the raucous electric version of "While My Guitar Gently Weeps" is superior to the somber acoustic version is a judgment call; in retrospect, it seems unfortunate that the Beatles did not do what they did with "Revolution"—release both versions. The problem was, they already had more songs in hand than even a double album could accommodate; thus such fine compositions as George's "Not Guilty" and John's "Child Of Nature," both of which were taped during the May demo sessions at George's house, never made it onto an album until George and John's respective solo careers. What's more, George Martin had wanted to narrow the field even further. Unconvinced after listening to the May demo tapes that the Beatles had enough quality material to warrant a double album of thirty songs, he had advised them to separate the wheat from the chaff and put out "a really super album" with just fourteen to sixteen titles.

Martin had a point. There are plenty of great songs on the White Album, probably as many as on any Beatles album, but the album's overall effect was not as powerful as, say, *Sgt Pepper* or *Revolver*. Critics have attributed this shortcoming to the Beatles' diminished unity during this period, noting that the ensemble playing and song development of previous albums had now given way to more individually oriented recording; as John said of the White Album, "it was just me and a backing group, Paul and a backing group." But this reasoning doesn't quite persuade. For one thing, John was exaggerating; the four Beatles did work together on many of the tracks on the White Album. And, as "While My Guitar Gently Weeps" so powerfully demonstrated, internal turmoil did not have to result in mediocre music.

A second, more mundane explanation for the diffused effect of the White Album is simply that some of the songs that ended up on the album were not that strong to begin with. It's not, however, that they were downright bad, which is why it is difficult to take the next step from Martin's statement and list exactly which songs should have been cut from the album. (Martin never bit this particular bullet either.) For if tracks like Paul's "Wild Honey Pie," Ringo's "Don't Pass Me By," George's "Savoy Truffle," and John's "Glass Onion" did not match the Beatles' usual high standards, they were interesting enough in their various ways and certainly the equal of most other pop songs of the era. To abort such offerings would have required keen discipline and self-criticism, neither of which the Beatles seemed to possess at this moment. As Harrison would later remark about McCartney's solo career, everybody needs someone who can tell them the truth when their work isn't up to par. But when Martin tried to play that role on the White Album, the Beatles wouldn't hear of it. The egoism they had warned others against was now sapping their own strength; the happy unit they had once been was beginning to unravel.

But this is hindsight speaking. At the time, the White Album was judged by the music it contained; its songs were seen not as shards of glass reflecting the band's internal dissension but as a musical outpouring of overwhelming quantity, richness, and diversity. To be sure, careful listeners could detect more individuality in this collection—the paucity of group vocals and harmonies was especially noticeable—but this was not necessarily the album's most striking feature. For the White Album coincided as well with a general scaling-back of the studio tricks and production techniques that had distinguished every Beatles album since *Revolver*. Because so many of the songs were written in India, they were guitar-based, and, apart from such exceptions as "While My Guitar Gently Weeps," they did not sound all that different as demos than they did as finished album tracks. This move back to musical basics was complemented by the album's cover, an expanse of pure white whose minimalist elegance punctured the pretensions of the many garish imitations that had sprung up in the wake of *Sgt Pepper*. Indeed, the White Album's cover alone demonstrated that, creatively, the Beatles remained a good step and a half ahead of everyone else in popular music.

Almost as if to prove that all the fussing and fighting had not alienated their muse, the Beatles opened the White Album with "Back In The U.S.S.R.," the song Ringo had quit over. Paul had taken over the drum kit in Ringo's absence, and his performance gave credence to George Martin's separate remark that technically Paul was an even better drummer than Ringo was. Paul might not coax as much emotion from the drums as Ringo did, but "Back In The U.S.S.R." was straightahead rock 'n' roll, and Paul's tight, pounding beat was more than adequate for that. He got plenty of help from George and John, too; this was but one of the tracks that contradicted John's claim that there was no real, collective Beatlemusic on the White Album.

When Ringo walked out during the August 22 session, the other Beatles had kept working; by evening's end they had finished the rhythm track of "Back In The U.S.S.R." Actually, "evening's end" is a misnomer, for the Beatles were now literally recording all night. The August 22 session, for example, did not end until nearly five in the morning, and when George, John, and Paul returned to Abbey Road the following night to add overdubs, they did not end up leaving the studio until 3:00 A.M. But they left with the song completed, a remarkably quick piece of work. In addition to Paul's spirited lead vocal, George and John turned in some tearing lead and bass guitar work, as well as the high, swooping harmonies that validated Paul's reference to the song as "a kind of Beach Boys parody." None of these effects had been part of the "Back In The U.S.S.R." demo track, which featured only Paul singing to a briskly strummed acoustic guitar, along with very occasional, innocuous backing vocals from the other Beatles. Like "While My Guitar Gently Weeps," "Back In The U.S.S.R." was an exception to the White Album trend, in that it changed quite markedly between its demo and album incarnations. But in this case, the extra punch clearly improved the song.

After literally getting the album off to a roaring start, the jet engine sounds that had introduced "Back In The U.S.S.R." reappeared at the end of the song, providing a fade-in to John's lovely ballad "Dear Prudence." Because the Beatles happened to record "Dear Prudence" immediately after "Back In The U.S.S.R.," Paul again handled the drumming. But the instruments that stand out most are Paul's marvelously understated bass and John's deftly picked acoustic guitar. The guitar notes that gradually emerge from the engine's din are like the first rays of sun illuminating a gray dawn—calming yet vibrant, inexorable yet intriguing. John seems to have worked out this guitar pattern himself, for it is identical to what he plays on the demo of "Dear Prudence"; his vocal is also much the same.

At the end of the demo, John ad-libs a few lines of spoken commentary, smirking that the song is about a girl "who attended a meditation course in Rishikesh." No sooner have these words left John's lips than Paul is heard in the background harmonizing what sounds suspiciously like "Coo-koo." John barely manages to swallow a chuckle before rhetorically asking, "Who was to know that she would go completely berserk, under the care of Maharishi Mahesh Yogi?" "She" was Prudence Farrow, sister of the actress Mia Farrow; she had so deeply immersed herself in meditation at Rishikesh that she refused to come out of her bungalow for group activities. "So, we sang to her," John concludes wistfully, the result being this song. Yet like so much of Lennon's work, "Dear Prudence" transcends its specific origins to convey a larger message—the same message John had been spreading since "Nowhere Man": Don't hide from life, you have reason to smile, wake up and play your part in the grand scheme of things.

"Glass Onion," on the other hand, which came next on the White Album, was Lennon's reaction against people reading too *many* messages into his songs. Comprising a hodgepodge of references to earlier

Beatles songs, along with a few deliberately misleading "clues" like "the Walrus was Paul," it was a competent but unremarkable song; it probably would have been cut had the Beatles not overridden George Martin's advice and insisted on the White Album being double-sized. What's more, if John had had his way, the subsequent "Ob-La-Di, Ob-La-Da" probably would have met the same fate. Despite its infectious chorus and quirky story line, "Ob-La-Di, Ob-La-Da" was a prime example of the kind of schmaltzy McCartney music Lennon was growing increasingly impatient with. But at least "Ob-La-Di, Ob-La-Da" had a real melody. "Wild Honey Pie," which followed it, simply assaulted the ear; it sounded like someone had taken a hammer to a giant pocket watch until the springs inside collapsed in heavy, discordant agony. It was perhaps the most extreme case of self-indulgence on the album.

John's witty satire of a big-game hunter in "The Continuing Story of Bungalow Bill" was good, acerbic fun, despite Yoko's off-key warble of the line "Not when he looked so fierce," but it was the two concluding songs on side one that returned the album to the heights first scaled by "Back In The U.S.S.R." and "Dear Prudence." First came the humbling grandeur of "While My Guitar Gently Weeps," then the sprawling weirdness of "Happiness Is A Warm Gun." A favorite of John, Paul, and George's, "Happiness Is A Warm Gun" was a quintessential Lennon composition. It was three separate songs rolled into one; it changed tempos often and unexpectedly (in fact, the Beatles needed seventy takes to perfect the rhythm track); it was inspired in part by an item in the mass media, a magazine cover whose headline unironically declared, "Happiness Is A Warm Gun"; it featured John's deadpan humor; and it made plain his love for Yoko—his Mother Superior.

John had help writing the song. Derek Taylor contributed the opening line and helped shape the first passage's lyrics while he and Lennon were tripping on LSD one day. The song's second passage, however, invoked a different drug. To the distress of the other Beatles, Yoko had introduced John to heroin sometime in the summer of 1968; hence the line "I need a fix." (Lennon would drift toward outright addiction the following year, as described in his gut-churning 1969 single, "Cold Turkey.") Finally, the overtly sexual, spoken overdub in the third passage of "Happiness Is A Warm Gun," which begins, "When I hold you in my arms," seems to have been a satirical takeoff on the trite moon–June lyrics found in such fifties pop songs as the Everly Brothers' "All I Have To Do Is Dream." This is a speculation, but it is based directly on the May demo tapes, which captured an amusing moment during the recording of Lennon's "I'm So Tired." Near the end of the take, John breaks into a speech that sounds very similar in pace and intonation to what later appeared on "Happiness Is A Warm Gun." On the demo tape, however, John's tone is earnestly tongue-in-cheek as he half croons the words, "When I hold you in my arms / When you show each one of your charms / I wonder should I get up / And go to the funny farm."

Lennon once said that he preferred the White Album to *Sgt Pepper* because his own songs were better on the White Album. That may sound unfair to such *Pepper* gems as "A Day In The Life" and "With A Little Help From My Friends," but those were joint compositions with McCartney; John's White Album songs were very much solo creations. Their quality was indeed high, and far more consistently so than Paul's, as side two of the White Album in particular illustrates. Paul wrote five of the nine songs on side two, but only "Blackbird" belonged in the same company as John's "I'm So Tired" and "Julia." (Ringo's plodding "Don't Pass Me By" seems to have been more a concession to group equality than a serious musical offering, while George's "Piggies" kept the Beatles' countercultural flame alive with its withering portrait of bourgeois gluttony.)

Four of McCartney's five songs on side two were virtually one-man tracks—only "Rocky Raccoon" featured much input from the three other Beatles—and their erratic quality foreshadowed the ups and downs of Paul's solo career. "Blackbird" was a triumph of simplicity that worked very well as a solo track. The slight sentimentalism of "Martha My Dear" and "I Will," on the other hand, cried out for Lennon's corrective edge. "Why Don't We Do It In The Road" was somewhere in between. A belting blues number whose lyrics took the sixties ideal of free love to exhibitionist lengths, it showed off Paul's bad boy side and prodigious vocal powers but could have amounted to much more. Paul later said he wrote the song as "a ricochet off John," yet he invited only Ringo to play on the track. Too bad: some primal Lennon vocals and stinging Harrison guitar work could have elevated a good song to greatness.

The most beautiful and important song on side two of the White Album was "Julia," Lennon's paean to his dead mother. John recorded numerous demos of "Julia," but all of them sound very similar to the version found on the album, itself the only instance where John recorded a Beatles song completely solo. Like "I'm So Tired," "Julia" was one of the last songs recorded for the White Album, yet both songs had been written months before, during John's visit to India. Officially, he and Yoko were not yet a couple at that point, but certainly "Julia" and perhaps also "I'm So Tired" contain hints that Yoko was already much on his mind. The reference to Yoko in "Julia," via the line "Ocean child calls me," was explicit but disguised; Yoko means "ocean child" in Japanese. Given that the future lovers were regularly exchanging letters at this time, it seems reasonable to guess that the verse in "I'm So Tired" declaring that "my mind is set on you," was also directed at Yoko.

But again, one need not be aware of the personal subtext to appreciate the emotions Lennon conveys in these songs. In "I'm So Tired," his confusion and frustration produce an insomnia so profound that he would "give you everything I got for a little peace of mind." In "Julia," his tender, haunting plea for human connection begins with the disarming admission that "Half of what I say is meaningless" (a quote he lifted from Lebanese poet and novelist Kahlil Gibran's *The Prophet*). He then lays bare even more of his vulnerability by adding, "But I say it just to reach you." The song is filled with minor chords, reinforcing his melancholy and uncertainty, while the lyrics summon images of female beauty that seem as fleeting and bewitching as a vivid but incompletely remembered dream. In the end, alas, it is his need and longing that are most real, and since his heart remains unsatisfied, he must be content to speak his mind: song as therapy.

Side three is the rock 'n' roll segment of the White Album, and while none of its songs have the melody or mass appeal of, say, "Day Tripper" or "Paperback Writer," they leave no doubt that the Beatles were fundamentally a rock band, not a pop band that just happened to play rock 'n' roll. "Helter Skelter" in particular was, as Paul said, "the loudest, nastiest, sweatiest" rock song they could conceive of. Although an English person recognized "helter skelter" as a type of amusement park ride, to an American the term signified disorganized chaos. And, indeed, the first time the Beatles recorded the song at Abbey Road, they got so caught up in its heavy, screeching fury that they jammed on for more than ten minutes on one version, over twelve minutes on a second, and an epic, yet still tightly played, twenty-seven minutes on a third. On September 9, the night they taped the version of "Helter Skelter" heard on the record, they held the length down to four and a half minutes but went just as wild, both on tape and off. Ringo's impassioned scream, "I've got blisters on my fingers," was caught on tape, but had the Beatles also been filming a video that night, it would have shown George setting fire to an ashtray and running around the studio, wearing it on his head like a crown of fire.

As a young rocker, John used to tell Dylan that he listened to the sound of a song, not its words. The songs on side three reverted to that primitive conception of rock 'n' roll, both in their creation and in their performance, and one can feel the Beatles glorying in the rawness of it all. "Birthday," the opening number, was literally written on the spot in the studio. "Yer Blues" was essentially the same grinding guitar riff played over and over while Lennon screamed about feeling suicidal. The next song, "Mother Nature's Son," was a piece of McCartney-light that had somehow wandered down the wrong alley and got lost among the rough boys; it belonged elsewhere on the album, if at all. (One might say the same of Harrison's side-closer "Long, Long, Long," but it did provide a calm landing pad after "Helter Skelter.") "Everybody's Got Something To Hide Except Me And My Monkey" was, again, less a song than, as John admitted, a good opening line. But he teased that line into enough of a tune that he and the lads could have a good time with it, especially whoever was in charge of the clanging cowbell. Only "Sexy Sadie" on side three was more significant for its lyrics than its sound, even though its melody in the middle eight was a piece of loveliness, as befit the idealized vision of the heroine offered lyrically at that point. "Sexy Sadie" was, of course, not a woman but a man, specifically John's old friend the Maharishi. The song had been written in India, in a flash of shattered idealism, in the minutes after John had packed his bags and was waiting to leave following an unpleasant confrontation with the Maharishi.

John also dominated the fourth and final side of the White Album, largely by virtue of the two versions of "Revolution" featured there. (Of the three songs placed between these two tracks, Paul's "Honey Pie" offered yet another dollop of his endless supply of syrupy nostalgia,

George's "Savoy Truffle" was most notable for its beefy horns and a lyric that seemed to vent frustration at Paul—"We all know 'Ob-La-Di-Bla-Da' / But can you tell me where you are?"—while John thought so little of "Cry Baby Cry" that years later he denied having written it.) But back to "Revolution." By the time the White Album was released on November 22, 1968, the single version of "Revolution" had been out for nearly three months; people were used to hearing the song played fast and loud. Opening side four with a radically different arrangement gave the audience a glimpse inside the Beatles' creative process, and this sensation was heightened by the burst of studio chat from John and Paul at the top of the song. Politically interested listeners who now heard John sing to "count me out, in" of a revolution of destruction might have concluded that Lennon had grown more militant in the intervening months. This he had in some ways, but the lyrical correspondence was pure coincidence. As noted earlier, the album version of "Revolution" had actually been recorded first, as was the baffling "Revolution 9" sound collage. There was method as well as madness to the latter—as critic Tim Riley has observed, "no musical novice would have arrived at just this set of combinations" of sounds—and it was shrewdly introduced by the McCartney snippet "Can you take me back where I came from?" Still, most listeners were undoubtedly relieved when the last chants of "Block that kick" faded away and they found themselves transported to the Walt Disney–like wonderworld of "Goodnight."

Composing against type, it was Lennon who wrote "Goodnight," intending it as a lullaby for his son Julian, then five. John was right when he later said that the strings on "Goodnight" were "possibly overlush," but he was the one who told Martin to arrange them "like Hollywood." Ringo's warmly down-to-earth vocal saved the song from preciousness, however, and his whispered farewell at song's end to "everybody, everywhere" reestablished the personal connection between band and audience that had always been so vital to the Beatles' mass appeal.

The trouble was, the Beatles' connections with one another were now fraying as never before. They had thought of naming the White Album after Henrik Ibsen's play *A Doll's House*, but there was nothing childish or make-believe about their collective existence anymore. This was real life, and it was about to get grim.

CHAPTER 21

In My Hour of Darkness (*Let It Be*)

OF ALL THE FOURTEEN HUNDRED LIVE PERFORMANCES GIVEN BY THE BEATLES IN THE COURSE OF THEIR CAREER, PERhaps none was as famous as their final show: the rooftop concert that concluded the film *Let It Be*. Although the *Let It Be* film was not released until May 1970, its songs were actually recorded well over a year earlier; the rooftop concert itself took place on January 30, 1969. The Beatles had not played a truly live show since the end of their last American tour in August 1966, but the excitement they generated atop the Apple building that January afternoon showed they remained as charismatic and musically alive as ever. With the winter wind blowing back their shoulder-length hair and a lunchtime crowd of astonished office workers gathering down below, the Beatles played a forty-two-minute set consisting of five songs: "Get Back," "Don't Let Me Down," "I've Got A Feeling," "Dig A Pony," and "The One After 909," with the first three songs being played twice. If the performance was not one hundred percent studio-perfect, it came remarkably close, and the sheer joyful energy of the occasion more than compensated for the occasional forgotten lyric or misplaced harmony.

Indeed, one of the loveliest moments in the show occurred when John Lennon suddenly found himself at a loss for words at the start of the third verse of "Don't Let Me Down." Paul McCartney had been

263

singing harmony on the chorus, but the verses of this love song to Yoko were John's alone. So John did exactly what he had done at the Woolton church fete so many years ago, on the day he and Paul first met as Liverpool teenagers: He made up new words on the spot. Actually, this time they were more sounds than words, but they were real enough to bluff John's way through, and when he paused for breath after the next line, he flashed a huge grin of triumphant complicity Paul's way.

For the most part, though, the Beatles were in fine form throughout the set. The rhythm section of McCartney, Harrison, and Starr, augmented by guest keyboardist Billy Preston, was exceptionally tight. From the very first warm-up rehearsal of "Get Back," Ringo in particular was right on target, blasting the beat forward with clean, snapping strokes. Meanwhile, Paul's exuberant lead vocals showed just how glad he was to be in front of an audience again, even if he couldn't see most of them. The rooftop venue had been Paul's idea, an inspired outwitting of the fame monster that continued to dog the Beatles' every step. The Apple rooftop was about the only place left where the Beatles could play live without being overwhelmed by the mass hysteria that had driven them off the world stage in the first place. And if blasting rock 'n' roll through downtown London at midday disrupted business and caused a fuss, well, all the better; it made the show that much more of a happening.

The rousing vitality of the Beatles' performance made it plain that none of them had lost their musical touch, but it was John and Paul who seemed to have the most fun. John's famous closing line about hoping that the band passed the audition was but one of the jokes he and Paul dispensed in the course of their almost nonstop stage banter. Thus when the warm-up rehearsal of "Get Back" was greeted by a smattering of applause from the Beatles' rooftop entourage, Paul likened the reaction to that of a cricket match audience, quipping, "It looks like Ted Dexter [a famous English cricketer of the time] has scored another." Not to be outdone, John, in a laconic singsong voice, chimed in, "We've had a request from Martin and Luther." And when the police finally arrived to call things to a halt while the Beatles were reprising "Get Back" one last time, Paul was inspired to ad-lib to Loretta, the song's heroine, "you've been playing on the roofs again, and that's no good. . . . [Your mother's] gonna have you arrested!" The inside jokes, the wacky wordplay, the gleeful nose-thumbing at authority—it almost seemed as if the intervening years of glory and madness had somehow fallen away and the Beatles were back at the Cavern Club, four young phenoms out to conquer the world and have a rocking good time doing it.

Yet by the time *Let It Be* was actually released, on May 13, 1970, the Beatles had passed irrevocably into history. Those four young phenoms had indeed conquered the world and had lots of fun along the way, but after "having scaled every known peak of show business, [they] quite deliberately never came home again," as McCartney phrased it in a mock press release he read during the shooting of the film. *Let It Be* thus came to be regarded as the group's farewell album, even though *Abbey Road*, recorded in the summer of 1969, was actually the last album they made. Moreover, because both the album and film of *Let It Be* were released just after the Beatles' split had become public knowledge in April 1970, many journalists, critics, and other outsiders focused as much on what the film and album revealed about the breakup as they did on the music contained therein. The overclarity of hindsight caused the *Let It Be* film in particular to be regarded primarily as an exposé of the personal tensions that supposedly made the band's breakup inevitable. Indeed, to hear most Beatles books tell it, the entire *Let It Be* project was little more than a spotty, uninspired swan song by four jaded musicians who could barely stand one another anymore.

This gloomy view was not entirely groundless, at least as regards the Beatles' quarrelsomeness. Lennon later called the *Let It Be* recording sessions "the most miserable . . . on earth." Harrison dubbed them "the low of all time," and even the irrepressible McCartney recalled them as being "very sticky." As with the White Album, not every *Let It Be* session was blackened by nasty arguments and lost tempers, but a sufficient number of them were to make George Martin conclude that the group was self-destructing and that it was time for him to leave: "I thought, 'This is the end. I don't want to be part of this anymore.' "

One small but revealing measure of the Beatles' internal estrangement was their attitude toward the fan club Christmas disc of 1968. Every year since 1963, all four Beatles had put real effort into these discs, conceiving and performing skits and songs and gathering around a common microphone to tape good-humored holiday greetings. For the 1968 disc, however, each Beatle recorded his own contribution separately. What's more, John's contribution gave voice, albeit in code, to his anger at Paul, George, and Ringo for their less than welcoming attitude toward Yoko. John recited an absurdist prose poem describing how "two balloons called Jock and Yono" had "battled on against overwhelming oddities, including some of their beast friends," a veiled reference to the three other Beatles.

Meanwhile, the business of running Apple was proving more difficult than expected, engendering more and more disagreements and turning the Beatles into what none of them, save perhaps Paul, really wanted to be: businessmen. The most significant conflict was also the most explosive: who to name as the group's new business manager. On February 3, 1969, just four days after the rooftop concert, Allen Klein, a controversial figure who had negotiated lucrative record deals for the Rolling Stones and other pop musicians, was appointed to the post at the insistence of John, George and Ringo and despite the adamant opposition of Paul, who preferred lawyers Lee and John Eastman, the father and brother of his new fiancée, Linda Eastman. Clearly, the earlier all-for-one-and-one-for-all unity of the Beatles had evaporated.

Although he lost the argument over Klein, Paul continued to act as the Beatles' career planner and organizer, but this, too, proved a source of conflict. As Ringo later remarked, "Paul would want us to work all the time, because he was the workaholic." The other Beatles agreed to the *Let It Be* project only after McCartney, in his words, "slightly badgered them into it." Recalling the meeting in which he proposed the idea, Paul said that in late 1968 John, George, and Ringo were "very happy to not really work, because they were enjoying the rewards of their success . . . I was like, 'Hey, guys! C'mon! We can't sit around, we gotta do something. We're the Beatles!' "

McCartney favored a return to live performing, but the other Beatles, especially Harrison, wouldn't hear of touring. A compromise was eventually struck in which the band would give a single spectacular concert—perhaps in a Roman amphitheater—which would be filmed for later viewing. Rehearsals for this concert would also be filmed, so the public could eavesdrop on the Beatles' creative process. Finally, at John's insistence, the songs for the project were to be recorded as simply as possible, forsaking the overdubbing and other studio techniques that had distinguished the band's previous work. The Beatles would be shown "as nature intended . . . warts and all." In keeping with this return to basics, the working title of the project was *Get Back*.

But making plans did not vanquish the underlying lethargy, and before long fresh trouble was brewing. As Martin recalled, "In order to get everything together and organized, Paul would be rather over-bossy, which the other boys would dislike. But it was the only way of getting together. John would go wafting away with Yoko, George would say he wouldn't be coming in the next day. It was just a general disintegration." The most famous example of Paul's bossiness was captured on film, in a scene where he and George have a spat after Paul tells the guitarist how he should be playing his instrument. Paul had long been in the habit of giving such instructions, but apparently George had finally had enough. In a cold, sarcastic voice, he tells Paul, "I'll play whatever you want me to play, or I won't play at all if you don't want me to play. Whatever it is that will please you, I'll do it." Before the day was over, George had walked out, making him the second Beatle to quit the group in five months, even though, like Ringo before him, he returned to the band some days later.

Nevertheless, it oversimplifies a complex situation to think that the Beatles' feelings for one another during this period were unrelievedly bitter or that the discord afflicting them was entirely of their own making. In a sense, their rows were a measure of how much they still loved one another; after all, one doesn't bother to fight with someone one doesn't care about. Nor were all the words they exchanged harsh ones. At one point in the project, for example, George tells Paul, "When you write a song, I get into it completely, I feel as if I wrote it," adding, "There's so much [music] to get out, and there's no one better to get it out with than us." The problem was, the rest of the world felt the same way. It wanted the Beatles to keep putting out music constantly and indefinitely, regardless of what that meant for the Beatles themselves. The endless, adoring expectations of the outside world imposed immense personal and professional pressures, pressures the

Beatles had endured in the past but which now were catching up with them. Harrison snuck a barbed complaint into his 1968 Christmas disc contribution, declaring with transparent falseness that it was the Beatles' "faithful fans" who had "made our lives worth living." George and John were especially frustrated by the limitations imposed by the Beatles myth; to use George's word, each of the Beatles was "pigeonholed" into a certain role within the band, and there seemed no escape. If each of them had "been sick of the group" at one time or another in the past year, as even Paul admitted during filming, it was partly because of "the awful tension of being locked in each other's arms" without cease.

Yet whatever problems the Beatles had among themselves, the performance they gave on the Apple rooftop that January afternoon showed that they could still rise to the musical occasion when they chose to. And they proved the point again a day later when they stayed indoors to record the final versions of "Let It Be," "The Long And Winding Road," and "Two Of Us," again before cameras. These two performances yielded fully half of the twelve tracks included on the *Let It Be* album, and they would seem to discredit the notion that the Beatles' music had been diminished during this period by their personal difficulties.

That is not the full story, however. For prior to these two performances the Beatles had taped dozens of hours of rehearsals, many of which later surfaced on bootleg recordings. These tapes revealed that the same band that had thrilled the world with its televised performances of "All You Need Is Love" and "Hey, Jude" could also sound quite dreadful when its members put no effort into their playing. One may reasonably argue that it is unfair to judge a musical group on its private practice sessions; as with an actor or athlete, what matters is the public performance. Yet the discrepancy between the dispirited, incohesive, often out-of-tune-and-tempo rehearsals of the *Get Back* project and the purposeful yet fun-loving professionalism that the Beatles had displayed in the studio in years past was too dramatic to brush off so easily. At this point in their career, Lennon later said, "nobody was really into" rehearsing, and it showed.

The original *Get Back* album contained more than a hint of this lassitude and sloppiness, which probably explains why it was never issued. Assembled by Glyn Johns, an engineer drafted by Paul to assist on what would be the first album recorded at the Beatles' new studio in the Apple basement, the original *Get Back* album was markedly different from the *Let It Be* album that later replaced it. The only overlaps were "The One After 909," "Let It Be," "For You Blue," "Maggie Mae," and "The Long And Winding Road." Otherwise, *Get Back* included a different take of the title song (the same version released as a single); opted for studio versions of "Dig A Pony" and "I've Got A Feeling," rather than the rooftop versions found on *Let It Be*; featured neither "I Me Mine" nor "Across The Universe"; and filled its remaining space with songs not found on *Let It Be*, including "Don't Let Me Down," a cover of "Save The Last Dance For Me," an instrumental titled "Rocker," and a song Paul later released on his first solo album, "Teddy Boy."

There was also lots of studio chat wedged in among the various tracks, in keeping with the cinema verité aim of the project. Some of these spontaneous moments were very charming. For example, just before "The Long And Winding Road" began, an apparently straight-faced John asked Paul, "Are we *supposed* to giggle during the solo?" But for the most part, the unpolished nature of *Get Back* was distracting rather than exciting. The idea of releasing a record that was so "live" it included live mistakes may have sounded good in theory, but in practice Lennon's extended ranting on "Dig It" and McCartney's self-involved elaboration of "Teddy Boy" were more tiresome than engaging. The astonishingly flat singing that the two of them did on "Save The Last Dance For Me" was simply embarrassing.

When the Beatles received acetates of the original *Get Back* album in the mail, recalled Lennon, "We were going to let it out in really shitty condition." This idea had a perverse appeal to Lennon because it would "break the myth" of the Beatles: "This is what we are like with our trousers off. So would you please end the game now?" But it didn't happen that way. Sometime in early 1970, well after the Beatles had finished recording *Abbey Road*—indeed, probably after they had decided to break up—Lennon and Harrison invited famed record producer Phil Spector to have a go at reproducing the *Get Back* album. The result was the *Let It Be* album released in May 1970.

Let It Be clearly was not as consistently strong an album as *Revolver* or *Sgt Pepper*, but neither was it "the nadir of the Beatles' career," as one book has maintained. An album that contained such Beatles classics as "Get Back," "The Long And Winding Road," "Across The Universe," and "Let It Be," along with such honorable mentions as "Two Of Us," "I Me Mine," and "I've Got A Feeling," cannot be so blithely dismissed. Although Spector was later criticized by both McCartney and George Martin for sweetening the album by overdubbing orchestration and choirs onto three tracks, in a sense he was more faithful to the original *Get Back* concept than Glyn Johns had been, for he used more of the live Apple rooftop and studio performances. Moreover, Spector wisely included just enough studio chat to give listeners the illusion of being flies on the wall at a Beatles session, while refraining from the maximum disclosure that had tarnished *Get Back*.

Thus the album opened with one of Lennon's oddball ad-libs, a bawling send-up hinting that the Beatles were no longer Sgt. Pepper's Lonely Hearts Club Band but the even more hapless "Charles Hawtrey and the Deaf Aids." It then slipped deftly into McCartney's fetching acoustic number, "Two Of Us." Glyn Johns had opened *Get Back* with "The One After 909" in an apparent effort to invoke the Beatles' youthful roots—the song was one of the very first Lennon ever wrote—and "Two Of Us" served the same function, even though McCartney had written it only recently. "Two Of Us" has been described, without documentation, as a song about Linda Eastman, but the mood it invokes is actually more buddy-movie than love story. And like "Hey, Jude," the lyrics of "Two Of Us" can easily be read as referring above all to Paul's relationship with John. The line about "burning matches, lifting latches" brings to mind two young lads skipping school in favor of illicit fun, something Paul and John did quite often; the line about "spending someone's hard-earned pay" recalls the "working class glee" that Paul said he and John felt when they first realized their songwriting could make them rich; and the one about "chasing paper, getting nowhere" corresponds to their Apple experience of finding themselves bureaucratically in over their heads. The most poignant line comes in the bridge, however, when Paul sings, "You and I have memories / Longer than the road that stretches out ahead." Such a sentiment made no sense if directed at Linda, whom Paul had known for barely a year, but it could well have been an (at least) unconscious appeal to John not to abandon such an old and close friendship.

Reinforcing the sense of partnership, Lennon and McCartney sang joint lead vocals on "Two Of Us." In fact, in contrast to the largely solo efforts found on the White Album, John and Paul sang together on six of the twelve *Let It Be* tracks, further confounding portrayals of the album as disunity run amok. "Dig A Pony," the next song on *Let It Be*, was one of those six tracks, and it's a lucky thing, too. A lyrically muddled love call to Yoko, it was hardly the most melodious tune John ever wrote, but Paul's high harmonies, along with Harrison's inventive lead guitar work, made it seem more interesting than it actually was.

One of the reasons Lennon admired Spector's reproduction of *Let It Be* was the brilliant salvage job he did on the next track, "Across The Universe." John considered this beautiful invocation of the seamless unity of all creation to be one of the best songs he ever wrote. Nevertheless, after the Beatles first recorded it in February 1968, during the same sessions that yielded "Lady Madonna," John chose not to release the song because he felt it had been so poorly realized. He blamed the failure on Paul, later charging that McCartney would "subconsciously try and destroy a great song" by encouraging an "atmosphere of looseness and casualness and experimentation" during its recording. Lennon made the same accusation about "Strawberry Fields Forever," but he had a stronger case with "Across The Universe."

It seems that after the Beatles had done seven takes of "Across The Universe," someone suggested adding very high background vocals to the song. But rather than hire professional singers, Paul simply walked outside to the crowd of fans who perpetually laid siege to Abbey Road and randomly selected two teenage girls to come in and sing the parts. The result was predictably amateurish, and the song was further weakened by a hurried tempo that made it sound almost jumpy rather than dreamy. When Spector resurrected the song, he slowed the tempo considerably and added a background of strings and choral singers, thus rescuing from oblivion what would have been the greatest lost masterpiece of the Beatles' entire career.

271

"I Me Mine" was also orchestrally enhanced by Spector, but the effect of his alterations was much less noticeable because the Beatles' playing on the track was already so compelling. A song that Harrison had variously described as "a heavy waltz" and a dissection of "the ego, the eternal problem" could well have been a pretty dreary affair, but George's surging guitar lines and the clever tempo change in the middle eight that unleashed Paul's backing vocals gave the song real bite. As it happens, "I Me Mine" was the last full song recorded by the Beatles. When the rough cuts of the *Let It Be* film were ready, they turned out to include a sequence featuring "I Me Mine"—George was shown unveiling the song to Ringo and joking, "I don't care if you don't want it in your show," and John and Yoko were seen waltzing around Twickenham Studios—so George, Paul, and Ringo returned to Abbey Road on January 3, 1970, to record a proper version for album release. (John, away on holiday, missed this session.)

After two consecutive studio pieces, Spector now paused to refresh the album's founding conceit with two more snatches of verité: a much and rightly shortened version of the Lennon chant "Dig It," followed by John's ironic, high-pitched introduction of "Let It Be" as "Hark, The Angels Come." John's line was meant to be funny, but it inadvertently touched on the creative origins of "Let It Be," for McCartney had written the song after being visited in a dream by his mother, Mary, who had been dead for some twelve years. "She died when I was fourteen, so I hadn't really heard from her in a while, and it was very good," Paul recalled, adding that he had been going through a difficult time and his mother's sudden appearance "gave me some strength."

It was unusual for McCartney to write about such intimate matters, but it led to one of the finest songs the Beatles ever recorded. As John had so often done, Paul managed in "Let It Be" to connect his personal situation with the larger communal reality. After describing how his mother comforted him "in my hour of darkness," he sang in the second verse of all "the broken hearted people living in the world," and averred that "though they may be parted / There is still a chance that they will see," a touchingly hopeful line. His vocal delivery was nothing less than perfect, coaxing the fullest emotions possible from the song without drifting into mawkish self-regard. The Beatles' backing track was equally superb, magisterial in its scope and power. The song began quietly, with just Paul playing the piano, then gradually added angelic backing vocals, Ringo's stately, almost somber drums, and Paul's discreet bass line before swelling in the middle eight into a pulsing yet controlled rock song, thanks to George's stinging guitar lead and George Martin's orchestration. Although the basic track of "Let It Be" had been recorded the day after the rooftop concert, most of the overdubs that gave the song its symphonic richness were added nearly a year later, during the band's very last recording session, on January 4, 1970. It was a fine and fitting farewell.

Side one of *Let It Be* ended with another of the rough edges associated with the *Get Back* project—a ragged but amusing run through of "Maggie Mae," a traditional standard about a Liverpool streetwalker, which the Beatles sometimes sang as a studio warm-up number. The live feeling continued on side two with the rooftop versions of "I've Got A Feeling" and "The One After 909," both boasting joint Lennon–McCartney vocals, before returning to the studio for Paul's "The Long And Winding Road" and George's "For You Blue." Why the latter, a slight blues boogie, was included on *Let It Be* at all is something of a mystery; Harrison would have been far better represented by any number of other compositions already recorded but left unreleased by the Beatles, including his subsequent solo releases "All Things Must Pass," "Not Guilty," or "Let It Down."

As for "The Long And Winding Road," this was another of the songs Phil Spector restyled with string and choral overdubs, but McCartney was so unhappy with the result that he cited it as an example of professional sabotage in his 1970 lawsuit seeking dissolution of the Beatles partnership. Comparing the Beatles' original recording of "The Long And Winding Road" with Spector's version, it's easy to see why Paul was so shocked. Whereas the original version featured a restrained, almost spare instrumental arrangement that lent a contemplative dignity to the song, the gushing, bombastic orchestration of Spector's remake threatened to reduce "The Long And Winding Road" to a mere nostalgic tearjerker. Luckily, the melody and sentiment were strong enough to withstand the intrusion.

"The Long And Winding Road" was a close cousin of "Let It Be"—a piano-based ballad examining themes of separation, sorrow and loss. The redemptive possibilities of faith and human connection acted as counterweights to these sobering themes, but they did not necessarily triumph; unlike his earlier songwriting persona, McCartney now seemed to accept that life did not always get better. What's more, his lyrics again seemed to invite the speculation that he was, at least in part, singing to John. "You left me standing here / A long, long time ago" went one especially wounded line. Even more plaintive was the plea, "Don't leave me waiting here." But if one listened very carefully to that line, it seemed to be followed by Paul singing in the background, "It's too late," an apparent acknowledgment that he and John could never return to the miraculous state of grace they had shared for so many years. At the end of the film version of "Get Back," as the credits rolled, Paul voiced a more upbeat version of his wish for reunification, ad-libbing in the song's fade-out, "Get back, get together, Ohhh, we got to get together." But the dream was ending by then, and all the king's horses and all the king's men couldn't put it back together again.

CHAPTER 22

The Breakup Heard 'Round the World

WHEN IT CAME, THE BREAKUP OF THE BEATLES TOOK THE WORLD BY TERRIBLE SURPRISE, LIKE THE SUDDEN DEATH of a beloved young uncle. The news broke on April 10, 1970, when Paul McCartney announced that he had left the group; confirming McCartney's departure, the Apple press office added that the activities of the Beatles might well remain "dormant for years." To most people, the breakup was not just shocking but baffling, for John, Paul, George, and Ringo could obviously still make great music together. Seven months earlier, in September 1969, they had released the magnificent *Abbey Road* album. In October, two of the finest songs from that album, "Something" and "Come Together," had been released as a single. And in March, a month before McCartney's stunning revelation, the "Let It Be" single had been issued. All of this material ranked among the very best the Beatles had ever produced, and it sold in very large numbers. Creatively and commercially, the Beatles were at the height of their powers. Why break up now?

That question would be analyzed and debated exhaustively in the months and years to come, and not just by heartbroken Beatles fans. For the Beatles were not simply the outstanding musical partnership of their time, they were also one of its most important cultural symbols. Thus their dissolution took on a far larger historical significance than the demise of mere pop stars; rather, like the assassination of presidents or the July 1969 moon landing, the breakup of the Beatles was regarded as one of the defining events of the 1960s. Indeed, seizing on the fact that the split came a scant four months into the new decade, media pundits invariably interpreted it as a sign that the sixties era of optimism and goodwill had conclusively ended.

Yet despite the widespread and intensive news coverage the Beatles' breakup received, the truth about it remained elusive, and not simply because of the press's usual preference for quick and easy answers. The public, for its part, often seemed to be in a state of denial, fascinated by the drama but insisting that the last act be rewritten and given a happier ending or, better yet, no ending at all. In their shock and anger, many latched on to oversimplifications—blaming Yoko Ono and Linda McCartney was a particular favorite—even as they refused to accept that the band they had loved all these years would not reunite.

The Beatles themselves were not much help. Fully human after all, they did not—with the exception of John Lennon in his famous *Rolling Stone* magazine interview, conducted nearly a year after the fact—want to speak much about what they were going through. What answers they gave tended to be opaque, one-sided, or otherwise incomplete. To the outside world, their breakup meant an end to the most widely and wisely loved music of the century. But to the Beatles themselves, the breakup was a painful, intimate matter, a personal crisis of untold proportion that tore at the heart of their identities and drove them apart from their dearest friends, their virtual blood brothers. The inevitable feelings of anger, sadness, fear, uncertainty, relief, and freedom were confusing enough on their own, but of course the Beatles had to experience them under the obsessive scrutiny of millions.

What was worse, the larger world seemed incapable of discussing the subject without demanding to know if and when the Beatles would get back together, a single-minded focus that drove the Beatles mad. "It's like asking a divorced couple: 'Are you getting back together?' . . . when you can't stand to look at each other," said McCartney. Lennon, too, likened the Beatles' breakup to a divorce, a comparison that suggested another possible reason for the foursome's reticence: They didn't explain what they were doing because they weren't entirely sure; few people are, in the middle of a divorce. In fact, there is considerable evidence to suggest that, contrary to the conventional wisdom that has taken shape in Beatles books over the years, the Beatles' breakup was not inevitable and that the four of them did not necessarily want to separate completely and forever.

As befit the Beatles' mythic stature, there was an operatic quality to their divorce. They had never intended to carry on forever, and they had promised one another that when the day came, they would go out on top, rather than fade into slow, ignominious decline. "One of the things we'd always been very conscious of with the Beatles was to have a great career and leave 'em laughing," McCartney later recalled. Yet like young adults who don't bother to draw up a will because death still seems impossibly remote, the Beatles never got around to formulating an actual exit plan. Thus their breakup was not a carefully thought out, coordinated affair, but a jumbled and sometimes nasty explosion of egos, lawyers, and bank accounts. This, too, complicated public understanding, for it meant that the story emerged in dribs and drabs and out of proper chronological order, and revolved more around volatile emotions than solid facts. In the process, appearances took on even more importance than usual and were often, though not always, deceptive.

Perhaps the best example was the event that set off all the alarm bells in the first place, McCartney's statement that he had left the Beatles. This announcement coincided with the release of Paul's first solo album, *McCartney*. Tucked inside review copies of the album was a printed interview in which Paul said he had enjoyed working solo, had broken with the Beatles because of "personal differences, business differences, musical differences," and did not foresee a resumption of his songwriting partnership with Lennon. Outsiders immediately leaped to the conclusion that the Beatles had split up and that McCartney had instigated the rupture. Yet a careful reading of the interview showed that, in fact, McCartney had said nothing about the Beatles splitting up; he said only that *he* had broken with them. Moreover, he twice specifically left open the question of whether the break would be temporary or permanent, saying, "Time will tell." Nevertheless, newspaper headlines around the world reduced the story to screaming variations of PAUL BREAKS UP THE BEATLES.

What made this so misleading was that it was actually Lennon who had pulled the plug on the band a full seven months earlier, as John himself later proudly admitted. The moment of truth came during a meeting of all four Beatles, held at Apple sometime in mid-September 1969. Lennon had just returned from Toronto, where he and the Plastic Ono Band had made an impromptu appearance at a concert on September 13. It was during the flight from London to Toronto, John later said, that he made his decision to quit. He immediately shared this portentous news with Allen Klein, the Beatles' new business manager, who happened to be aboard the flight. Whatever Klein thought of the merits of John's decision, he told him to keep quiet about it for the time being, for business reasons. Precise dates are uncertain, but Klein at this time either had just finished or was still in the midst of renegotiating the Beatles' contracts with their record company, EMI. He had secured a hefty increase in royalty rates, but it would be some time before the corresponding payments actually arrived, and Klein did not want them jeopardized by the news that John Lennon had left the group. Klein did not even want John to tell Paul about his decision, but this proved impossible.

McCartney, always the Beatle most intent on keeping the group together, had suggested during the meeting at Apple that one way to overcome their internal discord was to get back to being a working live band again, perhaps by making surprise appearances at the kinds of small clubs where they had first begun. After making his pitch, McCartney later recalled, "John looked me in the eye and he said, 'I think you're daft. In fact, I wasn't going to tell you . . . but I'm leaving the group.' To my recollection, those were his exact words. And our jaws dropped. And then he went on to explain that it was rather a good feeling to get it off his chest. . . . Which was nice for him, but we didn't get much of a good feeling." Lennon recorded a similar memory in his posthumously published memoirs, writing that "when I finally had the guts to tell the other three that I, quote, wanted a divorce, unquote, they knew it was for real, unlike Ringo and George's previous threats to leave."

"I started the band. I disbanded it. It's as simple as that," Lennon continued in his memoirs. But of course it wasn't that simple. True, if there was one factor above all others that accounted for the breakup of the Beatles, it was John Lennon's decision to leave the band. But that decision seems not to have been as clear-cut as Lennon liked to claim in later years, and in any case, why did he make it? And how and why did it lead to the eventual breakup of the Beatles? For four lads whose love and talent and miraculous togetherness had indeed changed the world, as *Sgt Pepper* had promised, how did it come to this?

There is no one answer to these questions. Although the sequence of relevant events in the Beatles' breakup can be reliably established, the whys and wherefores remain matters of opinion and perspective. The Beatles' own views, which are what matter most, have evolved over the years to where, instead of name-calling and sullenness, there are now large areas of agreement about what happened and why. But not total agreement. Paul, for example, has said that he wished the Beatles had never broken up, a view none of the others have shared. Yet, ironically, it was the other three who did work with one another quite a lot in the early 1970s. To take another example, no one much disputes that Yoko Ono was the main reason that John left the group. In his memoirs (the text of which Yoko controlled), John praised Yoko for giving him the "inner strength to look more closely at my other marriage. *My real marriage*. To the Beatles, which . . . had become a trap." In Paul's words, "John had to clear the decks of us to give space to his and Yoko's thing." Paul further observed separately, "Someone like John would want to end the Beatle period and start the Yoko period. And he wouldn't like either to interfere with the other." Fine. But Paul's additional assertion that George and Ringo took John's departure from the Beatles as a signal to leave the group themselves illustrates how tricky this story can be. Paul's interpretation is certainly consistent with *what* George and Ringo did—indeed, John later sneered that Paul's claim to have left the Beatles was laughable, given that the other three had already quit—but not necessarily with *why*, for it shortchanges the fact that George and Ringo had their own reasons for wanting out. John was guilty of the same mistake when he claimed sole credit for breaking up the Beatles. And John had less excuse, for unlike Paul, he shared many of George and Ringo's feelings.

Chief among these were issues of personal space and freedom. As

281

acrimonious as the Beatles' breakup turned out to be, it was not entirely their own fault. The adoring millions also played a part. Like moths to a flame, the Beatles' fans were ineluctably drawn to the four young men whose music and charisma made everyone feel so happy and alive. By overwhelming their heroes with the intensity and relentlessness of their passion, however, the fans ended up driving the Beatles into seclusion and, ultimately, retirement. As Harrison later said, in the best single explanation of why the Beatles finally decided to "burn down the factory" that was their collective identity, "It's just that it wasn't as much fun for us in the end as it was for all of you." Denying that Yoko and Linda were responsible for breaking up the Beatles, Ringo commented years later that, "From 1961, 1962 to around 1969, we [the four Beatles] were just all for each other. But suddenly you're older and you don't want to devote all that time to this one object. . . . We stopped because we'd had enough. We'd gone as far as we could with each other." George, too, referred to the Beatles experience as "stifling," adding that it finally came to resemble a situation where "you've got ten brothers and sisters and you've grown up and you're all forty years old and you still haven't moved out. . . . We had to try to help break that Beatle madness in order to have space to breathe, to become sort of human."

The problem of limited space was an artistic frustration as well. There was only so much room on any given album, and it wasn't enough to accommodate all the songs the individual Beatles were writing near the end. Harrison especially felt unhappy with his de facto quota of one or two songs per album, and with Ringo now writing the occasional tune as well, competition for album space was intense. Adding to the pressure was the longstanding feeling on the part of John, George, and Ringo that Paul considered himself first among equals. "You'd have to do fifty-nine of Paul's songs before he'd even listen to one of yours," George later complained. By the end, recalled Paul, the Beatles had agreed to divide future albums into "four Paul songs, four John songs, four George songs, four Ringo songs, which wasn't gonna be right, it wasn't the right balance. It was getting too democratic for its own good."

As knotty as these problems were, however, they did not have to mean the breakup of the Beatles. In fact, there was a fairly simple solution to them, which at least some of the Beatles not only discussed but put into practice. A conversation between George and John, captured on tape during the *Get Back* project in January 1969, laid out the essential idea. George, noting that he had already written "my quota of tunes for the next ten years, or albums," says that after *Get Back*, "I'd just like to maybe do an album of songs. . . ." "On your own?" John asks. "Yeah," George replies. John, who by now had already put out the first of his experimental albums with Yoko, quickly applauds George's idea, observing that it could easily coexist with Beatles work and it would offer "an outlet for every little note you want." George continues, "Any of us can do separate things as well. That way, it also preserves this, the Beatles bit of it, more." Doing solo projects alongside Beatles work was exactly what John and Ringo in particular did throughout 1969, thus providing an example of how all four Beatles could have continued to work together in years ahead: coming together from time to time to record a Beatles album while continuing to pursue solo careers as well. This would indeed have preserved "the Beatles bit" while still gaining them the independence they understandably craved.

All of which casts John's boast about unilaterally breaking up the Beatles in quite a different light. Notwithstanding his characteristically black-and-white declarations after the fact, many of John's statements and actions at the time of the breakup indicate that he was quite possibly prepared, even after his divorce speech, to keep working with the other Beatles, albeit in a form markedly different from that of previous years. In the aftermath of Paul's April 1970 announcement, for example, John snarled, "I put four albums out last year and I didn't say a fucking word about quitting." Exactly, not publicly he didn't. And that is a crucial distinction, for John's public silence effectively kept the door open to future collaboration. Whether John consciously intended to keep his options open is not known, but certainly one of the key unanswered questions about the Beatles' breakup is why Lennon did not publicly announce he was leaving the group sooner than he did. If, as he later claimed, he was so eager to free himself from the Beatles, why did he wait so long—from September 1969 to April 1970—to say so?

The "business reasons" explanation makes sense as far as it goes, but it cannot account for the entire delay, unless it took seven months for the newly negotiated EMI advance payments to arrive, which seems unlikely. John later ridiculed Paul for supposedly thinking that John's agreement during the September 1969 meeting not to tell the world he was leaving the Beatles meant that nothing had really changed. But in fact Paul and the other Beatles had good reason to take John's divorce statement with a grain of salt; after all, John was the guy who not long before had declared that he was Jesus Christ come back again. Moreover, John's behavior in the months following the September 1969 meeting was ambiguous. He spent most of his time on political activism and what little music he made was with the Plastic Ono Band, yet he maintained an office at Apple, continued to identify himself publicly as a Beatle, and worked on numerous Beatles projects. For example, he and Yoko made a tape for the 1969 Christmas fan club disc (as did Paul, George, and Ringo, each working separately for the second year in a row). More importantly, with George's support, John brought in Phil Spector to reproduce the *Let It Be* album. In sum, as much as John was consumed by his new passions, he had not cut all his ties with the Beatles and quite possibly did not wish to. Why should he? As long as those ties didn't interfere with his solo interests, he could have his cake and eat it too.

But any such scenario was rendered moot by the global media explosion ignited by McCartney's April 1970 announcement. Lennon resented what he considered a public relations ploy by McCartney, especially the implication that it was Paul who had walked out on *him*. Whatever chance there might have been for a reconciliation between the two longtime partners had now been lost. McCartney later called his questionnaire a "dumb move" that looked "very hard and cold" in retrospect; he wished he had gotten the approval of the other Beatles before issuing it. At the same time, he reiterated that he had not been willing to wait forever for the others to come back, especially since he did not think they would. He also maintained that it was high time to tell the world the truth: "The Beatles have left The Beatles, but no one wants to be the one to say the party's over."

With McCartney's announcement, the dissent that had been roiling within the Beatles for the past two years had for the first time burst into public view. And that very fact set in motion a chain of additional reactions that all but guaranteed the Beatles' demise. For now that the rift had become common knowledge, John could not work with Paul again, even if he did somehow get over his anger, without losing face. Thus any collaboration among all four Beatles was ruled out for the foreseeable future. Paul's behavior had also exacerbated the already very chilly relations among the four. It was not just the questionnaire that irritated John, George, and Ringo, it was the *McCartney* album itself and Paul's insistence that it be issued ahead of both *Let It Be* and the solo album that Ringo had recorded, *Sentimental Journey*. Although Ringo's album had long since been scheduled for release first, followed by *Let It Be*, Paul refused to accept third place in line. Sometime in early 1970, probably in March, Ringo was dispatched to reason with Paul on the subject. The drummer had been chosen as envoy because, unlike John and George, he still had a relatively friendly rapport with Paul. The meeting went badly, however. Suspecting the other Beatles of trying to sabotage his solo career, Paul, according to Ringo's subsequent sworn affidavit, "went completely out of control, shouting at me, prodding his fingers toward my face, saying, 'I'll finish you all now' and 'you'll pay!' "

The main quarrel, however, was between John and Paul. It had gotten steadily worse throughout 1969, despite an external threat that should have united the two men. Northern Songs, the music publishing company that owned the copyrights to the Lennon–McCartney song catalogue, had become the target of corporate predators. Northern Songs became vulnerable when Dick James, its founder, suddenly decided in March to sell his portion of the company to a London-based conglomerate, ATV Music. McCartney and Lennon were the second- and third-largest shareholders in Northern Songs behind James, and although James had made untold millions of pounds from their compositions over the years, he chose not to offer them the first chance to buy his shares. Without warning, he sold out to ATV, which then initiated a campaign to buy up enough of the outstanding shares to secure majority control.

Stunned by James's betrayal, Lennon and McCartney recovered

their wits in time to launch their own takeover campaign. It got off to a bad start when John discovered in April that Paul had for some time been quietly buying additional shares of Northern Songs, such that he now had 751,000 shares, compared to John's 644,000. The notion of McCartney buying a controlling interest in Northern Songs was mathematically far-fetched, yet Paul seemed unable to explain why he had kept his purchases secret from John, who immediately accused him of conniving behind his back. Such distrust bode ill for the Lennon–McCartney takeover bid, as did McCartney's refusal to put up his shares as collateral when the Beatles finally made their £2 million counteroffer to the ATV bid. However, Lennon and McCartney had the advantage of being the geese whose golden eggs made Northern Songs so valuable in the first place. Other shareholders were therefore reluctant to alienate them by siding with ATV.

By mid-May, it appeared that ATV, having captured forty-seven percent of all Northern stock, had fallen just short of victory. All that remained was for Lennon and McCartney to reach an agreement with the consortium of stockholders whose control of fourteen percent of total shares made them the swing vote. It was at this point that Lennon snatched defeat from the jaws of victory. The negotiations had been proceeding smoothly enough, with the Beatles assuring the consortium that the ill-reputed Allen Klein would not sit on the board of directors of Northern Songs, until Lennon lost his temper and insulted his potential allies. Apparently tired of compromising over the future of a company he considered rightfully his, Lennon announced that he was "not going to be fucked around by men in suits sitting on their fat arses in the City"—that is, in the London financial district. The deal duly collapsed, the consortium signed with ATV, and the Lennon–McCartney song catalogue fell irretrievably out of the composers' control. (In 1986, McCartney and Yoko Ono had the chance to regain the catalogue, but they were outbid by singer Michael Jackson.)

Under the circumstances, it is a wonder that Lennon and McCartney came as close to victory in the Northern Songs struggle as they did, for they were deeply divided over a more fundamental business question: Who should be taking the place of the long-departed Brian Epstein? John, of course, wanted Klein, a view eventually shared by

Ringo and George, while Paul wanted John Eastman, his new brother-in-law. The two candidates could hardly have been more different. Klein was a New York accountant whose foulmouthed personality and street-fighter instincts masked a razor-sharp financial mind but helped explain his propensity for attracting lawsuits and tax fraud accusations. Eastman was, contrary to myth, no relation to Eastman Kodak, but came from a very wealthy background in his own right. Lee Eastman, his father, had long been a prominent attorney in the entertainment business; John was following in his father's golden footsteps.

For a while during 1969, both Lennon and McCartney got their way. That is, Klein served as the Beatles' business adviser, John Eastman as their lawyer. But Klein and Eastman detested each other from the very start, and perhaps sensing that only one of them could survive, they criticized and undercut each other relentlessly. Paul's distaste for Klein did not deter him from backing Klein during the EMI negotiations, or during Klein's ruthless firing of much of the staff at Apple. Nevertheless, Paul continued throughout 1969 to distrust Klein and try to turn the other Beatles against him. He did not succeed, but his antipathy to Lennon's man put him increasingly at odds with John.

Indeed, it was probably Klein, more than Yoko Ono, who most significantly came between Lennon and McCartney. When Paul issued his *McCartney* questionnaire in April 1970, he went out of his way to stress that Allen Klein did not represent him. In fact, convinced that Klein was defrauding the Beatles, Paul wanted nothing further to do with him, but this was easier said than done. To escape Klein, McCartney had to leave the Beatles partnership. Toward that end, he requested in July that his fellow Beatles legally release him from the partnership, but he got no answer. Subsequent inquiries were no more successful. Finally, under counsel from Eastman, McCartney concluded that the only way to sever himself from Klein was to file a lawsuit. The catch was that, for technical reasons, the suit had to name not Klein but the three other Beatles.

McCartney later said that he agonized over the prospect of "suing my best mates and being *seen* to sue my best mates. That was the worst." Nevertheless, the suit was filed on December 31, 1970. The trial began in London on January 10, 1971, and two months later the

High Court issued its ruling. Siding with McCartney, the Court appointed a receiver for the Beatles' assets, thus freezing the group's money and disempowering Klein; it also ordered an independent inquiry into the group's finances. But not until January 9, 1975, nearly four years later, was the Beatles partnership finally dissolved formally.

If McCartney's questionnaire was the nail that sealed the Beatles' coffin shut, his lawsuit coated the coffin with a layer of cement. A reunion was now unthinkable. The irony was that the other Beatles soon turned against Klein themselves, John most dramatically of all. When Klein's management contracts with John, George, and Ringo expired in 1972, not one of the former Beatles renewed them; in fact, in 1973, joined by Paul, they sued Klein for fraud. And in 1974, John penned a song about Klein, "Steel And Glass," that was nearly as vicious an attack as the one John had launched against Paul with "How Do You Sleep?" in 1971. (The lawsuits between Klein and the former Beatles were settled in 1975. In 1979 a New York judge sent Klein to jail for two months for Apple-related tax offenses.)

"You know, it seems that my partings are always not as nice as I'd like them to be," Lennon mused years later. He was by no means sorry that the Beatles had broken up, he emphasized, but he did regret that it "had a bad taste to it." McCartney, too, thought it "a pity that such a nice thing had to come to such a sticky end. . . . I like fairy tales. I'd love to have had the Beatles go up in a little cloud of smoke and the four of us just find ourselves in magic robes, each holding an envelope with our stuff in it." But real life, added Paul, wasn't like that. If it were, the Beatles might never have split in the first place.

CHAPTER 23

A Final Masterpiece (*Abbey Road*)

THE MUSIC THE BEATLES MADE IN THEIR FINAL MONTHS TOGETHER WAS AS INSPIRED AND MASTERFUL AS ANY IN THEIR career, and there was no reason to think they could not have created more of it. Indeed, perhaps the most impressive thing about *Abbey Road*, the masterpiece they recorded in the spring and summer of 1969, was the continuing musical evolution it revealed. True, the album did an uncanny job of displaying the elements that had propelled the group's earlier rise to excellence: the singing and songwriting of Lennon and McCartney, the musical synergy of all four Beatles, the invisible hand of George Martin—to name but three. Yet *Abbey Road* was no mere rehash of past glories. Songs like "Come Together" and "Here Comes The Sun" were unique creations, as impossible to anticipate as they were to forget. Likewise, the suite of tracks that turned most of side two into one continuous piece of music illustrated that the Beatles were still pioneers, making up new rules as they went along. After seven years in which they had revolutionized popular music, *Abbey Road* demonstrated that the Beatles remained in a class by themselves. Equally important, it showed that they were still artists in progress, still moving forward, still growing and improving right up to the very end.

Although *Abbey Road* is generally recognized as a strong album—George Martin called it his favorite of all the Beatles' albums—its full quality often goes underappreciated in Beatles books. In most tellings of the story, the narrative focus at this point is directed so much at the group's impending breakup that the music gets lost in the backwash of who (may have) fought with whom while it was being made. The truly remarkable thing about this period in the Beatles' history, however, is not the personal tensions within the group but how the music survived and even flourished despite them. It was as if, as Lennon once said, the Beatles were just channels for a larger musical force that cared nothing for their petty squabbles and was determined to find its way into the world no matter what. It was the Beatles' special chemistry that had allowed that force to come through in the first place, and the flow didn't stop now just because the lads were sometimes at odds with one another. Indeed, it was during the recording of *Abbey Road* that George Martin made the statement quoted earlier in this book about the "inexplicable *presence*" felt in a room whenever all four Beatles were together. Whether the Beatles liked it or not, in the end the music was bigger than they were.

John and Paul provided a vivid case in point on April 14, 1969, the day they snuck into Abbey Road by themselves to record "The Ballad Of John And Yoko." Ten weeks had passed between the end of the contentious *Let It Be* sessions and this recording of John's brisk and biting complaint that the media's hounding of him and his new wife was "gonna crucify me." During those ten weeks, Paul and John had clashed over Allen Klein's possible role with the Beatles, Paul had married Linda Eastman, John had wed Yoko Ono and she and he had held their first "bed-ins for peace." John's and Paul's lives were plainly heading in quite different directions. Nevertheless, John unexpectedly showed up at Paul's door one day "on heat" to record his new song, Paul recalled, and he convinced Paul to come help him. The two old partners ended up going behind George's and Ringo's backs because Ringo was busy acting in a new film, *The Magic Christian*, and George was out of the country. A proper Beatles recording session was scheduled for April 16, but John, ever in a hurry to make his records, didn't want to wait the extra two days.

The Abbey Road archives tapes of this session contain some wonderfully revealing moments. The session takes place in Studio Three, with

Paul substituting for Ringo on drums, John playing acoustic guitar while singing his lead vocal, and George Martin monitoring the proceedings from the control room. The song is straight-ahead, three-chord rock 'n' roll, and the beat is all-important. Lennon seems pleased with McCartney's first attempt at drumming it. "That was a good speed," John comments after the first take. Before take two, John asks, "Okay, Paul?" before starting back into the song. Paul, affecting a mock-servile voice, replies, "Yassuh." Before take four, John murmurs, "You could go a bit faster, Ringo." Paul snickers, "Okay, George."

Those aren't bad lines. It must be said, however, that on the archives tapes they sound remarkably subdued, almost hollow. It's true that John and Paul aren't chewing each other's heads off—in fact, they seem to be trying very hard to get along—but there is a forced, polite quality to their joking and none of the enthusiastic electricity heard during earlier Beatles sessions (or John's solo sessions eighteen months later, for that matter). When they finish the eleventh and final take of the song, John and Paul don't say a word to each other. The silence is only broken when John calls out to the control room, "What did you think?" Making a record seems to have become a job.

Yet it is a job that John and Paul do extremely well. John's vocals are on target from the very start of take one, and Paul's drumming is consistently firm and vibrant. The recording keeps breaking down, however, because Paul can't quite master the pause and shift in the drum pattern that whacks the song into the homestretch, right after John yells "Think!" at the end of the middle eight. But when the two of them practice that passage separately after take five and John explains that "it speeds up a little on the middle eight," Paul immediately grasps what John is looking for. He raps out the beat, John says, "Yeah," and Paul answers, "Okay." Still, it's a tricky bit, and when Paul misses it again during take six John sighs, "Ah, buggers." But Paul finally clobbers it on take ten, and the two partners spend the rest of the seven-hour session overdubbing bass, piano, lead guitars, percussion, and Paul's backing harmonies. John and Paul work so efficiently that the session finishes an hour early.

By the end of the evening, "The Ballad Of John And Yoko" gallops like a thoroughbred. During the overdubs, Paul sounds off-key at times as he seeks and tries out different harmonies. But that is the nature of discovery, and the finished song, where Paul sings just a syllable of harmony at the end of each line in the fourth verse before launching into a virtual countermelody during the final verse, validates his approach. Released as a single six weeks later (backed by Harrison's "Old Brown Shoe," the song all four Beatles recorded two days later), "The Ballad of John And Yoko" became a number one hit, despite being censored by some American radio stations because of its lyrics—"the Christ bit," as John put it in a note to an Apple staffer.

The Beatles' relative civility during this and the other recording sessions of the *Abbey Road* era must be credited in part to George Martin. The days were long past when Martin could crack the whip on the Beatles, but he did manage to put them on their best behavior, apparently by threatening to leave them to their own devices. After the unpleasantness of the *Let It Be* sessions, Martin was as surprised as anyone to hear that a new album was being planned, and he didn't automatically agree to participate in *Abbey Road*. When McCartney approached him about serving as producer, Martin made it clear that he would return only if he were granted real authority and if the Beatles stopped squabbling so much. If, as Paul professed, the Beatles wanted to make an album like they used to make, then they themselves had to be like they used to be.

The Beatles' conduct during *Abbey Road* did not quite live up to that high standard, but it came close enough to get the job done. Tensions remained, of course, and sometimes they erupted into arguments and shouting. Paul later recalled that both Ringo and George told him off during the *Abbey Road* sessions for being too overbearing in the studio. The Yoko factor also became even more intrusive, and bizarre, when John insisted on bringing a bed into the studio so he didn't have to be separated from his newly pregnant wife, for whom doctors had ordered bed rest. One day, when Yoko helped herself to one of George's biscuits without asking, it sparked a nasty exchange between the two Beatles. And sometimes John did not bother to attend the recording sessions at all—he and Yoko were injured in an automobile accident on July 1, and they were also drifting back into occasional heroin use in the summer of 1969—which meant that parts of *Abbey Road*, especially the overdubs on side one, were recorded without him.

But there were plenty of friendly, happy moments, too, both with and without John. On August 8, the day the famous cover photo for *Abbey Road*—a color profile showing the four Beatles crossing the zebra stripe outside the studio building—was shot, the photo session ended early, leaving the Beatles with a couple of hours to kill before the afternoon recording session began. To hear most Beatles books tell it, John and Paul could barely stand to be in the same room at this point, but in fact the two of them slipped back to Paul's house together to pass the time while Ringo went shopping and George visited the zoo. On another occasion, John and Paul spent hours singing into the same Studio Three microphone, overdubbing wacky vocals and sound effects onto "You Know My Name (Look Up The Number), a comedy number later issued as the B-side to the "Let It Be" single. Lewisohn reports that there was also lots of good-natured banter among the Beatles during the taping of "Octopus's Garden" and "Here Comes The Sun."

One of McCartney's happy memories of *Abbey Road* came during a session for "Come Together," the monumental Lennon anthem that opens side one of the album. According to McCartney, Lennon was never liberal with his praise of the other Beatles—"If you ever got a speck of it, a crumb of it, you were quite grateful"—so Paul was very pleased when John complimented the "swampy and smoky" piano lick that Paul worked out for the song. And Paul wasn't the only one who played well on "Come Together." In fact, the song was a prime example of how tight and powerful a musical unit all four Beatles continued to be during the *Abbey Road* period. There is as much inventiveness and life in the first three seconds of "Come Together" as is found on whole albums by many other musicians.

Unfurling another in a long line of highly distinctive song openings, the Beatles combine four distinct sounds to create an instantly gripping musical mood at the start of "Come Together." First comes John's vocal, a half-sung, half-whispered command to "Shoot me"—ominous enough on its face, but downright spooky in view of John's murder eleven years later. Only the "shoot" part of John's vocal is audible, however; the "me" is obscured by the first note of Paul's snakelike, ascending bass line. Virtually simultaneous with the bass, a third sound appears, a quick, slapping noise that reverberates above the bass line like an arrow quivering in a target. Lennon produced this noise by clapping his hands the instant he sang "me" and then applying tape echo to the clap during the re-mix stage of production. Finally, these two rising rhythms are answered by Ringo's descending drum pattern, rolling in like thunder from on high.

Although the first line about "ol' flatop" was taken from a Chuck Berry song, Lennon was actually trying to write a political song when he began composing "Come Together." Hippie candidate Timothy Leary, the LSD prophet, was thinking about running for governor of California and asked Lennon to write a campaign song around the slogan "come together." As it happened, the only line in John's finished song with political overtones, besides the chorus, was "One thing I can tell you is / You got to be free." But like the chorus, that was a powerful cry—simple, inclusive, direct. When Lennon sang the song live in New York's Madison Square Garden in 1972, he changed the chorus to "Come together / Stop the war / Right now!" The crowd roared its agreement. Nevertheless, at song's end, John mumbled, in an apparent reference to the verses, "I've gotta stop writing such daft words." If even Lennon found them obscure, how can an outsider venture to say what, if any, larger point they made? Lennon seems to be singing about himself, but what stands out most are the familiarity and sly humor of such individual lines as "I know you, you know me" and "Got to be good lookin' / Cuz he's so hard to see."

Musically, it is hard to single out any one aspect of "Come Together" for praise; it is a brilliant group effort. Lennon's fierce lead vocal is insistent yet enveloping, and though it is entirely capable of standing on its own, the boost it gets from McCartney's deftly placed harmonies makes it even more urgent. Perhaps even more deserving of mention, and not simply because it so often gets overlooked, is the truly outstanding drumming done by Starr. "Come Together" is a good example of George Martin's point that two of Ringo's greatest strengths as a drummer are his great instinctive feel for a song and his distinctive individual sound. Both are apparent in the song's opening moments, but the real high point comes near the end, just after John has sung the last chorus. Heading for the fade-out, where John will sing "Come Together" over and over while George replies with high guitar phrases, the Beatles first repeat the opening "Shoot me" passage four times. On the fourth pass, Ringo kicks the band into the refrain with a drum fill like a lightning punch in the gut, so swift and strong it passes right through you before you have the chance to lose your breath. His drumming on the album's remaining tracks is no less impressive. It is almost as if he is determined to show that, despite McCartney's earlier criticisms, he was the musical peer of all his fellow Beatles.

Intentionally or not, Harrison makes the same point with the album's next song, his lovely ballad "Something." Both Lennon and McCartney reportedly thought that "Something" was the best song on *Abbey Road*. Frank Sinatra was quoted calling it "the greatest love song of the past fifty years." Considered together with Harrison's other *Abbey Road* gem, "Here Comes The Sun," "Something" was also compelling evidence that the Beatles as a band were still improving. For now they boasted not only the two "greatest songwriters on earth at the time," as Ringo put it, but also a third songwriter of truly major stature.

The working tapes of "Something" reveal that Harrison had trouble perfecting the lyrics; for a brief time, as a joke, the opening lines were, "Something in the way she moves / Attracts me like a pomegranate." But musically, George later said, the song boasted "probably the nicest melody line I've ever written." Many shared his opinion. More than 150 cover versions of "Something" were recorded by other artists in the first decade after its release, second only to "Yesterday" among Beatle songs. But as usual, the Beatles' own arrangement is hard to top. Ringo's drumming shines again, Paul offers his usual virtuoso performance on bass and George's liquidy guitar lead fills the middle eight with joyful yearning. The entirety is buoyed and framed by an orchestral score by George Martin that is not too sweet, not too tart, but just right.

If there is a track on *Abbey Road* that is too sweet, it is McCartney's "Maxwell's Silver Hammer." Paul said that this cheerfully macabre tale about a young man with a habit of bashing in people's skulls was a metaphor for the unpredictability of life's ups and downs. It was in the same vein as "Ob-La-Di, Ob-La-Da"—as Harrison said, "it's one of those instant, whistle-along tunes"—and like that song, Paul insisted on recording it over and over, until John and George were sick of it.

Harrison later called it a "really fruity" song. A jeering Lennon said that the Beatles were assured of a mainstream audience as long as they kept producing "nice little folk songs like 'Maxwell's Silver Hammer' for the grannies to dig."

But McCartney's next song, "Oh! Darling," certainly wasn't for grannies. In fact, John admired it so much he wished he could have sung it rather than Paul. He even maintained that he could have sung it better than Paul. Which is surely possible; John was one of the great singers of rock 'n' roll. But so was Paul, and he proves it on "Oh! Darling." McCartney later said that he came into the studio early every day for a week to sing the song before the others arrived, aiming to sound "as though I'd been performing it on stage all week." On his fifth try, he taped the version heard on the album: a raw, throaty vocal whose abandon harkened back to "Long Tall Sally" (complete with Little Richard falsettos) while hitting every note cleanly and fully. His vocal was augmented by another fine example of ensemble playing, especially George's opening guitar barks that gave way in the middle eight to astringent, hopping three-steps.

The ensemble is also the key to "Octopus's Garden," Ringo's vision of aquarian utopia. In years past, the other Beatles used to tease Ringo for bringing in compositions that were unwitting recyclings of other people's songs. But while "Octopus's Garden" bore more than slight resemblance to Paul's "Yellow Submarine," Ringo later said that he actually wrote it after quitting the Beatles the previous summer: "At the time, I just wanted to be under the sea, too. I wanted to get out of it for a while." In the *Let It Be* film, George Harrison is seen helping Ringo work out the chord sequence for the song, and he continues in that role on the finished record. His zippy opening guitar solo in particular helps create the impression that there is more to this slight song than there actually is. Paul's merrily clanking piano and the soaring backing harmonies he and George contribute further the illusion. Here was another of the Beatles' secrets on display: the way the group covered up the shortcomings of its various members. After all, how many other marginal singer-songwriters could rely on Paul McCartney and George Harrison to sing backing harmonies for them?

The last song on side one, "I Want You (She's So Heavy)," also was a monument to the Beatles' remarkable musical cohesion and rapport. Shortly after the Beatles broke up, Lennon said that one thing he missed about playing with them was "being able to just sort of blink or make a certain noise and know they'll all know where we are going on an ad-lib thing." It's easy to imagine John relying on this kind of telepathy to steer the other Beatles through "I Want You (She's So Heavy)." John's cry of love to Yoko may have been short on lyrical sophistication—the title itself, sung dozens of times over, was the song's only lyric—but musically "I Want You (She's So Heavy)" was quite complex, in that it shifted in and out of various tones and tempos that were subtly but unmistakably different. It took a tight band to negotiate all those twists and turns, but the Beatles (joined by keyboardist Billy Preston) finished the basic rhythm track in a single session, on February 22, 1969.

"I Want You (She's So Heavy)" also showed that the Beatles continued to have their avant-garde side. Doing so many separate iterations of a single riff was a risky choice that could have backfired into banality, but the pace of the song never flagged. The long, swelling fade-out was not exactly consistent with mainstream pop either. The sound gradually expanded to such massive dimensions that one would think classical orchestration was used, but in fact the effect was achieved by Lennon and Harrison taping countless electric guitar overdubs. John then boosted the sound further by deliberately injecting so-called white noise—static—into the mix, so that the last minute of the song resembled a windy night in the Arctic wilderness. And then, to add one last bit of strangeness, the storm vanished as abruptly as if the fuse box had blown out. This ending to "I Want You (She's So Heavy)" powerfully illustrated George Martin's separate observation, "There is nothing more electrifying, after a big sound, than complete silence," but it was apparently conceived of by John Lennon. During the final mixing session for *Abbey Road*, Lennon was listening to the playback of this song when he suddenly turned to engineer Alan Parsons and said, "There! Cut the tape there." As it happened, this mixing session, held on August 20, 1969, was the last time that all four Beatles were together inside Abbey Road Studios.

After the Beatles broke up, George Martin said on more than one occasion that he regretted not having devoted more attention to George Harrison as a songwriter. Martin's favoritism toward Lennon and McCartney was understandable, given the quality and quantity of their output, but as a result, said Martin, "George, poor George, didn't get much of a look until later on." Martin did not offer specifics, but "Here Comes The Sun," the opening song on side two of *Abbey Road*, may well have been one of the compositions that showed him the error of his ways. "Here Comes The Sun," Martin later said separately, "in some ways is one of the best songs ever written."

That is a very grand statement. But "Here Comes The Sun" certainly ranks as one of the best songs the Beatles ever recorded, and it is almost completely George Harrison's work. He wrote the song while strolling in Eric Clapton's garden on one of the first days of spring. Besides having composed it, he plays each of the many guitars that give it its frolic-in-the-grass sense of joy. He also plays the harmonium, does the handclaps and almost all the singing (except for some help from McCartney on harmonies)—in fact, he does everything but play Paul's bass and Ringo's drums and write Martin's score. For years, Lennon and McCartney had been writing songs whose excellence and accessibility were so widely and immediately apparent that they amounted to instant classics: "I Want To Hold Your Hand," "Help!" "Yesterday," "Norwegian Wood," "Eleanor Rigby," "We Can Work It Out," "Penny Lane," "A Day In The Life," "Hey, Jude." Now, after years of watching his big brothers, Harrison had done the same with "Here Comes The Sun."

"I wouldn't have minded being George, the invisible man, and learning what he learned" during the early Beatle years, said Lennon after the band broke up. And in fact, while "Here Comes The Sun" is very much its own creation, it does boast many of the same qualities that distinguish John and Paul's masterworks.

Above all, there is the ingenious blend of simplicity and sophistication. The melodic hook of "Here Comes The Sun" is so quick and pure that Harrison lodges it in the ear with less than two seconds of expertly picked acoustic guitar. Indeed, its five notes fit so snugly together that he doesn't even need words the second time he sings them—"Doo-doo-doo-doo"—and the rest of the song grows from there. The chords essentially follow the 1-4-5 routine, except a joker is thrown in at the end of the first verse, just before the line "And I said, it's all right," which precedes the bubbly strut that returns the tune to its beginning. In the middle eight—"Sun, Sun, Sun / Here it comes"—a second layer of simplicity is added when George plays another three-chord pattern. But this time the base shifts from A major to G major and the order is 4-1-5. And he introduces this key change with yet a third simplicity— the kind of unexpected but perfectly natural-sounding tempo change normally associated with John Lennon. The lyrics, too, have the strength of the innocent. Instead of preaching answers, they invoke universals: the warmth of the sun, the coming of spring, the smile of a human face. Like so much of the Beatles' best work, they gladden the heart and inspire faith in tomorrow.

Weaving together so much simplicity so intricately ends up creating a sublime form of sophistication. In another parallel with the Beatles' best work, there is far more going on within "Here Comes The Sun," far more textures and dimensions, than there is in most pop songs. Yet while "Here Comes The Sun" is structurally sophisticated, it is never obscure, because the essence is never lost. George had, in short, become quite a good musical architect. No doubt Paul and John's examples were crucial in this respect, but they, in turn, had learned from George Martin. Martin's advice to "think symphonically" had gotten all three Beatles thinking about how to make larger artistic statements within the pop format, and their innate talents and unquenchable curiosities had taken it from there.

Which helps explain another central characteristic of the Beatles' work that is illustrated by "Here Comes The Sun": Not only did they compose great songs, they gave the definitive interpretation of those songs. It is extremely difficult to think of a remake of any Beatles song that is superior to the original. How could a cover version improve on the Beatles' rendition of "Here Comes The Sun"? Their arrangement is airy yet grounded, gentle yet bombastic—contrasts that emerge from the combination of Harrison's delicate guitar work and diaphanous vocals on the one hand and Martin, McCartney, and Starr's vigorous instrumental contributions on the other. Martin brings in the strings on the very first syllable of Harrison's vocal in order to expand the total volume of sound, and then has the orchestra reinforce and counterpoint the main melodic themes for the rest of the song. After cleverly sneaking in unnoticed amidst the first rush of cellos, McCartney unleashes a bouncing, surfing bass line that gives the song an irresistible flow and momentum, which Starr accentuates with jolly, muscular drum bursts. The song conveys its mellow rapture as vividly as "Come Together" expresses its own confused vehemence at the start of side one, and the distance between those two moods only underlines yet another of the Beatles' strengths, their great emotional and musical range.

"Here Comes The Sun" is the one song on *Abbey Road* in which John Lennon played no role whatsoever. As such, it underscores that the three other Beatles were a pretty hot band in their own right. In fact, as instrumentalists, McCartney, Harrison, and Starr were in a different league than Lennon. His contribution to the group was something else altogether—a wild, searching, profound poetic sensibility that just happened to express itself most eloquently through music. The resulting foursome was a combustible mixture, in part because Lennon was such a multifaceted creative force. For every "I Am The Walrus," there was a "Julia," for every "Nowhere Man," a "Ticket To Ride." On *Abbey Road*, the hard edges of "Come Together" and "I Want You (She's So Heavy)" are balanced out by the lofty atmospherics of "Because," the second song on side two. Ringo is the odd man out on "Because," for this lovely meditation on the majesty of the round earth and its blue and windy skies is above all a vocal showcase for John, Paul, and George. Not since "This Boy," way back in the "I Want To Hold Your Hand" era, had they sung such complicated and exquisite three-part harmony.

Like the harmony singing on "Because," *Abbey Road* itself has been described as a very professional album. To stop there is to damn with faint praise, but it's true that *Abbey Road* is a highly competent piece of work, and in more ways than one. For example, part of the reason why Ringo's drumming and Paul's bass playing sound so potent is the great expertise with which they were recorded. The studio staff working with the Beatles on *Abbey Road* included some of the best technicians in the business. George Martin and Geoff Emerick in particular were veterans of the recording team that had revolutionized pop music recording methods during the making of the *Revolver* and *Sgt Pepper* albums.

Both men had in different degrees subsequently distanced themselves from the Beatles, largely because of the Beatles' own behavior, but they remained on the cutting edge of their craft when they returned to work on *Abbey Road*.

It was McCartney who, perhaps sensing that the Beatles had gotten too full of themselves and were veering offtrack, lured both Martin and Emerick back for *Abbey Road*. The other Beatles, especially John, sometimes resented this sort of managerial acuity on Paul's part, and with the *Magical Mystery Tour* film to his credit Paul's track record was by no means unblemished. But any fair reading of the Beatles' history has to concede that McCartney's organizational drive was a vital element in their accomplishments. Without it, *Abbey Road*, one of their three or four all-time best albums, would not have been made. For Paul was the one who hustled all the requisite people and parts into position and pushed this project through to completion. And of no aspect of the album was this more true than the long medley on side two, sixteen minutes of music that, in Ringo's words, contained "some of our finest work" ever.

The eight songs that constituted the medley were less songs than partially completed song fragments. It is a tribute to Martin and McCartney's musical abilities that they devised the many key and tempo changes that stitched these fragments into such a seamless continuum. But beyond that, it is a reflection of McCartney's keen organizational instincts that he realized that this was the way forward in the first place. Had it been left up to Lennon, those fragments probably would have remained unfinished, which in turn would have meant no album. Instead, the album was saved by Martin and McCartney's idea of transforming the fragments into a miniature symphony.

Lennon made no secret of his distaste for the *Abbey Road* medley, and while Martin was doubtless right that one reason was John's preference for straight-ahead rock 'n' roll, it was also true that the medley was McCartney's project and it involved conceptual complexities quite beyond Lennon's musical ken. It is also the case that Lennon's offerings are the least impressive parts of the medley. "Sun King," "Mean Mr. Mustard" and "Polythene Pam" have some good moments, especially the wicked humor of the latter. But they never hit the kind of high points reached by McCartney's contributions: the beautiful, aching sadness of "You Never Give Me Your Money," the rambunctious jauntiness of "She Came In Through The Bathroom Window," the world-weary yearning of "Golden Slumbers" and "Carry That Weight." Nevertheless, as a whole, the medley is a marvelous sleight-of-hand, somewhat akin to turning interesting leftovers into a holiday feast.

Appropriately enough, the most poignant moment in the medley comes during what is the last significant passage on the album, "The End." (The twenty-three-second ditty "Her Majesty" was tacked on after "The End" by a studio engineer and, for some reason, left in place by the Beatles.) Notwithstanding the hindsight-heavy accounts of this stage in the Beatles' career, it is important to remember that at the time the Beatles finished recording "The End," in early August 1969, they did not yet know they were going to break up. At least not consciously. But just as the *Abbey Road* album seems to sum up all the reasons why the Beatles became the most popular and accomplished musical force of their time, so "The End" gives each individual Beatle his turn in the spotlight before the curtain falls.

First comes Ringo's drum solo, the one and only of his career, a performance as solid and self-effacing as the drummer himself. Next follow a few bars of gloriously crunching guitar chords and "Love you" choruses as the Beatles return one last time to the pure rock 'n' roll that was always their greatest musical love. And then, going still further back, to the days when John, Paul, and George had no regular drummer and boasted that "the rhythm's in the guitars," each of the three guitarists lets rip with a distinctive farewell solo. Paul leads off, darting and soaring, then George shimmers in like quicksilver before John enters and slams the whole thing home. A bright, rapid piano emerges from the crash, setting the stage for the three former Quarry Men to reunite and sing a last piece of wisdom, Paul's line, "And in the end / The love you take / Is equal to the love you make." It had been a long, amazing road for the four lads from Liverpool. But in the end, Paul's sign-off line did not quite fit the Beatles themselves. For as much as the world loved them, the love they gave the world in return through their music was of a different, higher order—an extraordinary, miraculous gift, like no other before or since.

CHAPTER 24

The Classics of Their Time: The Beatles in History

"**H**APPY BIRTHDAY TO ME, HAPPY BIRTHDAY TO ME!" IT
IS OCTOBER 9, 1970, JOHN LENNON'S THIRTIETH BIRTHDAY, AND
he is spending the evening at Abbey Road Studios recording the first
studio album he will release since leaving the Beatles. In the background, his bandmates Ringo Starr and bassist Klaus Voormann
chuckle at John's tongue-in-cheek greeting to himself, but the jolly
studio atmosphere is nothing like what will be heard on the finished
record. Entitled *John Lennon/Plastic Ono Band*, the album will shock
listeners with its stripped-down production style and stark, confessional lyrics. The album's first lines refer to John's abandonment by his
mother when he was a child: "Mother, you had me, but I never had you
/ I wanted you, but you didn't want me." In "Working Class Hero,"
Lennon sings of a world where "as soon as you're born, they make you
feel small."

Plastic Ono Band became known as Lennon's "primal scream" album,
because he recorded it after spending four months in a form of psychological therapy that emphasized long sessions of howling and weeping
to purge the pain supposedly buried inside during childhood. John felt
that primal screaming had cured him, and perhaps it had. Despite the
album's often grim lyrics, the Abbey Road archives tapes reveal Lennon
in a buoyant, happy mood while in the studio. They contain lots of

307

funny, warmhearted exchanges between John and Ringo—wisecracking, joking and trading musical ideas with each other and with Voormann, the Beatles' old friend from Hamburg days. And John and Ringo both sound especially pleased when, later on John's birthday night, George Harrison unexpectedly drops into the studio.

At the time, John, Ringo, and Voormann are nearing the end of take four of the song "Remember." John hasn't figured out the song's ending yet, so the band just keeps vamping. At last, John stops playing and interrupts the others. "Okay, okay," he says, laughing. "If *one* of us doesn't stop—I mean, *somebody's* got to set a pattern." An instant later, John exclaims, with real life in his voice, "George!" and Ringo chirps, "Great!" as their old pal enters the studio. Harrison, who is working in a studio down the hall on his own solo album, *All Things Must Pass*, is apparently carrying a slide guitar, for the tape picks up a few of its notes, as well as John's question "Is it tuned to open E then?" George answers enthusiastically, "No, it's probably F-sharp, because it was strung so slack before." The tape runs out at that point, so the rest of the conversation is lost.

One of the most powerful songs on *Plastic Ono Band* is "God," in which Lennon delivers a litany of icons in whom he no longer believes, including Jesus, Elvis, Dylan, and, of course, the Beatles. But the Beatles that Lennon didn't believe in was the myth, not the men—the web of burdensome expectations, constraints, and pressures imposed by the outside world, not the three guys who went through the whole mad experience with him. As John said in 1980, "I still love those guys. The Beatles are over, but John, Paul, George and Ringo go on." Even McCartney, with whom Lennon was feuding at the time of the *Plastic Ono Band* sessions, and with whom he continued to have both public and private fights for the rest of his life, was by no means solely an enemy during the two men's solo years. To recall Harrison's metaphor for the Beatles' breakup, just because the four brothers had moved out and were now living on their own did not mean they stopped spending time with one another, and enjoying it when they did.

Notwithstanding Lennon's adamant disbelief, the myth of the Beatles survived and even grew in the years after the group's breakup. Because the Beatles quit at the height of their creative and commercial

powers, their artistic reputation remained largely untarnished by mediocre work; thus their mythic stature as the most beloved and accomplished musical partnership of their time was perfectly preserved, as if
in a time capsule. That mythic stature was then exalted to martyrdom
when Lennon was murdered outside his New York apartment building
by a deranged fan on December 8, 1980.

Long before that unspeakable tragedy, however, the myth of the
Beatles had flourished on a more mundane level. One of its many
manifestations was the continuing public interest in why the Beatles
had broken up and whether they would be getting back together again.
As usual, much of what the outside world came to believe about the
Beatles during this period bore only faint resemblance to the truth.
Perhaps because so much of the group's breakup had taken place in
courts of law and newspaper and magazine columns, many people
concluded that the Beatles had turned irrevocably against one another
(though this did not, paradoxically, silence the pleas that they reunite).
The truth was more complicated. To be sure, the former Beatles
continued to have their share of squabbles after breaking up, but they
had good times together as well, both professionally and socially; the
media portrayal of them as intransigent enemies was no more valid than
the innocent moptop image assigned to them in the 1960s. "We have
arguments and little fights," Ringo said in 1981. "We did when we were
touring, and we do now. But nothing like what the newspapers make it
out to be."

The basic rift had always been between Paul and the other three, and
relations between the two camps did remain quite frosty in the immediate aftermath of the breakup, especially during the 1971 court proceedings that McCartney initiated to dissolve the Beatles' partnership. But
by 1973, the situation had changed markedly. All four former Beatles
united that year to file suit against Allen Klein, the former business
manager who had been the proximate cause of their breakup. The four
also came together on vinyl, via separate contributions to Ringo's solo
album, *Ringo*. Although their collective dynamic had obviously
changed, their underlying friendship seemed to have survived the unpleasantness of the breakup. As long as they didn't talk about Apple
business, McCartney later recalled, they got along fine.

Whether they liked it or not, the four former Beatles were linked forever by the immensity of the Beatles experience. And as the breakup itself receded farther and farther into the past, it seemed that the bond forged during the good times was stronger than the bad feelings unleashed during the rupture. Beatles historian Mark Lewisohn has speculated that the former Beatles had "a level of kinship, brotherhood if you like, because of what they went through, that people will never really understand. I've always been pleased to see that even when they were slagging each other off, there was affection in it. It was like brothers who had fallen out. They were still brothers underneath." At a 1979 press conference, Harrison told a roomful of reporters, "Everybody's sued each other to their hearts' content and now we're all good friends. . . . We could all hang out together and have a great time, but the only thing that would spoil it would be all of you with the cameras and microphones."

"The men from the press," to borrow Lennon's phrase, didn't help much, but simpleminded journalism was not the only reason outsiders were unclear about how things stood among the former Beatles; they themselves often encouraged the confusion. They contradicted themselves in interviews, or provided deliberately misleading or vague replies, or simply changed their minds with the passage of time. Anyone reading Lennon's infamous "I'm a genius!" interview in *Rolling Stone* in early 1971, for example, would have thought he would never again have anything to do with the other Beatles; the same is true of the vicious attack he launched later that year against McCartney with the song "How Do You Sleep." But a few years later, Lennon distanced himself from both those outbursts. Notwithstanding his own denigration of the Beatles myth during the early 1970s, by 1974 Lennon was taking pleasure in recalling the Beatles' history. When McCartney passed through New York in mid-1974, the two ex-partners spent two or three nights together reminiscing about the old days in Hamburg and Liverpool.

At about that same time, Lennon and McCartney also began speaking positively about the Beatles playing music together again. Not exclusively or permanently, for each had his own life and career now, but a four-way collaboration of some sort. In an early 1975 interview, conducted shortly after the Beatles' legal partnership had at last been formally dissolved, Lennon said that there was a "good feeling among the guys" and "There's nothing [negative] going down between us. It's all in people's heads." Asked whether he shared Harrison's publicly stated reluctance to play again with McCartney, Lennon said of his old bandmates, "I could play with all of them. George is entitled to say that, and he'll probably change his mind by Friday. You know, we're all human. We can all change our minds. So I don't take any of my statements or any of their statements as the last word on whether we will."

Lennon's return to live with Yoko Ono in early 1975 put an end to that kind of talk, but the idea of some form of Beatles reunion never died completely. Although loath to fan reunion rumors—"The silliness goes on without us," complained Ringo in 1974—the former Beatles were also reluctant to absolutely rule out playing together again. "None of us want to be the first to say never," Lennon said in an interview just weeks before his death. "Never is such a long time. . . ." In fact, according to a legal deposition that Lennon gave a few days before his death, one specific project that had all four Beatles intrigued was the production of a collective video autobiography: the Beatles telling their life story on camera, and performing together again as part of the show. Tentatively titled *The Long And Winding Road*, the project remained in limbo throughout the 1980s.

The autobiography project was revived, however, after a massive legal settlement in 1989, which finally resolved all the lawsuits that had been pitting the Beatles against EMI Records since the 1970s and against each other since the 1980s. The three surviving Beatles decided to produce the autobiography themselves, through their Apple holding company. Retitled *The Beatles Anthology*, the multipart video was expected to air on television systems around the world sometime in 1995. The former Beatles also decided to open the vaults at Abbey Road and issue one or more CDs of previously unreleased music from their heyday. George Martin was asked to oversee this compilation of what he called "a historical outlook on the music" of the Beatles—an amalgam of live performances, alternate takes of already released songs, BBC radio performances, and selections from the Beatles' private collections.

Finally, the ex-Beatles also decided to perform together again. In February 1994, Paul, George, and Ringo went into a recording studio and added fresh vocal and instrumental tracks to a song that John had recorded but not completed before his death. "Free As A Bird," a willowy ballad that Lennon was said to have written after winning his legal fight against deportation from the United States in 1975, was also to be released in conjunction with the *Anthology* video series.

The *Anthology* project was described by Derek Taylor, the former Beatles press officer, as a means of the Beatles' reclaiming their own history. After years of watching outsiders define their legacy in books, films, and magazine articles that purported to be definitive but were usually far from it, the Beatles would at last tell their own story. The *Anthology* video and CDs would be their statement to history, their attempt to set the record straight about what they had done and what it meant. Thus, the *Anthology* autobiography also raised the related question of how the Beatles would be remembered in the future. Would their music continue to inspire critical respect and popular enjoyment in the decades and centuries ahead? When Paul McCartney said that people a century from now would be listening to the Beatles just like people today listen to Mozart, was that wishful thinking or an immodest but probably accurate prediction? Did the Beatles really belong in the same company as giants like Mozart and Beethoven, or would they fade from memory as soon as their generation of fans died off?

"I suppose it is pretentious to say that the Beatles are as important as those great people in the past, and it's not *really* for us to say," George Martin told me during an interview in 1993. Then, grinning, he added, "But we will say it all the same. Because the great value of the Beatles was in being the voice of the people, being the expression of music of their age. The music we did together in the 1960s was the best music that was happening in those times. It was the best also of *all* music at that time. I like not to have barriers in music. So if we're talking about contemporary music, we're talking about Boulez as well as the Beatles, and I claim the Beatles were the most important writers of contemporary music. On that basis, they've got to be recognized."

Martin is obviously prejudiced when it comes to the Beatles' musical accomplishments. The problem is, it is difficult to find *anyone* able to offer a truly unbiased judgment, simply because of the massive impact the Beatles' music has had. Perhaps all of us are still too close to the Beatles as a social phenomenon to hazard an objective judgment of their music in world historical terms. On the one hand, their songs are still heard so ubiquitously that one can easily take their beauty for granted. On the other, the songs still invoke such intense memories and feelings that it is impossible for many people to separate their emotions from the intrinsic quality of the music.

Moreover, the phenomenon cuts both ways. To this day, the news media in the United States and much of Europe is run by editors, reporters, and producers who came of age during the Beatles era. Their personal interest in the music (and in the Beatles themselves) may have resulted in news coverage that disproportionately inflated the Beatles' reputation among the public at large. However, the reverse is often true of later generations. Many who grew up with the music of the 1970s and 1980s all but closed their ears to the Beatles. The counterreaction was especially intense during the 1970s, when memories of the Beatles remained fresh and no one remotely comparable had arisen to supplant them. Trends in pop music are set largely by the young, who look to music in part to define their separateness from the adult world. In the 1970s, devotees of punk rock and new wave music actively denigrated the Beatles (and other sixties groups) as boring old farts who had to be swept away to make room for the new; many of their less zealous peers simply didn't bother to listen to the Beatles in the first place. Active or passive, such rebellions were a means of asserting generational identity. After all, to teenagers of the late 1970s and 1980s, the Beatles were the music of their parents.

Much the same argument was made back in the 1960s by young people who preferred the Rolling Stones to the Beatles. The Stones, it was said, were grittier, more dangerous and outrageous, more purely rock 'n' roll; one's parents might like the Beatles' music, but they would never stand for the overt sexuality and angry defiance of such Stones classics as "Let's Spend The Night Together" and "Street Fighting Man." This viewpoint understated the Beatles' own outlaw tendencies, but it was undeniably valid in another respect, one that links it to the post-sixties reactions against the Beatles. Bands like the Rolling

Stones—or, later, The Sex Pistols, Blondie, Talking Heads, Nirvana, or any number of other hot pop acts—were much more exclusively emblems of their respective generations than the Beatles were (using the word "generation" here in the pop music sense of two or three years of time). That is, anyone outside of that specific generation was unlikely to enjoy, or even know about, these acts; their following was strictly circumscribed by age, which meant that in almost every case their popularity plummeted as soon as their fans passed into full adulthood and stopped devoting so much time and passion to music.

Every generation needs and deserves its own cultural heroes and reference points, but to apply such criteria to the question of the historical standing of the Beatles is to confuse, yet again, emotional needs with artistic judgments. Whether one's parents like a given type of music or not is irrelevant to that music's actual worth. More to the point, the generational argument actually works in the Beatles' favor, for it underscores one of their greatest strengths: their appeal over time. The reason the Beatles can't be described as a generational band is that they were much more than that. To be sure, they were a symbol of their generation—was there anything more sixties than the Beatles?—but they also transcended that generation. Their music was so outstandingly universal that even older people who disapproved of the Beatles' lifestyles and beliefs often found they could not help but respond viscerally to their songs. "We always did songs which related to everybody from children to our parents and grandparents. . . . Everyone relates to 'Yesterday' and half the people still relate to 'I Am The Walrus,'" Ringo said in 1976.

It has now been more than thirty years since the Beatles' first number one record. Are we at last ready to see them for what they were? Returning to George Martin's point, the Beatles' status as the most important musical force of the late twentieth century seems indisputable. It's not simply that their music perfectly captured the spirit of its time; although essential, that achievement simply made the Beatles representative of their era. Rather, it was the revolutionary effect their music had on the world around them that most sets the Beatles apart. For example, before the Beatles, rock 'n' roll was strictly for teenagers; more than any other group, the Beatles were responsible for turning rock into the dominant pop music form of the late twentieth century. And they pushed musical history forward in other ways as well. They utterly transformed the way music was recorded and presented; they challenged the traditional role of pop stars as opinionless, plastic icons; they broadened and deepened the prevailing conception of pop music, forcing its recognition as a genuine art form. In terms of social resonance, lasting global popularity, and artistic excellence, no other contemporary artist, or group of artists, has achieved anything like what the Beatles did. As Ringo once observed, "Who else is there? . . . We were the monsters. There's been a lot of biggies, and very few monsters. That's the difference."

The sheer impact of the Beatles assures them a place in history, yet the question remains: What will their stature be on *artistic* grounds? It is one thing to be remembered for being historically significant; it is another to be ranked among the greatest musical artists in human history. The Beatles will surely be deemed "important" for many years to come. But will their songs be listened to merely as cultural artifacts, or will they be enjoyed for their own sake as well? Leaving aside their undeniable importance as a social phenomenon, is the Beatles' music alone of a quality to rank them as the enduring classics of their time?

Quite possibly yes. There is no single artist who dominates twentieth-century music the way Picasso dominates twentieth-century painting, but if one assembled even a short list of the century's musical giants, it would be very difficult to leave off the Beatles. Not only were they outstanding composers, having written dozens of songs that were both hugely popular and musically exceptional, they were also spectacular performers, both in their live shows and in their studio recordings. George Martin cited this dual achievement as the key reason for distinguishing between the Beatles, on the one hand, and, on the other, a performer as inspired as Elvis Presley and a songwriter as gifted as George Gershwin. "People don't remember Elvis Presley for 'Heartbreak Hotel' or the other songs, they remember Elvis Presley," contended Martin. "That's the first focus, the songs come after. With the Beatles, there is their enormous songbook. It's like Gershwin. Gershwin is not remembered as a performer at all, he's remembered for his music. The Beatles have been able to combine the two things—they've got this great songbook, à la Gershwin, and they've got the great performance record, à la Presley."

Replace Presley and Gershwin with Frank Sinatra and Cole Porter and the same point applies. Or plug in Bob Dylan—the greatest poet of his generation, and a very fine songwriter, but handicapped by a less than wonderful singing voice and persona. Of course there is Duke Ellington, the pianist, band leader, and composer who for decades created and performed music of rich and lasting quality, but there are not many others whose careers can survive comparison with that of the Beatles.

John Lennon used to say that the songs of the Beatles were nothing more nor less than the folk music of the electronic age. This truth is reflected in the fact that countless millions of people from all generations and walks of life, not to mention widely diverse cultures and countries, have enthusiastically applauded the Beatles' music over the years. This response is partly a tribute to the Beatles' extraordinary creative range. Offering everything from sweaty rock 'n' roll tunes like "I Saw Her Standing There" and touching love songs like "Here, There And Everywhere" to inspiring anthems like "All You Need Is Love" and children's sing-alongs like "Yellow Submarine" to mind-bending psychedelia like "Tomorrow Never Knows" and masterful social commentary like "A Day In The Life" meant that there was something for everyone in the Beatles' repertoire. In addition, the Beatles never forsook the common vernacular; unlike modern composers of classical music, the Beatles spoke in a language that the broad public could understand. And they spoke about things that mattered. They thought that making the world a better place was important, and their music encouraged people to take heart and join in. Without lapsing into the stridency that afflicts so many self-consciously "political artists," the Beatles spread values of love, justice, and liberation that not only contributed to such immediate political change as ending the Vietnam War but also helped foster a revolution in attitudes and behavior whose aftereffects are still visible. Like many folk poets, the Beatles were political rebels, but because their music was so widely beloved, they got away with it.

Because of the Beatles' uncanny ability to weave simplicity into sophistication, their "folk music" simultaneously ascended to the level of enduring artistic achievement. Perhaps the most fundamental reason that the Beatles' music "has cut through differences of race, age and class [and] is adored by the world," as Derek Taylor put it in 1964, is that it touches the essence of what it is to be human. Lyrically and musically, the songs of the Beatles both invoke and convey the joy, sorrow, struggle, laughter, wisdom, anger, love, fear, and other emotions and experiences that make up the human condition. To be sure, the Beatles did not consciously intend anything so grand; indeed, they seem to have often been unaware of all that was expressed in their songs. And while they never shirked from hard work, it was not perspiration so much as inspiration that imparted such special magic to their music. LSD guru Timothy Leary sounded silly in the late 1960s when he called the Beatles young gods incarnate who had been dispatched to earth to lead humanity to a new evolutionary stage, but his underlying point was not so outlandish. The music produced by the collaboration of the Beatles was, as they themselves recognized, something bigger than the four of them. When John, Paul, George, and Ringo all came together, they seemed to enter another dimension, as George Martin put it, and become a vehicle for whatever higher force is out there, urging us all on. Lennon described this phenomenon as being a channel for "the music of the spheres, the music that passes all understanding." But however one explains it, the Beatles tapped into the deepest, truest aspects of being human. And in so doing, they, like all great artists, put the rest of us in touch with the divine.

The music of the Beatles was, in short, high art for the mass public. And remarkably enough, it was recognized and embraced as such, virtually from the moment it first reached a wide audience. Yet precisely because the Beatles were such a gigantic popular success, there will always be those who refuse to accept that the music they produced might qualify as great art. The fact that men like Mozart and Shakespeare were immensely popular in their own times puts the lie to such elitism (though this is not meant to equate the Beatles with those two giants on strictly artistic grounds). When Paul McCartney says that people will be listening to the Beatles a hundred years from now just like we listen to Mozart today, he isn't—or shouldn't be—claiming that the Beatles are Mozart's musical equal. Comparing Mozart and the Beatles is, in that sense, like comparing apples and oranges. But the Beatles may well be regarded as the twentieth-century counterpart of Mozart. Like him, they created music that was not only the most popular of its time but also of the very highest quality artistically.

No serious history of twentieth-century music could fail to award a place of prominence and respect to the Beatles. In terms of influence, impact, originality, popularity, relevance, and excellence, their work is without modern peer. McCartney may be right that the music of the Beatles will transcend its time and place and be enjoyed in centuries to come. But ultimately that judgment is for future generations to make. The main message of the Beatles, as Lennon said shortly before his death, is "Be here now." And right here, right now, their music sounds as fresh as it ever did, and ever will.

The Released Recordings of the Beatles

(Listed according to the official, British order of issuance.)
(Singles in regular type, albums in *italics*)
(EPs listed only when containing otherwise unissued material)

1962

Love Me Do/P.S. I Love You, released October 5, 1962.

1963

Please Please Me/Ask Me Why, released January 11, 1963.

Please Please Me, released March 22, 1963.

    Side One: I Saw Her Standing There; Misery; Anna (Go To Him); Chains; Boys; Ask Me Why; Please Please Me.
    Side Two: Love Me Do; P.S. I Love You; Baby It's You; Do You Want To Know A Secret; A Taste of Honey; There's A Place; Twist And Shout

From Me To You/Thank You Girl, released April 11, 1963.

She Loves You/I'll Get You, released August 23, 1963.

With The Beatles, released November 22, 1963.

    Side One: It Won't Be Long; All I've Got To Do; All My Loving; Don't Bother Me; Little Child; 'Till There Was You; Please Mister Postman.
    Side Two: Roll Over Beethoven; Hold Me Tight; You Really Got A Hold On Me; I Wanna Be Your Man; Devil In Her Heart; Not A Second Time; Money (That's What I Want).

I Want To Hold Your Hand/This Boy, released November 29, 1963.

1964

Can't Buy Me Love/You Can't Do That, released March 20, 1964.

Long Tall Sally, Extended Play, released June 19, 1964.

    Side One: Long Tall Sally; I Call Your Name.
    Side Two: Slowdown; Matchbox.

A Hard Day's Night/Things We Said Today, released July 10, 1964.

A Hard Day's Night, released July 10, 1964.

    Side One: A Hard Day's Night; I Should Have Known Better; If I Fell; I'm Happy Just To Dance With You; And I Love Her; Tell Me Why; Can't Buy Me Love.
    Side Two: Any Time At All; I'll Cry Instead; Things We Said Today; When I Get Home; You Can't Do That; I'll Be Back.

I Feel Fine/She's A Woman, released November 27, 1964.

Beatles For Sale, released December 4, 1964.

    Side One: No Reply; I'm A Loser; Baby's In Black; Rock And Roll Music; I'll Follow The Sun; Mr. Moonlight; Kansas City/Hey, Hey, Hey, Hey!
    Side Two: Eight Days A Week; Words Of Love; Honey Don't; Every Little Thing; I Don't Want To Spoil The Party; What You're Doing; Everybody's Trying To Be My Baby.

1965

Ticket To Ride/Yes It Is, released April 9, 1965.

Help!/I'm Down, released July 23, 1965.

Help!, released August 6, 1965.

    Side One: Help!; The Night Before; You've Got To Hide Your Love Away; I Need You; Another Girl; You're Going To Lose That Girl; Ticket To Ride.
    Side Two: Act Naturally; It's Only Love; You Like Me Too Much; Tell Me What You See; I've Just Seen A Face; Yesterday; Dizzy Miss Lizzy.

We Can Work It Out/Day Tripper, released December 3, 1965.

Rubber Soul, released December 3, 1965.

Side One: Drive My Car; Norwegian Wood (This Bird Has Flown); You Won't See Me; Nowhere Man; Think For Yourself; The Word; Michelle.

Side Two: What Goes On; Girl; I'm Looking Through You; In My Life; Wait; If I Needed Someone; Run For Your Life.

1966

Paperback Writer/Rain, released June 10, 1966.

Eleanor Rigby/Yellow Submarine, released August 5, 1966.

Revolver; released August 5, 1966.

Side One: Taxman; Eleanor Rigby; I'm Only Sleeping; Love You To; Here, There And Everywhere; Yellow Submarine; She Said She Said.

Side Two: Good Day Sunshine; And Your Bird Can Sing; For No One; Doctor Robert; I Want To Tell You; Got To Get You Into My Life; Tomorrow Never Knows.

Bad Boy, released December 9, 1966. (The only original song released on the Christmas album *A Collection of Beatles Oldies*.)

1967

Strawberry Fields Forever/Penny Lane, released February 17, 1967.

Sgt Pepper's Lonely Hearts Club Band, released June 1, 1967.

Side One: Sgt Pepper's Lonely Hearts Club Band; With A Little Help From My Friends; Lucy In The Sky With Diamonds; Getting Better; Fixing A Hole; She's Leaving Home; Being For The Benefit Of Mr. Kite.

Side Two: Within You Without You; When I'm Sixty-Four; Lovely Rita; Good Morning Good Morning; Sgt Pepper's Lonely Hearts Club Band (Reprise); A Day In The Life.

All You Need Is Love/Baby, You're A Rich Man, released July 7, 1967.

Hello, Goodbye/I Am The Walrus, released November 24, 1967.

Magical Mystery Tour; Extended Play, released December 8, 1967.

Side One: Magical Mystery Tour; Your Mother Should Know.
Side Two: I Am The Walrus.

Side Three: The Fool On The Hill; Flying.
Side Four: Blue Jay Way.

1968

Lady Madonna/The Inner Light, released March 15, 1968.

Hey, Jude/Revolution, released August 30, 1968.

The Beatles, released November 22, 1968.

Side One: Back In The U.S.S.R.; Dear Prudence; Glass Onion; Ob-La-Di, Ob-La-Da; Wild Honey Pie; The Continuing Story Of Bungalow Bill; While My Guitar Gently Weeps; Happiness Is A Warm Gun.

Side Two: Martha My Dear; I'm So Tired; Blackbird; Piggies; Rocky Raccoon; Don't Pass Me By; Why Don't We Do It In The Road; I Will; Julia.

Side Three: Birthday; Yer Blues; Mother Nature's Son; Everybody's Got Something To Hide Except Me And My Monkey; Sexy Sadie; Helter Skelter; Long, Long, Long.

Side Four: Revolution 1; Honey Pie; Savoy Truffle; Cry Baby Cry; Revolution 9; Goodnight.

1969

Yellow Submarine, released January 17, 1969.

Side One: Yellow Submarine; Only A Northern Song; All Together Now; Hey Bulldog; It's All Too Much; All You Need Is Love.

Side Two: Seven instrumental tracks from the soundtrack to the film, *Yellow Submarine*; performed by the George Martin Orchestra.

Get Back/Don't Let Me Down, released April 11, 1969.

The Ballad of John And Yoko/Old Brown Shoe, released May 30, 1969.

Abbey Road, released September 26, 1969.

Side One: Come Together; Something; Maxwell's Silver Hammer; Oh! Darling; Octopus's Garden; I Want You (She's So Heavy).

Side Two: Here Comes The Sun; Because; You Never Give Me Your Money; Sun King; Mean Mr. Mustard; Polythene Pam; She Came In

Through The Bathroom Window; Golden Slumbers; Carry That Weight; The End; Her Majesty.

1970

Let It Be/You Know My Name (Look Up The Number), released March 6, 1970.

Let It Be, released May 8, 1970.

Side One: Two Of Us; Dig A Pony; Across The Universe; I Me Mine; Dig It; Let It Be; Maggie Mae.

Side Two: I've Got A Feeling; The One After 909; The Long And Winding Road; For You Blue; Get Back.

This book began as an article for *The New Yorker* magazine. Eventually published on January 24, 1994, the article broke the news worldwide that the three surviving Beatles—Paul McCartney, George Harrison, and Ringo Starr—had begun working together again for the first time since the band's breakup in 1970. The article reported that the three former Beatles were producing a multi-hour video autobiography of the group, *The Beatles Anthology*, whose release in 1995 would be accompanied by four to six CDs of previously unreleased music from the Beatles archives at Abbey Road Studios in London. It also reported that the surviving Beatles were planning to record new music for possible release in conjunction with the *Anthology* project.

This information about the *Anthology* project came to light only after the assignment of the article; the article was originally conceived of as a profile of Mark Lewisohn, a researcher and author who is recognized as one of the world's foremost authorities on the Beatles. Lewisohn is the only person (outside the Beatles themselves and Abbey Road Studios staffers) who has listened to all four hundred–plus hours of working tapes in the Beatles archives at Abbey Road Studios in London, a task he undertook in 1987 under commission for EMI Records, the Beatles' record company and the owner of the tapes. In the course of my *New Yorker* reporting on Lewisohn, I was granted access to the Abbey Road archives twice by EMI officials, making me the first outside journalist so fortunate. I eventually listened to some fifty hours' worth of archives tapes of the Beatles and of the solo work of John Lennon. I later supplemented my access to these official archives tapes by listening to dozens of additional hours of so-called bootleg tapes—copies of the Abbey Road tapes that have long circulated outside the copyright system. As noted in this book's Preface, these recordings were, along with the Beatles' commercially released song catalogue, the primary source materials for this book.

I decided to write *A Day In The Life* only after finishing my *New Yorker* article. While researching the article, I had read almost all the books about the Beatles that were still in print or in libraries. It was a mind-numbing but eye-opening experience, and at the end I realized that, despite the shelves full of books, there was no single volume that did justice to what matters most about the Beatles: their music. Most Beatles books concentrate more on the colorful private lives of the Fab Four than on their art. Of the books that do focus on the music, such critical analyses as Wilfrid Mellers's *Twilight of the Gods* and Tim Riley's *Tell Me Why* sometimes offer useful insights, but these insights are buried in prose that is written well over the head of anyone lacking a university degree in musical theory. Beatles producer George Martin's autobiography, *All You Need Is Ears*, and his memoirs of recording the *Sgt Pepper's Lonely Hearts Club Band* album, *The Summer Of Love*, contain valuable information and observations, but they are also limited; Martin is too close to the Beatles to put them into larger perspective, he has little to say about their lyrics, and his books cover only a limited portion of the Beatles canon. Mark Lewisohn's cataloguing of the contents of the four hundred hours of Abbey Road archives tapes, *The Beatles: Recording Sessions*, is superb, but superb in the way an encyclopedia is superb; *Recording Sessions* provides far more detail than the average reader wants and inevitably focuses more on the trees than on the forest.

I wanted to write a book that took the Beatles' music seriously but that also was accessible, a book that illuminated the creative process behind the art that has changed the lives of millions, while also putting that art into a larger historical perspective. This was impossible to do without simultaneously cutting through the barrage of myth and misinformation that had grown up around the Beatles and their work. For a second realization from my marathon of Beatles reading was that, despite the many Beatles books whose ad copy promises that they "set the record straight" on the Beatles, there was in fact no book that assembled in a single volume the best attainable—and genuinely reliable—version of truth concerning the lives and work of the foremost musical group of our time.

As an investigative reporter, I was shocked by how factually unreliable most Beatles books are. It is not that their "facts" are always wrong. Sometimes they are, sometimes not. The real problem is, there's usually no way of telling the difference, because the source of the information is not made clear. Very few Beatles books provide documentation to back up their claims; the reader is expected to accept them on faith. To be sure, the consequent damage to the truth is sometimes minor. One easy way to check the reliability of any Beatles book is to compare its version of a given Beatles quote with film or radio recordings of the actual statement. For example, after John Lennon's notorious 1966 remark about the Beatles being "more popular than Jesus," he faced reporters in Chicago where he explained himself thus: "I'm not anti-God, anti-Christ, or anti-religion. I was not saying we are greater or better. I believe in God, but not as one thing, not as an old man in the sky. I believe that what people call God is something in all of us." Philip Norman, on page 333 of his *Shout!*, gives instead the following quote: "I'm sorry I opened my mouth. I'm not anti-God, anti-Christ or anti-religion. I wouldn't knock it. I didn't mean we were greater or better." Such differences seem, and sometimes are, slight. But even slight differences can convey significantly different meanings. Moreover, such inconsistencies raise the question of whether there could be similar differences on larger, more complex or complicated points.

Beyond simple accuracy, there is the issue of journalistic honesty and fairness. Many authors of Beatles books use technically factual evidence in misleading ways—for example, by quoting a source who supports the author's point of view while ignoring countervailing evidence, or by presenting one source's perspective on a given event or situation as the *truth* of that event or situation, when in fact it was just one person's opinion about it. Standards of proof have, in short, been appallingly low; one simply cannot trust that the "facts" in most Beatles books are anything more than one-sided speculation, hearsay, or opinion. As a result, to quote George Martin's preface to Mark Lewisohn's *The Complete Beatles Chronicle*, "a great deal of misinformed rubbish has been avidly devoured."

One of the most controversial books in this regard was Albert Goldman's *The Lives of John Lennon*. Goldman seemed reflexively driven to interpret any and all evidence in the most sensational manner possible. One example among many was his claim (though, typically, he presented it as fact) that Lennon was a homosexual and had a long and intense relationship with the Beatles' manager, Brian Epstein (who was indeed gay). A careful reading of the relevant passages in Goldman's book reveals that the bulk of the evidence for his claim resided on the "must have been" and "according to someone who heard it from someone else" level of proof. Peter Brown, Epstein's former aide and a long-time senior staffer for the Beatles, made a less salacious and sweeping version of the same claim in his kiss-and-tell recounting of the Beatles story, *The Love You Make* (co-authored with Steven Gaines), again without adequately documenting the charge. The one solid piece of evidence on this subject has been provided by Pete Shotton, Lennon's closest friend since childhood; in Shotton's recollection of their friendship, *John Lennon In My Life* (co-authored with Nicholas Schaffner), Shotton provides a secondhand account of a single incident. Shotton writes that Lennon once told him that he, John, had on a single occasion allowed Epstein to give him a hand job. The difference between one such passing sexual encounter and a full-fledged homosexual relationship is, of course, vast, but Goldman in particular seems not to recognize any such distinctions.

At the other end of the spectrum is Lewisohn, whose books on the Beatles are models of rigorously researched and carefully presented information. Having interviewed Lewisohn extensively while preparing my *New Yorker* profile of him, I came to appreciate how dedicated and tenacious an approach he takes to certifiable fact. With Lewisohn, nothing goes into print unless it is documented in black and white; his motto seems to be that it is better to say nothing than to guess. In fact, the world has Lewisohn to thank for establishing the exact date that John Lennon and Paul McCartney first met, and the story of his research is instructive as regards the factual basis of much popular writing about the Beatles. Before Lewisohn's research, most books had properly reported that the two schoolboys met at an outdoor church fair, where John was performing with his band, the Quarry Men, but the date of this fateful meeting varied from anywhere in 1956 to 1958. (The Beatles' own authorized biography sets the date, wrongly, as June 15, 1956.) One day in London, Lewisohn invited me to the British

Library's Newspaper Library, just north of the city, where he showed me how he had pinpointed the true date: by painstakingly scanning every column of every page of the *South Liverpool Weekly News* for the summer months of 1956, 1958, and finally 1957 until he came across a small item reporting on the festival.

Because of his extraordinary access to primary sources and his tireless scholarship, Mark Lewisohn's books seem certain to be standard reference volumes for as long as people remain interested in the Beatles. Long after scores of other Beatles books—the half-baked biographies, the supposed insider accounts, the well-intentioned musical appreciations—have disappeared from bookshop and library shelves, Lewisohn's books will remain an enduring part of the historical record. *Recording Sessions* and *The Complete Beatles Chronicle* in particular are essential purchases for any serious student of the Beatles. Indeed, without the foundation of archival material provided in *Recording Sessions*, my own book could not have been written.

Because they are built on the solid ground of unimpeachable documentation and checkable fact, Lewisohn's books are cited frequently in the Notes that follow. I have of course drawn on other books, articles, and radio, television, and film recordings as well. Wherever possible, I have gone to the original source for the fact in question, and I have relied as extensively as possible on first-person, eyewitness accounts, judiciously cross-checking them against competing versions of events. The Beatles themselves have been interviewed often and at length over the years, especially in *Rolling Stone* and *Playboy* magazines, and I have relied on their direct statements whenever I could, bearing in mind that the Beatles, too, can express mere opinion or change their minds over time. As for other books, I have given precedence to those that are based on firsthand knowledge, such as George Martin's *The Summer of Love* and Pete Shotton's *John Lennon In My Life*, and to those based on original, firsthand reporting by an author, such as the official biography of the Beatles, *The Beatles*, written in 1968 by Hunter Davies, and the two-volume biography of John Lennon, *Lennon*, published in 1984 by journalist and Lennon friend Ray Coleman. Most other sources I have approached with caution for the reasons described above; I have used their facts only in limited instances, where the specific circumstances gave credence to their accounts, and I have explained my actions in the relevant passage of the Notes.

Only the names and authors of books cited are listed in the Notes that follow. For full publication references, see the Bibliography, which precedes the Notes, and be aware that in some cases (noted as such) the page numbers cited refer to a paperback edition. Magazine articles are referenced in full in the Notes. During my *New Yorker* reporting, I conducted interviews with a number of associates of and experts on the Beatles, including George Martin, Derek Taylor, Ken Townsend, and Mark Lewisohn; these interviews have been used in this book as well. I also requested interviews with Paul McCartney, George Harrison, and Ringo Starr; each of them declined.

B i b l i o g r a p h y

David Bennahum. *in their own words: the Beatles . . . after the breakup.* Omnibus Press, London, 1991, paperback.

Pete Best, *Beatle!: The Pete Best Story,* Plexus, London, 1985.

John Blake. *All You Needed Was Love: The Beatles After The Beatles.* Perigee Books, New York, 1981.

Peter Brown and Steven Gaines. *The Love You Make: An Insider's Story of The Beatles.* Penguin Books, New York, 1984, paperback.

Ray Coleman. *Lennon: The Definitive Biography.* Harper Perennial, New York, 1992, paperback.

Hunter Davies. *The Beatles.* McGraw-Hill, New York, 1985, paperback, second revised edition.

Richard DiLello. *The Longest Cocktail Party.* Playboy Press, New York, 1972.

William J. Dowlding. *Beatlesongs.* Simon & Schuster, New York, 1989, paperback.

Brian Epstein. *A Cellarful of Noise.* Doubleday, New York, 1964.

Vic Garbarini and Brian Cullman, with Barbara Graustark. *Strawberry Fields Forever: John Lennon Remembered.* Bantam, New York, 1980, paperback.

Geoffrey Giuliano. *The Beatles: A Celebration,* Methuen, Toronto, 1986.

Geoffrey Giuliano. *Blackbird.* Penguin, New York, 1992, paperback.

Geoffrey Giuliano. *Dark Horse: The Secret Life of George Harrison.* Stoddart, Toronto, 1989, paperback.

Albert Goldman. *The Lives of John Lennon.* William Morrow, New York, 1988.

John Green. *Dakota Days.* St. Martin's Press, New York, 1983, paperback.

Edward Gross. *Paul McCartney: Twenty Years on His Own.* Pioneer Books, Las Vegas, 1990, paperback.

George Harrison. *I Me Mine.* Simon & Schuster, New York, 1980.

Cynthia Lennon, *A Twist of Lennon.* Star Books, London, 1978.

John Lennon. *In His Own Write* and *A Spaniard in the Works*. New American Library, New York, 1967, paperback, 1980 reissue.

John Lennon. *Skywriting by Word of Mouth*. Harper & Row, New York, 1986.

Hal Leonard. *The Complete Beatles*. Hal Leonard Publishing, Milwaukee, 1988, Volumes 1 and 2.

Mark Lewisohn. *The Beatles: Recording Sessions*. Harmony Books, New York, 1990, paperback.

Mark Lewisohn. *The Complete Beatles Chronicle*. Harmony Books, New York, 1992.

Mark Lewisohn, Piet Schreuders, and Adam Smith. *The Beatles London*. Hamlyn, London, 1994.

Ian Macdonald. *Revolution In The Head: the beatles' records & the sixties*. Fourth Estate, London, 1994.

Paul McCartney. *The Paul McCartney World Tour*. Privately published, 1990.

George Martin, with Jeremy Hornsby. *All You Need Is Ears*. St. Martin's Press, New York, 1979, paperback.

George Martin, with William Pearson. *The Summer of Love*. Pan Macmillan, London, 1994.

Wilfrid Mellers. *The Twilight of the Gods: The Music of the Beatles*. Macmillan, New York, 1973, paperback.

Miles. *Beatles: In Their Own Words*. Omnibus Press, London, 1978, paperback.

Scott Muni et al. *Ticket To Ride*. Macdonald, London, 1989.

Philip Norman. *Shout!: The Beatles in Their Generation*. Warner Books, New York, 1981, paperback.

May Pang. *Loving John: The Untold Story*. Warner Books, New York, 1983, paperback.

Tim Riley. *Tell Me Why: The Beatles: Album by Album, Song by Song, The Sixties and After*. Vintage Books, New York, 1989, paperback.

Editors of *Rolling Stone*. *The Ballad of John and Yoko*. Rolling Stone Press, Garden City, N.Y., 1982, paperback.

Chris Salewicz. *McCartney*. St. Martin's Press, New York, 1986, paperback.

Nicholas Schaffner. *The Beatles Forever*. Stackpole Books, Harrisonburg, Pennsylvania, 1977.

A Day In The Life

Frederic Seaman. *The Last Days of John Lennon*. Dell, New York, 1991, paperback.

David Sheff and G. Barry Golson. *The Playboy Interviews with John Lennon and Yoko Ono*. Playboy Press, 1981.

Pete Shotton and Nicholas Schaffner. *John Lennon In My Life*. Stein & Day, New York, 1983, paperback.

Derek Taylor. *As Time Goes By*. Davis-Poynter, London, 1973.

Derek Taylor. *It Was Twenty Years Ago Today*. Simon & Schuster (Fireside), New York, 1987, paperback.

Elizabeth Thompson and David Gutman, editors. *The Lennon Companion: Twenty-five Years of Comment*. Macmillan, New York, 1987.

Jann Wenner. *Lennon Remembers*. Popular Library, New York, 1971, paperback.

Jon Wiener. *Come Together: John Lennon in His Time*. Random House, New York, 1984, paperback.

Films:

It Was Twenty Years Ago Today, Granada Television, 1987.

Let It Be, directed by Michael Lindsay-Hogg, executive producers The Beatles, United Artists, 1970.

The Compleat Beatles, directed by Patrick Montgomery, Delilah Films, 1982.

The Making of Sgt Pepper, directed by Alan Benson, executive producer George Martin, A Really Useful Group, 1992.

Notes

CHAPTER ONE:
Inside Abbey Road Studios
("A Day In The Life")

Page 1:   The description of the Beatles archive room at Abbey Road is based on interviews conducted by the author with various Abbey Road sources during visits to Abbey Road in December 1992 and April 1993.

The figure of ten and a half hours is based on a tabulation of all the individual songs released on the Beatles records. Note that the reference to fourteen albums includes both the twelve bona fide albums the group released *and* the EPs *Long Tall Sally* and *Magical Mystery Tour*, but excludes the 1966 album *A Collection Of Beatles Oldies* because the latter contained only songs that had been previously released as singles or on other albums, except for the song "Bad Boy."

The figure of four hundred hours for the amount of unreleased recordings in the Beatles archives was provided by Abbey Road archivist Mark Lewisohn in an interview with the author.

The dates of the music contained in the Abbey Road archives are based on Lewisohn's book *The Beatles: Recording Sessions*. The description of the actual tape boxes is based on the author's eyewitness observation.

Page 2:   Lennon's "a peak" quote is from page 138 of Jann Wenner's book *Lennon Remembers*.

Page 2:   Lennon's "eyeball to eyeball" quote is from page 117 of the *Playboy Interviews*. His "I needed a middle-eight" quote is from page 49 of *The Ballad of John and Yoko*.

Page 3:   Lennon's "I was reading the paper" quote is found on page 155 of the *Playboy Interviews*.

The commentary about the significance of the lyrics about the Guinness heir is the author's own analysis.

Page 3:   Wilfrid Mellers's remark is found in his book *The Twilight of the Gods*, page 98.

Lewisohn's "While Paul or George's 1-2-3-4 count-ins" quote is from page 39 of his *Recording Sessions*.

That the four-track tape machine is the only one on the Abbey Road premises capable of playing the four-track tapes used during the 1960s was confirmed by the author during interviews with Abbey Road staff members.

Page 4: The drug connotation of "Sugarplum fairy" is noted on page 52 of George Martin's book *The Summer of Love.*

Page 5: The information on the date and times of the recording sessions for "A Day In The Life" is from page 94 of Lewisohn's *Recording Sessions.* George Martin's "We left it in" quote is found on page 208 of his autobiography, *All You Need Is Ears.*

Page 7: McCartney's "was based on some of the ideas" quote is from his interview in the December 1984 issue of *Playboy.* Martin's "a tremendous build-up" quote is found on page 209 of *All You Need Is Ears.*

That Lennon and McCartney were musically illiterate is discussed by Martin on pages 138–39 of ibid.

Page 7: Martin's recollections of the scoring of "A Day In The Life" are found on pages 209–12. His "And whatever you do" quote is found on page 96 of Lewisohn's *Recording Sessions*, which also confirms the February 10 date of the session. McCartney's "It was interesting" quote is found on page 14 of ibid.

The Beatles evening wear request is recalled by Martin on pages 210–11 of *All You Need Is Ears* and noted on pages 244–45 of Lewisohn's *Chronicle*, which also lists the other guests and notes the existence of the film shot that evening. A copy of the film was viewed by the author. The other videos previously shot by the Beatles are described on pages 221–22 and 243 of ibid.

Page 8: McCartney's "In the future" quote is found on page 111 of Miles, *Beatles: In Their Own Words.*

Page 8: The reasons for the BBC's banning of "A Day In The Life" are noted on page 255 of Lewisohn's *Chronicle.* McCartney's "as a deliberate provocation" quote is from page 92 of Miles, *Beatles: In Their Own Words.* George Harrison's "to wake up as many people" as we could quote is found on page 150 of Derek Taylor's book *It Was Twenty Years Ago Today.* McCartney's "It wasn't a willful arrogance" quote is from page 13 of Lewisohn's *Recording Sessions.*

Page 9: The applause and Martin's "When we'd finished" quote are noted on page 97 of Lewisohn's *Recording Sessions.* The tapes containing the long hum were heard by the author. Lennon's "a sound like the end of the world" quote is referenced to the May 30, 1987, issue of the London *Times* on page 181 of William Dowlding's *Beatlesongs*.

Page 10: Tim Riley's "is ultimately hopeful" quote is found on page 229 of his book *Tell Me Why*.

McCartney's Mozart quote appeared in the January 24, 1994, issue of *The New Yorker*, for which the remark was fact-checked with publicist Geoff Baker in McCartney's London office. Lennon's remarks about the Beatles being more popular than Jesus were widely reported—see, for example, page 212 of Lewisohn's *Chronicle*—and are described in greater depth in Chapter 16 of this book. Kroll's remark in *Newsweek* is cited on page 155 of Martin's *The Summer of Love*.

CHAPTER TWO:
Four Lads from Liverpool

Page 13: Lennon's comments about his kinship with previous writers and artists comes from the *Playboy Interviews*, pages 133–34. His childhood remark about seeing God sitting by the fire is reported in Coleman's *Lennon*, page 114.

Page 14: An early example of Lennon's penchant for referring to Yoko Ono as "Mother" comes in his 1968 composition, "Happiness Is A Warm Gun," when he sings, "Mother Superior jumps the gun." Later, in the *Playboy Interviews*, done two months before his death, he also repeatedly refers to Yoko as Mother, and admits on page 160 that it is a habit. The "As our relationship . . ." quote from Pete Shotton is found on pages 21 and 24 of his book, *John Lennon In My Life*. Lennon's "a little gang of guys" quote is from the *Playboy Interviews*, page 136.

Page 14: The details of Lennon's birth during an air raid are based on his aunt Mimi's recollections, as reported in Coleman's *Lennon*, page 98, and also on the account on pages 6–7 of the Beatles' authorized biography, *The Beatles*, by Hunter Davies.

Ringo's mother's story about holding him upside down is found on page 142 of the Davies book. The birthdates of Paul and George are documented on pages 22 and 35, respectively.

Page 15: The end of Britain's national conscription, in 1960, is reported in *McCartney*, by Chris Salewicz, page 37. McCartney himself also refers to it in a

December 10, 1987, interview in *Rolling Stone*, calling it a miracle, "like Moses and the sea opening."

The details of Ringo's childhood are reported in the Davies biography, chapter 18.

Page 15: The paragraph on George Harrison's youth is drawn from both Geoffrey Giuliano's *Dark Horse*, pages 4–11, and from the Davies biography, pages 35–40.

Page 16: The paragraph on McCartney's parents is based on Salewicz's *McCartney*, pages 7–21, except for the "fatty" comment, which is found in both the Davies biography, page 26, and, in more colorful form, in Geoffrey Giuliano's *Blackbird*, page 15. Paul's remark about "sing-songs" is quoted in Bennahum, *in their own words: the Beatles . . . after the break-up*, page 76.

The "absolutely natural" quote from McCartney's former teacher is found in Salewicz, pages 66–67. McCartney recounts his remark about his mother's money in the Davies biography, page 27, alongside his brother Michael's testimony that "for months we both regretted" the statement. Davies also reports that both boys cried themselves to sleep.

Uncle George's death is described in Coleman's *Lennon*, page 104. Elsewhere in the book, Coleman describes John's warm relationship with Uncle George, who was so much gentler than his aunt Mimi, and who would often take young John for walks and read stories to him at night. John himself told Hunter Davies (page 16) that the night that Uncle George died, John's cousin Lelia came to the house and both she and he went upstairs and broke into hysterical, continuous laughter, a nervous reaction that made him feel "very guilty afterwards."

Page 17: The circumstances of Lennon's life during his toddler years, and the relationship between his biological parents, are recounted in Coleman's *Lennon* on pages 86–89 and in Albert Goldman's *The Lives of John Lennon*, pages 29–34. Goldman's book has been rightly criticized for its vituperative tone and its many undocumented, opinionated conclusions, yet in this instance it provides useful additional perspective—provided it is read along with Coleman's and others' accounts of these events—if only because it gives more credence to Freddy Lennon's version of events and suggests alternative interpretations of facts that are not in dispute, such as Julia's turning young John over to Mimi to raise. While Mimi blamed this action on Julia's new man, Dykins, asserting on page 25 of the paperback edition of Philip Norman's *Shout!* that "no man wants another man's child," Goldman proposes that it was perhaps the care-free Julia herself who made the decision, on the grounds of simply not wanting the responsibility of tending to a child.

The story of John's having to choose between his biological parents is told in the Davies biography, pages 7–9, in Coleman's *Lennon*, pages 89–94, and in Goldman's *Lives*, pages 33–37. When John finally left Mimi's house, which was called Mendips and located at 251 Menlove Avenue, Woolton, Liverpool, he moved into the flat of his college friend and soon-to-be-fellow-Beatle Stuart Sutcliffe. This was a short-term arrangement, for the Beatles soon left for Hamburg, and when they returned, in December 1960, John moved back in with Mimi; Stuart had remained in Germany with his fiancée, Astrid Kirchherr.

Page 18: Lennon's remark about seeing his mother sporadically was made in the *Playboy Interviews*, page 137. That John was unaware of how close his mother lived to him during childhood has been attested directly by his best friend, Pete Shotton, on page 23 of *John Lennon In My Life*. Shotton also describes Mimi's values and personality, as does Davies, in chapter 1 of the authorized biography, and Coleman in chapter 1 of *Lennon*, where the two mummies quote is found on page 91.

Examples of Lennon's claims to be working class are found in his March 1971 interview with *Red Mole*, a leftist magazine in London, which was reprinted in *The Lennon Companion*, edited by Elizabeth Thompson and David Gutman, pages 165–80; and in his own book, *Skywriting by Word of Mouth*, page 15. John describes the kind of neighborhood where he grew up in the *Playboy Interviews*, page 131. Pete Shotton likewise confirmed on page 19 of his book that John's "semi-detached home was, in those days, a sign of impressive middle class affluence." The affluence derived from Uncle George's stature as owner of the local dairy farm. Philip Norman reports in *Shout!* on page 27 of the paperback edition that a man who worked for George at the dairy came to garden twice a week. That George also owned rental properties is reported in Goldman's *Lives*, page 41. Even at a young age, John had a sense of Britain's class hierarchy, judging from a story Aunt Mimi told Hunter Davies. Trying to teach John the value of money, she told him that his uncle George had to work for his money. "No, he doesn't," John shot back. "All his men do the work" (page 10).

Page 18: Shotton's remarks about John and Aunt Mimi are found on page 23 of his book, chapter 2 of which contains many funny and warmhearted stories of the two boys' exploits at Quarry Bank, including stories of their being "caned" and John's reading tastes. Shotton did not attend primary school with Lennon, but John's Dovedale days, as well as his Quarry Bank experiences, are described in Coleman's *Lennon*, pages 103–13. Both Shotton (page 37) and Coleman (also page 37) confirm the "Twitchy" nickname, as does Lennon himself on page 16 of the Beatles' authorized biography, though only Coleman claims this word was never used to Dykins' face. Likewise, both Shotton and Coleman mention John's fascination with deformities, Shotton on page 34 and Coleman in various passages, including page 176, which contains the Thelma Pickles quote.

John's quote about rock 'n' roll getting through to him comes from page 100 of *Lennon Remembers*.

Page 19: Lennon's story about Elvis and Little Richard is quoted in Goldman's *Lives*, page 63.

Sources differ on what song John first learned to play. Davies, on page 20 of the authorized biography, says Buddy Holly's "That'll Be The Day." Pete Shotton claims it was Fats Domino's "Ain't That A Shame," adding that he is virtually sure it was Julia who bought John his first guitar, and not Mimi, as some biographers have claimed.

The world has Mark Lewisohn to thank for establishing the exact date that John Lennon and Paul McCartney first met, and, as noted earlier, the story of Lewisohn's efforts is instructive as regards the factual basis of much popular writing about the Beatles. Before Lewisohn's research, most books had properly reported that the two schoolboys met at an outdoor church fair, where John was performing with the Quarry Men, but the date of this fateful meeting varied from anywhere in 1956 to 1958. (The Beatles' own authorized biography sets the date, wrongly, as June 15, 1956.) One day in London, Lewisohn invited me to the British Library's Newspaper Library, just north of the city, and showed me how he had pinpointed the true date by painstakingly scanning every column of every page of the *South Liverpool Weekly News* for the summer months of 1956, 1958, and finally 1957 until he came across a small item reporting on the festival.

Page 19: The story of the day McCartney and Lennon first met is based on accounts in the Beatles' authorized biography, pages 31–33, in Coleman's *Lennon*, pages 145–47, in Shotton and Schaffner's *John Lennon In My Life*, pages 53–56, and in Miles, *Beatles: In Their Own Words*, page 9, which contains McCartney's "Wow, he's good" quote.

McCartney's musical background is described in the Davies biography, pages 29–31, and in Miles, *Beatles: In Their Own Words*, pages 9–10. His brother's comments are on pages 28 and 31 of Davies. Paul's quote about his and George's learning the guitar from the same book is from Geoffrey Giuliano's *Dark Horse*, page 20.

Page 20: John's quote about being the kingpin is from the Davies biography, page 33. His quote about deciding to make the group stronger is found in *Lennon Remembers*, page 160; in the same passage, he also discusses how George was invited into the group. George's hero-worshiping behavior is noted in Coleman's *Lennon*, page 161, and also in the *Playboy Interviews*, pages 126–27.

The precise date when George Harrison, Paul McCartney, and John Lennon began playing together on a regular basis is unknown. Lewisohn, in his book *The Complete Beatles Chronicle*, identifies February 6, 1958, as the probable date when Harrison first *met* the Quarry Men (though of course George had known Paul for years already). Lewisohn notes, however, that the date might also have been March 13, a night on which the Quarry Men performed, though with or without Harrison is unclear. The first date that all three definitely played together at a public event was December 20, 1958, at the wedding of George's brother. The mid-1958 date for the taping of the demonstration record is cited on page 13 of Lewisohn's *Chronicle*. The recording later surfaced on bootlegs, which were heard by the author of this book.

Page 21: As reported on page 143 of Coleman's *Lennon*, Aunt Mimi used to pester John to put away the guitar and get back to his studies, remarking, "The guitar's all very well, John, but you'll never make a living from it." The quote from Julia Baird is from her book *John Lennon, My Brother* (Grafton Books, London, 1988), as quoted in *Dark Horse*, page 22.

The paragraph on Julia's death is based on the accounts in the Davies biography, page 48, Coleman's *Lennon*, pages 169–70, and Goldman's *Lives*, 76–78, which lists the exact date of death, based on the police report.

Page 22: Shotton's recollections of John's nasty behavior after his mother's death are found on page 61 of his book.

Isaacson is but one of Lennon's former classmates who is quoted to the same effect in Coleman's *Lennon*, pages 152, 192. Lennon's reference to ending up like his father comes from page lxxv of the 1985 introduction to the Hunter Davies biography.

Page 22: McCartney's "don't real on me" quote is from Bennahum, *in their own words: the Beatles*. . . page 76. Cynthia Lennon's quote is found on page 190 of Coleman's *Lennon.*

CHAPTER THREE:
Starting a Reputation
(*Please Please Me*)

Page 25: Lennon's repertoire during the Madison Square Garden show, and his remark that he "wanted to have some fun" are found in *Lennon*, by Ray Coleman, pages 614–15. Lennon's desire to "go all the way back" and his seconding of Elton John's suggestion of "I Saw Her Standing There" are related by John's lover at the time, May Pang, in her book *Loving John: The Untold Story*, pages 270–71.

Lewisohn points out on page 24 of *Recording Sessions* that "Please Please Me" did reach number one on three of the British pop charts—those compiled by *Melody Maker, New Musical Express*, and *Disc*—but only number two in the charts of *Record Retailer* and *New Record Mirror*. The Beatles' first single, "Love Me Do," rose no higher than number seventeen.

The February 11, 1963, recording date for "I Saw Her Standing There" is documented in Lewisohn's *Recording Sessions*, page 24. Its inclusion in the Beatles' stage repertoire is attested, first, by its appearance on the album *The Beatles At the Star Club Live!*, recorded on December 31, 1962, in Hamburg on amateur equipment and released, against the Beatles' wishes, in 1977, and second, by the stage show song lists compiled by Nicholas Schaffner and printed in his book *The Beatles Forever*, page 15.

Page 26: McCartney tells the story of writing "I Saw Her Standing There" with Lennon in Lewisohn's *Recording Sessions*, page 9.

Page 26: On pages 163–64 of the *Playboy Interviews*, Lennon says of "I Saw Her Standing There," "That's Paul doing his usual good job of producing what George Martin used to call a 'potboiler.' "

Page 27: "Twist And Shout" was written by Bert Berns under the pseudonym "Medley/Russell" and first recorded by the Isley Brothers and released in May 1962, according to Dowlding's *Beatlesongs*, page 39, which also recounts the Beatles' use of it in their stage shows from 1962 through 1965, and reprints the Lennon quotes, drawn from Ray Coleman's biography and from Lennon's 1971 interview with *Red Mole* magazine, as reprinted in *The Lennon Companion: Twenty-Five Years of Comment.*

Page 28: Lennon's "what we generated was fantastic" quote comes from page 45 of *Lennon Remembers.*

Page 29: The story of the Beatles' resisting "How Do You Do It" is related in Lewisohn's *Recording Sessions*, pages 7, 8, and 18. A quote from McCartney on page 7 suggests that despite their dislike of the song, the Beatles nevertheless took it to a higher level, to the later benefit of Gerry and the Pacemakers, who copied the arrangement the Beatles had devised.

Page 30: McCartney's authorship of "Love Me Do" is attested by Lennon in the *Playboy Interviews*, page 129. George Martin's lack of enthusiasm for the song was expressed in his 1992 documentary film, *The Making of Sgt Pepper.*
  The description of the recording sessions and commercial release of "Love Me Do" comes from *Recording Sessions*, pages 8, 18, 20, and 22. McCartney's remark about sensing the Beatles were going to make it comes from Dowlding's *Beatlesongs*, page 34.

Page 30: Lennon's Orbison reference regarding "Please Please Me" comes from the *Playboy Interviews*, page 142. George Martin's criticism of the original version of the song is based on page 20 of *Recording Sessions*. McCartney's quote about Martin is from *Beatles: In Their Own Words*, by Miles, page 79. Martin's "Gentlemen" quote comes from his *All You Need Is Ears*, page 130.

Page 31: The release date and chart action of the single "Please Please Me" are found in Dowlding's *Beatlesongs*, page 27. The punishing performance schedule of the Beatles at this time is chronicled in Lewisohn's *The Complete Beatles Chronicle*, where the sites of the next-day concerts are recounted on page 100. George Martin's remarks about releasing a follow-up album to the hit single are found in *Recording Sessions*, page 24.
  Lennon named *Please Please Me* as one of his favorite Beatles albums in the *Playboy Interviews*, page 161. Norman Smith's quote is found in Lewisohn's *Recording Sessions*, page 24.

Page 32: The description of the marathon recording session to finish *Please Please Me*, as well as the specific quotes from Norman Smith and Lewisohn, come from Lewisohn's *Recording Sessions*, pages 24 and 26. The listing of the differing estimates of how long it took to complete the day's work on February 11 is found in Dowlding's *Beatlesongs* on page 18 and demonstrates just how wrong even some of the careful writers of Beatles books have been. There's no arguing with Lewisohn's figure of 585 minutes (which amounts to nine and three-quarters hours), for it is based on the actual studio time sheets. Yet Ray Coleman, whose two-volume biography of Lennon is distinguished by an impressive amount of reliable first-hand reporting, somehow cites a figure of eleven hours, and George Martin, who of course was present at the session, also gets it wrong in his autobiography, claiming thirteen hours.

Page 33: Lennon recalled the Disney inspiration for "Do You Want To Know A Secret" in the *Playboy Interviews*, page 140. The charting of the song is noted in Dowlding's *Beatlesongs*, page 37.

The description of the evening portion of the *Please Please Me* recording session, including quotes, is drawn from Lewisohn's *Recording Sessions*, page 26, except for the George Martin quote about John's "tearing flesh" while singing "Twist And Shout," which comes from Martin's autobiography, page 131.

Page 34: The release date and chart action of *Please Please Me* come from Lewisohn's *Recording Sessions* and Dowlding's *Beatlesongs*. The refusal of Capitol Records to release the Beatles' first album, and indeed their first three singles, on the grounds that they would not be popular in America, is recounted by George Martin in his autobiography, pages 159–60. The role of Vee Jay Records is noted by Martin and documented by Lewisohn in *Recording Sessions*, pages 200–01. Lewisohn also documents the number one charting of the subsequent singles, pages 32, 35, and 37.

CHAPTER FOUR:
Mach Shau!:
The Hamburg–Liverpool Apprenticeship

Page 37: The rejections by HMV and Columbia are reported in Lewisohn's *Recording Sessions*, page 16, which cites "confidential letters on file" within the EMI archives, explaining that executives at the two labels had heard the record the Beatles made in Hamburg playing backup on singer Tony Sheridan's version of "My Bonnie," but had not been sufficiently impressed to audition the group. George Martin adds additional details in his autobiography, *All You Need Is Ears*, on page 121.

Page 38: Rowe's quote about guitar groups being on the way out is, in fact, not a first-hand quote from Rowe but rather Brian Epstein's version of what Rowe told him while rejecting the Beatles; there is no record, however, of Rowe's repudiating the remark, which is reported on page 131 of the 1985 paperback edition of the Beatles authorized biography by Davies. The McCartney and Lennon banter about Rowe's kicking himself after the fact is found on page 20 of Miles, *Beatles: In Their Own Words.*

Martin's negative judgment of the Beatles' demonstration disc is found in his autobiography, page 122.

The confusion over whether the June 6 session was an audition or a recording test, and the solution to the mystery, are found in Lewisohn's *The Complete Beatles Chronicle*, page 56. It should be noted that Martin, on pages 27 to 33 of his book *The Summer of Love*, offered a different account of events, suggesting that the Beatles had in fact auditioned in March 1962, three months earlier than previously thought. His chief piece of evidence for this claim is that he would never have offered a group a recording contract without first meeting them. However, Martin did not address the point made by Lewisohn that the contract sent to Epstein was not a genuine offer, since it had not been signed by anyone at EMI. Moreover, had an audition taken place in March 1962, a record of same presumably would have been found during Lewisohn's search of company files for his *Sessions* and *Chronicle* books, but he makes no mention of this.

Page 39: Martin's "saleable future" quote comes from his autobiography, page 123.

That four songs were recorded during the June 6 session and only "Besame Mucho" still survives on tape is reported on page 17 of *Recording Sessions.* The existing "Besame Mucho" tape was listened to by the author.

Page 39: Martin's "just great people" quote comes from his autobiography, pages 122–23. The first Smith quote comes from *Recording Sessions*, page 17, the second from *Beatlesongs*, page 35.

Page 40: As to the details of the contract, Martin himself admitted on pages 123–24 of his autobiography that the terms of the Beatles' initial contract with EMI were niggardly.

The statistics on the number of trips the Beatles made to Hamburg and when, and how many hours they played there, are found in Lewisohn's *Chronicle*, especially pages 62 and 86.

Lennon's "It was Hamburg" quote comes from the Davies biography, page 93.

Page 40: McCartney's "People would appear" quote is found in an interview in the August 1980 issue of *Musician* magazine, as reprinted (in full and without the rewritten quotes found in the magazine) in *Beatlefan* magazine, vol. II, no. 5.

Page 41: The Hunter Davies "vital year" quote is from his biography, page ix.

The Quarry Men's difficulties and the joining of young George Harrison with Lennon and McCartney are noted in Lewisohn's *Chronicle*, pages 13 and 16.

Sutcliffe's date of joining the Beatles is pinpointed by Lewisohn in *Chronicle*, page 18. His lack of musical ability is described there as well, and also in Coleman's *Lennon*, page 187, and Shotton and Schaffner's *John Lennon In My Life*, page 62. The latter, and Lewisohn, note that Sutcliffe bought his bass guitar with the 65 British pounds prize money he won when one of his paintings was purchased by a local collector that January. Shotton saw Lennon's insistence that Sutcliffe join the early Beatles as further evidence of John's wish to turn friends into musical partners: "Since music came so naturally to John, it simply never occurred to him that *anyone* to whom he felt especially close could not also participate."

The "rhythm's in the guitars" quote comes from McCartney's August 1980 *Musician* interview, as reprinted in *Beatlefan*, vol. II, no. 5. Lewisohn describes the Scottish tour in detail, and its aftermath, in *Chronicle*, pages 18–22.

Page 41: Beginning on page 18 of *Chronicle*, Lewisohn traces the development of the Beatles' name(s) using handbills, performance contracts, newspaper stories and advertisements, and the like, as well as the letter Sutcliffe wrote in 1960, reproduced on page 18. Lewisohn further notes that Lennon, McCartney, and Harrison, with supporting players, called themselves Johnny and the Moondogs briefly at the end of 1959, but soon jettisoned the name, and that on two other occasions, April 23 and 24, 1960, John and Paul played as a duo, calling themselves the Nerk Twins. From Lewisohn's individual entries it is clear that the name Beatles did not stick until the first trip to Hamburg. The roles of Sutcliffe and Lennon in formulating the name are recounted in the

Davies biography, page lxvii, in Coleman's *Lennon*, pages 195–96, and in Shotton and Schaffner, page 63, among others; John's interest in the word "beat" is consistently noted throughout. The rest of his possible intent concerning the word, regarding beatniks and rock 'n' roll's beat, are speculations on the part of the present author.

Page 42: The information on Allan Williams and Pete Best is based on Lewisohn's *Chronicle*, pages 21–22.

Lewisohn's *Chronicle* is the best source for the specific dates that the Beatles played the various Hamburg clubs. The general atmosphere along the Reeperbahn is best conveyed in the Davies biography, chapters 11, 12, and 14, and in *Shout!*, by Philip Norman, pages 107–29. Harrison's "We knew that by the end of the evening" quote is found on page 32 of Giuliano, *Dark Horse*; Lennon's "I've never seen" comes from Davies, page 80.

Page 43: Pete Best's recollections of the groupie scene in Hamburg are found in his book *Beatle!: The Pete Best Story*, pages 53–56. Lennon's quote is from *Blackbird*, page 38. Like Lennon, McCartney has downplayed some of the wilder stories from the Hamburg era, such as the allegation that John once urinated off the roof onto a group of nuns walking on the sidewalk below. Paul told Lennon biographer Ray Coleman that John had indeed "had a pee over the edge" one time, but not when anyone was passing underneath him. The confusion, McCartney said, arose from another incident when the boys did shout down to some nuns. "The two stories got together, so we get this really outrageous story where John's peeing on nuns. It never really was like that," says McCartney on page 258 of Coleman's book.

The protests against the Beatles came in the form of a letter from the group Derry and the Seniors, according to Lewisohn's *Chronicle*, page 21, which also gives information on page 25 on the Litherland Town Hall Ballroom appearance. See also the Davies biography, especially pages 92–93.

Page 44: The dates of the Beatles' shows following the Litherland appearance and of their beginning at the Cavern come from Lewisohn's *Chronicle*, especially pages 30–51.

The sexual escapades the Beatles got used to in Hamburg were carried over to their Cavern days, at least in John's case, according to his friend Pete Shotton. On page 69 of his book, Shotton recalled that "the enthusiasm of John's predominantly female audience was often turned to particularly good account." Noting that girls at the Cavern "tended to come in pairs," Shotton wrote that John always made sure that both he and Shotton were pleased with the pair they went home with: "As often as not, these girls not only lived together, but also slept together in a double bed. So we all generally wound up piling into one bed, to screw away the afternoon in one big happy heap."

Page 45: Harrison's "eating our lunch" quote comes from the Davies biography, page 99.

Lewisohn emphasizes on page 42 of his *Chronicle* that the *probable* dates of the Tony Sheridan sessions were June 22 and 23, 1961, though he notes that information about these sessions is sketchy and contradictory. A compact disc of the recordings has been issued, which the author listened to.

The exact text of Epstein's telegram is found on page 56 of Lewisohn's *Chronicle*.

Page 45: George Martin's initial dealings with Brian Epstein and his reactions to the Beatles are detailed in his autobiography, pages 120–24.

Pete Shotton's recollections, which include the fact that Pete Best was very popular among the Cavern crowd, are found on page 71 of his book, *John Lennon In My Life*. Confirmation of Best's popularity and of the general outlines of the story are found in the Davies biography, pages 137–40, as is Paul McCartney's "nonsense" rejoinder, on page 371. See also Best's own account, on pages 165–76 of his book, which agrees on the basic facts with other accounts. McCartney's "wacky trio" quote comes from page 6 of *Recording Sessions*.

When Lennon learned from Epstein that Martin wanted to use another drummer for studio recordings, he saw the chance to get rid of Best that he and the others had been waiting for. "Okay," he told Brian, "but you tell Pete he's out and I'll get Ringo in." Later, John alone owned up to what low, selfish behavior this was on the part of the three original Beatles. "We were cowards," he said of their decision to delegate their dirty work to Epstein. The Beatles manager called the Best dismissal "the first real problem I'd had." See page 140 of the Davies biography.

Page 46: Best's resentment at being called not good enough and his hurt at missing their ascension to the big-time, is found on pages xxxv–vi of the Davies biography and pages 165–76 of his own book, *Beatle!*

Martin's "last chance" quote comes from page 124 of his autobiography.

The planned approach to Philips in the event of a George Martin rejection of the Beatles is reported in *Recording Sessions*, page 16.

John's confirmation of the "bigger than Elvis" quote is found in *Lennon Remembers*, page 70. His quote about the Beatles being the best band in the world is from the *Playboy Interviews*, page 60.

CHAPTER FIVE:
Where Music Had to Go
(*With The Beatles*)

Page 49: The God Almighty quote is on page 165 of the *Playboy Interviews*. The best band in the world remark is from page 60. In the same interview, he used the term "piece of garbage" (or "piece of rubbish") six times to describe songs that he and McCartney, or he alone, had written as Beatles. The reference to "Little Child" as a "knock-off" came in a 1972 interview with *Hit Parader* magazine, as quoted in Dowlding's *Beatlesongs*, page 51; the reference to "Tell Me Why" is on page 164 of the *Playboy Interviews*. The Buddy Holly quote is on page 129.

Page 49: McCartney's reference to "work songs" is found on page 10 of *Recording Sessions*. His "You'd hear about Big Bill Broonzy" quote is from an interview found on a privately compiled video of Beatles material that was viewed by the author. His "If the Beatles ever wanted a sound" quote is from page 7 of *Recording Sessions*.

Page 50: The Dylan in Colorado quote comes from Anthony Scaduto's book *Bob Dylan* (Grosset & Dunlap, New York) page 175.

Page 51: McCartney's "A lot of our songs" quote is found on page 9 of *Recording Sessions*, his quote about going to G minor on page 10.
    The date and place of composition for "She Loves You" is given in Lewisohn's *Chronicle*, page 114. The recollection of writing it on twin beds comes from McCartney, on page 10 of *Recording Sessions*.

Page 51: The quote from Norman Smith is from page 32 of *Recording Sessions*.
    Lennon's quote about the hook, line, and sound comes from the *Playboy Interviews*, page 118.

Page 52: That John and Paul had written songs individually by this time is attested by, for example, John's claim in the *Playboy Interviews*, page 142, that "Please Please Me" was "my song completely." On page 12 of Lewisohn's

Recording Sessions, Paul says much the same about "I'll Follow The Sun," a song he wrote when he was sixteen.

Regarding the joint authorship of "She Loves You," Paul's admission is on page 10 of *Recording Sessions*. John's is on page 143 of the *Playboy Interviews*.

Lennon's 1971 interview was with *Rolling Stone* magazine; the specific quote is found on page 124 of *Lennon Remembers*. His memory of writing "I Want To Hold Your Hand" is on page 117 of the *Playboy Interviews*.

Page 53: The loss of fidelity on the German version of "I Want To Hold Your Hand" occurred because George Martin and the Beatles chose merely to add a new vocal track onto the existing English rhythm track. Thus, the rhythm track had to be "mixed down" from four-track to two-track, making room for the German-language vocals. The same fidelity loss did not occur on "She Loves You" because in that case the Beatles recorded an entirely new rhythm track before overdubbing German vocals. For more details, see page 38 of Lewisohn's *Recording Sessions*.

Page 54: For the Dylan quote, see Scaduto's *Bob Dylan*, op. cit. Riley's observation is found on page 63 of *Tell Me Why*. George Martin's close harmony quote comes from page 36 of *Recording Sessions*.

Page 54: Lennon's remarks about "This Boy" are found on pages 117 and 163 of the *Playboy Interviews*. McCartney's quote is on page 10 of *Recording Sessions*; page 36 of same documents the October 17, 1963, recording sessions for "This Boy" and "I Want To Hold Your Hand."

The sales figures and chart action for "I Want To Hold Your Hand" are found on page 136 of Lewisohn's *Chronicle*, page 37 of his *Recording Sessions* and page 59 of Dowlding's *Beatlesongs*.

Page 55: The George Martin–Brian Epstein business plan is described in a quote from Martin found on page 28 of *Recording Sessions*.

The Beatles' schedule during 1963 is documented in Lewisohn's *Chronicle*, pages 88–135.

Page 56: Derek Taylor's quote was made during an interview with the author of this book. McCartney's cotton socks quote is on page 10 of *Recording Sessions*.

Page 56: The chord patterns of "It Won't Be Long" are reproduced in the songbook *The Complete Beatles*, published by copyright owners Hal Leonard Publishing Corporation (Milwaukee, 1988), vol. 2, pages 4–7.

Page 57: McCartney's recollections about writing "All My Loving" are found on page 10 of *Recording Sessions*. John's remarks are on page 145 of the *Playboy Interviews*.

Lennon and McCartney's lukewarm views about "Little Child" and "Hold Me Tight" have already been noted in the text. About "All I've Got To Do," Lennon, on page 163 of the *Playboy Interviews*, had nothing more to say than "That's me trying to do Smokey Robinson again." On page 145, he dismissed "I Wanna Be Your Man" as "a throwaway," noting that it grew out of a lick that McCartney had. The first time the Beatles met the Rolling Stones, John and Paul played them the unfinished song. When the Stones agreed that it was their style, Paul and John went off in a corner and finished writing it in front of the Stones' very eyes, an episode that Lennon claimed was what inspired Mick Jagger and Keith Richards to start writing their own songs. "I Wanna Be Your Man" was the first song the Stones recorded, but the fact that Lennon and McCartney gave it away, John said, "shows how much importance we put on it: We weren't going to give them anything *great*, right?"

In his autobiography, *I Me Mine*, Harrison wrote that "Don't Bother Me" was the "first song I wrote—as an exercise to see if I *could* write a song." He was sick in bed at the time and later felt that it wasn't "a particularly good song," but it convinced him that if he kept at it "maybe eventually I would write something good."

Page 58: The release dates and charting action of "I Want To Hold Your Hand," *Please Please Me*, and *With The Beatles* are reported in Dowlding's *Beatlesongs*, pages 47 and 59.

The date of the Royal Variety Performance, as well as the Beatles' song list, is noted in Lewisohn's *Chronicle*, pages 127–28. This was, of course, the occasion where John Lennon charmed the entire audience by quipping, "For our last number I'd like to ask your help. Will the people in the cheaper seats clap your hands? And the rest of you, if you'll just rattle your jewelry." The remark provoked warm laughter and applause, and was greeted with profound relief by Beatles manager Brian Epstein, who had feared Lennon would make good on his pre-performance threat to tell them to "rattle their fuckin' jewelry."

Extensive excerpts from the London *Times* article were reprinted in Nicholas Schaffner's *The Beatles Forever*, page 23.

Page 58: Lennon's remark about the chords of "Not A Second Time" is found on page 79 of Miles's *Beatles: In Their Own Words*. The quote about exotic birds is on page 74 of the *Playboy Interviews*.

The December 29, 1963, article in the London *Sunday Times* is quoted on page 188 of the Davies biography, *The Beatles.*

The statements of Alexander Kendrick are quoted on page 129 of Lewisohn's *Chronicle.*

The Dylan quote comes from Scaduto's *Bob Dylan*, pages 203–04.

CHAPTER SIX:
Life with Brian:
Manager Brian Epstein

Page 61: The chamber pot photograph is printed in Davies's biography, though its caption incorrectly lists the date of the dinner as January 1963.

Page 62: The details of Brian Epstein's business missteps on behalf of the Beatles, and the consequent effects on his relationship with them, are detailed in the text later in the chapter. The quote from George Martin appears in the video *The Compleat Beatles.* The Lennon quote comes from page 32 of Miles's *Beatles: In Their Own Words.*

Page 63: The Epstein quotes about observing the Beatles in the Cavern and in his record shop are drawn from the Davies biography, pages 124 and 129. The Harrison quote is from page 125.

Page 63: Epstein's "hobby" quote is from page 125 of the Davies biography.

Among the books charging that Epstein's homosexuality was the spur of his involvement with the Beatles are *The Love You Make*, by Peter Brown and Steven Gaines, especially pages 60–61; *Shout!*, by Philip Norman, especially page 171; and, most sensationalistically, *Lives*, by Albert Goldman, especially pages 110–16 and 139–42.

Page 64: Lennon's remark that Epstein was in love with him is found on page 76 of the *Playboy Interviews.* Pete Shotton reveals Lennon's interlude with Epstein on page 73 of his book *John Lennon In My Life.* Ray Coleman's testimony is found on page 245 of his *Lennon.*

The Beatles' handling of their own bookings, and their falling out with Allan Williams, is described on pages 30–32 of Lewisohn's *Chronicle.* It was actually Pete Best and his mother, Mona Best, who did the work, having had previous experience owing to Pete's father's work as an impresario. The Beatles fell out with Williams when they decided not to pay him a commission for their gigs at the Top Ten Club during their second Hamburg trip. The Beatles apparently reasoned that since they had arranged and negotiated the deal themselves, Williams didn't deserve any pay. He himself naturally felt differently, pointing out in a strongly worded letter to the Beatles, reprinted in *Chronicle*, that they "would not even have smelled Hamburg if I had not made the contacts" and threatening to have them deported. As it happens, Paul McCartney's father also felt that the group was "in the wrong" in its dispute with Williams; his letter to Paul is found on page 39 of McCartney's 1989 World Tour concert program.

Page 64: The changes made in the Beatles' organization by Brian Epstein have been widely reported. See especially pages 128–29 of the Davies biography and pages 247–50 of Coleman's *Lennon*.

Epstein's "lovely" quote is found on page 115 of the Davies biography; his "didn't *change* them" quote on page 129.

Page 65: That Lennon rebelled against Epstein's changes is noted in Coleman's *Lennon*, pages 247–50.

The arrangements of the Decca audition are described in the Davies biography, pages 130–32. The fifteen songs that the Beatles played that day, January 1, 1962, are listed on page 63 of Lewisohn's *Chronicle*. Lennon's ire with Epstein is noted on page 56 of *Chronicle* and, more fully, on page 299 of Coleman's *Lennon*.

Page 66: Epstein's "bigger than Elvis" boast is reported on page 131 of the Davies biography. A comprehensive listing of all the Beatles' live performances is found in Lewisohn's *Chronicle*. The most commonly cited date for the onset of Beatlemania is October 13, 1963, the date that the Beatles performed at the London Palladium, but Lewisohn observes on page 88 of *Chronicle* that "it is clear from the local newspaper coverage that Beatles-inspired hysteria had definitely begun by the late spring, some six months before it was brought to national attention by Fleet Street newspapers."

The dates of the Beatles' three Sullivan show appearances were February 9, 16, and 23 of 1964. The size of the television audience and other details are found in Lewisohn's *Chronicle*, pages 144–47. Philip Norman reports on pages 257–58 of *Shout!* that Sullivan had witnessed Beatlemania, that the Beatles were paid $3,500 for each appearance on the show, plus $3,000 more for the taping, and he quotes the Sullivan show's producer saying, "Even for an unknown act, that was about the least we could pay."

Page 67: George Martin's "He loved the helter-skelter" quote is from page 6 of his book *The Summer of Love*. Lennon's "Brian contributed as much as us" quote is found on page 32 of Miles's *Beatles: In Their Own Words*. Pete Shotton's remarks are found on pages 71 and 116 of his book, *John Lennon In My Life*.

Page 67: The negotiations for "A Hard Day's Night" are described on page 121 of Peter Brown's *The Love You Make* and on page 248 of Norman's *Shout!*
  The ten percent merchandising deal is described on pages 334–35 of Goldman's *Lives* and, in greater depth, in Norman's *Shout!*, pages 260–64, 285–87, and 315–16. Brian Epstein's gift of ten percent of NEMS to the Beatles is attested by his financial adviser, Dr. Walter Strach, in *Shout!*, and further detailed on page 253 of the Davies biography, which notes that of the ten thousand one-pound-sterling shares in NEMS, Brian owned seven thousand, his brother, Clive, owned two thousand, and each of the Beatles owned two hundred and fifty. Peter Brown's $100 million estimate is found on page 149 of *The Love You Make*.

Page 68: McCartney's "Green" quote is from the Davies biography, page 371.
  Epstein's difficult relationship with McCartney is noted on page 224 of the Davies biography and pages 306–09 of Coleman's *Lennon*. Lennon's closeness with Epstein is attested by Lennon himself on page 32 of Miles's *Beatles: In Their Own Words*. His put-downs of Epstein are quoted on pages 298–99 of *Lennon* and on page 348 of Norman's *Shout!*
  Derek Taylor's press conference quote comes from Norman's *Shout!*, page 313.

Page 68: That Epstein had a history of insecurity and unhappiness is testified to by Taylor in his interview in the video *Yesterday*, by Martin in his autobiography, pages 174–78, and by Brown in the Davies biography on page 221 and in his own book *The Love You Make*, passim, especially pages 58, 174–75, and 219–21.
  The Beatles' flight from New Delhi to London on which Epstein broke out in hives is described on pages 189–90 of Brown's book. Brown goes on to assert on pages 194–97 that Epstein actually missed attending the Beatles' final concert in San Francisco because of a bout of depression stemming from a theft and attempted blackmail by a young hustler with whom he had had a long and unhappy sexual relationship. According to Brown, Nat Weiss was also the target of the hustler's theft, though Weiss had had no relationship with him and in fact had strongly advised Epstein to stay away from the man.

Weiss's quote about Epstein looking pathetic is found on page 211 of the Davies biography. Brown's eyewitness account of Epstein's suicide attempt is related on pages 197–98 of his book.

The date that the first properly executed management contract between the Beatles and Brian Epstein was signed is reported as October 9, 1962, in Goldman's *Lives* and elsewhere. The Beatles had signed an earlier agreement with Epstein on January 24, 1962, but it was not binding because both McCartney and Harrison were under twenty-one years of age and Epstein, in any case, did not affix his own signature to the contract, explaining that he didn't want "the boys" to feel bound to him until he had produced for them. For more details, see the Davies biography, pages 126–27.

That the Beatles had begun grumbling about Epstein's handling of their original EMI contract is noted by George Martin in his autobiography, pages 177–78, and by Brown on pages 225–26. Brown adds that McCartney, when asked later what moment with Epstein he regretted most, recalled that he had put Epstein down in front of the other Beatles by saying, "Yeah, well Klein got the Stones a million and a quarter, didn't he? What about us?"

Page 69: The appalling terms of the Beatles' initial EMI contract are conceded by George Martin on pages 123–24 and 177 of his autobiography; the American equivalents are found in Goldman's *Lives*, pages 331–32. Epstein's failure to renegotiate the EMI contract promptly, as well as the date and terms of the new deal consummated in November 1966, are noted in Brown's *The Love You Make*, pages 224–26, and in Goldman's *Lives*, pages 331–32.

Epstein's insertion of the clause stipulating continued payment of EMI royalties through NEMS is divulged on page 226 of Brown's *The Love You Make*.

Page 70: Epstein's addiction to stimulants and tranquilizers has been widely reported. See especially pages 224–25 in the Davies biography, page 177 in George Martin's autobiography, and pages 114, 164, 174, 196–98, 212–13, and 244 of *The Love You Make*. Lennon's concern about Epstein, and the audiotape he received from him, are described on page 142 of Shotton's book.

Brian Epstein's death scene and the results of the coroner's inquest are recorded in Brown's *The Love You Make*, pages 244–48, and in the Davies biography, pages 216–26. Davies's quote about an emotional suicide is on page 1 of the biography. Martin's quote is on page 178 of his autobiography.

Page 71: The TV footage of Lennon and Harrison is included in the film *The Compleat Beatles*, Lennon's private remarks to Shotton are recounted on page

143 of Shotton's book. Those to Coleman are on pages 430–32 of Coleman's *Lennon*. Lennon's subsequent comments about the Beatles being in trouble after Epstein died are found on page 52 of *Lennon Remembers*.

CHAPTER SEVEN:
I Heard a Funny Chord
(*A Hard Day's Night*)

Page 73: Lennon's "creating without even being aware" quote comes from page 120 of the *Playboy Interviews*.

That it was Ringo who said "It's been a hard day's night" is reported in, among many other accounts, Lewisohn's *Recording Sessions*, page 43. John, on page 148 of the *Playboy Interviews*, later dubbed the remark "a Ringoism, where he said it not to be funny, just said it." The odd thing about this Ringoism, as John pointed out, was that John had written the very same phrase in passing a few months earlier in his book of nonsense prose, *In His Own Write*. The actual phrase from *In His Own Write* is: "He'd had a hard day's night that day, for Michael was a Cocky Watchtower," found on page 37 of the paperback edition. True, Ringo may have read it there and unconsciously recalled it later, but since Ringo was not known as a big reader, this seems unlikely. Was Ringo's quip then simply a case of two peculiar minds thinking alike—further indication that the Beatles were, as they sometimes said, four parts of the same person?

The seizing of Ringo's remark as the title of the film is noted on page 345 of Coleman's *Lennon*. Lennon's recollection of bringing in the song the following morning is from page 148 of the *Playboy Interviews*.

That the Beatles completed recording "A Hard Day's Night" in nine takes is reported on page 43 of *Recording Sessions*. The description of the atmosphere and chat inside the studio is based on the author's having listened to the session tapes.

Page 74: Wilfrid Mellers, on page 43 of *Twilight of the Gods: The Music of the Beatles*, writes that "the opening sustained chord is arrestingly a dominant ninth of F," while Tim Riley, on page 99 of *Tell Me Why*, states that the chord is "a G7 with added ninth and suspended fourth."

The Beatles did not smoke marijuana for the first time until August 1964, a story related in Chapter 16.

Martin's remark about *A Hard Day's Night* and the second era of Beatles music is found in his autobiography on page 132.

Page 75: The Beatles first used four-track-tape technology while recording "I Want To Hold Your Hand" on October 17, 1963, as is documented in *Recording Sessions* on page 36.

The judgments of the relative standing of the Beatles' various compositions to date are, needless to say, those of the author.

Page 75: The date of the release of the *Long Tall Sally* EP, and of the Beatles' trips to America and elsewhere, are found in Lewisohn's *Chronicle*, pages 136–65.

Lennon's authorship of ten of the thirteen songs on *A Hard Day's Night* is documented in most compact form in Dowlding's *Beatlesongs*, pages 67–79, which in turn is based on comments by Lennon and McCartney drawn from a variety of sources, especially Lennon's *Playboy Interviews*.

It has been widely reported that the songs for *A Hard Day's Night* were written in the George V hotel in Paris in January 1964 on a rented grand piano. This assertion is based on the liner notes, written by the Beatles' press officer, Tony Barrow, which were included with the album. Doubtless there is some truth to this claim, but it is hard to say how much, for neither Lennon nor McCartney later specifically mentioned writing any of their songs in this setting, though they did refer to other settings, such as Lennon's recollection of writing "A Hard Day's Night."

Page 78: Lennon describes his authorship of "I'm Happy Just To Dance With You" in the *Playboy Interviews*, pages 164 and 140. His comments about "And I Love Her" are from page 146. Ringo's switching from drums to bongos is noted on page 40 of *Recording Sessions*, which also reports on page 39 that the first two takes of the song "were much heavier than the final version, with a different guitar intro . . . and a lead guitar solo in the middle eight." McCartney's comment about "And I Love Her" is from his December 1984 interview with *Playboy*.

Lennon's dismissal of "Tell Me Why" is on page 164 of the *Playboy Interviews*.

Page 79: The recording of "Can't Buy Me Love," on January 29, 1964, is described on page 38 of *Recording Sessions*. George Martin's quote is from his autobiography, page 133. The passage on the early takes of the song are based on the author's listening to the outtakes.

Page 79: The release date and sales records of "Can't Buy Me Love" are documented on page 43 of *Recording Sessions.*

The Mellers quote is from page 47 of *Twilight of the Gods.* Lennon's quote is from page 164 of the *Playboy Interviews.*

The chart action of the single and album of "A Hard Day's Night" is reported on pages 66–67 of Dowlding's *Beatlesongs.* The differing contents of the U.K. and U.S.A. versions of *A Hard Day's Night* are documented on pages 200–201 of *Recording Sessions.*

Page 80: The seven-week duration of filming for *A Hard Day's Night*— beginning on March 2, 1964, and concluding on April 24—is documented in Lewisohn's *Chronicle,* pages 149–58.

John Lennon's remark in Paris is quoted on page 54 of Miles's *Beatles: In Their Own Words.* Ringo's remark about fan mail is on page 47 of same.

Page 81: Harrison's "Fame makes relationships difficult" quote was made in the mid-1980s in *The Hollywood Reporter* and reprinted in Geoffrey Giuliano's biography of Harrison, *Dark Horse,* page 185.

The concept for the movie coming from John's remark about touring Sweden is noted on page 344 of Coleman's *Lennon.* The original working title of the movie was simply *Beatlemania,* according to Brown and Gaines on page 120 of *The Love You Make.*

Page 82: John Lennon's complaints about the distortions of the Beatles' individual personalities in *A Hard Day's Night* are from *The Beatles in Richard Lester's "A Hard Day's Night,"* page 107, edited by J. Philip Di Franco, (Chelsea House, New York, 1977), as cited in Jon Weiner's *Come Together,* page 29. Lennon nevertheless concedes that the movie worked "*precisely because we were what we were, realistic.*" The same page contains also a relevant quote from McCartney, further supporting the author's interpretation that the caricatures in the film were more right than wrong. Toward the same end, George Martin's quotes are from his autobiography, *All You Need Is Ears,* pages 166 and 161.

Page 82: According to page 46 of *Recording Sessions,* the Beatles had issued four previous EP records, but *Long Tall Sally* was the first to contain all new material: Lennon's "I Call Your Name," plus cover versions of three American songs drawn from the Beatles' live stage act. Lewisohn is also the source for the fact that the Beatles recorded "Long Tall Sally" in one take.

The chart action of both the Beatles' version of "Long Tall Sally" and of Little Richard's 1956 version is detailed on page 62 of Dowlding's *Beatlesongs*.

McCartney's recollections of playing the song the day he first met Lennon are found in his December 1984 interview with *Playboy*, where McCartney added: "All my screaming songs, the early Beatles screaming stuff—that's me doing Little Richard. I would often fall a little bit short, not have that little kick, that soul, and it would be John who would go, 'Come on! You can sing it better than that, man! Come on, come on! Really throw it!' All right, John, OK. . . ."

Page 83: Ringo's "greatest songwriters" quote comes from page 96 of Bennahum's *in their own words: the Beatles . . . after the break-up.*

CHAPTER EIGHT:
The Burdens of Fame:
Beatlemania

Page 88: George Harrison's quote about fame is cited in Giuliano's *Dark Horse*, page 40.

Page 88: The view that touring was a sine qua non of a successful pop music career is noted in Lewisohn's *Chronicle*, page 214. The media's speculation that the Beatles were breaking up is noted there as well, but also in the film *It Was Twenty Years Ago Today*. The idea of letting the *Sgt Pepper* album tour in the Beatles' place was explained by Paul McCartney in George Martin's 1992 documentary film, *The Making of Sgt Pepper*.

The quotes from Ringo Starr are found on pages 214–15 of the Davies biography. Lennon's quote comes from page 210 of Lewisohn's *Chronicle*.

Page 89: Although 1963 is the best date for the onset of full-fledged Beatlemania, the truth is that the Beatles were exciting crowds on a local basis even earlier than this. Lewisohn notes in *Chronicle* that Beatlemania experienced its first birth pangs during the Beatles gig at Liverpool's Town Hall Ballroom on December 27, 1960. His book offers the most detailed accounting of how the hysteria steadily grew over time, until by 1963 it had become a social phenomenon impossible to ignore.

See page 124 of *Chronicle* for more information about the show at the London Palladium. The theater was home to the weekly broadcast of *Val Parnell's Sunday*

Night at the London Palladium, the British equivalent of America's *Ed Sullivan Show* in that it was a top-rated show that could make an entertainer's career. The press coverage of the Palladium gig is noted in *Chronicle*, in the Davies biography on pages 180–81, and in Norman's *Shout!*, pages 237–38.

The allegation that the crowds outside the Palladium were in fact quite small was made by photographer Dezo Hoffman in Norman's *Shout!*, page 238. Hoffman, who had been photographing the Beatles with their agreement for some weeks by then, is quoted as saying, "There were *no* riots. I was there. Eight girls we saw—even less than eight." Journalist Norman goes on to report that the photos published in newspapers the next day were always carefully cropped so that only a handful of the allegedly one thousand "screaming teenagers" could actually be seen, and he concludes on page 241 that the riots had been "faked."

Lewisohn's survey of local newspaper coverage is summarized on page 88 of *Chronicle*.

Page 90: The Beatles' citation of the Heathrow Airport welcome back from Sweden on October 31 as the start of Beatlemania is noted on page 182 of their authorized biography. The media's practice of covering the Beatles' comings and goings in future years is noted on page 183 of same and in various other accounts of their lives during those years; see, for example, the photos on pages 136 and 181 of Lewisohn's *Chronicle*.

Lennon's joke in front of the royals has been misquoted in small ways in various Beatles books. The version quoted here comes from film footage of their actual performance, which also reveals the look on John's face the moment after he delivered this famous bon mot: a mixture of puckish humor and self-satisfied delight. As has been reported in various books (see, for example, page 92 in Lewisohn's *Chronicle*), John had alarmed Beatles manager Brian Epstein backstage by threatening to tell the assembled denizens of the British ruling class to "rattle their fuckin' jewelry."

The Beatles' tour itineraries for 1964 through 1966 are most reliably reported in Lewisohn's *Chronicle*, which also cites the 300,000 figure from Adelaide. The practice of middle-aged men wearing Beatles wigs was reported in contemporaneous newspaper stories, as well as recalled by George Martin on page 160 of his autobiography.

Page 90: Harrison's quote about being in a rut comes from page 214 of the Davies biography. Lennon's "sameness" quote is on page 215 of same.

The Shea Stadium figures are found on page 208 of the Davies biography and on page 199 of Lewisohn's *Chronicle*. The practice of taking brown bag money is disclosed by Epstein's business aide Peter Brown in his book, *The Love You Make*, on pages 138 and 189, who adds that Epstein customarily demanded official fees of between $25,000 and $50,000, plus upward of fifty percent of gross receipts. The Finley story is also found in *The Love You Make* (among other places), on page 145.

Page 91: George Martin's "audience started singing" story is told in his autobiography on page 161. Ringo Starr's quote is from the compilation by Miles, *Beatles: In Their Own Words*, page 22.

There are many tapes of Beatles live performances, and there is no doubt that their playing in these years could be erratic, but listen, for example, to the tapes of their August 14, 1965, performance for *The Ed Sullivan Show*, or their December 1965 shows in London or even their final concert in San Francisco in August 1966. The screaming crowds are always there, but the Beatles, whether by rote, instinct, or simple luck, turn in fairly respectable performances, with harmonies on target, solos in the right place, and remarkably animated banter between songs.

The acoustical expert in Australia was Anita Lawrence of New South Wales University in Sydney; her findings were reported in a newspaper story that was replicated on page 163 of Lewisohn's *Chronicle*.

Page 92: Lennon's quote about hating it and loving it is found on page 610 of Coleman's *Lennon* biography. His remark about digging fame is on page 22 of Miles's *Beatles: In Their Own Words*. The Beatles' policy of affecting indifference regarding their fame is disclosed on page 79 of Pete Shotton's book, *John Lennon In My Life*. The film inside the Beatles' limousine was shot by a crew that, operating with the Beatles' consent and under some form of editorial control by Epstein's NEMS company, was documenting the Beatles' entire American visit. The film was later broadcast in both England and the United States. For more details, see page 144 of Lewisohn's *Chronicle*. The radio announcers' obsession with Beatles time and weather is evident on the film itself, and is further noted in various accounts of the visit, including page 194 of the Davies authorized biography and page 107 of Brown's *The Love You Make*.

Page 92: Shotton tells the Cadillacs story on page 96 of his book, adding that the Beatles, to their surprise, were never sent a bill for the cars they demolished. It was typical that the Beatles were not called to account for their actions, according to Shotton.

The role of Mal Evans in procuring girls for the Beatles is recounted on page 79 of Shotton's book, and on page 141 of Peter Brown's *The Love You Make*, where Aspinall's role is also noted. Brown, of course, was a colleague of both Aspinall and Evans and thus in a position not only to have observed such activities for himself but also to receive candid replies in his interviews with them for his book, such as Aspinall's orgies quote, found on page 134. According to Brown, there would sometimes be as many as fifteen girls waiting to "meet" one of the Beatles, some of whom would pass the time ironing their stage costumes in Aspinall's or Evans's rooms.

Lennon's story about the party of starlets and models is found on page 94 of Shotton's book. His *Satyricon* and Caesars quotes are from pages 84–88 of *Lennon Remembers*.

Page 93: That the Beatles smoked marijuana inside Buckingham Palace before being knighted was later disclosed by John in an interview with *L'Express* and is noted in Coleman's *Lennon* biography, pages 403 and 712. Brown's *The Love You Make*, page 167, and Norman's *Shout!*, page 311, and other sources contend that while McCartney, Harrison, and Starr were thrilled by the award, Lennon initially wanted to turn it down, regarding such cooperation with the Establishment as hypocrisy. Shotton claims, however, on pages 96–97, that his friend John was also pleased by the honor initially, and only turned against it in retrospect.

Harrison's "a thousand years" quote is from his interview with *Rolling Stone*, December 10, 1987. Lennon's "elevator man" quote is from the *Playboy Interviews*, page 79.

Page 93: The Beatles' practice of speaking in code was revealed by Lennon in the Davies biography, page 290. The "cripples" password is recounted in numerous books, including page 16 of *Lennon Remembers* and page 165 of George Martin's autobiography.

Lennon, Harrison, and Starr moved out to the so-called stockbroker belt of London in 1964, settling into houses that were within a couple miles of one another. The houses are described in the Davies biography, in chapters 31, 33, and 34. McCartney remained in London, first at the home of his then-girlfriend, Jane Asher, and later in a house he purchased in St. John's Wood, very near Abbey Road Studios.

Derek Taylor's story about the mayor's wife is found on pages 16–18 of his book. Though he coyly describes the city where these events took place merely by the letter "M," it can only be Milwaukee. As revealed by the itinerary printed on page 139 of Lewisohn's *Chronicle*, Milwaukee was the only city on the 1964 tour whose name begins with "M," except for Montreal. The hint that clinches the case for Milwaukee is the haughty remark by the mayor's wife, in which she takes pains to distinguish her city from nearby Chicago, which she calls "a dirty, corrupt and badly administered city." Lennon refers to this same story on page 18 of *Lennon Remembers*.

Page 94: Lennon's "unreality" quote comes from pages 18–20 of *Lennon Remembers*.

The description of the Manila fiasco is based primarily on Peter Brown's eyewitness account in his book, *The Love You Make*, pages 185–90, with supporting and counterchecking information from Lewisohn's *Chronicle*, pages 211–12 and Shotton's *John Lennon In My Life*, page 127, where Lennon's quote is found.

Page 95: That the Beatles sometimes had to leave the stage in mid-performance is noted in Lewisohn's *Chronicle*, with two examples being the September 1964 shows in Cleveland and Kansas City, described on page 171. The crushing of the limousine is recalled by Ringo Starr in the Davies biography, page 214; Starr places the incident in San Francisco, though other Beatles books claim that it happened in Seattle. The Houston airport story was told by George Harrison in an interview with *Rolling Stone*, published December 10, 1987. The Memphis incident is described on page 213 of Lewisohn's *Chronicle*, by Lennon himself in a radio interview quoted on page 13 of Jon Wiener's book, *Come Together*, and on page 129 of Pete Shotton's memoir.

Page 96: Ringo's "potty" quote is found on page 54 of Miles's *Beatles: In Their Own Words*.

Lennon's "This isn't show business" quote comes from page 54 of Miles's *Beatles: In Their Own Words*. The August 29, 1966, San Francisco concert ranking as the Beatles' last live show is documented on page 230 of Lewisohn's *Chronicle*; the grand total of fourteen hundred live performances comes from page 214. The story of the group photo at the concert is told by Harrison in an interview with *Rolling Stone*, published December 10, 1987.

Page 96: Lennon's "moving hothouse" quote is from page 28 of Miles's *Beatles: In Their Own Words*. McCartney's "jovial moptops" quote is found on page 179 of Chris Salewicz's *McCartney*.

CHAPTER NINE:
War Weary
(*Beatles For Sale*)

Page 99: Regarding the interpretation of the cover photos from *Beatles For Sale*, a devil's advocate might contend that the pictures merely captured a mood that the Beatles happened to be in on the day of the photo shoot. True. On the other hand, there is so much other evidence of their generally despondent mood during this period, as noted in the text of this book and in comments by the Beatles themselves, that this interpretation seems warranted.

Page 100: Derek Taylor's books include *As Time Goes By, It Was Twenty Years Ago Today*, and *Fifty Years Adrift in an Open-Necked Suit*. None of them deals exclusively with the Beatles, though the group does figure prominently in each book. Taylor served as Beatles press officer twice: first in 1964, and again from 1968 through 1970. In 1965, he migrated to California, where he promoted The Byrds, the Beach Boys, and The Doors, among others, and helped to organize the Monterey Pop Festival, before returning to work for the Beatles in their Apple period. Amidst all his comings and goings, Taylor ended up being at the epicenter of much of the musical aspect of the countercultural revolution of the 1960s, and his books recount those times, and the people who made them, with discernment and affection. He was the perfect ambassador to the world for the Beatles.

George Martin's quote about *Beatles For Sale* is found on page 53 of Lewisohn's *Recording Sessions*, which likewise notes that this album is widely regarded as the Beatles' weakest. For other supporting views, see Tim Riley's *Tell Me Why* (which notes that the album is "critically unpopular" but maintains, in something of a stretch, that the album nevertheless reveals an "essential" side of the Beatles' musical personality).

Page 101: The release dates and chart action of "I Feel Fine" and *Beatles For Sale* are documented in Lewisohn's *Recording Sessions* on pages 52–53, and in Dowlding's *Beatlesongs* on pages 80 and 82.

Page 101: George Martin's consideration of alternative singles releases is disclosed in the liner notes to *Beatles For Sale*. The four exceptions to the Beatles' practice of recording only original compositions in years to come were Ringo's version of "Act Naturally" and John's of "Dizzy Miss Lizzy" on

Help!, John's version of "Bad Boy" (released in the U.K. on the December 1966 compilation album, *A Collection of Beatles Oldies,* and in the United States on the June 1965 *Beatles VI* album), and John's take of "Maggie Mae" on *Let It Be.*

Page 102: The album's recording dates and general schedule in the second half of 1964 are documented in Lewisohn's *Chronicle,* pages 166–76.

Lennon's feedback quote is found on page 147 of the *Playboy Interviews.*

Page 102: Lewisohn mentions the press speculation about an "electronic accident" on page 50 of *Recording Sessions,* in the same entry in which he dismisses such speculations. The vibrating wine bottle story is found on page 159 of *Recording Sessions.* The other two "accidents" are described on pages 183 and 116.

Page 103: Lennon's quote about marijuana and "She's A Woman" is found on page 147 of the *Playboy Interviews.*

The statement that "Eight Days A Week" would most likely have been this period's single in the absence of "I Feel Fine" is a speculation by the author, based on the following evidence: (1) the *Beatles For Sale* liner notes state that it was one of three songs considered for this role, the others being "No Reply" and "I'm A Loser"; (2) it was "Eight Days A Week," not those other two songs, that became the single in the United States; and (3) "Eight Days A Week" featured a more upbeat tempo and lyric, not unimportant considerations for hit singles.

Paul's recollection of Ringo's remark came in his December 1984 interview with *Playboy.* John's "lousy" quote came from *his* sessions with the same magazine, the *Playboy Interviews,* pages 147–48. It should be noted, however, that John seemed confused in his recollections of the song, contending that it "was Paul's effort at getting a single for the movie" that later was titled "Help!" John claimed that "Eight Days A Week" had been the working title of the movie, but this was incorrect; the title had actually been "Eight Arms To Hold You." Moreover, work on the film did not begin until February 1965, a full four months after the Beatles finished recording "Eight Days A Week." For details, see Lewisohn's *Chronicle,* pages 173–74 and 183.

Page 104: That "Eight Days A Week" was the first pop song to receive a fade-in is noted on page 49 of Lewisohn's *Recording Sessions.* The George Martin quote comes from page 83 of same and actually was spoken in reference to the harmonies he had the Beatles sing on the lovely "Here, There and Everywhere" from *Revolver.*

Lennon's reference to "I'm A Loser" as belonging to his Dylan period is found on page 165 of the *Playboy Interviews* and is the basis for critics' remarks.

Page 104: Lennon's recounting of Dick James's reaction to "No Reply" is found on page 83 of Dowlding's *Beatlesongs*.

Page 105: McCartney's quote about "I'll Follow The Sun" is found on page 12 of *Recording Sessions*.

The original recording artists and related information concerning "Mr. Moonlight" and "Leave My Kitten Alone" are found on page 48 of *Recording Sessions*. A bootleg tape of the Beatles' rendition of "Leave My Kitten Alone" was made available to the author by a private collector. George Martin's query regarding "Baby's In Black" is found on page 47 of *Recording Sessions*.

CHAPTER TEN:
The Naturals:
The Lennon–McCartney Collaboration

Page 109: Ringo Starr's "The song is what remains" quote is cited on page 297 of Dowlding's *Beatlesongs*. George Martin's quote about "absolutely no evidence," came in an interview with the author of this book.

Page 110: The information on the writing and recording of "From Me To You" is found on page 28 of *Recording Sessions*. The takes written about in this book were listened to by the author.

Page 110: The good-natured jibes exchanged during the "From Me To You" session were nothing new between the two top Beatles. Back when they were still the Silver Beetles, "John and Paul were always at it, trying to outdo each other" on stage, recalled drummer Tommy Moore on page 94 of Philip Norman's *Shout!*. On page 106 of Chris Salewicz's *McCartney*, Liverpool promoter Sam Leach emphasizes that their rivalry was, however, a "very healthy" one. John and Paul, he says, were "good mates" who "never tried to upstage each other. While one was at the front of the stage, the other would do the backing, and vice versa. But whoever was doing the lead singing would put so much into it, that it was as though he was saying to the other, 'Go on, follow that!' That was the rivalry they created: they pushed each other on."

Page 111:   George Martin's "two people pulling on a rope" quote is found on page 364 of Ray Coleman's *Lennon.* Lennon's reference to his partnership with McCartney as a love affair and his "It wasn't resentment" quote are from his *Playboy Interviews,* pages 120 and 148. Martin's "Meeting John" quote is found on page 280 of the Davies biography. McCartney's "He'd write 'Strawberry Fields' " quote is from Martin's 1992 film, *The Making of Sgt Pepper.*

Page 112:   The temperamental similarities of Lennon and McCartney were pointed out by Martin on pages 363–64 of Coleman's *Lennon:* "Some people accentuated the differences between them—John being the acrid, bitter one and Paul the soft one. That was basically an image built up by the press. The truth is that deep down they were very, very similar indeed. Each had a soft underbelly, each was very much hurt by certain things. John had a very soft side to him. But you see, each had a bitter turn of phrase and could be quite nasty to the other, which each one expected at certain times. They did love each other very much throughout the time I knew them in the studio. But the tension was there mostly because they never really collaborated." Martin's contention about good but not blisteringly great is found on page 98 of his own book, *The Summer of Love.*

Page 112:   Pete Shotton's "Paul's presence" quote is from page 121 of his book, *John Lennon In My Life.*

McCartney's "You know, I could sit down" quote is from page 73 of Edward Gross's *Paul McCartney: Twenty Years on His Own.*

Page 113:   Lennon tells the story behind writing "Michelle" on page 116 of the *Playboy Interviews* and takes credit for the middle eight of "We Can Work It Out" on page 150. His contribution of the middle eight to "She's Leaving Home" is noted on pages 170–71 of Dowlding's *Beatlesongs.*

Page 114:   George Martin's "sauce vinaigrette" quote is found on page 371 of Coleman's *Lennon.* Lennon's reference to McCartney as "quite a capable lyricist" is found on page 118 of the *Playboy Interviews,* as is his citation of "Yesterday." The citations of "The Fool On The Hill" and "Fixing A Hole" are on pages 157 and 166. Among Lennon's attacks on McCartney were his reference to him as Engelbert Humperdinck, a treacly pop singer, referenced on pages 629–30 of Coleman's *Lennon,* and his bitter song, "How Do You Sleep," from the *Imagine* album. See also his open letter to McCartney in the English pop music publication *Melody Maker,* as reprinted on pages 485–88 of *Lennon.* McCartney's "I've become known" quote is found on page 11 of

Recording Sessions. That McCartney taped "Yesterday" and "I'm Down" on the same day is reported on page 59 of ibid.

Page 115: McCartney's "When we got in a little room" quote is from page 85 of his 1989–90 World Tour program booklet. His story about Lennon's liking McCartney's songs more than his own is from his December 1984 interview in *Playboy*.

Page 115: Lennon's "I was lying" quote is from page 117 of the *Playboy Interviews*; the original quote to which he is referring is found on page 55 of *Lennon Remembers*. His "partly because the demand" quote is from page 118 of the *Playboy Interviews*. His admission about the routinized nature of his early songwriting is found on page 80 of Miles's *Beatles: In Their Own Words*. McCartney's "We just knocked them out" quote is from page 8 of *Recording Sessions*. Lennon's Tin Pan Alley quote is from page 82 of *Beatles: In Their Own Words*.

Page 116: Lennon's quotes about Dylan and his own "Dylan period" are found in Coleman's *Lennon*, pages 383 and 343.

Page 116: Martin's "That was just the way their collaboration worked" quote is from page 364 of Coleman's *Lennon*. Shotton's account of the writing of "Eleanor Rigby" is found on pages 123–24 of his book, *John Lennon In My Life*.

Page 117: Hunter Davies's eyewitness description of the writing of "Magical Mystery Tour" and "With A Little Help From My Friends" is found in Chapter 30 of his book, along with reproductions of the handwritten lyrics of "Yesterday" and "I Want To Hold Your Hand."

Page 118: Lennon and McCartney's high opinion of their abilities as songwriters is noted by Paul on page 10 of *Recording Sessions*. His "pulling it out of the air" quote is from page 71 of Miles's book. His quotes about "written in one go," "the good thing about working with John" and "nearly always a sign" are from page 78 of his World Tour program booklet. Lennon's "my joy is when you're like possessed" quote is from his December 6, 1980, interview with Andy Peebles of the BBC. His references to "Nowhere Man," "In My Life," and "Across the Universe," and the quote about the latter, are from page 163 of the *Playboy Interviews*. McCartney's story about "Yesterday" is told in his December 1984 *Playboy* interview.

Page 118: Lennon's statement about egomaniacs is from *Lennon Remembers*, page 162. His quotes about "the music of the spheres" and "you have to be in tune" are from pages 120 and 103 of Garbarini and Cullman's *Strawberry Fields Forever: John Lennon Remembered*. His "after you come out" quote is from page 47 of the *Rolling Stone* book *The Ballad of John and Yoko*.

McCartney's "not necessarily worse" quote is on page 274 of the Davies biography, where he adds, "The last four songs of an album are usually pure slog. If we need four more we just have to get down and do them." This quote, combined with the information on page 263 about Paul and John writing the song near the end of *Sgt Pepper* because they needed a song Ringo could sing, is the basis for the assertion that this song was one of those that was "forced."

Page 119: McCartney's "That's the beauty of working at random" quote is from page 82 of Miles's book. The studio chat from the *Let It Be* sessions was listened to by the author of this book. McCartney's "the nice thing" quote is from page 14 of *Recording Sessions*. Martin's "I have often been asked" quote is from page 137 of his autobiography.

Page 120: Martin's "They were the Cole Porters" quote is from page 167 of his autobiography.

Page 120: The quotes from Dick James are found on page 365 of Coleman's *Lennon*. McCartney's "the collaboration I had with John" quote is from his December 1984 *Playboy* interview.

CHAPTER ELEVEN:
Fresh Sounds
(*Help!*)

Page 123: The swimming pool quote is found on page 19 of Bennahum, *in their own words: the Beatles . . . after the break-up*, where McCartney dismisses the notion of the Beatles being antimaterialistic as "a huge myth." He claims that he and Lennon made such comments "out of innocence, out of normal fucking working-class glee that we were able to write a swimming pool. For the first time in our lives, we could actually do something and earn money."

As far as "dropping out," it is true that the Beatles went to India in 1968, but this was necessarily a very abbreviated form of dropping out, since the Beatles' record contract with EMI bound them to produce two albums and three singles a year through 1970, hardly a schedule that allowed for much relaxation, much less an extended retreat from the material world.

Lennon's "when everybody else was just goofing off" quote is from page 79 of the *Playboy Interviews*. Lennon's "Watching The Wheels" appeared on the *Double Fantasy* album in 1980.

Page 124: That Lennon wrote "Help!" no earlier than the spring of 1965 is suggested by his memory of writing the song "bam-bam, like that," after director Richard Lester told him, in the middle of filming, that "Help!" was going to be the title of the movie the Beatles were making in the spring of 1965, a story Lennon relates on pages 148–49 of the *Playboy Interviews*. The evidence on whether Lennon originated the idea for the song is not conclusive, but it is the most likely interpretation. Although Coleman asserts the contrary on page 345 of his *Lennon* biography, he provides no proof or citation. Lennon, on the other hand, speaks in the *Playboy Interviews* of being "commissioned" to write the song for the movie, and in reply to the specific question of why the title of the movie was changed to *Help!* from the previous *Eight Arms To Hold You*, he does not claim any credit for himself but simply explains that "Help!" was a better title.

That "Help!" is the first Beatles song where the words are the point at least as much as the music is an assertion by the author.

"Help!" entered the U.K. charts at number one and remained there for four weeks, while in the United States it was number one for three weeks, according to Dowlding's *Beatlesongs*, page 97.

Lennon's reference to his "fat Elvis period" and his state of mind and health at that point is found on page 149 of the *Playboy Interviews*, except for the quote about Weybridge, which is reported on page 348 of Coleman's book.

Page 124: The Beatles' discontent with the movie *Help!* is noted, among other places, on page 180 of Lewisohn's *Chronicle*.

Lennon's "because I meant it" quote is from page 115 of *Lennon Remembers*. McCartney's "sitting there" is from *in their own words: the Beatles . . . after the break-up*, page 112. His recollection of driving out to Weybridge is found in his December 1984 interview with *Playboy*.

Page 125: Lennon's criticism of the quickening of the tempo of "Help!" is found on page 115 of *Lennon Remembers*.

The date of the "Help!" recording session is documented in *Recording Sessions*. Tapes of the session were heard by the author.

Page 126: The Silver Beatles' claims about "the rhythm's in the guitars" comes from McCartney's August 1980 *Musician* interview, as reprinted in *Beatlefan*, vol. II, no. 5.

Page 126: Lennon's references to his "fat Elvis" period are noted above. His references to his "Dylan period" are found, among other places, on page 165 of the *Playboy Interviews*. Coleman, on pages 343–44 and 383–84 of *Lennon*, also documents Lennon's fascination with and respect of Dylan in late 1964–65, noting that he, Coleman, and Lennon spent considerable time trying to work out the lyrics to Dylan's 1965 single "Subterranean Homesick Blues."

McCartney says of Dylan, on page 50 of his 1989 World Tour program, "We were highly influenced by him and he was quite influenced by us in fact as well." Harrison's regard for Dylan is noted by Pete Shotton on page 105 of his book, by Lennon on page 103 of the *Playboy Interviews*, where he recalls that George used to sit him down and make him listen to Dylan's albums, and by Harrison himself in his December 1987 interview with *Rolling Stone*, where he says, "Five hundred years from now, looking back in history, I think he will still be the man, Bob, he just takes the cake."

Page 127: Lennon's reference to the "abysmal" lyrics of "It's Only Love" is on page 150 of the *Playboy Interviews*.

The story of Lennon's changing the lyric while first singing "You've Got To Hide Your Love Away" is told by Pete Shotton, who says it was the first Beatles song composed in his presence and who adds that he himself "contributed the sustained 'hey's' that introduce the main chorus." See page 122 of his book.

The reference to "You've Got To Hide Your Love Away" as the first gay love song is credited to Tom Robinson, a gay singer and rock band leader, on page 302 of Coleman's *Lennon*. Robinson felt the song was a message from Lennon to Brian Epstein.

Page 128: McCartney's "You put your own meaning" quote was said in reference to the song "Doctor Robert" and is found on page 88 of *in their own words: the Beatles.* . . .

That the flutes on "You've Got To Hide Your Love Away" were the first instance of an outside musician joining the Beatles is noted on page 54 of Lewisohn's *Recording Sessions*. The same book cites the other new instruments the Beatles played during the sessions for *Help!*, except for the reference to Harrison's sitar, which is found on page 228 of the Davies biography.

Page 129: Outtakes of "If You've Got Trouble" and "That Means A Lot" were listened to by the author. Their recording dates and related information, as well as the fact that they remain locked up in the Abbey Road archives, are documented on pages 55–56 of Lewisohn's *Recording Sessions*. McCartney's "we just couldn't get behind" quote is found on page 12 of same.

That there are no undiscovered Beatles masterpieces still secreted away in the Abbey Road archives was confirmed by Lewisohn in an interview with the author.

Page 130: "Ticket To Ride" was a number one hit in the U.K. for five weeks and in the United States for one week, according to page 101 of Dowlding's *Beatlesongs*.

Lennon's "one of the earliest heavy-metal" quotes is from page 165 of the *Playboy Interviews*, where he also credits McCartney for originating the song's drum pattern. That Paul also played the opening guitar lick is noted on page 54 of *Recording Sessions*.

Page 131: Regarding "Yesterday," Dowlding reports in *Beatlesongs*, page 107, that more than 2,500 artists had recorded versions of "Yesterday" by 1980, and on page 105 that the song was not released as a single in the U.K. until 1976 (though it was released as a single in the United States in 1965).

Page 131: McCartney's recollection of "Yesterday" coming to him in his sleep as a dream is found in his December 1984 *Playboy* interview. McCartney doesn't mention the Hotel George V, but since George Martin says, on page 59 of *Recording Sessions*, that this is where he first heard the song, in January 1964, and it is known that there was a grand piano in the room for the Beatles to compose on, the author has surmised that this must have been where McCartney actually set down the tune.

The June 14, 1965, recording date for "Yesterday" is documented on page 59 of *Recording Sessions*. McCartney reveals his working title and opening line on page 78 of his 1989 World Tour program, where he adds that it took him a mere two weeks to finish the words and confirms that he felt the tune too beautiful to burden it with silly lyrics about eggs. His "we didn't think it fitted our image" quote is found on page 12 of *Recording Sessions*.

Page 132: McCartney's "most complete thing" quote is found on page 174 of Salewicz's *McCartney*.

Page 132: George Martin recalls conceiving of the string quartet for "Yesterday" on page 59 of *Recording Sessions*, where he adds that McCartney worked closely with him, adding his own ideas. The same page documents McCartney's recording schedule on June 14, 1965.

CHAPTER TWELVE:
Four-way Synergy:
That Inexplicable Charisma

Page 135: George Martin's "absolutely true" quote came in an interview with the author. Among examples of the Beatles speaking of themselves as four aspects of the same person, see Lennon's quote on page 45 of *Lennon Remembers*, and McCartney's quote on page 310 of the Davies biography, part of which is quoted here—"We're individuals . . ." George Harrison's "magic" quote is found in *Beatlefan* magazine, vol. 1, no. 3. John Lennon's "IT happens" quote is found on page 75 of Miles's *Beatles: In Their Own Words.*

The number of hours of Beatles music stored in the archives at Abbey Road Studios was attested by Lewisohn in an interview with the author.

Page 135: For documentation of the method of recording used on the Beatles' music, see *Recording Sessions*, pages 67, 70, and especially 54; the latter explains that, beginning in 1965, the Beatles began "to rehearse songs with a tape machine running, spooling back to record properly over the rehearsed material." Thus rehearsals *would* be recorded, but not permanently; each take would be obliterated by the succeeding take. This is what makes the "Think For Yourself" session so unusual; individual takes were preserved, not erased.

Martin's "I was saving money" quote came in an interview with the author.

The recording of the Christmas discs during the "Think For Yourself" rehearsals is noted on page 67 of *Recording Sessions.*

Page 136: Tapes containing the studio chat from the "Think For Yourself" session were listened to by the author in the course of writing this book, as were the Beatles' Christmas gift records.

Page 140: Ringo's own amazement at his good fortune is reported on page 335 of Hunter Davies's authorized biography of the Beatles. John's "would have surfaced" quote is from page 141 of the *Playboy Interviews.* His "every bit as warm" quote is found on page 204 of Geoffrey Giuliano's *The Beatles: A Celebration*.

Page 140: Journalist Maureen Cleave of the London *Evening Standard* was the first to liken the Beatles to the Marx Brothers, as noted on page 174 of the Davies biography, but as time passed the comparison circulated more widely; see page 29 of Jon Wiener's *Come Together*.

Martin's "John, that's crap" quote comes from page 100 of his book *The Summer of Love*.

McCartney's "bad enough mood" quote comes from his interview in *Playboy*, December 1984.

Page 141: The mange-tout peas story is found on page 226 of Philip Norman's *Shout!*, where it is attributed by name to George Martin. John's Lufthansa joke is told on page 354 of Coleman's *Lennon*.

Paul's "Little Elvis" quote about John comes from an interview in the December 10, 1987, issue of *Rolling Stone*.

Page 142: Ringo's "brothers" quote is found on page 109 of David Bennahum's *in their own words: the Beatles . . . after the break-up*. Paul's "a right slagging session" quote comes from page 373 of the Davies biography.

Page 142: Astrid Kirchherr's "sparks would fly" quote is found on page 33 of Geoffrey Giuliano's *Dark Horse*. Paul's quote about riding in the back of the limo comes from an interview in the November 5–December 10, 1987 issue of *Rolling Stone*. Pete Shotton's quote comes from page 105 of his *John Lennon In My Life*.

Jeff Jarratt's "inexplicable charismatic thing" quote is from page 174 of Lewisohn's *Recording Sessions*.

Page 143: George Martin's "brotherhood" quote comes from an interview with the author.

Page 144: McCartney's "it made us very tight" quote comes from an interview in the December 1984 issue of *Playboy*. His remark about doing it to a live audience is made in the film *Let It Be*.

Page 144: Ringo's "play real well together" quote is found on page 34 of David Bennahum's *in their own words: the Beatles . . . after the break-up*. Paul's "great band" quote comes from an interview in the December 10, 1987 issue of *Rolling Stone*.

Ringo's "worst band" quote is from page 48 of *in their own words: the Beatles . . . after the break-up*.

Regarding the Beatles' internal democracy-meritocracy dynamic, see Paul's comment, reported on page 303 of Coleman's *Lennon*, that while John "was probably the deciding vote" in the group, "we were all sort of leaders." See also John's remark, on pages 279–80 of DiLello's *The Longest Cocktail Party*, that the Beatles' general practice was to do "what any three of us decided."

Page 145: John's "technical musicians" quote is from page 142 of the *Playboy Interviews*. George Martin's "all-rounder" quote is from page 137 of his autobiography; separately, on page 86 of his book *The Summer of Love*, Martin goes so far as to say that Paul could play the drums, technically, even better than Ringo, though without Ringo's distinctive sound. John's description of himself as a musical primitive, and his rating of his guitar ability, is found on page 46 of *Lennon Remembers*. Martin's quote about Ringo's drumming is from page 127 of his autobiography.

Page 146: Martin's quote about George and Ringo being "very much part of the magic" was made in an interview with the author. John's quotes about John and Paul's creating it without George and Ringo come from page 142 of the *Playboy Interviews*.

McCartney's quote about "there was nobody else" comes from page 85 of his 1989–90 World Tour program. The history of John's inviting the other three Beatles to join the band has been told, and referenced, in Chapters Two and Four of this book. Lennon's quote about "four of us" is found on page 22 of Miles's *Beatles: In Their Own Words*.

CHAPTER THIRTEEN:
Coming of Age
(*Rubber Soul*)

Page 149: Van Gogh's letter to Gauguin is printed in *Vincent by Himself*, edited by Bruce Bernard (Macdonald & Co., London 1985), page 213.

The precise release date for *Rubber Soul* and "We Can Work It Out" / "Day Tripper" single, December 3, 1965, is documented on page 69 of *Recording Sessions*.

George Martin's quotes are from the video *The Compleat Beatles*.

Page 149: Among those who praise *Rubber Soul* are the American critics Robert Christgau and John Piccarella, who called the album "the Beatles' most unqualified triumph, the record claimed by their *Sgt Pepper* faction and their Hamburg faction both," on page 248 of *The Ballad of John and Yoko*.

Page 150: That Paul wrote the verses and John the middle eight of "We Can Work It Out" is confirmed by John on page 150 of the *Playboy Interviews*. The recapitulation of the chord writing for the song is informed speculation on the part of the author, based on the record itself and the sheet music found in *The Complete Beatles*, pages 315–17.

The number of takes and recording date and times for "We Can Work It Out" is documented on page 64 of *Recording Sessions*. Outtakes of the session were listened to by the author.

Page 153: That "We Can Work It Out" and "Day Tripper" were issued as a double A-sided single is confirmed on page 69 of *Recording Sessions*, which notes that this was the first instance of such a release. Lennon and McCartney's recollection of "Day Tripper" as "forced" is mentioned on page 64 of ibid.

Page 153: Lennon's authorship of "Day Tripper" and his comments about its lyrics referring to "weekend hippies" are noted on page 150 of the *Playboy Interviews*. His reference to smoking pot for breakfast is on page 149 of ibid. For documentation of the four Beatles' relationship to both pot and LSD at this time, see Chapter Sixteen of this book.

Page 154: Lennon's description of writing "Nowhere Man" is found on page 163 of the *Playboy Interviews*.

Page 155: Martin's harmonium contribution to "The Word" is noted on page 68 of *Recording Sessions*. The reference to having played the instrument on "If I Needed Someone" is qualified because it is not specifically mentioned in *Recording Sessions*—the relevant entry, on page 64, refers only to "additional instruments"—although it is cited in Dowlding's *Beatlesongs* on page 125.

McCartney's reference to the Beatles' borrowing "that jangly thing" from The Byrds was stated in the film "It Was Twenty Years Ago Today," based on Derek Taylor's book of the same name.

Page 156: Lennon's remarks about "In My Life" are from page 151 of the *Playboy Interviews.* McCartney's claim was made in his interview in the December 1984 issue of *Playboy.*

Page 156: The information about the piano solo of "In My Life" is based on page 65 of *Recording Sessions* and Martin's interview in the July 1987 issue of *Musician.*

Page 156: The instruments employed on *Rubber Soul* are noted in the relevant entries of *Recording Sessions.* Tim Riley's quote is found on page 154 of his book *Tell Me Why.*

Page 157: The information on the rewrite of "Drive My Car" is found on page 114 of Dowlding's *Beatlesongs* and page 78 of McCartney's 1989–90 World Tour program, the latter of which provides the original version of the song's lyrics.

Page 157: The number of remakes of "I'm Looking Through You" are reported on pages 65–68 of *Recording Sessions,* which also list the instruments used and include Lewisohn's nomination.

Page 158: The re-creation of Lennon's chord structures on "Norwegian Wood" is informed speculation on the part of the author, based on the information on instruments and capoes found on page 115 of Dowlding's *Beatlesongs* and the sheet music in *The Complete Beatles* songbook.

Page 159: The author listened to takes one and four of "Norwegian Wood" himself. Takes two and three are described on page 65 of *Recording Sessions.*

Lennon admits that "Norwegian Wood" was based on an affair he'd had, on page 150 of the *Playboy Interviews.*

Page 160: McCartney takes credit for the idea of arson in the February 1985 *Musician.*

CHAPTER FOURTEEN:
"Think Symphonically":
Producer George Martin

Page 164: McCartney's recitation of the Beatles' musical influences, and his "Big Bill Broonzy" quote, are from an interview contained in an untitled collection of video outtakes, which was obtained by the author.

Page 164: Derek Taylor's remark came during an interview with the author of this book.

The Beatles' inability to read or notate music is discussed in Martin's autobiography on pages 137–40. Martin's course of studies at Guildhall is noted on page 27, and his family background on pages 13–15, of same.

Martin had shown his own willingness to flout convention in one of the very first decisions he made about the Beatles. In 1962, right after deciding to sign them to a recording contract, Martin was wondering which of the four he should choose as the band's lead singer and star. In those days, every pop group comprised a front man and backing players: Buddy Holly and the Crickets, for example. Martin was leaning toward making McCartney the leader when he suddenly realized this would violate the essence of the Beatles' appeal. "Why not keep them as they were?" he asked himself. "It hadn't been done before— but then, I'd made a lot of records that hadn't been 'done before.' " (See page 124 of Martin's autobiography.)

Martin had indeed acquired a reputation as a maverick since joining EMI in 1950. As he describes in his autobiography, in 1955, at the age of twenty-nine, he had taken over EMI's struggling Parlophone label and, despite the doubts of superiors, had carved out an identity for it by making comedy records with such figures as Peter Sellers and the Beyond the Fringe gang. He also produced classical, jazz, and pop music, recording such stars as Sophia Loren and Peter Ustinov. (After the Beatles broke up, Martin was sometimes annoyed that people seemed ignorant of the breadth and richness of his career, both pre- and post-Beatles. In a 1993 interview with the author of this book he explained, "I thought, 'Good God, don't people know I've done other things?' It obviously is the most important thing I've done, but not necessarily the most interesting.")

Page 165: Ringo's "very twelve inch" quote is noted on page 69 of Martin's book *The Summer of Love*. John's quote about the Beatles "learning together" with Martin is from a television interview from the early 1970s included on an unpublished collection of video footage about the Beatles that was obtained by the author.

Page 165: The dates, instrumentation, and Martin's quoted recollections of the respective recording sessions for "I Am The Walrus" are documented in *Recording Sessions*, pages 122–23 and 127. The outtakes of the song were listened to by the author of this book in the course of his research.

Martin confirms his disapproval of drugs on page 206 of his autobiography, noting that the Beatles knew he didn't approve.

Page 167: Martin's "organized chaos" quote comes from page 122 of *Recording Sessions*, Ken Scott's from page 126.

On pages 6–8 of *Recording Sessions*, McCartney describes the Beatles' efforts to find B-sides they could perform in concert in their early days. His "funny hat quote" comes from page 283 of the Davies biography.

Page 167: Lennon's quote about *Rubber Soul* comes from page 83 of *Lennon Remembers*. McCartney's "louder, further" quote is from page 13 of *Recording Sessions*.

Martin's "two directions at once" quote is from page 133 of his autobiography.

Page 168: Martin tells the Lewis Carroll story on pages 12 and 13 of his autobiography. It is worth noting, as yet another example of how unreliable human memory can be, that Martin told a somewhat different version of the same story to Lewisohn. On page 38 of *Recording Sessions*, Martin is quoted saying that within minutes of receiving the Beatles' "roguish apologies" they all made their way to the recording studios to make the German version of "I Want To Hold Your Hand." In his book, however, Martin says that the record was made the following day, because when the Beatles "wanted to be charming, as they did then, it was impossible to maintain anger for very long, and within a few minutes I had calmed down and joined the tea party—though in what guise it's hard for me to say: the Mad Hatter perhaps."

Martin's quote about the "White Album" is found on page 163 of *Recording Sessions*.

Page 168: Martin's citation of *Help!* and especially "Yesterday" as the key turning point is found on pages 166–67 of his autobiography. That "You've Got To Hide Your Love Away" was the first Beatles song to feature an outside musician (flautist John Scott) is noted in *Recording Sessions*; Lewisohn is careful to recall the one exception, the use of session drummer Andy White on the Beatles' debut single, "Love Me Do," in 1962. Townsend's "workshop" quote is found on page 36 of *Recording Sessions*.

Martin's description of the studio routine during the early years of working with the Beatles is found on pages 132–33 of his autobiography.

Page 169: Martin describes his decision to leave EMI, and the mean and greedy corporate behavior that led him to that decision, on pages 179–83 of his autobiography. The Beatles' insistence that he continue to produce them is noted on page 209 of Lewisohn's *Chronicle*.

Martin's and McCartney's quotes about "She Loves You" are found on pages 10 and 32 of *Recording Sessions*.

Page 169: The studio chat from the "Think For Yourself" sessions was listened to by the author of this book.

Page 170: Martin's attempt to learn guitar, and Lennon's confusion about saxophones, are described in Martin's autobiography on pages 138–39. That the song in question was "Good Morning Good Morning" is noted on page 74 of Martin's later book *The Summer of Love*, though some of the dialogue is slightly different in that account.

The criticisms by professional musicians are noted by Martin on pages 201–02 of his autobiography. His praise of the Beatles as being superior to himself is on page 167, and his quote about "Penny Lane" is on page 259.

Page 171: McCartney's "Try it" quote is from page 13 of *Recording Sessions*.

McCartney describes distorting an acoustic guitar so that it sounded "hot" while recording "Ob-La-Di, Ob-La-Da" on page 11 of *Recording Sessions*. The backward cymbal sound is extensively deployed on *Sgt Pepper's Lonely Hearts Club Band*; how the trick worked is best demonstrated on George Martin's 1992 documentary film about the album. "Rain" was but one of the many songs on which the Beatles recorded their instruments and vocals overly fast, to be slowed down on replay; see page 74 of *Recording Sessions*. Page 150 recounts the time McCartney had drums moved into the corridor at Abbey Road Studios while recording "Mother Nature's Son." The quote from Emerick about pianos and guitars sounding like one another is from page 114.

Page 171: The stories about Lennon's efforts to change the sound of his voice when recorded come from *Recording Sessions*. The milk bottle incident is mentioned on page 114, the "Revolution 1" session on page 136, Ken Townsend's invention of "Automatic Double Tracking," or ADT, on page 70, John's request to sound like someone from the moon on page 144, and Martin's neck operation quote on page 95.

Martin's "main influence" quote is from page 104 of his book *The Summer of Love*. Harrison's quote about inventing sounds in 1967 is found on page 27 of Derek Taylor's book *It Was Twenty Years Ago Today*. Martin's quote about assembling digital information is from his interview with *Q* magazine, May 14, 1993.

Page 172: Martin's remark about painting pictures in sound is found on page 280 of the Davies biography. His reference to Picasso is on page 278 of same. His quote about the historical significance of *Sgt Pepper's Lonely Hearts Club Band* is from his autobiography, page 214.

McCartney's "bitterness" quote is found on page 93 of Miles's book, *Beatles: In Their Own Words*. Lennon's angry remarks about Martin are found in *Lennon Remembers*, pages 27 and 62. Martin's reply is found on page 114 of *Recording Sessions*.

Page 173: McCartney's "tools" quote is found on page 6 of *Recording Sessions*, Ken Scott's on page 126.

Martin's absence from many of the sessions for *The Beatles* is noted on pages 135 and 149 of *Recording Sessions*, and page 143 notes McCartney's stinging retort when Martin dared critique his vocal on "Ob-La-Di, Ob-La-Da": Emerick recalled that Martin suggested that Paul "should be lilting onto the half-beat or whatever and Paul, in no refined way, said something to the effect of, 'Well, you come down and sing it.' " Emerick quit working for the Beatles that day.

Martin's desire to quit the Beatles himself after *Let It Be* was expressed in *The Compleat Beatles* video, as was his recollection of Paul's efforts to lure him back for *Abbey Road*. His pride in the album's second side is noted on page 192 of Lewisohn's *Recording Sessions*.

Page 173: Martin's "good team" quote is found on page 259 of his autobiography.

CHAPTER FIFTEEN:
Listen to the Color
of Your Dream
(*Revolver*)

Page 175: McCartney describes his Mayfair Hotel meeting with Bob Dylan on page 50 of his 1989–90 World Tour program.

Page 176: McCartney's "sounds" quote is noted on page 60 of Nicholas Schaffner's book *The Beatles Forever*.

Page 177: The patch job on "Taxman" is described on page 76 of *Recording Sessions*.

Page 177:   The ninety-six percent tax rate faced by the Beatles is noted by their business staffer Peter Brown in *The Love You Make*, page 253. Regarding the praise of Harrison's writing of "Taxman," the caveat should be added that it is possible it was Lennon who wrote the line about "Declare the pennies . . ."—he claims on page 127 of the *Playboy Interviews* to have contributed to the song's lyrics—but impossible to verify.

Page 178:   The recording dates and studio techniques related to "Tomorrow Never Knows" are documented on pages 70–72 of *Recording Sessions.* Geoff Emerick's "*Revolver* very rapidly became" quote is found on page 74.

The Beatles' three months of inactivity in early 1966 are documented on pages 210, 215–16 of Lewisohn's *Chronicle*, and the comparison to the schedule of the Quarry Men is supported by the listing of the band's work dates from late 1959 through to 1966, provided in passim in *Chronicle.*

That Lennon did a lot of LSD during the months prior to and during the recording of *Revolver* is recalled by, among others, Pete Shotton on page 118 of his book. The drug connections of Lennon's six songs from the *Revolver* period will be discussed in the text in the course of this chapter. Of the six, only "And Your Bird Can Sing" lacked a direct connection to drugs.

Lennon is commonly reported to have drawn the lyrics of "Tomorrow Never Knows" from the *Tibetan Book of the Dead*—indeed, he himself said as much on page 153 of the *Playboy Interviews*—but the opening line of the song is actually a word-for-word transcription of Leary's book (which was itself based in part on the *Tibetan Book of the Dead*), as explained on pages 197–98 of Albert Goldman's The *Lives of John Lennon.*

Page 178:   Lennon's "Dalai Lama" quote is found on page 72 of *Recording Sessions.* Martin's Leslie speaker recording technique is described on the same page, as is the amazement and requests for additional treatments that the experiment provoked. Lennon's reference to monks is on page 278 of the Davies biography.

Martin's "strangled cry" quote is found on page 370 of Ray Coleman's *Lennon.*

The backward guitar on "Tomorrow Never Knows" is noted on page 70 of *Recording Sessions;* the techniques of making tape loops are described on page 72.

Page 179:   Lewisohn's description of take one of "Tomorrow Never Knows" is found on page 70 of *Recording Sessions*, as is the information relating to Geoff

Emerick. The change in the recording technique for the drums is described on page 72.

Page 180: The information about the liberation of the bass sound is found on page 74 of *Recording Sessions*, except for the reference to McCartney's new style of playing, which he himself mentions in his interview with Lewisohn on page 13 of ibid.

Lennon's quote about McCartney's bass playing is found on page 142 of the *Playboy Interviews*.

Page 180: Lennon's comparison of "Paperback Writer" with "Day Tripper" is found on page 151 of the *Playboy Interviews*.

Starr's quotes about his drumming on "Rain" were made to Max Weinberg and reported in Weinberg's book *The Big Beat*, as cited on page 130 of Dowlding's *Beatlesongs*.

Page 181: Lennon claimed on page 167 of the *Playboy Interviews* to have originated the idea of putting backward vocals on "Rain," but George Martin told Lewisohn on page 74 of *Recording Sessions* that it was actually he who did so. It is impossible to know which man's memory is closer to the truth.

Geoff Emerick's explanation of the use of the vari-speed technique on "Rain" is found on page 74 of *Recording Sessions*. That the Beatles now began to attend the mix sessions at Abbey Road is noted on page 77, ibid.

Lennon's "boring people doing boring things" quote is from page 166 of the *Playboy Interviews*.

Page 182: Lennon's rejection of the Beatles' leadership role in the 1960s is expressed on pages 32, 70–73, and 78–79 of the *Playboy Interviews*.

Page 182: The reconstruction of the collaborative effort that created "Eleanor Rigby" is based on the author's cross-checking of the three separate versions of the story offered by McCartney, Lennon, and Lennon's friend Pete Shotton. Lennon and McCartney differ significantly about the authorship of this song, and the dispute would be difficult to resolve had Shotton not offered his own eyewitness account of events. Lennon's version is found on page 123 of *Lennon Remembers*, and on pages 118–19 of the *Playboy Interviews*; McCartney's is found on page 82 of Miles's *Beatles: In Their Own Words*, with additional information from his interview in the December 1984 *Playboy*; and Shotton's is found on pages 122–24 of his book, *John Lennon In My Life*. Shotton's account is persuasive not simply because he is a third party, but because his book is a loving remembrance of his friend Lennon that nevertheless does not shrink from pointing out the full dimensions of the man, good and bad. In this case, Shotton directly contradicts Lennon's claim to have written most of the lyrics to "Eleanor Rigby," noting that his friend's memory "could be extremely erratic" and adding that John's contribution to the song was in fact "virtually nil."

There is no dispute that McCartney wrote the tune of the song and the entire first verse. John admits as much, Shotton's account supports this, and Paul explains the process in the Miles book. Paul's changing the name from Daisy Hawkins to Eleanor Rigby is documented in the Miles book and also the 1984 *Playboy* interview. The brainstorming scene at John's house comes from Shotton and is not inconsistent with Lennon's recollection, and is reinforced by McCartney's remark, cited in Dowlding's *Beatlesongs*, page 134, about taking the song down to Lennon's place and laughing and getting stoned while working on it.

There is still a gap in the story, between the session at John's house and the polishing touches applied at Abbey Road. It is conceivable it was at this point that Lennon's memory of events kicks in, wherein McCartney supposedly tosses the lyrics of the partially finished song at John and Beatles assistants Mal Evans and Neil Aspinall and asks them to finish it up. Yet even in John's account, the song ends up being finished not by John alone but by John and Paul together, a scene also consistent with McCartney's recollections in the Miles book.

Page 183: That it was Martin who wrote the score of "Eleanor Rigby," with the benefit of McCartney's inspiration, is based on McCartney's comment on page 135 of Dowlding's *Beatlesongs*, on Lennon's comment on page 119 of the *Playboy Interviews*, and on Martin's remark to Lewisohn on page 77 of *Recording Sessions*, which also includes his reference to *Fahrenheit 451*.

Page 184: That "Here, There And Everywhere" was Paul's favorite among his many songs is noted on page 83 of *Recording Sessions* by Lewisohn, who, besides his authoritative knowledge about the Beatles, also works for McCartney personally. The text qualifies John's regard for "Here, There And Everywhere" only because he never said explicitly that the song was his favorite by Paul. He did say the next best thing, however, on page 152 of the *Playboy Interviews*, calling it "one of my favorite songs of the Beatles."

McCartney's recollection of writing the song beside the pool at Lennon's house while waiting for John to awaken is found in his 1984 *Playboy* interview.

Page 185: The Frère Jacques backing vocals on "Paperback Writer" can be plainly heard on the record, but are also noted on page 73 of *Recording Sessions*.

Paul and Ringo's disavowals of hidden meanings in "Yellow Submarine" are found on pages 82–84 of Miles's *Beatles: In Their Own Words*. The details of the special effects recording session, which took place on June 1, 1966, are documented on page 81 of *Recording Sessions*.

Page 185: The description of the origin of "She Said She Said" is based on Lennon's recollections, found on page 76 of *Lennon Remembers* and on page 152 of the *Playboy Interviews*, and Fonda's account of the day in question, found on pages 217–18 of *Rolling Stone* magazine's book *The Ballad of John and Yoko*. The recapitulation of Lennon's writing of the song is based on the raw composing tape, which the author listened to in the course of writing this book.

Page 186: Lennon's explanation of writing the middle eight of "She Said She Said" was given to *Rolling Stone* magazine in 1968 and is cited on page 140 of Dowlding's *Beatlesongs*.

McCartney's "in one go" quote is found on page 78 of his 1989–90 World Tour program. He said he wrote "Good Day Sunshine" by Lennon's pool in the December 1984 *Playboy* interview. Lennon's quotes about both his and McCartney's being "channels" for "the music of the spheres" are from pages 120 and 103 of Garbarini and Cullman's *Strawberry Fields Forever: John Lennon Remembered*.

Page 187: The Wilfrid Mellers quote is found on page 76 of his book *Twilight of the Gods*. John's "horror" quote about "And Your Bird Can Sing" is cited on page 141 of Dowlding's *Beatlesongs*. The story behind "Doctor Robert" is revealed by McCartney on page 88 of *Beatles: In Their Own Words*. The Shotton quote is found on page 122 of his book.

Lennon's reference to "For No One" as one of his favorite McCartney songs is found on page 152 of the *Playboy Interviews*.

Page 187: The musical effects used on "For No One" are described on pages 78–79 of *Recording Sessions*. The sentence listing McCartney's contributions to "I Want To Tell You" is based on the information on pages 81–82 of ibid. and on that found on page 144 of Dowlding's *Beatlesongs*; the sentence contains one piece of speculation, crediting McCartney for the song's opening fade-in, which is an educated guess based on Paul's other contributions to the song but primarily on the fact that McCartney was the source of most of the ideas for production and arrangement in most of the Beatles' songs, as pointed out by, among others, Abbey Road engineer Norman Smith on page 178 of Salewicz's *Mc-Cartney*.

Lennon's remarks about "Got To Get You Into My Life" are found on page 153 of the *Playboy Interviews*.

McCartney's initiation of the brass for "Got To Get You Into My Life" is noted on page 79 of *Recording Sessions*, as are the names and London club connections of the players and the recording techniques of Geoff Emerick; see page 77 of ibid. for the information about "Eleanor Rigby."

Page 188: McCartney's "That *was* an LSD song" quote is from his interview in the December 1984 *Playboy*. Lennon's "you don't realize what they mean" quote is found on page 47 of the *Rolling Stone* book *The Ballad of John and Yoko*. It was partly to soften the heaviness of the lyrics to "Tomorrow Never Knows" that John borrowed one of Ringo's malapropisms for the title of the song, as he explains on page 153 of the *Playboy Interviews*.

Lennon's interest in reincarnation was recalled by his friend Elliot Mintz on pages 173–74 of *Rolling Stone*'s book *The Ballad of John and Yoko* and expressed by Lennon himself, albeit in terms of its Eastern equivalent term, karma, on page 14 of the *Playboy Interviews*.

CHAPTER SIXTEEN:
We All Want to Change the World:
Drugs, Politics, and Spirituality

Page 191: Derek Taylor's "an abstraction, like Christmas" quote comes from a video interview he gave years after the Beatles disbanded, contained on a reel of privately collected footage that was viewed by the author.

The Beatles' press conference remarks about success and nuclear war are reported on page 58 of Miles's *Beatles: In Their Own Words*.

Page 192: George Harrison's "For a while we thought we were having some influence" quote is found on page 136 of Derek Taylor's *It Was Twenty Years Ago Today*. His the "desire to *find out*" quote is from an interview in the October 22, 1987, issue of *Rolling Stone*.

Page 192: McCartney's "U-turn" remark is found on page 50 of his 1989–90 World Tour program, where he also describes how pot led the Beatles to abandon drink and pills. Lennon's comment about drink is found on page 82 of *Lennon Remembers.*

Dylan's confusion about the actual lyrics of "I Want To Hold Your Hand" is noted by McCartney in his World Tour program. His recollection is reinforced by Coleman's *Lennon*, page 343, where Coleman recalls a 1964 interview he did with Dylan in which Dylan expressed astonishment that "I Want To Hold Your Hand" was not a drug song and the Beatles not marijuana smokers. The story of the meeting during which Dylan got the Beatles high for the first time is told most expansively in Brown and Gaines's *The Love You Make*, pages 143–44, though it must be noted that neither of the authors claims to have been present that night, nor do they cite specific sources for the detailed descriptions and specific dialogue they present in the book. However, central elements of their story are supported by Lennon's remarks on page 52 of *Rolling Stone*'s book *The Ballad of John and Yoko*, which also contains his "We've got a lot to thank him for" quote.

Page 193: The daily smoking habits of the Beatles during *Help!*, and the reshooting this sometimes made necessary, are recounted by Lennon on page 149 of the *Playboy Interviews*, which also contains his "in our own world" quote. The "Let's have a laugh" code phrase is qualified in the text with the word "reportedly" because it is based not on a direct statement by one of the Beatles but on the account in *The Love You Make.*

McCartney's "It was a move away from accepted values" quote is from page 50 of the World Tour program and is supported by a quote from George Harrison, found in the October 22, 1987, issue of *Rolling Stone*, saying that before acid and marijuana, the Beatles were always rushing around too much to have time to think about what was happening to them.

Derek Taylor's "taller and broader of mind" quote is found on page 88 of his book *It Was Twenty Years Ago Today.* Harrison's "It was like opening the door" quote is from the November 5, 1987, issue of *Rolling Stone*, which also includes his citation of 1966 as the year of LSD for the Beatles.

Page 194: Lennon has offered the fullest description of the night with the LSD-dispensing dentist, found on pages 73–75 of *Lennon Remembers*, and the fact that the acid was given to them without their knowledge is supported by Harrison on page 120 of Miles's *The Beatles: In Their Own Words.*

The description of the second LSD trip, in Los Angeles, is based on the Lennon recollection just cited, as well as Peter Fonda's comments on pages 217–18 of *The Ballad of John and Yoko* and Lennon's 1980 comments in the

Playboy Interviews. The fact that McCartney declined to take LSD that day is supported both by the Lennon recollections and by an interview of McCartney in the September 11, 1986, *Rolling Stone.*

That McCartney took his first acid trip with Lennon after John took it by mistake one night in the studio is based on the McCartney interview just cited. The actual date and the other details reported are found in a variety of sources, including that interview, Lennon's comments on page 76 of *Lennon Remembers,* George Martin's memories, as reported on pages 206–07 of his book *All You Need Is Ears,* Hunter Davies's eyewitness account on pages 270–71 of his *The Beatles,* and page 104 of Lewisohn's *Recording Sessions.*

Page 194: McCartney's "this fantastic thing" quote is found on page 21 of Taylor's *It Was Twenty Years Ago Today.* His "opened my eyes" quote is reported on page 136 of Shotton's book, *John Lennon In My Life,* page 118 of which contains Shotton's "brought enthusiasm back" quote.

Extremist that he was, Lennon later went too far with LSD, taking it so often that its benefits were lost on him and the battering of his ego became intolerable. He therefore stopped taking acid sometime in the summer of 1967, only to return to it one weekend the following spring under the guidance of Derek Taylor, who assured Lennon of the many reasons he had to believe in himself. The story is told on pages 77–78 of *Lennon Remembers* and on pages 322–23 of Coleman's *Lennon.* Lennon, as quoted on pages 116–19 of *Beatles: In Their Own Words,* later credited Taylor for helping him to shed the depression that had been haunting him and recover the confidence he had lost in himself, a process reinforced, he said, by the arrival of Yoko Ono in his life. The spring 1968 date is based by deduction on Lennon's reference to Ono, with whom he became lovers sometime in May 1968 (probably on May 19, reports Lewisohn on page 283 of his *Chronicle*), and on Taylor's own recollections, as found on pages 62–63 of his book *As Time Goes By.*

Taylor's "We felt liberated" quote is found on the video documentary *The Compleat Beatles.*

Page 195: McCartney's "It started to find its way" quote is from page 88 of Taylor's *It Was Twenty Years Ago Today.*

That "She's A Woman" contained the Beatles' first direct musical references to drugs is based on Lennon's comment on page 147 of the *Playboy Interviews* and the lack of any such supporting information regarding any previous Beatles song. Subsequent references to drugs are, in this book, cited in the order of their appearance.

Lennon's "didn't write the music" quote is found on page 78 of *Lennon Remembers*.

Page 195: Ringo's "we found out very early" quote is from page 110 of Martin's book *The Summer of Love*.

Lennon's "gettin' smart . . . the love-and-peace thing" quote is found on page 173 of the *Playboy Interviews*.

George Martin's "had no idea they were also into LSD" quote is found on page 207 of *All You Need Is Ears*.

Page 196: The BBC banning order and McCartney's LSD admission are noted on pages 255–56 of Lewisohn's *Chronicle*.

McCartney's lack of shame is supported by his quote that acid "opened my eyes," as reported on page 136 of Shotton's book, *John Lennon In My Life*. Before long, however, in the face of the onslaught of media and political criticism, McCartney spoke differently. He never disavowed LSD, but he blamed the media for making too much of his statement. In a testy exchange with an English television reporter, recounted on page 116 of Taylor's *It Was Twenty Years Ago Today*, McCartney denied trying to spread the word about LSD, saying it was the media itself that was doing so. Asked if he didn't have a responsibility as a public figure for what he said, Paul replied, "I mean that you are spreading this now *at this moment*. This is going into all the homes in Britain, and I'd rather it didn't. You're asking me the question, you want me to be honest, I'll be honest. But it's you who have got the responsibility not to spread this now." (Taylor's account is also the source regarding the subsequent admissions by John, George, and Brian Epstein.)

That two of the Beatles were "flying" during the *Sgt Pepper* photo session was revealed by John during an interview contained in unreleased video footage from the early 1970s, which was viewed by the author. With a smirk at the camera, John divulged that two of the Beatles were flying and two weren't during the session. Although the second flying Beatle might have been Paul or Ringo, it seems most likely that it was George, since George was the one who did the most LSD during this period and Paul in particular would have been unlikely to take LSD during such an important photo session.

The stories of John's and George's drug arrests are told on pages 288–91 and 308–10 of Peter Brown's *The Love You Make*, and, in John's case, pages 458–59 of Coleman's *Lennon*, and in George's, pages 62–65 of Geoffrey Giuliano's *Dark Horse*. The latter source provides the information about Sergeant Pilcher.

Page 197: The ad in the *Times* of London is described on pages 78–79 of ibid., as well as page 117 of *It Was Twenty Years Ago Today.*

The Beatles' renunciation of drugs is described in their own words on pages 32 and 36 of *Beatles: In Their Own Words* and cited as well on page 243 of *The Love You Make*, which also described their relationship with the Maharishi on pages 239–44, and on page 703 of Coleman's *Lennon.*

McCartney's "open a few doors" quote, and the remarks by John and George in the same paragraph, are found on page 115 and page 37, respectively, of *Beatles: In Their Own Words.*

Page 198: Lennon's "Trojan Horse" quote is on page 123 of ibid.

The story of Lennon's "more popular than Jesus" remark is based on pages 404–09 of Coleman's *Lennon*, pages 212–13 of Lewisohn's *Chronicle*, pages 191–94 of Brown's *The Love You Make*, and pages 28 and 32 of *Beatles: In Their Own Words.* Coleman and Brown also report on John's subsequent Vietnam remarks.

Page 198: The observations about the Beatles becoming newly interested in social and political issues in 1966 are found on page 164 of Taylor's *It Was Twenty Years Ago Today* and page 117 of Shotton's *John Lennon In My Life.*

Lennon's explanation of the Beatles speaking out on Vietnam is found on page 123 of *Beatles: In Their Own Words.* Among many other statements by the Beatles against the war were those made on August 23, 1966, by all four, as documented on page 17 of Jon Wiener's *Come Together*; in January 1967 by Paul, as noted on page 164 of Taylor's book; and in April 1968 by John, as noted on pages 73–74 of Wiener's book, the latter of which also contains his statement about the Establishment.

Page 199: Harrison's "We felt obviously that Vietnam was wrong" quote is found on page 150 of Taylor's book, page 165 of which reports Abbie Hoffman's "Beethoven coming to the supermarket!" quote, and page 24 of which notes Ginsberg's "They had, and conveyed" quote.

Page 200: Lennon's "Maybe the Beatles were in the crow's nest" quote is from page 78 of the *Playboy Interviews*, as is Ono's "mediums" quote. Supporting Lennon's remark are statements Harrison made in his interview in the November 5, 1987, *Rolling Stone.* Martin's "The great thing about the Beatles" quote is from the video documentary *The Compleat Beatles.*

CHAPTER SEVENTEEN:
Rock 'n' Roll as Art
(*Sgt Pepper's Lonely*
Hearts Club Band)

Page 203: Lennon's "Genius is a form of madness" quote is found on page 64 of *Lennon Remembers*. His childhood realizations and his "see through walls" quote are from pages 132–34 of the *Playboy Interviews*. The story about his getting down on his knees is told by Pete Shotton on page 117 of his *John Lennon In My Life*.

Page 203: The EMI record company's demand for a single while waiting for *Sgt Pepper* to be finished is described on page 202 of George Martin's *All You Need Is Ears*. The childhood theme intended for *Sgt Pepper's Lonely Hearts Club Band* is noted in Dowlding's *Beatlesongs*, page 147, in Norman's *Shout!*, page 359, and alluded to in a Lennon interview reprinted in *The Ballad of John and Yoko*, pages 49–50. McCartney's "[Strawberry Field] was the place right opposite" quote comes from George Martin's 1992 documentary film, *The Making of Sgt Pepper*.

   The date the Beatles began recording "Strawberry Fields Forever" is documented on page 87 of *Recording Sessions*. Martin's "set the agenda" quote is from page 13 of his book *The Summer of Love*. For Lennon's "badly recorded" quote and his blaming of this on McCartney, see page 162 of the *Playboy Interviews*.

Page 204: Martin's "a gentle dreaming song" quote is found on page 278 of the Davies biography.

   To write the passage on the demo tapes of "Strawberry Fields Forever," the author of this book listened to the tapes himself, which were made public in 1987 by Lennon's widow, Yoko Ono.

   Lennon describes the process of writing the song in Spain on page 130 of the *Playboy Interviews*.

Page 205: Lennon's explanation of the "No one I think . . ." lyrics to "Strawberry Fields Forever" is found on page 133 of the *Playboy Interviews*. For the discussion of the rest of the lyrics and the wordplay involved, see especially the reproduction of an early, handwritten draft of Lennon's lyrics, on page lix of Davies's *The Beatles*.

Page 206: George Martin's "Absolutely lovely" quote is found on page 89 of *Recording Sessions.* His wish to have taped and released the acoustic version of "Strawberry Fields" is found on page 14 of his book *The Summer of Love.*

The statement that Lennon had added a final verse to the song is a deduction, based on the fact that the verse does not appear on Lennon's demo tapes but is heard on the Beatles' take one, recorded November 24, 1966. The other comments about the song's lyrics are analysis offered by the author of this book. The final sentence about escaping to endless fields filled with strawberries is supported by his comment, "I have visions of strawberry fields," found on page 47 of *The Ballad of John and Yoko.*

Page 207: The capabilities of the mellotron, and the fact that it is McCartney who plays it on "Strawberry Fields Forever," are reported on page 87 of *Recording Sessions.* Martin's recollection of the mellotron being John's idea is found on page 16 of his book *The Summer of Love.* His quote, "It's Strawberry Fields . . ." comes from his 1992 documentary film, *The Making of Sgt Pepper.*

The description of how the song changes throughout the various takes is based on the author's listening to first the demo tapes, then takes one through seven, fifteen, and twenty-four through twenty-six.

Page 207: Lennon's requests to Martin about retaping "Strawberry Fields," and the fact that it took fifteen additional takes to perfect the second rhythm track, are described on pages 89–90 of *Recording Sessions* and pages 199–201 of Martin's *All You Need Is Ears.*

Page 208: That Lennon said "cranberry sauce" is evident on the record, and reinforced by his statement to this effect on page 74 of the *Playboy Interviews.*

The account of Martin splicing together the two different versions of "Strawberry Fields" at Lennon's request is based on pages 90–91 of *Recording Sessions* and pages 200–201 of Martin's *All You Need Is Ears.* Phil McDonald's "There's no such word as *can't*" quote is on page 114 of *Recording Sessions.*

Page 209: The premature fade-out on "Strawberry Fields," Martin explained on page 23 of his book *The Summer of Love,* was undertaken to disguise the fact that the rhythm section had gone out of tempo during those moments that were eliminated.

Martin's judgment of "Strawberry Fields / Penny Lane" as the greatest record of the Beatles is found on page 202 of *All You Need Is Ears.* Among references to the record as the greatest single of all time, see page 98 of *Recording Sessions*.

Page 209: The November 1965 genesis of "Penny Lane" is documented on page 91 of *Recording Sessions*. The sentence about competitive impetus is an informed speculation by the author of this book, based on Paul's comment about John, quoted and sourced in Chapter Ten, that, "He'd write 'Strawberry Fields,' I'd go away and write 'Penny Lane.' . . . To compete with each other," and also on George Martin's recollection, found on page 14 of his book *The Summer of Love*, that Paul wrote "Penny Lane" "immediately after" John wrote "Strawberry Fields."

John's memory of Paul feeling full of confidence is found on page 118 of Miles's *Beatles: In Their Own Words*.

That John helped with some of the words on "Penny Lane" is suggested by Paul's quote, on page 88 of ibid., where he uses the pronoun "we" when describing the writing of the lines about both the banker and the finger pie, and also by John's quote, on page 50 of *The Ballad of John and Yoko*, where he also uses "we" in describing the creation of "Penny Lane."

Page 210: The number of recording sessions for "Penny Lane," and the instruments used, are documented on pages 91–93 of *Recording Sessions*.

Page 211: The passage about the piccolo trumpet overdub is based on page 93 of ibid. and pages 201–02 of Martin's *All You Need Is Ears*. Mason's "jolly high notes" quote is from page 93 of *Recording Sessions*.

Page 211: News stories speculating on the Beatles' imminent demise appeared, among other places, in the *Sunday Times* of London and on the BBC, according to page 214 of Lewisohn's *Chronicle*. In fairness, it should be noted that journalists were not completely without plausible cause; no other entertainment act in history had succeeded as purely recording artists, there had always been a premium placed on live performing. But the Beatles naturally refused to allow such traditional notions to get in their way. There is some interesting footage of reporters questioning George, John, and Ringo as they arrived, separately, at Abbey Road that autumn to begin recording what would become the *Pepper* album. John, when asked if the Beatles were breaking up, said, "I could see us not working together for a period, but we'd always get together for one reason or another. I mean, you need other people for ideas as well." George, less patient with what has obviously become a too frequently asked question by then, doesn't stop to chat on his way into the studio the way

John did, but simply looks back over his shoulder to say with no little exasperation, "No!" Ringo, exuding his usual calm good cheer, also denies the reports, adding that, with any luck, he will have arrived just in time for the tea break.

On the studio as clubhouse theme, see Harrison's quote on page 27 of Derek Taylor's *It Was Twenty Years Ago Today*.

Page 212: Regarding press reaction to the "Strawberry Fields" and "Penny Lane" single's failing to hit number one, Derek Taylor notes in ibid. the "fuss" that was made, via such headlines as HAS THE BUBBLE BURST? Taylor also reports that the Beatles remained serene anyway, and John's happiness in the studio, on page 21. Shotton's "plainly felt" quote is found on page 135 of his book, *John Lennon In My Life*. McCartney's "great glee" quote is on page 111 of Martin's book *The Summer of Love*.

Regarding the recording of "A Day In The Life," the Beatles began it on January 19, 1967, two days after completing "Penny Lane" on January 17, according to pages 93–94 of *Recording Sessions*.

Page 212: The films made for "Strawberry Fields Forever" and "Penny Lane" were shot on January 30–31 and February 5 and 7, respectively, according to Lewisohn's *Chronicle*, pages 242–43. These films marked another artistic advance, for they included not a single shot of the Beatles playing or singing; the songs instead served as soundtracks for a series of images meant to amplify or somehow comment on the songs. The "Strawberry Fields" film features a scene, shot in a meadow near a large oak tree, where McCartney appears to leap up from a piano, run to the base of the tree, and suddenly leap up onto a branch that is well above his head, an impossibility that was in fact contrived by filming Paul dropping down from the tree and then playing the film in reverse. The most arresting images in the "Penny Lane" film are those of John walking along a crowded city street on a sunny day, shots of the Beatles riding white horses through a stone archway and, later, of them sitting at an immaculately set table in the middle of a field, where they are served tea in what is very plainly bitterly cold weather.

The idea of a Sgt Pepper's Lonely Hearts Club Band has been credited, in various accounts, to McCartney, to Neil Aspinall, and to Mal Evans. Shotton claims on page 133 of his book that it was Evans, but adds no specific supporting details. Ringo, however, has been quoted saying the same thing; see page 159 of Dowlding's *Beatlesongs*. George Martin, however, says on page 64 of his book *The Summer of Love* that the idea had originated in the "fertile imagination" of Paul McCartney. Certainly that is how Paul himself remembers it, claiming in his December 1984 *Playboy* interview that "it was an idea I had . . . [that] it would be nice to lose identities, to submerge ourselves in the persona of a fake group." Lewisohn, the most reliable arbiter of such matters, likewise credits Paul, on page 95 of *Recording Sessions*.

As for McCartney's spearheading the cover campaign, see the comments from Peter Blake, the artist who designed the cover collage, on pages 37–38 of Taylor's *It Was Twenty Years Ago Today*, as well as pages 113–118 of Martin's *The Summer of Love*. The latter notes that EMI chairman Sir Joseph Lockwood had at first vetoed the cover and then, in the face of the Beatles' insistence, had demanded that the group obtain legal clearances from all the personages pictured, and even then had declared that under no circumstances could Gandhi be used, since EMI wanted no trouble in India. According to Martin, McCartney shot back, "All right, I'll trade him two Marlon Brandos for a Gandhi!"

Although reported elsewhere, McCartney's avant-garde activities during the 1966–67 era are described most fully by Paul himself, on pages 50–51 of his 1989–90 World Tour program, which also includes his observation about the difference between Lennon and himself regarding the mainstream.

Page 213:   The "If you want to know about the Sixties" quote by Copland is found on page 1 of Ian Macdonald's *Revolution In The Head*. The release of *Sgt Pepper* was called "a decisive moment in the history of western civilization" by British critic Kenneth Tynan, according to page 161 of Dowlding's *Beatlesongs*. Martin's "turned the Beatles" quote is found on page 214 of his book *All You Need Is Ears*.

Page 214:   Lennon's "absolutely nothing to do with" quote is from pages 166–67 of the *Playboy Interviews*. Ringo's "out the window" quote is from the February 1982 *Musician* magazine, as cited on page 160 of Dowlding's *Beatlesongs*.

Page 215:   The composition of "With A Little Help From My Friends" by John and Paul is described in Chapter Ten of this book. Mellers's "He's the least talented" quote is from page 88 of his book *Twilight of the Gods*.

Page 215:   Lennon's explanation of "Lucy In The Sky With Diamonds" is found on pages 153–54 of the *Playboy Interviews*. The BBC's ban is noted on page 167 of Dowlding's *Beatlesongs*. The celeste-like organ, and Harrison's playing of a tamboura, is described on page 100 of *Recording Sessions*. Martin's "a most wonderful phrase" quote comes from his 1992 documentary, *The Making of Sgt Pepper*. McCartney's comments about the lyrics of the song are found on page 89 of Miles's *Beatles: In Their Own Words*.

Geoff Emerick's praise of *Pepper* is from his interview in the July 1987 issue of *Musician*.

Page 216: Jerry Boys' "still impossible to make" quote is from page 114 of *Recording Sessions*. George Martin describes his mallet and piano technique on page 108 of his book *The Summer of Love*.

Paul's "Typical John" quote is from his December 1984 *Playboy* interview. Martin's claim about John's writing his "It can't get no worse" line on the spot is found on page 112 of *The Summer of Love*. The problem is that Hunter Davies, on pages 268–69 of his authorized biography of the Beatles, describes from what appears to be eyewitness knowledge how John and Paul actually wrote the song together at Paul's house one afternoon. If the Davies account is true, this might be why John could walk into Studio Two and sing out his line on the spot, without seeming ever to have heard the song before. On the other hand, Martin may be right and Davies may have been reporting a version of the songwriting according to John's and/or Paul's less than precise memories.

Page 217: The original running order of side one of *Sgt Pepper* is listed on page 108 of *Recording Sessions*. It begins the same, with the title track followed by "With A Little Help From My Friends," but the remainder is as follows: "Being For The Benefit Of Mr. Kite," "Fixing A Hole," "Lucy In The Sky With Diamonds," "Getting Better," and "She's Leaving Home." This plan was dated April 6, 1967; on April 21, Martin forwarded the new, and final, sequence to EMI, as documented on page 113 of *Recording Sessions*.

Martin's praise of the guitars on "Fixing A Hole" is found on pages 85–87 of *The Summer of Love*. John's praise of the lyrics is from page 166 of the *Playboy Interviews*.

McCartney says on page 89 of Miles's *Beatles: In Their Own Words* that "She's Leaving Home" was inspired by a report in the *Daily Mirror*.

Page 217: Regarding the score of "She's Leaving Home," it seems that McCartney was in a hurry to record the song and asked Martin to drop a preexisting engagement with another artist to write a score for him. When Martin declined, McCartney engaged freelance arranger Mike Leander instead. Martin recalled the incident with some bitterness years later in his autobiography, *All You Need Is Ears*, pages 207–08, calling it "one of the biggest hurts of my life." On page 134 of *The Summer of Love*, Martin also questioned whether the Leander score should not have been a bit more "astringent." McCartney owned up to his behavior in his December 1984 *Playboy* interview, saying he hadn't realized at the time that Martin would be offended.

Page 218: Martin's favoritism toward "Being For The Benefit Of Mr. Kite" and his theory of the *Sgt Pepper* running order are described on pages 149 of *The Summer of Love*. Lennon's lack of admiration for "Kite" is expressed on pages 275 and 284 of the Hunter Davies authorized biography, *The Beatles*. He was less critical of the song in the *Playboy Interviews*, where he says on page 155 that the song was "pure, like a painting." Martin's description of the recording of the song is found on pages 203–05 of his *All You Need Is Ears* and pages 90–93 of *The Summer of Love*.

Page 218: Martin calls "Within You Without You" dreary on page 203 of his *All You Need Is Ears* and a dirge on page 124 of *The Summer of Love*. The latter includes his mention that the other Beatles were impressed with the song, which is reinforced by John's very positive comments about it on page 157 of the *Playboy Interviews*.

Martin's "the biggest mistake of my life" quote is from his 1992 documentary film *The Making of Sgt Pepper*. His admission about cutting "When I'm Sixty-Four" and "Lovely Rita" is found on page 150 of his book *The Summer of Love*. Paul described writing "When I'm Sixty-Four" in his December 1984 *Playboy* interview. Its speeded-up vocals are noted on page 91 of *Recording Sessions*. Martin's remark about the clarinets is from page 34 of *The Summer of Love*.

Page 219: The "Lovely Rita" recording sessions and effects are described on pages 95–97 of ibid. and page 91 of *Recording Sessions*.

Page 220: Lennon's cornflakes inspiration for "Good Morning Good Morning" is noted on page 155 of the *Playboy Interviews*. The demo tape of the song was heard by the author. That it is Paul who plays the guitar solo is noted on page 105 of *Recording Sessions*. Martin's "Sgt Pepper himself was breathing life" quote is from page 109 of ibid. His contention that *Sgt Pepper* was not the Beatles' musically greatest album but their most important is found on page 159 of *The Summer of Love*.

CHAPTER EIGHTEEN:
Organized Chaos
(*Magical Mystery Tour*)

Page 223: The date and programming specifics of the *Our World* broadcast are documented on page 259 of Lewisohn's *Chronicle*, including the names of the various countries and television systems that participated. Virtually all of Western Europe was covered, as well as the United States, Canada, Mexico, Japan, and Australia. Seven Soviet-bloc countries had agreed to transmit the program, but changed policy at the last minute.

The total number of viewers has been estimated at anywhere between 200 million and 400 million people in various accounts of the event. Lewisohn, who typically has researched the event in the greatest depth, revised his own estimate from the 400 million figure used in his 1987 *Recording Sessions* book down to the 350 million figure found on page 237 of *Chronicle*.

Page 224: Lennon's "Oh, God, is it that close?" quote is found on page 116 of *Recording Sessions*. That both he and McCartney wrote songs for the broadcast is reported on page 257 of *Chronicle*, where the possibility that Paul's song was "Your Mother Should Know" is also raised. Lewisohn is careful to say that this "is not known for sure"—hence, the qualification in the text of this book—but it seems most likely, especially given that "Your Mother Should Know" was the first song that the Beatles recorded after returning from some eight weeks away from the studio in the summer of 1967 following the *Our World* broadcast.

The first-take information about "La Marseillaise" is found on page 116 of *Recording Sessions*. Harrison's "But when you question" quote is reported in Geoffrey Giuliano's *The Beatles: A Celebration*, as cited on page 187 of Dowlding's *Beatlesongs*.

Page 225: One of the first people to call Lennon's music "bumpy" was the Beatles' Hamburg friend photographer Astrid Kirchherr, as quoted on page xliii of the 1985 preface to their authorized biography, by Hunter Davies.

The recording history of "All You Need Is Love" is described on pages 116–21 of *Recording Sessions*.

Page 225: Richard Lush's "Lennon was very nervous" quote is found on page 120 of *Recording Sessions*.

The BBC film of the Beatles' *Our World* performance was viewed by the author. Additional photos and information are found on pages 120–21 of ibid. Derek Taylor's "Pop music never really had a finer moment" quote is from a television interview contained in an untitled collection of video clips, viewed by the author.

Page 226: Brian Epstein's "cannot be misinterpreted" quote was reported by *Melody Maker* magazine, as cited on page 188 of Dowlding's *Beatlesongs*. Taylor's "people who'd never really liked the Beatles" quote is from the same television interview just cited. That "All You Need Is Love" was a worldwide best seller is documented on page 121 of *Recording Sessions*.

For examples of dismissive criticism of "All You Need Is Love," see pages 368–69 of Norman's *Shout!*, page 228 of Brown's *The Love You Make*, and pages 233–34 of Riley's *Tell Me Why*. On pages 103–04 of Mellers's *Twilight of the Gods*, the song is not dismissed so much as simply misinterpreted as an "infinitely sad" song that supposedly suggests that love is in fact unattainable.

Page 227: Lennon's reference to Elvis Costello is found on page 191 of *The Ballad of John and Yoko*. His "Maybe in the Sixties we were naive" quote is from an interview with RKO Radio, as quoted on pages 305–06 of Wiener's *Come Together*. Václav Havel's "I do not believe that certain values" quote is cited in an article by Jefferson Morley in the March 19, 1990, issue of *The Nation* magazine.

Page 228: Epstein's hope that "Yellow Submarine" would fulfill the Beatles' United Artists contract is noted by business aide Peter Brown on page 199 of *The Love You Make* and by Lennon on page 172 of the *Playboy Interviews*. Martin's "bottom of the barrel" quote is from page 226 of his book *All You Need Is Ears*. The rejection of "Only A Northern Song" from *Sgt Pepper* is noted by Lewisohn on page 276 of *Chronicle* and by Martin on page 124 of *The Summer of Love*; indeed, as noted on page 97 of *Recording Sessions*, "Only A Northern Song" was one of the first songs recorded for *Sgt Pepper*. Lennon describes the songwriting division on "Baby, You're A Rich Man" on page 155 of the *Playboy Interviews*, saying that he wrote the verses and the hook was Paul's. Recording of "Hey Bulldog" took place on February 11, 1968, according to page 134 of *Recording Sessions*, which also contains the "really fun" quote from Emerick.

The Beatles were filmed while working in the studio that day, the footage to be used to help promote "Lady Madonna," the result being that their singing and the soundtrack are out of sync.

Page 229: McCartney's "We goofed, really," quote was made in an interview with journalist Ray Connolly of the London *Evening Standard*, as quoted on page 253 of *The Love You Make*, which also cites other highly critical press reviews of the film.

The listing of the songs the Beatles recorded in the period between *Sgt Pepper* and leaving for India, where they would write much of the material for their next album, is based on *Recording Sessions*, pages 97, 109–34.

George Martin's "If the Beatles' professional career" quote is found on page 159 of his book, *The Summer of Love*.

Page 229: McCartney's generation of the *Magical Mystery Tour* idea is described many places but most reliably and concisely on page 253 of Lewisohn's *Chronicle*, which also includes a reproduction of the filming notes that Paul made on his flight back from the United States. The recording sessions for *Magical Mystery Tour* are documented on pages 110–11 of *Recording Sessions*. The Beatles' return to work at the end of the summer is indicated by the lack of intervening entries in *Chronicle*, pages 260–61, where the September 1 meeting at McCartney's house is also described. The achievements of the first two days of work are described on pages 122–23 of *Recording Sessions*.

Page 230: Hunter Davies's description of hearing Paul play "The Fool On The Hill" to John on a guitar is found on page 268 of his authorized biography. The September 6 demo version was listened to by the author of this book. Lennon's criticism of the lyrics of "Yesterday" is found on page 118 of the *Playboy Interviews*.

Lennon's acid trip genesis of the opening lines of "I Am The Walrus" is noted on page 156 of ibid., as are the Lewis Carroll and Allen Ginsberg references. The "Dead Dog's Eye" story is told on page 124 of Shotton's book, *John Lennon In My Life*.

Page 231: Lennon's conception of songwriting as "doing little bits which you then join up" was George Martin's phrasing of what John had once told him, as reported on page 281 of the Davies biography. The police siren inspiration for the melody of "I Am The Walrus" is documented on page 276 of ibid., as well as on page 51 of *Rolling Stone* magazine's book *The Ballad of John and Yoko*.

Page 231:   The Shakespeare insertion is documented most fully on pages 128–29 of *Recording Sessions*, where Lewisohn reproduces the playlist of the BBC for that evening, as well as the portion of *Lear*—Act IV, Scene 4—that Lennon ended up recording. That John had no previous intention of using Shakespeare is indicated by his quote on page 156 of the *Playboy Interviews*, as well as by the unlikelihood that he would have known that *Lear* was being broadcast that evening before actually hearing it on the radio. For a description of the innovations of Picasso and Braque, see pages 126–37 of Pierre Daix's *Picasso: Life And Art* (paperback, HarperCollins, New York, 1994), as well as pages 118–20 of Timothy Hilton's *Picasso* (paperback, Thames and Hudson, London, 1976).

Page 232:   Lennon's irritation about "I Am The Walrus" being the B-side to "Hello, Goodbye" is noted by Pete Shotton on page 180 of *John Lennon In My Life*. McCartney's "almost wrote itself" quote is from page 15 of *Recording Sessions*. The marketing strategy behind "Lady Madonna" is noted on page 132 of ibid.

Page 233:   Among those who claimed the *Mystery Tour* began the end of the Beatles were Lennon himself, on pages 51–54 of *Lennon Remembers*, which in turn heavily influenced subsequent writing on the topic. The Beatles' Greek island plans are noted on pages 235–37 of *The Love You Make*.

CHAPTER NINETEEN:
The Ballad of John and Yoko

Page 235:   Lennon's "That ain't bad picking" quote is from December 1980 and is found on page 187 of *The Ballad of John and Yoko*. His "overawed" and "sixteen track voice" quotes are from 1971 and found on pages 114–15 of ibid.

   Shotton's "she was the best thing" quote is from page 171 of his book, *John Lennon In My Life*.

Page 236:   McCartney's "In fact she wanted more" quote is found on page 53 of his 1989–90 World Tour program.

Lennon's "I know I'm sounding" quote is from pages 157–58 of the *Playboy Interviews*.

Page 236: McCartney describes meeting Yoko Ono first at a charity event in the October 1986 *Musician* interview.

Lennon describes his first meeting with Yoko on pages 173–76 of *Lennon Remembers* and on pages 86–88 of the *Playboy Interviews*.

Cynthia Lennon's recollections of Yoko's pursuit of Lennon are recounted on pages 428–29 of Coleman's *Lennon*. Shotton's account of his meeting with Ono at Apple are found on page 161 of *John Lennon In My Life*.

Page 237: Shotton's description of "the morning after" is from pages 168–69 of ibid., the Jesus Christ story from pages 167–68.

Page 238: Lewisohn estimates the date of John and Yoko's first night together as May 19, 1968, on page 283 of *Chronicle*, though he emphasizes that it is only the probable date. Shotton agrees on the late May date, though the details of his account make the May 19 date, a Sunday, impossible. That the May evening at John's house was indeed their first sexual encounter is qualified in the text because both John and Yoko were later quoted saying that they were "dating on the side" prior to that time, despite the fact that both were married. For John's quote, see page 21 of the *Playboy Interviews*; for Yoko's, page 88.

That Lennon now insisted on having Yoko at his side in the recording studio is noted on page 135 of *Recording Sessions*, which also describes the work done on "Revolution" that day.

Page 238: Lennon credited Ono with the montage on "Revolution" on page 159 of the *Playboy Interviews*; he expressed his desire that it be a single on page 158.

Lewisohn notes the demo taping session at Harrison's house on pages 283–84 of *Chronicle*. The author listened to copies of the recordings made that day.

Page 239: The dates of and activities of other Beatles during the overdubbing sessions for "Revolution," and McCartney's distaste for "Revolution 9," are noted on pages 136, 138, and 142 of *Recording Sessions*.

Martin's "Yoko is now part of me" quote is from the 1988 film *Imagine*, produced by Andrew Solt and David Wolper.

Page 240: Ono's ignorance of rock 'n' roll is attested by Lennon's remark that the only Beatle she had heard of before meeting John was Ringo, on page 174 of *Lennon Remembers* and her own comments on page 114 of *The Ballad of John and Yoko*, as well as on page 47 of the *Playboy Interviews*. Her practice of criticizing during Beatles sessions has been widely reported—by Shotton on page 175, by Brown on page 269, by Coleman on page 454, by Lewisohn on page 277 of *Chronicle*. John's "Well, maybe *I* can" quote is from page 144 of *Recording Sessions*.

Martin's remark about Yoko Ono and Linda Eastman is found on page 488 of Coleman's *Lennon*.

The Beatles' "no outsiders" policy has likewise been widely noted; for example, on page 453 of ibid. For some reason, many of the descriptions suggest that this was a matter of male chauvinism when, in fact, as Coleman's own words make plain, the policy extended to men and women alike.

Page 240: Lewisohn's "had an undeniably negative bearing" quote is from page 277 of *Chronicle*.

Taylor's "No one in this building" quote is from page 321 of Brown's *The Love You Make*.

McCartney describes John's warning to him regarding Yoko in his interview in the December 1984 *Playboy*.

Yoko's explanation of John's jealousy appears as a postscript to Norman's *Shout!*, on page 498.

John's "goddess of love" quote is from page 42 of the *Playboy Interviews*, "as barmy as me!" and "me in drag" from page 169 of Shotton's *John Lennon In My Life*.

Page 241: Yoko's "with a real need" quote is from page 117 of *The Ballad of John and Yoko*.

Cynthia Lennon's "I knew immediately" quote is found on pages 440 and 446 of Coleman's *Lennon*.

Lennon's "She got it" quote is from page 88 of the *Playboy Interviews*, the "Don Juan" reference on page 85.

Regarding Ono's appreciation of Lennon's understanding her, see pages 113–25 of *The Ballad of John and Yoko*, especially page 125, and also page 102 of Garbarini, Cullman, and Graustark's *Strawberry Fields Forever*.

Page 242: Ono's "I was probably the successor" quote is from page 419 of Coleman's *Lennon*.

Lennon's admission about "Getting Better" is from page 154 of the *Playboy Interviews*. Ono's denial that he ever hit her is on page 33 of Coleman's *Lennon*.

One woman who apparently was not so lucky was May Pang, who nonsensationalistically recounts, on page 201 of her book, *Loving John*, the time that a blindly drunk and enraged Lennon tried to strangle her not just once but twice, all the while screaming that he hated Yoko for leaving him.

Ono's family background and schoolchild behavior is described in the very positive portrait drawn of her in *The Ballad of John and Yoko* on pages 14–29, especially pages 22 and 27.

Shotton's "a strong-willed, domineering tigress" quote and the related stories about Ono are from pages 172, 179, 185, 198, and 200 of *John Lennon In My Life*.

Page 242: John's denial that Yoko controlled him is from page 42 of the *Playboy Interviews*.

Christgau's "As both of them were happy" quote is from page 302 of *The Ballad of John and Yoko*.

Lennon's admission that it was Yoko who kicked him out in 1973 is on page 19 of the *Playboy Interviews*, his quote about "taught me everything" is on page 85.

Page 243: Lennon's "That's how the Beatles ended" quote is from page 101 of Garbarini, Cullman, and Graustark's *Strawberry Fields Forever*.

Lennon's confession to Shotton is described on page 187 of *John Lennon In My Life*. Ringo's "just John being John" quote is from page 292 of Brown's *The Love You Make*.

Page 244: Paul's "Looking back, it was largely" quote is from page 473 of Coleman's *Lennon*.

John's "The old gang of mine" quote is from page 41 of the *Playboy Interviews*.

The footage of the "Hey, Jude" rehearsals and live performance was viewed by the author. The dates of the events are found on pages 291, 296–97 of Lewisohn's *Chronicle*.

Page 244: Lennon's "You see, I presumed" quote is from page 66 of *Lennon Remembers*.

CHAPTER TWENTY:
Inner Turmoil, Creative Abundance
(*The Beatles*)

Page 247: The founding of Apple Corps has been widely described; see pages 253–57 of Brown's *The Love You Make* and pages 145–54 of Shotton's *John Lennon In My Life*.

McCartney described the White Album as "the tension album" in an interview in the February 1985 issue of *Musician*, adding, "It was the weirdest experience, because we were about to break up." The counterpart quote by Lennon is found on page 221 of Dowlding's *Beatlesongs*.

The quitting of Ringo Starr is described later in this chapter. The release date of the *Yellow Submarine* movie is documented on page 289 of Lewisohn's *Chronicle*.

Page 248: The author viewed the "Hey, Jude" and "Revolution" clips himself. For details about date and location, see pages 296–97 of ibid.

For criticisms of "Revolution" by the militant left, see pages 60–61 of Wiener's *Come Together*, which quotes the American magazine *Ramparts* calling the song "a betrayal," and the London-based *New Left Review* calling it "a lamentable petty bourgeois cry of fear."

Page 249: Lennon's switching back and forth on the question of whether to count him in or out of revolutions of destruction is based on the author's listening to the demo tapes from May 1968 and on the descriptions of the subsequent recording sessions as found on pages 136 and 141 of *Recording Sessions* and, regarding the September television performance, page 297 of *Chronicle*.

Page 249: Lennon's reference to "Hey, Jude" as a masterpiece is found on page 157 of the *Playboy Interviews*. That everyone else but John thought it should be the A-side of the next single is recalled by Shotton on page 180 of *John Lennon In My Life*. The huge sales generated by "Hey, Jude" are described on page 203 of Dowlding's *Beatlesongs*, which notes that the song placed second in a 1976 *Billboard* magazine chart listing the biggest hits of the past two decades; Chubby Checker's "The Twist" placed first. Documentation of John's defense of the "movement you need is on your shoulder" line is found on the same page, which cites a quote from McCartney to *Rolling Stone*, printed January 31,

1974. The chords of "Hey, Jude" are notated in *The Complete Beatles*, the songbook published in 1988 by Hal Leonard Publishing Corporation, which controlled the rights to the Beatles song catalogue at that time.

Page 250: Lewisohn gives the exact length of "Hey, Jude" at seven minutes, eleven seconds on page 145 of *Recording Sessions*, noting it was the group's longest single ever. ("Revolution 9" on the White Album was even longer, of course, but did not qualify as a song proper.) The thirty-six-piece orchestra is described on page 146.

The inviting of the three hundred extras for the Twickenham performance is described on page 296 of *Chronicle*.

Page 250: The events surrounding Ringo's quitting of the group and his later return are documented on page 151 of *Recording Sessions*, on Ringo's own quotes, as found on page 218 of Dowlding's *Beatlesongs*, on page 176 of Shotton's *John Lennon In My Life* (Shotton attended the peacemaking meeting between Ringo and the other Beatles), and on page 287 of Brown's *The Love You Make*. There is a discrepancy concerning the date of Ringo's return to the band; *Recording Sessions* suggests it was the night of the Twickenham filming—that is, September 4—while *Chronicle* claims it was the night before that, September 3. Since *Chronicle* was published four years after *Sessions* and corrected certain small errors and confusions of the earlier book, it is the *Chronicle* date of September 3 that is cited here.

Page 251: Harrison's "There was a definite" quote is found on page 114 of Bennahum's *in their own words: the Beatles . . . after the break-up*.

The deterioration in civility during the recording sessions for the White Album is based on page 141 of *Recording Sessions*, which cites the unanimous views of the Abbey Road studio staff; Emerick's quitting is described on page 143. Further supporting this are the quotes from Lennon and McCartney cited above and Shotton's recollections from pages 175–76 of *John Lennon In My Life*.

Page 251: Lennon's prolific period is attested by the fact that he wrote thirteen of the songs found on the White Album (assuming "Revolution 9" can be classified as a song), thus nudging out Paul, who wrote twelve, for the first time since *Rubber Soul*; the text refers to *A Hard Day's Night* because Lennon and McCartney were more or less evenly matched on the *Rubber Soul* and *Help!* albums.

The complete listing of the songs taped during the May 1968 demo sessions at Harrison's house is found on pages 283–84 of *Chronicle*. Harrison's "I worked on that song" quote is found on page 229 of Dowlding's *Beatlesongs*.

Page 252: The dates of the July 25 demo tape session and of the overdubs in subsequent sessions are found on pages 145, 149, 153–54 of *Recording Sessions*; page 154 also describes Harrison's invitation to Clapton, as does page 229 of *Beatlesongs*. The July 25 demo tape was heard by the author.

Page 253: Martin's wish to shrink the White Album, and his "really super album" quote are found on page 163 of *Recording Sessions*. Lennon's "it was just me" quote is from page 51 of *Lennon Remembers*.

Page 254: Harrison's remark about McCartney is found on page 115 of Bennahum's *in their own words: the Beatles . . . after the break-up*.

Page 255: Martin's ranking of McCartney as a drummer is found on page 86 of his book *The Summer of Love*.
The dates and hours of the recording sessions for "Back In The U.S.S.R." and "Dear Prudence" are found on pages 151–52 of *Recording Sessions*.

Page 255: McCartney's Beach Boys quote is from the December 1984 *Playboy* interview.
The author listened to the demo tapes of all songs described in this chapter.
Lennon's explanation of Prudence Farrow's role in his writing of "Dear Prudence" is found on page 168 of the *Playboy Interviews*.

Page 257: Shotton recalls that Lennon hated "Ob-La-Di, Ob-La-Da" on page 180 of his book, *John Lennon In My Life*. Page 141 of *Recording Sessions* contains recollections from Abbey Road Studios staff supporting this contention.
John, George, and Paul's high regard for "Happiness Is A Warm Gun" is documented on page 231 of Dowlding's *Beatlesongs*. The need for seventy takes is noted on page 157 of *Recording Sessions*. John recalls the gun magazine's stimulus on page 159 of the *Playboy Interviews*. Derek Taylor described his contributions to the song in an interview with the author.

Page 257: The most reliable and unbiased sources of information about Lennon's heroin use are Lennon himself, who calls it "not much fun" on page 38 of *Lennon Remembers;* Ono, who admits having turned John on to the drug on page 275 of Brown's *The Love You Make*, though she defends herself from what she said was Harrison's charge that it was her fault that John agreed to take it; Pete Shotton, who describes John's heroin use on page 194 of *John Lennon In My Life;* Paul McCartney, on page 51 of his World Tour program and in his December 1984 *Playboy* interview; and again Lennon himself, who refers to the nude album cover photo he and Yoko released in late 1968 as a "sight of two slightly overweight ex-junkies" on page 18 of *Skywriting by Word of Mouth,* his private diaries that were published after his death.

Lennon's preference for the White Album over *Sgt Pepper* is found on page 138 of *Lennon Remembers.*

Page 258: The all but one-man-band nature of McCartney's songs on side two of the White Album is documented on pages 137, 155, and 159–61 of *Recording Sessions.*

McCartney's "ricochet" quote is found on page 369 of the Davies biography, *The Beatles.*

Page 259: That "Julia" represented the only time Lennon recorded a Beatles song solo is noted by Lewisohn on page 161 of *Recording Sessions,* which also notes the October 13 date of taping. That he wrote the song, and "I'm So Tired" as well, in India is noted on pages 160 and 168 of the *Playboy Interviews* and reinforced by the fact that both were recorded at Harrison's house during the May 1968 demo sessions.

That Yoko means "ocean child" in Japanese is noted on page 448 of Coleman's *Lennon.*

That "Half of what I say is meaningless" was borrowed from Gibran is divulged by McCartney in an interview found on page 85 of Edward Gross's book, *Paul McCartney: Twenty Years on His Own.*

The frequency of minor chords in "Julia" is observable from the sheet music of the song, found on pages 16–21 of *The Complete Beatles.*

Page 259: McCartney's "the loudest, nastiest, sweatiest" quote is from an interview in the February 1985 issue of *Musician.*

The lengths, dates, and studio activities of the Beatles while recording the various versions of "Helter Skelter" are documented on pages 143 and 154 of *Recording Sessions.*

Lennon's remark to Dylan is reported on page 383 of Coleman's *Lennon.*

Lennon recalls the Beatles enjoying the uncomplicated nature of the music on the White Album on page 51 of *The Ballad of John and Yoko,* calling it "a great release."

Page 260: That "Birthday" was written on the spot in the studio is based on the recollection of Lennon, as expressed on page 160 of the *Playboy Interviews,* and of Abbey Road staffer and White Album de facto producer Chris Thomas, as quoted on page 156 of *Recording Sessions.*

Lennon's explanations of the genesis of "Everybody's Got Something To Hide Except Me And My Monkey" and of "Sexy Sadie" are found on page 161 of the *Playboy Interviews.*

Page 261: Lennon's denial of authorship of "Cry Baby Cry" is found on page 169 of the *Playboy Interviews.* That he did indeed write the song is plain from the May 1968 demo tapes, and from his description of working on the song's hook, found on page 277 of the Davies biography.

The release date of the White Album is documented on page 163 of *Recording Sessions.*

Riley's "no musical novice" quote is from page 286 of his book, *Tell Me Why.*

Page 261: Lennon's comments about "Goodnight" are found on page 169 of the *Playboy Interviews,* except for the Hollywood direction to Martin, reported on page 250 of Dowlding's *Beatlesongs.*

The Beatles' consideration of the title *A Doll's House* is documented on page 163 of *Recording Sessions.*

CHAPTER TWENTY-ONE:
In My Hour of Darkness
(*Let It Be*)

Page 263: The dates and other specific recording information concerning the Beatles' *Abbey Road* and *Let It Be* albums, as well as of their Apple rooftop concert and McCartney's breakup announcement, are documented in Lewisohn's *Chronicle*—see especially pages 230, 312, 332, and 349—and his *Recording Sessions,* see pages 192, 193, and 196.

Page 264: The description of the rooftop concert and the various Beatles' behavior therein is based on the author's viewing of *Let It Be* and his listening to the complete audio outtakes of the performance.

That the rooftop concert was Paul's idea is noted on page 169 of *Recording Sessions.*

Page 265: McCartney's "having scaled every known peak" quote is found in the printed booklet that was originally sold with the *Let It Be* album.

Lennon's "most miserable" quote is from Miles's *Beatles*, page 113. Harrison's "the low of all time" quote is found on page 165 of *Recording Sessions.* McCartney's "very sticky" is from an interview in the September 11, 1986, issue of *Rolling Stone.*

Page 265: Martin's "I thought, 'This is the end' " quote is found in the film *The Compleat Beatles.*

That 1967 was the last year that the four Beatles jointly made their annual Christmas disc is documented on page 131 of *Recording Sessions.* The Lennon quote was transcribed from the 1968 Christmas disc and checked against the version in Lennon's diaries, *Skywriting by Word of Mouth*, page 39. Confirmation of his intent with the quote is found on page 69 of *Lennon Remembers.*

Page 266: The date of Allen Klein's appointment is documented on page 705 of Coleman's *Lennon;* his background, and McCartney's opposition to him, is described on pages 475–76 and on pages 301–03 of Brown's *The Love You Make.*

Ringo's "Paul would want us" quote is from the film *The Making of Sgt Pepper,* 1992.

Paul's "slightly badgered them" and "very happy to not really work" quotes are found on page 59 of his World Tour program.

The various Beatles' differing attitudes about the *Get Back* project are described in various sources, including ibid., as well as pages 306–08 of Lewisohn's *Chronicle*, pages 253–56 of Dowlding's *Beatlesongs*, pages 118–22 of *Lennon Remembers*, and the soundtrack and accompanying booklet of the *Let It Be* film.

Page 267: Martin's "In order to get everything together" quote is from the film *The Compleat Beatles.*

Harrison's quitting of the Beatles after his fight with Paul is documented on page 306–07 of Lewisohn's *Chronicle*, which also mentions press reports that George also had a bitter argument with Paul that day, but there is no independent confirmation of those reports.

Page 267: Harrison's "When you write a song" quote is found in the booklet originally sold with the *Let It Be* album, as are Paul's "been sick of the group" and "the awful tension" quotes. George's quote about being "pigeonholed" is found in the February 1977 issue of *Crawdaddy* magazine.

The songs recorded by the Beatles inside Apple Studios the day after the rooftop concert are documented on page 170 of *Recording Sessions.*

Page 268: The author himself listened to many hours of the *Get Back* rehearsals; Lewisohn also describes them in *Recording Sessions*, especially on pages 163–68.

Lennon's "nobody was really into" quote is from page 118 of *Lennon Remembers.*

Regarding the original version of *Get Back* assembled by Glyn Johns, it should be noted that Johns actually compiled two slightly different versions of the album, both of which were listened to by the author. The original version of *Get Back* was completed by Johns on May 28, 1969, as documented, along with its contents, on page 176 of *Recording Sessions.* When this version failed to meet the approval of all four Beatles, Johns assembled a second version, completing the task on January 5, 1970; see page 196 of ibid.

Page 269: Lennon's "We were going to let it out" and "break the myth" quotes are from page 120 of *Lennon Remembers.*

The role of Lennon and Harrison in inviting Spector to work on the *Get Back* tapes is documented on page 199 of *Recording Sessions.*

Page 270: The "nadir of the Beatles' career" quote is found on page 252 of Dowlding's *Beatlesongs.* Lewisohn expresses a similarly negative view of *Let It Be* on page 199 of *Recording Sessions;* the criticisms of Spector by McCartney and Martin are noted on that same page, and on page 197.

The three tracks that Spector overdubbed were "The Long And Winding Road," "I Me Mine," and "Across The Universe," as noted on pages 197–99 of *Recording Sessions*, which also documents that these were the first and only Beatle songs since "She's Leaving Home" during the *Sgt Pepper* album whose orchestral scores were not composed by George Martin.

The comparisons of Glyn Johns' *Get Back* with Phil Spector's *Let It Be* are based on the author having listened to both.

Page 270: Lennon's claim of authorship for "The One After 909" is found on page 172 of the *Playboy Interviews.*

The suggestion that McCartney wrote "Two Of Us" for Linda Eastman is Coleman's, on page 555 of *Lennon.* Lennon actually said the song was his, on page 172 of the *Playboy Interviews,* but this is extremely doubtful; John's remark was made when his mind was clearly focused on a different subject, and in the *Let It Be* film it is Paul who sings lead on the song throughout, which would not be the case if John was the composer.

Paul's "working class glee" quote is found on page 19 of Bennahum's *in their own words: the Beatles . . . after the break-up.*

Page 271: Lennon's regard for "Across The Universe" is expressed in his quotes on page 162 of the *Playboy Interviews* and page 259 of Dowlding's *Beatlesongs;* the former also includes his quotes about the "atmosphere of looseness." The original February 4, 1968, recording date of "Across The Universe" and McCartney's drafting of the teenage fans is documented on page 133 of *Recording Sessions;* Spector's remake on April 1, 1970, is described on pages 198–99, as well as by an appreciative Lennon on page 555 of Coleman's *Lennon.*

Page 272: Spector's enhancement of "I Me Mine" is described on pages 198–99 of *Recording Sessions.* Harrison's "heavy waltz" phrase is from the *Let It Be* film; his "the ego, the eternal problem" quote is from his autobiography, *I Me Mine,* as cited on page 261 of Dowlding's *Beatlesongs.* The date of the "I Me Mine" recording session, and the fact that it was the Beatles' final recording of a full song, is found on page 195 of *Recording Sessions.*

Page 272: McCartney's explanation of "Let It Be" and his "She died when I was fourteen" quote are from his interview in the October 1986 issue of *Musician* magazine.

Page 273: The date and other specifics of the Beatles' overdub session for "Let It Be" are documented on page 195 of *Recording Sessions.*

The listing of the various Harrison compositions that the Beatles recorded before or during the *Get Back* sessions is based on the contents of the relevant bootleg tapes, as listened to by the author.

McCartney's unhappiness with Spector's overdubbing on "The Long And Winding Road" and his citing of the song in his 1970 lawsuit are noted on pages 197–99 of *Recording Sessions.*

CHAPTER TWENTY-TWO:
The Breakup Heard
'Round the World

Page 277:   The date of McCartney's resignation from the Beatles is documented on page 712 of Coleman's *Lennon.* The Apple press office's "dormant for years" quote is found on page 223 of Salewicz's *McCartney.*

The release dates for the *Abbey Road* album and subsequent singles are found on pages 200–201 of *Recording Sessions.* The sales figures are found on page 272 of Dowlding's *Beatlesongs.*

Page 278:   Lennon's dissection of the Beatles' breakup was found in his famous interview with *Rolling Stone* magazine, conducted on December 8, 1970, released in two parts in the January 21 and February 11, 1971, issues and finally published as a book, *Lennon Remembers,* as documented on pages 712–73 of Coleman's *Lennon.* The interview is a fascinating document, but its claims must be evaluated with care and skepticism, for as Lennon later admitted to George Martin, he was, as Martin told this author in an interview, "out of his skull" at the time, both because of drugs and because of his recent immersion in primal scream therapy, and he later apologized to Martin and others for his remarks. See also Lennon's explanation of his remarks in a second interview with *Rolling Stone,* printed June 5, 1975.

Ironically, John later explained that none of the Beatles, himself included, had really wanted to talk about their breakup. See his 1980 interview with Barbara Graustark, pages 125–26 of Garbarini and Cullman's *Strawberry Fields Forever: John Lennon Remembered.*

Page 278:   McCartney's "It's like asking a divorced couple" quote is found on page 482 of Coleman's *Lennon.* His "One of the things" quote is from page 123 of Bennahum's *in their own words: the Beatles . . . after the break-up.*

Page 279:   Excerpts from McCartney's questionnaire have been printed in many books; an especially complete version is found on pages 224–25 of Salewicz's *McCartney.*

The news media's hypercharged reaction to the news is noted on page 341 of Lewisohn's *Chronicle.*

Page 280:   The date of the Toronto concert at which the Plastic Ono Band (which at this point included Lennon, Ono, Eric Clapton, Klaus Voormann, and Alan White) appeared is documented on page 708 of *Lennon*. All accounts agree that the Apple meeting occurred shortly after Lennon's return, but none document the date precisely.

Lennon's own description of the September 1969 Apple meeting is offered in *Lennon Remembers*, pages 60–61, which is one basis for the information found in the remainder of the paragraph. Other sources include McCartney's December 1984 *Playboy* interview and page 329 of Brown's *The Love You Make*.

The date of the new contracts that Klein had negotiated with EMI and its American subsidiary, Capitol, was September 1, 1969, according to page 340 of Goldman's *The Lives of John Lennon*, which also provides figures on the exact increases in royalties. This runs contrary to the accounts found in most Beatles books, for it indicates that the deal with EMI had already been consummated *before* Lennon's demand for a divorce. Of course, it is possible that the contracts were not signed and executed until sometime later than September 1, which would explain why Klein still wanted silence, as would the fact that in any case the actual royalties had not yet been paid.

McCartney's "John looked me in the eye" quote is found in his interview in the September 11, 1986, issue of *Rolling Stone*.

Page 280: Lennon's "When I finally had the guts" and "I started the band" quotes are found on page 18 of his *Skywriting by Word of Mouth*.

McCartney expressed his wish that the Beatles had never broken up in his interview in the December 1984 issue of *Playboy*.

Page 281: Among the joint recording activities of the former Beatles during the early 1970s, Ringo drummed on both of John's first two solo albums and on George's first solo album, George played on John's second solo album and, like both John and Paul, contributed (albeit separately) to Ringo's 1973 album, *Ringo*. For details, see especially Schaffner's *The Beatles Forever*, chapters 6 and 7.

Lennon's "inner strength" quote is found on page 17 of *Skywriting by Word of Mouth*. That Ono controlled the text of the book is plain from the copyright information and from her own rather self-reverential afterword, found on pages 199–200.

McCartney's "John had to clear the decks" quote is from his interview in the November 5, 1987, issue of *Rolling Stone*. His "someone like John" quote is from his December 1984 *Playboy* interview. His remark about John's being a signal for George and Ringo to leave is found on page 10 of *in their own words: the Beatles . . . after the break-up.*

Lennon's sneer at Paul's claim to have left the Beatles was made in an interview printed in *Rolling Stone* on May 14, 1970.

Page 282: Harrison's "It's just that it wasn't as much fun" quote is from a 1979 press conference, as transcribed in *Beatlefan* magazine, vol. I, no. 3. Ringo's "From 1961, 1962 to around 1969" quote is from page 116 of *in their own words: the Beatles . . . after the break-up.*

Page 282: Harrison's "you've got ten brothers" quote is from a 1979 press conference, as transcribed in *Beatlefan* magazine, vol. I, no. 3. His unhappiness with his album quota and his "You'd have to do fifty-nine of Paul's songs" quote is found in his interview in the October 22, 1987, issue of *Rolling Stone.*

McCartney's "four Paul songs" quote is from page 59 of his 1990 World Tour program.

Page 283: The dialogue between John and George, found on one of the many *Get Back* outtakes tapes, was listened to by the author.

John's solo work during 1969 included the albums *Unfinished Music No. 2: Life With The Lions* and *The Plastic Ono Band—Live Peace In Toronto* and the singles "Give Peace A Chance" and "Cold Turkey." See pages 706–10 of Coleman's *Lennon.* Pages 334–39 of Lewisohn's *Chronicle* describe Ringo's projects, including the film *The Magic Christian* and the album *Sentimental Journey,* and George's onstage appearances with the band Delaney, Bonnie And Friends.

Page 283: Lennon's "I put four albums out" quote is from an interview printed in *Rolling Stone* on May 14, 1970. His ridicule of Paul is found on page 90 of *The Ballad of John and Yoko.* The best coverage of his activities in late 1969 and early 1970 is found in Coleman's *Lennon,* especially the chronology found on pages 708–12. For evidence of his continuing to identify himself as a Beatle, see his comments to reporters following his meetings with Canadian prime minister Pierre Trudeau in December 1969, found on pages 66–73 of *The Ballad of John and Yoko.*

Page 284: That John and Yoko, as well as the other Beatles, did their own separate tapes for the 1969 fan club Christmas disc is plain from listening to the disc and is confirmed by Lewisohn on page 131 of *Recording Sessions.*

Lennon's resentment of McCartney's April 1970 announcement is reported by, among others, Coleman on page 480 of his book *Lennon*, who adds that at the time Lennon told him by telephone for quotation in the *Melody Maker*, which Coleman then edited, that Paul had not left—John had fired him.

McCartney confirms Lennon's anger about his questionnaire in his December 1984 *Playboy* interview, and on page 9 of *in their own words: the Beatles . . . after the break-up*, which contains his "dumb move" quote. Page 8 of *in their own words* contains his "The Beatles have left The Beatles" quote.

Page 285: The background to the fight over the release of Paul's *McCartney* album has been widely reported; see, for example, pages 341–44 of Brown and Gaines, *The Love You Make*. Starr's affidavit is quoted on page 252 of Dowlding's *Beatlesongs*.

Page 285: The best descriptions of the struggle over Northern Songs are found on pages 311–15 of *The Love You Make* and pages 458–64 of Norman's *Shout!* Regarding Lennon's suspicion that McCartney was trying to buy up Northern Songs secretly, see pages 369–70 of Davies's *The Beatles*.

Page 286: Michael Jackson's purchase of the ATV song catalogue in 1986 for $47.5 million is noted on page 339 of Goldman's *The Lives of John Lennon*. In an interview in the November 5, 1987, issue of *Rolling Stone*, McCartney implicitly blamed Yoko for allowing their joint effort to obtain the catalogue to fail, saying that she insisted on offering a very low bid that Paul knew would not succeed. Why McCartney, an extremely wealthy man, did not mount his own independent bid for his songs he did not explain.

Page 287: The descriptions of Eastman and Klein and the events that surrounded them are based on the above-cited accounts in *The Love You Make*, *Shout!*, and *The Lives of John Lennon*, reinforced by Paul's and John's separate remarks in such interviews as *Lennon Remembers* and the 1985 postscript to the Davies biography of the Beatles.

Page 287: The machinations and reasoning surrounding McCartney's lawsuit are described in his interview in the October 1986 issue of *Musician* magazine, on pages 343–44 of *The Love You Make*, and on pages 149–50 of Giuliano's *Blackbird*.

McCartney's "suing my best mates" quote is found on page 482 of Coleman's *Lennon*. The dates and results of the court actions are described most reliably on pages 713 and 720 of ibid. and pages 344–46 of *The Love You Make*.

The lawsuits against Klein are described on page 718 of *Lennon* and on pages 379–80 of *The Love You Make*, the latter of which adds that Klein filed countersuits of his own, claiming damages of more than $100 million. Page 722 of *Lennon* reports that all claims were resolved in 1977 via a settlement that cost Apple Corps $5 million and Klein $800,000.

Page 288: Lennon's "Steel And Glass" appeared on the 1974 album *Walls And Bridges*; his "How Do You Sleep?" appeared on the 1971 *Imagine* album. Klein's jail sentence is described on page 492 of Norman's *Shout!*

Lennon's "You know, it seems that my partings" quote is from page 161 of the *Playboy Interviews*. His "bad taste to it" quote is from page 128 of *Strawberry Fields Forever: John Lennon Remembered*.

McCartney's "a pity that such a nice thing" quote is found on page 150 of Giuliano's *Blackbird*.

CHAPTER TWENTY-THREE:
A Final Masterpiece
(*Abbey Road*)

Page 291: As documented on pages 170–91 of *Recording Sessions*, the dates of recording for *Abbey Road* extended from April 16 to August 20, 1969, with the exception of a single session on February 22.

Page 291: Martin's naming of *Abbey Road* as his favorite Beatles album is found on page 159 of *The Summer of Love*.

Lennon's channels remarks are found on pages 103 and 120 of *Strawberry Fields Forever: John Lennon Remembered*.

Martin's "inexplicable *presence*" remark is reported on page 174 of *Recording Sessions*, referring to the April 26, 1969, session where "Oh! Darling" and "Octopus's Garden" were taped.

The date and location of the session for "The Ballad Of John And Yoko," as well as the competing activities of Harrison and Starr, are listed on page 173 of ibid.; McCartney's "on heat" quote is found on page 14. The tapes of all eleven takes of the session, plus overdubs, were listened to by the author, at Abbey Road Studios in April 1993.

Page 294: The recording of "Old Brown Shoe" on April 16 is noted on page 173 of ibid., the number one charting of "The Ballad Of John And Yoko" on page 177. Lennon's "Christ bit" quote is found on a note he scrawled to Apple staffer Tony Bramwell, which is reproduced on page 319 of Lewisohn's *Chronicle*, which also reports on the censorship practiced by some radio stations.

Martin's attitude toward producing the *Abbey Road* album is made clear in his comments in the film *The Compleat Beatles*, and in his quote on page 177 of *Recording Sessions*.

Page 294: McCartney's recollection of being told off by Starr and Harrison is based on his interview in the October 1986 issue of *Musician* magazine.

The installation of a bed in the studio for Yoko Ono has been widely reported; see specifically page 179 and 193 of *Recording Sessions*, which offer quotes from Abbey Road staffers.

Lennon and Ono's car accident is described on page 177 of ibid and page 707 of Coleman's *Lennon*. Lewisohn notes the return of John, and Yoko, to the Abbey Road Studios on July 9, but John is not mentioned in the entries for the sessions from July 11 to July 21, during which time the three other Beatles were adding overdubs to "Maxwell's Silver Hammer," "You Never Give Me Your Money," "Here Comes The Sun," "Something," "Oh! Darling," and "Octopus's Garden."

Regarding the return to heroin use by Lennon and Ono during the summer of 1969, refer first to the sources listed in the note for page 257, regarding their dabbling in heroin in 1968. For the 1969 period, see pages 326–27 of *The Love You Make*, where Ono is directly quoted explaining Lennon's and her decision to quit heroin "cold turkey," without medical assistance. Her testimony is believable because she and Brown were personal friends (see pages 383–84), but also because John himself described his heroin addiction in chilling terms later that summer, when he wrote the song "Cold Turkey," which he released with the Plastic Ono Band.

The *Abbey Road* cover photo session is described on page 186 of *Recording Sessions* and again, with updated, apparently more accurate detail, on pages 328–29 of *Chronicle*. The tomfoolery of the "You Know My Name (Look Up The Number)" session is described on page 175 of *Recording Sessions*, the high spirits of the other sessions on pages 174 and 178.

Page 295: McCartney's "If you ever got a speck" quote is from his interview in the December 1984 *Playboy*.

The recording tricks employed on "Come Together" are noted on page 181 of *Recording Sessions*.

Page 296: Lennon describes the origin of "Come Together" on pages 169–70 of the *Playboy Interviews*.

Film of Lennon's appearance at the August 1972 concert at Madison Square Garden was viewed by the author. It is also described on pages 248–50 of Jon Wiener's *Come Together*.

Page 296: Martin's remarks about Starr's drumming are found on page 127 of his own book *All You Need Is Ears*, and on page 95 of *Recording Sessions*.

Page 297: McCartney's high regard for "Something" is documented on page 193 of *Recording Sessions*, Lennon's and Sinatra's on pages 124–25 of Schaffner's *The Beatles Forever*.

Ringo's "greatest songwriters on earth" is from page 96 of Bennahum's *in their own words: the Beatles . . . after the break-up*. The pomegranate line in "Something" was heard by the author on the working tapes. George's "probably the nicest melody" quote is from page 279 of Dowlding's *Beatlesongs*, as is the 150 cover versions figure (attributed to Harrison's autobiography, *I Me Mine*).

Page 297: Paul's explanation of "Maxwell's Silver Hammer" is from page 102 of Miles's *Beatles: In Their Own Words*. George's "it's one of those instant" and "really fruity" quotes are from page 281 of *Beatlesongs*. Lennon's "nice little folk songs" quote is from page 125 of Schaffner's *The Beatles Forever*. He also disparages the song on page 171 of the *Playboy Interviews*.

Lennon's remarks about "Oh! Darling" are in the *Playboy Interviews*, also page 171. McCartney's comment about coming in early to sing the song is from page 102 of Miles's *Beatles: In Their Own Words*, and is confirmed by Abbey Road engineer Alan Parsons on page 180 of *Recording Sessions*; page 181 reports that McCartney taped the final vocal on July 23, which, calculating from previous entries, was his fifth attempt.

Page 298: Ringo's comments about the other Beatles teasing him and the actual genesis of "Octopus's Garden" are found in the April 30, 1981, issue of *Rolling Stone*. The various contributions to the song by Paul and George are documented on pages 174 and 180 of *Recording Sessions*.

Lennon's "being able to just sort of blink" quote is found on page 70 of *Lennon Remembers*.

Page 299: Billy Preston's participation and the number of takes required for "I Want You (She's So Heavy)" are documented on page 170 of *Recording*

Sessions. The overdubbing and remix techniques are described on pages 173 and 191 of ibid., the latter of which reports that the August 20 session was the last time the Beatles were together inside Abbey Road. Martin's "There is nothing more electrifying" quote is from page 212 of his book *All You Need Is Ears.*

Page 300:   Martin's regrets regarding Harrison are noted on page 124 of his book *The Summer of Love,* on page 11 of Bennahum's *in their own words: the Beatles . . . after the break-up,* and in an interview with the author of this book, which is where his "poor George" quote comes from. His quote about "Here Comes The Sun" being "one of the best songs ever written" is from page 174 of the book *Ticket To Ride,* by Scott Muni.

Harrison's description of writing the song in Clapton's garden is from page 285 of Dowlding's *Beatlesongs,* citing Harrison's autobiography, *I Me Mine.* His musical contributions to the recording of it are noted on pages 178–80, 185, and 190.

Page 300:   Lennon's "invisible man" quote is from page 162 of *Lennon Remembers.*

The description of the chord patterns is based on the sheet music found in *The Complete Beatles,* vol. 1, pages 298–302.

Page 301:   Martin's "think symphonically" quote is found on page 139 of *The Summer Of Love.*

Page 302:   Lennon's lack of participation in "Here Comes The Sun" is documented by the nonappearance of his name in any of the relevant entries in *Recording Sessions;* see pages 178–80, 185, and 190.

Page 302:   The recording of "Because," including Ringo's tapping of a beat for the other Beatles to hear in their headphones but not for inclusion on record, is documented on page 184 of ibid.

Among the descriptions of *Abbey Road* as professional, see Lennon's remark on page 102 of Miles's *Beatles: In Their Own Words,* as well as page 310 of Riley's *Tell Me Why.*

Regarding Martin's return for *Abbey Road,* see the note above for page 294. Emerick describes his recruitment by McCartney on page 181 of *Recording Sessions.*

Page 303:   Regarding McCartney's role on *Abbey Road,* see the above note.

Ringo's "some of our finest work" quote is from page 275 of *Beatlesongs*, citing a direct quote in Max Weinberg's *Big Beat*, Contemporary, New York, 1984.

Martin takes credit for the medley idea on page 192 of *Recording Sessions*, but Paul does likewise on page 14 of ibid.

For Lennon's dislike of the medley, see his own quote on page 102 of Miles's *Beatles: In Their Own Words*, as well as Martin's quote on page 124 of Schaffner's *The Beatles Forever*.

Page 304: The story of how "Her Majesty" was placed on the album is told on page 183 of *Recording Sessions*.

Page 304: The order of the guitar solos during "The End" was revealed by Lennon on page 48 of *Lennon Remembers*.

CHAPTER TWENTY-FOUR:
The Classics of Their Time:
The Beatles in History

Page 307: The archives tapes of the *Plastic Ono Band* sessions were listened to by the author during his visits to Abbey Road Studios. Lennon's "I still love those guys" quote is found on page 128 of the *Playboy Interviews*.

The relationship between Lennon and McCartney during their solo years is complex enough to fill an entire chapter on its own. Their fights often became publicly known, such as when they exchanged views in the pages of the English pop music paper *The Melody Maker* in 1971, following John's attack against Paul with the song "How Do You Sleep" from the *Imagine* album; see pages 482–88 of Coleman's *Lennon*. See also Lennon's remarks on pages 49–51 of *Lennon Remembers*. See also Paul's references to John's attacks in pages 368–74 of the 1985 postscript of Hunter Davies's *The Beatles*. In an interview in the September 11, 1986, *Rolling Stone*, McCartney admitted that there was "incredible bitterness" between him and John that they "didn't get over for a long, long time," until just before John's death, when they realized that if they didn't talk about Apple, everything was fine. Nevertheless, the two old friends and partners were still prone to blowups and apparently never succeeded in straightening out all their differences, a failure McCartney regretted after John's death. See Paul's December 1984 *Playboy* interview, as well as page 4 of Giuliano's *Blackbird*.

Acts of kindness and friendship between the two men did not usually make news. In the same pages in the Davies book cited above, for example, Mc-Cartney mentions that he flew to Los Angeles during Lennon's so-called lost weekend to talk him out of his self-destructive behavior and urge him to return to Yoko. And in the just cited *Rolling Stone* interview, McCartney recalls that both he and John eventually realized how other people were constantly pitting one of them against the other. It was to break through that sort of interference, Paul once explained, that he wrote the song "Dear Friend" to John on his 1971 *Wildlife* album. See page 33 of Gross's *Paul McCartney: Twenty Years on His Own.* See also pages 69–70 of the *Playboy Interviews,* where John describes watching television with Paul one night in New York and the two of them almost taking a cab down to the NBC Studios, where the producer of the program *Saturday Night Live* was, with tongue in cheek, offering a $3,200 reward for a Beatles reunion on his show. See also the comments cited on pages 110–14 of Bennahum's *in their own words: the Beatles . . . after the break-up,* which indicate that John had privately told Yoko that while Paul had hurt him terribly in the past, he still loved Paul and respected their collaboration together.

Page 308: Harrison's brothers metaphor is from a 1979 press conference, as transcribed in *Beatlefan* magazine, vol. I, no. 3. Lennon describes primal scream therapy on pages 103–05 of the *Playboy Interviews.*

Page 309: Ringo's "We have arguments" quote is found on page 116 of Bennahum's *in their own words: the Beatles . . . after the break-up.*

The former Beatles' lawsuits against Allen Klein are described on page 718 of *Lennon* and on pages 379–80 of *The Love You Make,* the latter of which adds that Klein filed countersuits of his own, claiming damages of over $100 million. Page 722 of *Lennon* reports that all claims were resolved in 1977 via a settlement that cost Apple Corps $5 million and Klein $800,000.

The former Beatles' collaboration on one another's albums, and specifically Ringo's 1973 album, is described in chapters 6 and 7 of Schaffner's *The Beatles Forever.* See also McCartney's quote on page 122 of Bennahum's *in their own words: the Beatles . . . after the break-up.* Regarding Paul's comments about getting along as long as Apple wasn't discussed, see page 372 of Davies's *The Beatles* and his September 11, 1986, interview with *Rolling Stone.*

Page 310: Lewisohn's "a level of kinship" quote is from an interview with the author. Harrison's "Everybody's sued each other" quote is from a 1979 press conference, as transcribed in *Beatlefan* magazine, vol. I, no. 3.

Regarding the Beatles' misleading interview replies, see Lennon's remark on page 125 of Garbarini, Cullman, and Graustark's *Strawberry Fields Forever: John Lennon Remembered* about the Beatles often giving glib answers to questions about their internal relations because they didn't want to talk about it.

Lennon's "I'm a genius!" interview was published in the January 21 and February 4, 1971, issues of *Rolling Stone* and subsequently reprinted in the book *Lennon Remembers*. His later distancing from the angry sentiments of that interview is documented on page 610 of Coleman's *Lennon*, where he likens the outbursts to "an abscess bursting," and on page 114 of *Recording Sessions*, where George Martin recounts Lennon's subsequent apology for his remarks. Regarding "How Do You Sleep," Lennon said in the *Imagine* film produced by Yoko Ono that he realized later the song had actually been about himself and that he and Paul "were okay about it." His evenings of reminiscing with McCartney are also described on page 610 of Coleman's *Lennon*.

Page 310: McCartney's positive remarks in 1974 about the Beatles playing together again are found on pages 122–24 of Bennahum's *in their own words: the Beatles . . . after the break-up*. Lennon's 1975 remarks are found on pages 144–45 of *The Ballad of John and Yoko*.

Regarding the apparent connection between Lennon's return to Yoko Ono after an eighteen-month separation and the halt to his remarks about playing again with the other Beatles, the simple coincidence of events is striking enough on its own. However, there is additional supporting evidence in the form of eyewitness testimony from May Pang, Lennon's lover during his time apart from Yoko. According to pages 286–310 of Pang's book, *Loving John*, McCartney in late 1974 invited Lennon to join him in a few weeks in New Orleans, where Paul planned to record a new album (subsequently titled *Venus And Mars*). Pang adds that John seemed enthusiastic about accepting Paul's invitation, but that a week later, he went to Ono's hypnotist in order to stop smoking, after which he suddenly left Pang without explanation and returned to live with Yoko.

Ringo's "The silliness goes on without us" quote is from page 125 of Bennahum's *in their own words: the Beatles . . . after the break-up*.

Lennon's "None of us want" quote is from page 125 of Garbarini, Cullman, and Graustark's *Strawberry Fields Forever: John Lennon Remembered*.

Page 311: Lennon's legal deposition was reported in the Special Summer issue of *Rolling Stone* in 1986 on page 15. See also McCartney's confirmation of the deposition and the film project in his own interview with *Rolling Stone* on November 5, 1987.

The 1989 legal settlement among the Beatles was described by Beatles researcher Mark Lewisohn in an interview with the author.

Regarding the plans for *The Beatles Anthology*, see the article in the January 24, 1994, issue of *The New Yorker*, written by the author and based on interviews with such Apple and EMI officials as Derek Taylor, the Apple press officer, and David Hughes, the head of communications for EMI Records.

That the three surviving Beatles recorded Lennon's "Free As A Bird" was reported in the March 3, 1994, issue of *The New York Times*, which described how Yoko Ono gave working tapes of the song to Paul McCartney at the January 1994 ceremony to induct Lennon into the Rock 'n' Roll Hall of Fame.

A copy of Lennon's solo version of "Free As A Bird" was listened to separately by the author.

Page 312: Derek Taylor's remark about the Beatles reclaiming their history was made in an interview with the author.

McCartney's remark about Mozart was reported in the author's article in the January 24, 1994, issue of *The New Yorker*, for which the remark was fact-checked with McCartney's London office.

Page 312: Martin's "I suppose it is pretentious" quote is from an interview with the author.

Page 314: Ringo's "Everyone relates" and "Who else is there?" quotes are from John Blake's *All You Needed Was Love*, page 262.

Page 315: Martin's "People don't remember" quote is from an interview with the author.

Page 317: Taylor's "has cut through differences" quote is from the liner notes to the Beatles' *Beatles For Sale* album.

Page 317: Lennon made the remark about folk music a number of times, including on page 121 of Garbarini, Cullman, and Graustark's *Strawberry Fields Forever: John Lennon Remembered*.

Page 317: Timothy Leary's full quote is found on page 365 of Norman's *Shout!*

Page 318: Lennon's "Be here now" quote is from page 70 of the *Playboy Interviews*.

Index

A

Abbey Road, 143, 173, 269, 277, 291–304

Abbey Road Studios, 1–2, 4, 9, 129, 135–136, 164, 324

"Across The Universe," 118, 269, 270, 271

"Act Naturally," 129

"All I Have To Do Is Dream," 258

"All My Loving," 50, 57, 75

All Star Club, Hamburg, 42

"All Things Must Pass," 273, 308

"All Together Now," 228

All You Need Is Ears (Martin), 325

"All You Need Is Love," 112, 116, 165, 223–227, 230, 268, 316

"And I Love Her," 75, 76, 78–79

"And Your Bird Can Sing," 184, 187

"Another Girl," 130

"Any Time At All," 80

Apple, 247, 266, 287

Asher, Jane, 52, 168

"Ask Me Why," 31, 39

Aspinall, Neil, 92, 93, 168, 237

Astaire, Fred, 164

As Time Goes By (Taylor), 94

ATV Music, 285–286

Augustine, Saint, 87

Australia, 90

B

"Baby, You're A Rich Man," 228–229

"Baby's In Black," 100, 105, 106

Bach, Johann Sebastian, 211

"Back In The U.S.S.R.," 251, 252, 255–257

Baird, Julia, 17, 21

"Ballad of John and Yoko, The," 292–294

Beatles '65, 101

Beatles, The. *See also* Harrison, George; Lennon, John; McCartney, Paul; specific songs; Starr, Ringo

Abbey Road album, 143, 173, 269, 277, 291–304

The Beatles Anthology, 311–312, 324

Beatles '65, 101

Beatles For Sale album, 99–106, 127, 129, 131

Pete Best leaves, 46

breakup and events leading to, 244, 247, 251–252, 254, 265–267, 277–288

at Cavern Club, Liverpool, 27, 31, 40, 41, 44–45, 62, 63

Christmas records, 136, 137, 140, 233, 265–266, 268, 284

closeness of, 142–146

death threats toward, 95–96, 206

drug use by, 6, 93, 97, 103, 123, 138, 153–154, 178, 185, 188, 192–198, 237, 257, 294

Dylan and, 50–51, 54, 56, 59, 103, 104, 116, 126–127, 175, 192–193

Eastern philosophy and, 192, 197

Ed Sullivan Show appearances, 66

end of touring years, 88–89, 96

Brian Epstein's management of, 61–71, 233

everyman identification of, 26

fame, consequences of, 88–97, 143

M